RETHINKING THE SPACE FOR RELIGION

Rethinking the Space for Religion

New Actors in Central and Southeast Europe
on Religion, Authenticity and Belonging

Edited by
Catharina Raudvere, Krzysztof Stala
& Trine Stauning Willert

NORDIC ACADEMIC PRESS

Nordic Academic Press
P.O. Box 1206
S-221 05 Lund
Sweden
www.nordicacademicpress.com

© Nordic Academic Press and the Authors 2012
Typesetting: Frederic Täckström, www.sbmolle.com
Jacket design: Design för livet
Printed by ScandBook AB, Falun 2012
ISBN: 978-91-87121-85-2

Contents

Preface

Generous funding from The Danish Research Council made it possible to establish the project "Between Conservative Reaction and Religious Reinvention. Religious Intellectuals in Central and South-East Europe on Community, Authenticity and Heritage" at the Department of Cross-Cultural and Regional Studies, University of Copenhagen, during the period 2008–2010. The editors had the pleasure of organizing several guest-lectures, seminars and workshops on themes related to the space for religion in contemporary Central and South-East Europe.

The final activity of the project was to organize the international conference "Cracks in the European Project. Quests for Heritage and the New Uses of History, Religion and (Trans)National Identities" in June 2010. Ten colleagues joined the three editors for presentations and discussions about religion, authenticity and belonging, and colleagues from the Centre for Modern European Studies at the Faculty of Humanities gave their responses.

The completion of the present volume was made possible thanks to The Danish Research Council, Centre for Modern European Studies at the Faculty of Humanities, University of Copenhagen, and especially its director at the time Professor Ib Bondebjerg; and, finally, the research project "The Many Roads in Modernity" funded by the Carlsberg Foundation. The editors want to express their most profound thanks to the funding bodies, the authors of the book, and colleagues in Copenhagen who took substantial interest all along the way.

Copenhagen 2012

Catharina Raudvere, Krzysztof Stala and Trine Stauning Willert

CONFLICTING CONSTRUCTIONS –
NATIONAL NARRATIVES IN EUROPE

CHAPTER I

Rethinking the Space for Religion

New Actors in Central and Southeast Europe on Religion, Authenticity and Belonging

Catharina Raudvere, Krzysztof Stala & Trine Stauning Willert

The point of departure for this volume is a growing dissatisfaction with the promotion of religion as the missing link in modern identity constructions and the way the issue is frequently approached in journalism, art and academia. It is apparent that many theological positions are also taken in the academic discussions on secularism. Concepts such as political theology, multiple modernities and authenticity are shared in wide circles of public intellectuals, and it is not always easy to distinguish between analytical and political purposes (Vries 2006; Kirwan 2008; Žižek & Milbank 2009; Casanova 2011). There are many aspects of the zone between politics, journalism and academia that confuse the discussions about how religion and history are used as rhetorical tools for identity politics, social cohesion and processes of inclusion and exclusion. The emphasis on religion as an actor in its own right in the public sphere is analytically unsatisfactory when no identification of agency is made and no reflection on power structures and changing means of influence by the religious institutions is provided – notwithstanding the consequences that the absence of reflection on the impact of various combinations of religious narratives and nationalism can have when employed by individual thinkers or state policymakers (Haynes & Hennig 2011). Another issue to be brought up when discussing the uses of references to religion as an argument for a shared cultural background and a national home is the question of why the post-secular paradigm has been so widely accepted (Calhoun,

Juergensmeyer & Vanantwerpen 2011; Stuckrad 2012). Critical analytical questions should be raised about who is making such claims and why. The chapters in this book do not provide an unanimous answer to questions about religion and rhetoric; rather, they offer localized cases where the relations between a variety of actors with fluid agendas indicate the complex relations between history, religion, identity and belonging in contemporary Europe.

While the present volume was being prepared, the uprisings in the Arab Mediterranean world were taking place. The events and their aftermath provoked media discussions about the borders of Europe and brought up unwanted memories of a European colonial past. The revolts have so far not been religiously motivated, but nevertheless these tense events and discussions provided perspectives on the profound changes some twenty years ago in Central and Eastern Europe that the chapters in the volume offer analyses of. An important difference between the non-violent revolts in the European communist countries and the current Arab wave of changes and transformation is that the citizens of the countries in Eastern Europe had the expectation of a reunion with Western Europe, and Western Europe was, at least on the surface, welcoming the Eastern countries "back home" to their original cultural setting. For the developing Arab democracies there is no welcome committee embracing them back in the family. Irrespective of the outcome of the revolts, European identity and European borders have been challenged again and questions raised about borders, belonging and loyalties.

European Belonging(s)

There is an apparent tension in contemporary European politics, and certainly not only from an EU perspective, about whether there are common European values or not (Judt 2005; Joas & Wiegandt 2008; Checkel & Katzenstein 2009). On the one hand there are attempts to formulate a shared European identity (often failing on where to draw the geographical and cultural borders in the age of globalization) and, on the other, a strong desire is noticeable to give space to regional particularities (Pagden 2002; Herrmann et al. 2004; Stråth 2000). A controversial political issue in this context of unity in diversity is what space religion and history may occupy in late-modern collective identity constructions. The issue is often raised: who claims the authority and legitimacy to define collective identities and for whom? In a more democratic Europe, the last two decades have seen the appearance of many new actors who claim attention on religious grounds in the public sphere (Berger & Lorenz 2008; Bjerg 2011).

Europe has a complex background when it comes to historical multicultural environments, and for centuries the borders of Europe followed the expansion and decline of empires (Todorova 2004). The history of a multiplicity of religions, ethnicities and cultures has deeply affected the violent conflicts of the nineteenth and twentieth centuries. Both world wars furthermore caused conflicts within and across national units, and provoked hitherto accepted borders and identities. The linkages to this traumatic heritage and issues about how to write history have generated academic as well as military conflicts. The outcome has been at one and the same time liberating and restraining when it comes to the features of contemporary identity politics. Ethnic belonging was a tool of resistance in the Soviet Union, and local identities in the Scandinavian welfare states were to a great extent invisible in the definition of the modern project; while in countries like Finland and Ireland, promoting cultural particularities/legacies went hand in hand with the formation of the modern nation-state. The north-western parts of Europe have been comparatively homogeneous in cultural terms, and various versions of the welfare state today deal with supposedly new issues about not only migration, but also regarding the very construction of sustainable meeting grounds for people with different religious and cultural backgrounds. In contrast, many parts of what used to be called Eastern Europe have to cope with the fact that old multireligious communities were brutally destroyed and transformed during and after the Second World War (Todorova 1997). The history of this region relates to a broad cultural legacy where Moscow and Istanbul were significant centres, and grand-scale modernization projects of varying political denominations had difficulties in transforming an imperial past and at the same time keeping multicultural communities alive. Homogeneity – either in nationalist terms or classless Marxist experiments – was the easier way out. To some extent the EU has taken upon itself the role of the old empires, attempting to provide a cultural, political and economic umbrella. The political dominance of the EU triggers local debates about belonging. The question is what the price and the benefits are of belonging to Europe in terms of cultural memory. Being present and accepted in Europe has consequences for the way each country constructs citizenship in the broadest sense.

Both countries and citizens have faced new demands of adaptation to EU standards. These processes have undoubtedly been successful, but the complexity of national identity has been downplayed and even marginalized. Religious narratives have definitely had an impact on the development away from authoritarian regimes. The question is, however, what actors and what agendas have played a role and in what arenas.

Parallel to these internal changes, the era of globalization, transnationalism and the even more visible diaspora communities have also had a significant impact. At this peak of EU expansion, the presence of the world outside Europe is more imperative than ever. However, most Europeans think of Europe as a distinct cultural unit. This becomes very apparent when its complicated relation to Turkey and Russia is brought up and is met with categorical claims of inclusion and exclusion. The chapters in the present volume tell different stories of how intellectuals and other public figures in various parts of Europe have challenged identity politics over the last two decades. Not even as individuals have their positions been unambiguous: they have contested hegemonic identities, but also willingly played the game conducted by nationalist forces. Conservative cultural and religious institutions that were supposed to have a much weakened position after decades of secularization turned out to be influential parts of political processes and debates (Calhoun, Juergensmeyer & Vanantwerpen 2011). Instead of repeating the simplistic phrase about "the return of religion", this volume focuses on the platforms and the agents of influence that make use of religion as a political and cultural argument.

The history of secularization has from its beginning been a long, varied and global process (Asad 2003; Bock, Feuchter & Knecht 2009; Calhoun, Juergensmeyer & Vanantwerpen 2011). It has also been an essential part of most national modernization projects worldwide. The combination of legal reforms and constitutional secularism meant radical changes in power relations at all societal levels, and targeted religious institutions and their representatives, who lost power and influence. A glance at the European map tells us a highly varied history of how these changes took different paths in the twentieth century, and contradicts the common misconception that secularization is always programmatically anti-religious (Roy 2010). However, under the influence of modernity and constitutional secularism, religious life took new and different forms. The old links between religious institutions on the one hand and state administration on the other were broken. This development pushed religious expressions towards more privatized spheres of piety. In other words, religion became a private concern and thus legally connected to civil liberties. The freedom of religion was directly linked to the freedom from religion and to the public recognition of religious and ethnic minorities. At its best, this also meant a conscious inclusion of minorities in collective memory. Several of the chapters in the present volume touch upon the issue of which groups are given space in national collective memory and on what criteria, which also gives an indication of who is left outside the national narrative.

In Europe today most religious institutions, groups and public persons accept the conditions of constitutional secularism – even if they sometimes argue in other directions. The difference between rhetorical emphasis and social practice is noticeable. In this volume we therefore find it relevant to speak of secularized religion, i.e. the acceptance of spaces defined by secular constitutions where religious actors in public and private follow given codes. Most Europeans expect their religious communities to act under the law and to a very great extent follow social consensus, thus most European religious communities are integrated well, and have negotiated relations to civil rights, democracy and secular constitutions. In some parts of Europe, such as Scandinavia, this is a more than century-long history. The focus of many secularization studies is on the institutional transformations, but the change has been equally – if not more – considerable when it comes to community concerns. The position of laymen, the authority of local clergy and the roles of women are but a few examples of changing conditions at grassroots level under the impact of secularization and modernity.

Rethinking the Space for Religion

The present collection of essays aims at a broad discussion of how history and religion are used as tools in the production of narratives about origin and belonging in contemporary Europe. In several places, authoritarian religious movements and discourses have gained significant political influence by skilfully navigating between narratives about the past and visions of the future. The religious institutions have not regained their traditional positions as copies of the past. They have not returned to the former monopoly of setting the agenda and have instead been forced into negotiations with media, ideological positions and trends. New intellectual voices play a role when it comes to defining the relationship between religion and belonging in a mode that matches late-modern living conditions. Both conservative and liberal interlocutors find attractive spaces outside the institutions.

The impact of the authoritarian religious movements has not been so substantial, since many of them have not been able to cope with religion in its secularized form and with new modes of religious expressions. Polarized religious discourse makes use of the contrasting conceptions of religion and anti-religion, hence having difficulties in dealing with interpretive alternatives within its own tradition. Another forceful factor is the intra-religious resistance against excluding definitions of religion and the greater willingness among these new voices to accept plurality as a condition of late modernity. Among certain intellectuals there is a pronounced opposition to what they regard as secular modernism, as that excludes a cultural heritage that involves religious identity.

The discussion in this volume has been regionally limited to Central and Southeast Europe, including a broad spectrum of religious positions taken on culture, identity and belonging. The broad term "religious intellectuals" comprises writers, debaters and academics who use the public sphere as an arena for their arguments of religion as the copestone of societal structure. This does not, however, imply that the intellectuals represent a homogeneous stand in national matters. The observed trend does not lie in common political denominators, but in the use of references to authenticity as a rhetorical tool. The religious dimensions of the agendas have been downplayed by an emphasis on authenticity. Given that individual religious practice, through the course of secularization processes, has been confined to the private sphere, and no country in Europe today can display a completely unifying religious narrative, cultural authenticity has been employed as the glue between history and religion. The construction of a common past has been the explicit goal despite global and transnational challenges. Historical narratives are made into tools for the construction of excluding identities, which stand in sharp contrast to the contemporary emphasis on individual choice and flexible opportunities. In societies confronted with a violent past, the chosen trauma can serve as a solid ground for social cohesion that replaces religion as a collective narrative. As some cases analysed in this volume indicate, experiences of totalitarian truth monopoly justify claims of authentic values, as is apparent in recently reclaimed religious and historical narratives.

In the 1990s, with its individualism, fluid identities and globalization, the need for new universalistic narratives emerged. In the cases of Poland, the Czech Republic, Romania and Slovenia, the intellectuals attempted to revive humanist, Western, liberal, and Christian narratives in order to integrate their societies back into Europe, or more generally into the Western world. In contrast to the stereotypical image of Orthodoxy, an aspiration to pronounce universalistic values can be observed in some strands of the Greek Orthodox Church. The ambition to denationalize, to universalize Greek Orthodoxy, by stressing the ecumenical dimension of Orthodox Christianity, is yet another example of this trend.

Secularization theory has repeatedly contested the links between national and religious identities (Berger & Lorenz 2008; Özkirimli & Sofos 2008; Halikiopoulou 2011). According to the stereotypical view, religion, at least in Western Europe, gradually ceased to function as the master narrative of nationalism. The process of desacralization of the nation has been observed in the West, especially since 1945, whereas in Eastern Europe it was possible to notice a recurrent sacralization of the nation, reinforcing the bonds between religion and nation in the post-Communist era. Historically, varying intensities of confessional-national identity could be observed in Eastern Central Europe and the Balkans: strong links between religions and the nation in Romania, Poland, Serbia, and Greece; weaker in Estonia, Hungary and the Czech Republic.

In the (re)definition and sacralization of the nation in post-Soviet Eastern Europe the dominant denominations have often positioned themselves as authentic sources for national identities, opposed to an inauthentic, coercive and monochrome socialist identity. In a time of transition, the sacralization of the nation has been an effective tool when promoting social and political cohesion of a certain ideological kind. An alternative use of religion can be observed in the tendencies to surpass traditional "nationalist" religion with the ideological aim of re-establishing modern, humanist, European (or universal) identities. These secular, humanist or transnational uses of religious pasts are discussed in the chapters on Greece, Poland, Romania, Bosnia and the Czech Republic.

Borders and Boundaries

One motivational factor in preparing this volume has been the recognition that the very concept of Eastern Europe is problematic; it raises more questions than it provides answers. This was also the point of departure for the research project "Between Conservative Reaction and Religious Reinvention: Religious Intellectuals in Central and South-East Europe on Community, Authenticity and Heritage", under the aegis of which this volume emerged. Today's national borders of the former Eastern Bloc are contested by a blurred image of the past. The lands east of the Oder river have for long been conceived as an indistinct part of Europe, historically squeezed between empires and communism. The aim of the chapters in this volume is to discuss both the significant features of the past and the complex contemporary situation where the category "Eastern Europe" is more or less obsolete. To complicate the picture further, four contributions deal with countries (Russia, Germany and Greece) that do not fit into the conventional Eastern picture, but function as prime examples of the both contested and blurred East–West divide. The objective is to mirror complex historical contexts and a multidimensional present, and to distance the discussion from any one-sided "Eastern European" development. The approaches in the chapters are related to three discursive domains. The first domain deals with how religious actors argue in public when they want to place contemporary issues in historical frameworks and construct collective identities. The second domain points to what religious themes and symbols are accentuated as significant for an authentic lifestyle, as well as the contemporary values these debaters distance themselves from. In most cases the arguments come from a self-understanding directed against contemporary decline, consumerism and liberalism. The third discursive domain is less focused on analyses of arguments and value discussions; from a cultural studies perspective it seeks rather to identify what social arenas are open to this kind of religious discourses. Here, special attention will be paid to social movements, mass media, virtual worlds, NGOs and educational systems as disciplining tools.

In their efforts to (re)invent modern national identity in the time of post-communist transition, some religious intellectuals seek to apply certain communicative strategies. Reinventing tradition and reviving religious discourses are means to strengthen hitherto "weak" national identities as well as to activate a latent European identity. Post-Communist intellectuals have disclaimed the imposed "Eastern" legacy epitomized by Soviet hegemony by strengthening the links to the West.

In the case of Romania, as analysed by Adrian Velicu, that struggle has been exemplified by the debate between, on the one hand, followers of the Latin legacy discourse claiming ancient Romanian bonds to the

Latin European culture and, on the other, advocates of an "enlightened" Romanian Orthodoxy. Velicu argues that references to the Latin heritage have frequently been used in order to justify modernization, while the argument pointing to the Orthodox legacy served as a tool for nationalist discourse. The complex dialogue between these discourses, and the efforts to dissolve the bipolarity of Romanian identity myths, are clarified by the author.

Another strategy employed by the elites is presented in Krzysztof Stala's chapter on the alliance between the Catholic Church and the dissidents in their struggle against the Communist regime in Poland. The strategy of reconciliation between the liberal intelligentsia and the progressive Catholic elites has established a common platform based on human rights, encompassing the universal values of human dignity, dialogue, tolerance and ecumenism. Such a de-ideologized platform served as a paradigm for the mass opposition movement against the Communist regime, which peaked with the Solidarity revolution in the 1980s. Later development, during the democratic period in the 1990s and 2000s, witnessed the breakdown of that alliance, due to the natural pluralization of the political and ideological outlooks on the democratic public scene. Stala contests the simplistic model launched by José Casanova, who claims "natural" and apparent links between democracy and religion in the modern world.

A different chapter dealing with communicative strategies is Stefan Arvidsson's musings on the role of myth in the modern world. In his historical overview, the author presents a variety of strategies of mythologization and demythologization in nationalist and political discourses, in modern philosophy as well as in the popular culture industry. Myths in late modernity have been transferred from the area of politics and ideology (the death of the grand narratives) into the culture industry and private culture consumption. The consequences of that transfer are, however, ambiguous. Arvidsson poses the closing question: Is the mythological symbolic potential a (malicious) impediment on the way towards the rationalistic Popperian open society, or rather, is it capable of producing a free space for creativity and human imagination?

The second discursive domain regards how religious and cultural actors choose between various themes and symbols in their interpretation and representation of a national or regional past or of a specific religious tradition. At the same time, though, the debaters often also claim that their proposals and interpretations can lead to a more contemporary (modern), relevant and viable version of cultural identity, including a supranational European identity.

In the case of the Czech Republic, Jitka Malečková shows how two seemingly contrasting public figures, a Catholic priest and a secular historian, choose the same national myths in their quest for an authentic, modern and European Czech identity. Both give prominence to the humanistic Hussite and the Catholic traditions as genuine European characteristics while they downplay, for instance, the aspect of gender equality as a specific Czech tradition connecting the Czech Republic to a supposedly Western European value system.

Trine Willert's chapter provides an introduction to various ethno-religious discourses that have claimed an authentic modern Greek identity by stressing the value of the anti-Western regional cultural heritage in the Byzantine or folkloric tradition. Such discourses are challenged today by a new generation of theologians and religious intellectuals, who use the Bible as source of a common European heritage symbolizing Greece's rightful place in the Christian European family. The same discourses that position Greece and Greek Orthodoxy closer to Europe and the West also challenge the "nationalization" of religion and suggest that nationalism has brought about a fall for Christianity, which should return to its original roots in early Christianity and, thus, revive religion as denationalized, purely religious and authentic.

With his contribution, Peter Lambert provides insight into the different uses of two historical heroic figures, the Catholic Charlemagne and the pagan Saxon Count Widukind (both eighth to ninth centuries), in German identity history. Lambert traces the "fate" of Charlemagne and Widukind from the internal disputes among Nazi leaders about whether to claim a pagan or a Christian German (Third Reich) heritage over contemporary local uses of Widukind in Saxony to the public debates about the uses of these two figures and their symbolic significance in relation to the Nazi past.

Peter Aronsson argues that national museums are authoritative spaces for the display and negotiation of community and citizenship. As meaning-generating and value-creating institutions related to nation-building and maintenance, museums play a role similar to the role churches used to play for religion. Through his analysis of official representations of history in a range of European countries, he concludes that the museums' strategies of presenting national and regional history are highly varied, ranging from the universalizing via the multiculturalizing to the strong ethnically based canon; each case depending on the contemporary local political situation, recent conflicts, threats and state-making processes.

The field where collective memory and stories about the past meet claims of authenticity and belonging opens up for the use of religious arguments where divine demands decide who is included and who is excluded (Gillis 1994; Nora 1996–98; Smith 2009). Europe has witnessed many variants of the theme, from the vulgar to the violent, from the philosophical to the political. Broad mobilization with high proficiency in contemporary modes of communication must therefore be regarded as a third discursive domain to take into consideration. In their contribution, Jörg Hackmann and Marko Lehti bring up the conflicts in Estonia about the statue of a Second World War soldier that served a vehicle to deal with a traumatic past as well as to petrify ethnic and political positions. This originally local conflict turned into a major diplomatic issue with consequences in world politics.

In his chapter, Victor Roudometof provides an account of selected issues of ecclesiastical involvement in the Greek public sphere and the impact of these in relation to the politics of memory and issues of national heritage. So-called 'hot' topics, such as the building of a mosque in Athens or the promotion of the positive role of the Church in history textbooks, provide arenas where two competing groups of intellectuals offer radically opposite interpretations on these issues. The author proposes viewing the cultural battles between these groups as an ongoing public negotiation of the relationship between Greece and the broader European project.

The supposed dichotomy between the intellectuals and the populists cannot be automatically accepted, especially when it comes to religion (Todorova 1997). Both parties are making use of the other. Karin Hyldal Christensen shows in her chapter how Soviet martyrs and saints are constructed and venerated in contemporary Russia by means of a combination of popular liturgies and historical investigations. The case is a clear example of how difficult it is to separate the intellectual from the populist, and religion as spiritual commitment from religion as a rhetorical tool.

The social arenas outside the conventional domains of the intellectuals, high-profile journalism and academia are made accessible through alliances with religious institutions and the political establishment.

Both the intellectuals and the traditional authorities in the religious institutions are facing the same challenges: new professional groups are competing for authority and the right to interpret religion and history from new arenas and with new modes of communication. In her chapter on how some Muslim theological writers in Bosnia relate to Sufism as a Muslim heritage, Catharina Raudvere discusses how references to Sufism serve both as a statement of liberal theological inclination and a quest for Islamic roots and authenticity. The case shows how new global impulses in terms of a flow of contacts, ideas and money challenge the established religious authorities and open up for alternative claims of authority and new kinds of agents.

The Rhetorical Potential of Authenticity

The impact of the criticism and arguments from the intellectuals is often questioned, not the least by themselves. The portrait of the thinker in the ivory tower or the contempt for "experts" are used in populist discourse to emphasize the distance between the intellectuals and "the people", often based on simple dichotomies and polarized arguments.

Several of the cases presented deal with intellectuals trying to combine discussions about national identity (or lack of it) with analyses of political and cultural conditions. The comments from the intellectuals on trends and conflicts seldom fit into broader political debates and campaigns, but not without exceptions: the iconic status of some intellectuals is sometimes attractive for use in politics, though mostly the intellectuals' views have turned out to be too complex for broader mobilization. The development in Poland tells us that the once powerful unity of workers, intellectuals and Church has turned out to be difficult to maintain as the liberties in post-1989 society paved the way for open forums, new lifestyles and transnational links that did not always support national unity, as other identities were stronger.

By way of conclusion: Our hypothesis is that conceptions of the pure, original and authentic have rhetorical potential that can easily be linked to religious eschatological promises. In contrast to the essentialist narratives religions often provide, these references seem to function as tools in the late-modern space of fluid identity boundaries. As several of the cases in the volume indicate, a vaguer reference to authenticity can sometimes be a more effective argument than polarized religious declarations. Earlier studies on "the return of religion" in Europe have far too often been generalizing, and the aim here is to highlight individual intellectual voices in order to uncover arguments and rhetorical figures, strategies and positions taken inside and outside communities and institutions. It is essential to analyse the present strength of nineteenth-century ideas of folk, territory, language and belief in detailed cases that show how public spaces – under the influence of globalization – can merge these romantic visions with the living conditions of late modernity.

References

Asad, Talal (2003): *Formations of the Secular. Christianity, Islam, Modernity*, Stanford: Stanford University Press.

Berger, Stefan and Chris Lorenz (ed.) (2008): *The Contested Nation. Ethnicity, Class Religion and Gender in National Histories*, New York: Palgrave Macmillan.

Bjerg, Helle, Claudia Lenz and Erik Thorstensson (2011): *Historicizing the Uses of the Past. Scandinavian Perspectives on History Culture, Historical Consciousness and Didactics of History Related to World War II*, Bielefeld: Transcript.

Bock, Heike, Jörg Feuchter and Michi Knecht (eds) (2009): *Religion and Its Others. Secular and Sacral Concepts and Practices in Interaction*, Frankfurt: Campus-Verlag.

Byrnes, Timothy A. and Peter Katzenstein (2006): *Religion in an Expanding Europe*, Cambridge: Cambridge University Press.

Calhoun, Craig, Mark Juergensmeyer and Jonathan Vanantwerpen (2011): *Rethinking Secularism*, Oxford: Oxford University Press.

Casanova, José (2011): Cosmopolitanism, the Clash of Civilizations and Multiple Modernities, *Current Sociology*, 59: 251–267.

Checkel, Jeffrey and Peter J. Katzenstein (eds) (2009): *European Identity*, Cambridge: Cambridge University Press.

Gillis, John R. (1994): *Commemorations. The Politics of Identity*, Princeton: Princeton University Press.

Halikiopoulou, Daphne (2011): *Patterns of Secularization. Church, State and Nation in Greece and the Republic of Ireland*, Farnham, UK: Ashgate.

Haynes, Jeffrey and Anja Hennig (2011): *Religious Actors in the Public Sphere. Means, Objectives and Effects*, London: Routledge.

Herrmann, Richard K., Thomas Risse and Marylynn B. Brewer (eds) (2004): *Transnational Identities. Becoming European in the EU*, Lanham: Rowman and Littlefield.

Joas, Hans and Klaus Wiegandt (eds) (2008): *The Cultural Values of Europe*, Liverpool: Liverpool University Press.

Judt, Tony (2005): *Postwar. A History of Europe since 1945*, London: Arrow Books.

Kirwan, Michael (2008): *Political Theology. A New Introduction*, London: Darton.

Lincoln, Bruce (2003): *Holy Terrors. Thinking about Religion after September 11*, Chicago: University of Chicago Press.

Nora, Pierre (1996–98): *Realms of Memory. Rethinking the French Past*, 1–3, New York: Columbia University Press.

Özkirimli, Umut and Spyros Sofos (2008): *Tormented by History. Nationalism in Greece and Turkey*, London: Hurst.

Pagden, Anthony (ed.) (2002): *The Idea of Europe. From Antiquity to the European Union*, Cambridge: Cambridge University Press.

Roy, Olivier (2010): *Holy Ignorance. When Religion and Culture Part Ways*, London: Hurst.

Smith, Anthony (2009): *Ethno-Symbolism and Nationalism. A Cultural Approach*, London: Routledge.

Stråth, Bo (ed.) (2000): *Europe and the Other and Europe as the Other*, Brussels: Peter Lang.

von Stuckrad, Kocku (2012): Secular Religion. A Discourse-Historical Approach to Religion in Contemporary Western Europe, *Journal of Contemporary Religion*, 27 (in press).

Todorova, Maria (1997): *Imagining the Balkans*, Oxford: Oxford University Press.

Todorova, Maria (ed.) (2004): *Balkan Identities. Nation and Memories*, London: Hurst.

Törnquist, Barbara Plewa and Krzysztof Stala (eds) (2011): *Eastern Europe in Focus: Social and Cultural Transformation after Communism*, Lund: Nordic Academic Press.

de Vries, Henk (2006): *Political Theologies. Public Religions in a Post-Secular World*, New York: Fordham.

Žižek, Slavoj and John Milbank (2009): *The Monstrosity of Christ. Paradox or Dialectic?* Boston: MIT Press.

NEGOTIATING EUROPEAN BELONGING
AND THE USES OF RELIGION

CHAPTER 2

Religion, Gender and History
Why the Czechs Belong in Europe
Jitka Malečková

All the historical development of the Czech state and Czech nation
points to three basic ideas: integration, humanity and Christianity,
and the latter two to a large extent coincide. From the beginnings
of its history, apart from a twenty-year period between the First
and Second World Wars, the Czech state was an integral part of a
higher entity. Nevertheless it never stopped existing in any of these
entities either de jure, or de facto. (Marklík 2007:95)

Surveys suggest that, in the early twenty-first century, Czechs are among
the least religious people in Europe. Only 19% of the respondents in
the 2005 Eurobarometer said that they believe in God, while 30%
answered that they "don't believe there is any sort of spirit, God or life
force" (Special Eurobarometer 2005:9). This makes the proportion of
self-proclaimed "non-believers" among the Czechs the second highest
in Europe.

At the same time, religious figures and symbols, and particularly
Hussitism, the early fifteenth-century Czech brand of religious reform,
have a central place in Czech national identity. The interpretation of the
role of Hussitism, the Reformation and the Counter-Reformation in
Czech history has been a crucial aspect of the historical discourse since
František Palacký's founding work in the first half of the nineteenth
century, and has instigated long-lasting and often heated debates over
the higher purpose and meaning of Czech history.

In his master narrative of Czech history, the impact of which can
still be felt today, Palacký used religion to support his claim about the

existence of the Czech nation as a European nation, and the right of this nation to exist. Today, only small groups of intellectuals discuss the place of religion in the Czech past. Nevertheless, the way references to religion in history keep reappearing in various contexts suggests its surviving relevance in Czech historical consciousness.

In a 1992 article entitled "The End of Czech Messianism?" Ivo Budil divided Czech political representatives of the early 1990s according to their attitude to Czech historical specificity. Although, he emphasized, Czech society does not need to explain the legitimacy of its state by Hussite or legionary traditions[1] any more, some politicians (the Civic Forum) still support the myth out of idealism, and others (e.g. the Social Democrats) "are shamelessly and cynically parasitical on this myth". In contrast, those parties (e.g. the conservative Civic Democratic Party) that find their model in Western market democracies and are supported by a public mistrustful of nationalism do not pay attention to Czech specificities (Budil 1992: 17–18). Nearly two decades later, the political map may look different, but references to religion and Czech specificity have not disappeared from the political dictionary, including that of intellectuals close to the current Civic Democratic Party.

Despite the intellectuals' allusions to a Czech specificity, the Czech case is far from unique in the uses of religion in national discourse. James Kennedy (2008:104–134) distinguishes three ways in which historians have constructed the relationship between religion and nation: supersession, sacralization and conflict. He shows how historians could both downplay religion as well as amplify and transform it in order to magnify its role in the past, and how they fought over determining the relationship between religion and the nation. Czech historiography offers examples of all the three processes and, generally, it seems productive to think about the Czech historical discourse as a part of broader tendencies that appeared throughout nineteenth and twentieth-century Europe.

This chapter examines how Czech intellectuals in the nineteenth and twentieth centuries constructed the relationship between religion and the nation in Czech history. It asks what role religion plays in the historical discourse of a nation that shows a rather limited interest in religion and has consistently, though not without strong opposition, defined itself as secular. It looks at two essential periods of the shaping and re-shaping of Czech national identity: the constitutive period of Czech nationalism in the nineteenth century, when the paradigm relevant at least until the mid-twentieth century and in some respects to this day was constructed, and the efforts to redefine Czech identity after 1989. It does not attempt a systematic overview of the development of Czech historical discourse on religion. Instead, it focuses on intellectuals, both historians and non-historians, whose views on religion and the nation have a wider public resonance, and follows how they relate to the nineteenth-century master narrative of Czech history. Since images of women had an important place in that narrative, alongside religion, reflections on gender in Czech history are included to indicate not only the continuities, but also discontinuities in the Czech historical consciousness.

While extensive research analyses the relationship between gender and nationalism from various perspectives (Yuval-Davis 1997; Blom, Hagemann & Hall 2000; Mayer 2000) and gender aspects of history writing attract increasing attention (Smith 1998; Epple 2003; Porciani & O'Dowd 2004; Malečková 2008), religion in modern gender history receives considerably less coverage (Starkey 2006). The intersections between religion, gender and nationalism, despite some exceptions (McLaren 2002), tend to be studied rather in societies outside Europe (Reeves-Ellington, Sklar & Shemo 2010) and have been completely neglected in Czech history to date.

The article argues that religion (and gender, when it appeared in historical discourse) has been mobilized particularly to support Czech national consciousness as a small nation: first, when trying to prove its right to existence in the nineteenth century, in the context of the multi-national Habsburg Empire, and later to redefine its place vis-à-vis the Western world and its international structures after the fall of Communism.

The first part of the article briefly outlines the place of religion and gender in the master narrative of Czech history, as formulated in the nineteenth century and in some of the later revisions. The second part draws out arguments on religion in the historical discourse after 1989, including works for the general public by secular and religious intellectuals. The third part deals with the ways in which gender was (or was not) linked with Czech history in the 1990s and 2000s.

The Constitutive Period of Czech Nationalism

The central place of history in the construction of Czech nationalism is embodied in the work and personality of František Palacký. Called "The Father of the Nation", Palacký authored a programme for the emerging modern Czech nation as well as its historical narrative. His views formed the basis of nineteenth-century Czech national identity and political arguments, grounded on the Czechs' "historical rights". Palacký saw the meaning of Czech history in the contacts and clashes with the Germans. In the fight of the two forces that influenced each other, the Slavs represented freedom, peace and democracy, and the Germans feudal hierarchy and authority based on written (i.e. undemocratic) law (Palacký 1908: 7–8, 45–46).[2] The Czechs' democracy was manifested in the Hussite movement, which Palacký considered the peak of national history, when world history depended on the direction of Czech history (Palacký 1908: 646).

Palacký's emphasis on the democratic character of the Czech nation is also reflected in his treatment of gender. The idealized family relations and the position of women among the pagan Czechs, displaying their democratic inclinations, were contrasted with the customs prevailing among the Germans. The mythical founder of the Czech ruling dynasty, Libuše, was presented as another sign of the Czechs' democracy: she was elected ruler despite being a woman and the youngest of her sisters (Palacký 1908: 30, 48). Palacký thus contributed to the creation of "the myth of gender harmony" (Malečková 2000), according to which the Czech nation has distinguished itself by the rights it acknowledged to women and by a peaceful cooperation between women and men. It is symptomatic of the myth that historians felt obliged to explain the "women's revolt", which, according to the medieval chronicle of Kosmas, followed the death of Princess Libuše: Palacký considered it the "strangest legend" and preferred to interpret it as a personal fight between the female and male leaders, rather than an "unnatural" revolt of women against men (1908: 30).

Palacký was not the first historian to praise the role and achievements of women in the Czech past. Václav Hanka, one of the authors of early nineteenth-century forged "Manuscripts", presented as the earliest sources on Czech history, depicted in his "Czech History" women both as (glorious) individual heroines and as a group distinguished by great courage (Hanka 1824: 11, 31–33, and passim). Among the national movements that created idealized images of women as heroines, whether mothers or fighters, the Czech national discourse is characterized by an emphasis on equality and cooperation between men and women, often interpreted as a consequence of the democracy inherent to the Czech nation.

The incorporation of women in national history characteristically occurred at a time when male patriots were increasingly interested in the support and participation of women in their patriotic activities. In the early periods of the Czech national movement in the first half of the nineteenth century, stressing women's place in and contribution to Czech history was intended to manifest the qualities of the Czech nation. In the debates over the woman question in the second half of the nineteenth century, the alleged equality and achievements of women in history served as a model and legitimization of the improvement of their position. Eliška Krásnohorská, one of the late nineteenth-century writers and women's leaders, argued in her "Czech Woman Question" in 1881 that women should regain the high standing and equality known from old sources in order to be able to benefit the nation; this included women's participation in education and employment (Krásnohorská 1881: 4–6). In the struggle for suffrage in the early twentieth century, women often referred to the idea of gender equality, which had been constructed by the earlier national discourse, starting with Hanka, Palacký and their contemporaries (Malečková 2000).

Palacký's interpretation of Czech history and national character created a cornerstone of the historical concepts formulated by the intellectual and political elites of the following generations. The next major contribution to the Czechs' perception of the role of religion in the national past was made by the professor and later first Czechoslovak president, Tomáš Garrigue Masaryk. In his search for the sense of Czech national life in the 1890s, Masaryk adapted Palacký's historical philosophy to the needs of the day and connected it with his own Protestant ethic. Masaryk used historical arguments to support his theses and buttress the consciousness of the Czech nation. He identified the main purpose of the Czech nation's existence as "humanity" ("humanita"), sometimes expressed in the form of reformation and democracy: "the ideal of humanity is the entire meaning of our national life" (Masaryk 2000: 148). Most importantly, Masaryk saw the emergence of the modern Czech nation as the fulfilment or crowning of the spiritual struggle of the "Hussite reformation" (Petráň 2006: 512).

The influence of the Protestant ethic was also evident in Masaryk's views on the place of women in society. An ardent supporter of the women's movement, Masaryk repeatedly stated that the so-called woman question was also a men's question and criticized particularly the Catholic view of women as subordinate to men. Inequality between men and women is not natural, but has developed historically, and a religion that sees women as lower beings comes from a barbaric period when women were enslaved. Women have both the abilities and the right to participate in public and political life and should be accepted as equal to men rationally, emotionally, and religiously, as well as economically and politically (Masaryk 1929:109–119, 1930:61–69).[3]

Masaryk dealt with the conditions of women as universal, all-human matters, rather than as specifically Czech (or Slavic) national issues. Concurrently, he supported the *Czech* women's education and emancipation in his speeches in the Austrian parliament and his collaboration with various women's organizations in Bohemia and Moravia. In a 1904 article, which summarizes his views on women's emancipation, he both praised and recommended collaboration between Czech women and men, emphasizing that the nation consists of millions of men and women connected into a whole, and both men and women should make sure that this whole is "organic": "As far as I can see into the Czech conditions it is gratifying that women and men so often act together: there are both few modern women as there are few modern men, and therefore they can well support each other in their efforts" (Masaryk 1930:67).

The long-lasting debates over "the meaning of Czech history", which began as a response to Masaryk's work, have been analysed quite extensively elsewhere (Havelka 1995, 2006, 2008). Here, suffice it to point out the centrality of the debates in Czech national discourse. This was manifested by the participation of leading intellectuals of various ideological persuasions in each phase of the debates (1910s, 1920s, 1930s and up to the 1960s), including the prominent historian Josef Pekař, the musicologist and first Minister of Culture of socialist Czechoslovakia, Zdeněk Nejedlý, and the famous dissident philosopher Jan Patočka. The intellectuals' ethical-religious beliefs and understanding of the role of religion in history formed, along with nationalism, the bases for their evaluation of the Czech past and its "meaning". Pekař criticized the Protestant bias in Masaryk's evaluation of Hussitism and saw the meaning of Czech history instead in "national existence itself". Catholic historians formulated a version of national history that identified the periods of Counter-Reformation and Baroque as peaks of Czech history. Rudolf Voříšek, for example, stated that the Czech nation is predestined by its history to understand the importance of Christianity and its consequences for national life (Havelka 2006:11–17). At the same time, a strong continuity can be followed in the debates, which always focused on the same key periods of the past – the Hussite movement, the White Mountain and Counter-Reformation, the National Revival and the establishment of the Czechoslovak Republic – though interpreting them differently. Even Pekař, known as a fierce opponent of Masaryk's philosophy of history, namely his appraisal of Hussitism as the peak of the Czech past, and a critic of the destructive consequences of the Hussite movement, acknowledged Hussitism as a historical phenomenon of European dimensions (Pekař 1929:28). The close relationship between the meaning of Czech history and the Czechs' place in Europe is, in fact, another feature of the debates. "[W]here the ardour of patriotic love encountered and united with enlightened and moral progress of Europe, we rose to greatness, where it weakened or disappeared, we declined", as Pekař put it (1929:22).

At the beginning of The Second World War, Karel Stloukal, a well-known historian who saw the meaning of Czech history in the struggle for freedom, described women in the Hussite period as a specifically Czech type: religiously and nationally conscious, educated and even emancipated (Stloukal 1940:26). Gender did not figure as an argument in the debates over the meaning of Czech history, but was treated in separate historical works, such as the monumental volume entitled "Czech Queens, Princesses, and Great Women", which Stloukal edited and introduced with an overview of Czech women's history (Stloukal 1940:11–45).

History and gender were linked in the works of the most influential figure of the Czech women's movement in the first half of the twentieth century, Senator Františka Plamínková. Connecting the fight for women's emancipation and the Czech nation's place in the world, Plamínková promoted the myth of gender harmony:

Our nation is democratic in its character and filled with love of justice. The whole course of Czech history shows the fine character of Czech women, their good-heartedness, their fine relations to the men, the esteem and hearty collaboration between both sexes ... Only those who know Bohemia as it was in its independence before Habsburg rule, can appreciate the development which has taken place in the Czechoslovak Republic since the revolution of the 28th of October

1918. To all others the liberties with which the Czechoslovak nation invests the people, including women, may seem too sudden and instable for the future (sic!) (Plamínková 1920:5–6).

Nineteenth-century patriots and feminists created, and intellectuals before the Second World War reinforced, an image of a glorious past of Czech women, in a society which favoured equality and which women, for their part, supported wholeheartedly (Malečková 2000). Early national history was illuminated by the examples of pious women, including the first Czech female saint Ludmila, and influential queens. The peak came with Hussitism, the "most glorious epoch of Czech history": Hussite women in the early fifteenth century were more educated than men in many European countries, "as full of enthusiasm for the reformation of moral life and as determined" to sacrifice their lives "in defence of the known truths and for freedom of thought, as ever was any man" (Plamínková 1920:5). Later, the Czech Brethren kept up the tradition of women's literacy and participation of common women in the life of the community, and their bishop, Comenius, explicitly supported women's education. Finally, in the "dark age" of the Counter-Reformation, when following the revolt of the Czech Estates many men were executed or had to emigrate, women preserved the national tradition and identity (Plamínková 1920:5–6).

The aim of the women's movement was to "harmonize the relationship between both sexes", which, Plamínková argued, might be a "typically Czech or Slavic aim" (1930:13). Another interesting feature of the Czech women's movement was a dedicated cooperation of many men, both theoreticians and practitioners. In a footnote, she compared the contemporary Czech women's movement to the traditions of the Hussites and the Czech Brethern in the fifteenth and seventeenth centuries, respectively, characterized by the same qualities and cooperation between men and women (Plamínková 1930:13).

Rather than being understood as a reflection of exceptionally friendly gender relations, characteristic of the traditional Czech society, the image of the important place of women and their collaboration with men in national history is interesting as a symptom of an effort to invent such a tradition. Both female and male proponents of this view closely tied the fate of women to that of the nation and, like Plamínková in the above quote, used it to support the perception of the new Czech/oslovak nation as progressive abroad.

Communist Czechoslovakia inherited the image of women's past alongside the concept of national history, with the peaks in Hussitism and the national revival, and the "dark age" in the period of Counter-Reformation. While gender aspects silently disappeared from historical discourse, the narration of national history could easily be modified for Communist purposes.

Zdeněk Nejedlý, who had participated in the struggle over the meaning of Czech history since the early twentieth century, summarized the Communist concept in 1947 in a work entitled "Communists – heirs of the great traditions of the Czech nation". After the challenge by Catholic historians before the war, Nejedlý rehabilitated the Hussite movement as the peak of Czech history, but interpreted it as a movement for social equality, not a religious movement. He emphasized the role of "the people" as the bearer of national traditions, from the Hussite period and the Czech Brethren in the sixteenth century, through the national revival to current patriotic working classes. He described these traditions as uniquely progressive, compared to other nations, especially the Germans (Nejedlý 1947:23).[4]

Communist rule thus brought a return to Palacký's concept of national history, though with new emphases, drawing on the interwar works of the Czech Left. There was a strong continuity in the master narrative of Czech history and the historical consciousness of the Czech public, which was still mainly shaped by the popularized version of Palacký's work.[5]

Post-1989 Reconstructions

Although after 1989 religion gained a more prominent place in public life, and to some extent in politics, the Czech public was interested more in disputes over the restitution of Church property, confiscated by the Communist regime, than the role of religion and Church in society. The fall of Communism did not engender a new phase of debates over the meaning of Czech history, either. Historical arguments appear particularly in efforts to redefine the relations of the Czechs with their neighbours and with Europe more generally. Nevertheless, religion and history intersect, often inconspicuously, in a wide spectrum of contexts. This section looks at how the relationship between religion and national history is constructed in the historical and religious discourses.

The first broad group of intellectuals touching on this relationship can be considered "secular". Regardless of the personal beliefs of the authors, both professional historians and non-historians, their popular works are not written from a religious point of view and focus primarily on the Czechs' place in Europe. They oscillate around three main claims: First, the Czechs are part of (a Christian) Europe because they are Christians, despite their Communist past and widespread atheism. Second, they belong to Europe because they have participated in all the European historical trends, including those concerning Christianity, and on occasion were even ahead of Europe. Third, due to their democratic and religious traditions the Czechs differ from other post-Communist nations and thus deserve a special place in Europe.

Of particular interest in this respect are histories of European integration. Their authors, often not professional historians, try to show that unification has a long tradition in Europe to which the Czechs have contributed since the beginnings of their history. They reflect the master narrative of Czech history and share the belief in its "mission".

According to economist and diplomat Václav Marklík (2007), the Czech nation broke up with fundamentalist Catholicism in the Hussite movement and with Communism in 1989. Thus rejecting collectivism, it has only one alternative – the secular liberal integration system of Euro-American capitalism heading towards globalism. However, even this system needs moral borders and a spiritual inspiration; otherwise it is threatened by a moral and civilizational collapse as a result of "the materialism and hedonism of the society and the rise of fundamentalist militant Islam, controlled by terrorists" (2007: 93). Yet, "the tolerant, kind and sincere Christian Churches turned towards people, like the Catholic, Protestant, or Orthodox Church", can restore the moral order (2007: 92–93). If the Czechs want to preserve their state, even if integrated in Europe, the nation has to have a moral mission or a meaning, which Marklík finds in spiritual values: integration, humanism and Christianity (2007: 95). Finally, he emphasizes that the Czechs are Christians because their civilization is Christian, even if they do not practise Christian faith and consider themselves atheists (2007: 97).

Political scientist Alexandr Ort (2008) offers an account of Czech history reminding us of traditional historical textbooks. The Czechs became acquainted with Christianity through the missionaries requested from Byzantium, Constantine and Methodius, who translated the Bible to the Old-Slavonic language the Czechs could understand. This had implications for the Czechs' higher rates of literacy compared to the rest of Europe, where Christianity was based on the Latin text of the Bible

(2008: 5–6). The Hussite movement included an effort to learn to read and write and was ahead of its time by a hundred years. Ort quotes Aeneas Silvius Picolomini (Pius II) who wrote that many a Hussite woman know the Bible better than many Catholic priests (2008: 6). Czechs generally were quite advanced throughout their history, Ort claims, e.g. in Palacký's Austroslavic programme or when interwar Czechoslovakia was accepted as a factor of stabilization in European politics and a democratic island in the centre of Europe (2008: 11–19). The Prague Spring demonstrated the strength of the democratic roots of the Czech nation, which other nations of the Soviet Bloc lacked (2008: 42).

Professional historians reflecting on the European dimension of the Czech past depict the relationship between the Czechs and Europe as more complex, but their views show strong parallels to those of non-historians. Thus Jiří Rak, a respected historian and author of works on nineteenth-century Czech national myths, writes in an exhibition catalogue on Czech Europeanism, addressed to general readers, that from the very beginnings of their history, the Czechs had embraced European civilization and at times contributed to its development (2006: 11). They share with other European nations both the positive and the negative aspects of history, including religious wars and national intolerance as well as openness and rich cultural exchange. "Therefore, the Czech membership in the European Union, which is a brand new chapter in the history of the old continent, should be understood as a quite natural phenomenon" (2006: 13). Rak describes the Hussite period as "another high period of the Czech Middle Ages", alongside the reign of Charles IV, and the Hussite wars as "a specific Czech phenomenon, which was unparalleled in Europe"; emphasizing, however, that the Czech followers of Jan Hus did not try to break away from the Church and from Christian Europe of that time (2006: 41–47).

References to religion in the works of secular intellectuals seem to be pragmatic, mainly aimed at showing the advanced character of the Czech nation and its struggle for peace and integration. A rather sophisticated example of this approach can be found in the works of Dušan Třeštík (d. 2007), a prominent historian of the early Middle Ages and author of numerous articles on the implications of Czech history for the present (Třeštík 1999, 2005). As a medievalist, he naturally dealt with religion and often mentioned religious figures, symbols or holidays in his popular newspaper articles. In an essay on Constantine and Methodius, who in traditional Czech historiography brought Christianity – in its Eastern form – to the Czechs, Třeštík argued that the matter was not a religious struggle between Eastern and Western Christianity, but the aim was to incorporate Great Moravia into Europe on an equal footing (2005: 279). Similarly, St. Wenceslas (Václav) was not primarily a religious figure for Třeštík, but a symbol of Czech statehood, demonstrating that Czechs were in the early tenth century rather advanced within Europe (2005: 270–271). Concurrently, Třeštík showed that the figure of Václav could become a symbol of the opposition to the state – thus confirming his purely secular interpretation of the major Czech saint.

While repeatedly criticizing various forms of Czech nationalism, Třeštík also made an effort to distance the Czechs from other Slavs, particularly Eastern Slavs, as with his interpretation of the role of Constantine and Methodius. He tried to show that the Czechs have belonged to Europe since their early history and belong there (again) today. Current Czech national self-identification, he argued, is exactly the same as that of the Western state-nations. Traditionally, Czechs saw the peak of their history in Hussitism, in which the Czech fighters for the Truth fought against the whole of Europe and (morally) won (though in another sense they lost everything, including their economic and political future). Today they see the peak in the reign of Charles IV because they do not want to be "against everybody" and win morally, but gain some (material) rewards, Třeštík concluded (2005: 177). It is worth noting that this enfant terrible of the Czech historical community belonged among the most popular historians of the late twentieth century, although he challenged, from a postmodernist standpoint, many long-held myths dear to the Czech audience and wrote, for instance, about the *invention* of the Czech nation. Třeštík's ambivalent relationship to nationalism is of particular interest in this respect.

Religious intellectuals[6] who reflect on religion in the Czech past do not form a single group; even if we limit the analysis to the most numerous Catholic intellectuals, it is clear that their views are rather diverse. Leaving aside the disputes and more systematic divisions, three approaches relevant for their treatment of religion and the nation can be mentioned here: the (conservative) voice of the official Catholic Church, "liberal" or non-conformist intellectuals, and extreme conservatives (sometimes called "fundamentalists"). Despite the differences between these approaches, intellectuals belonging to each of these streams display a surprising regard for national interests.

The public usually does not follow statements of Church representatives. However, Cardinal Vlk made the news in 2010 with his remarks
on the Muslim threat to Europe. His talk on the "historical roots of
the values that form today's Europe: A Czech experience from 2009"
is worth quoting here for the parallel with the interpretative paradigm
typical of secular intellectuals, including the implicit notion of the
mission of Czech history and the Czech contribution to Europe. In
the talk, Vlk stated:

> [that] my country, the Czech Republic, did not become a part of
> Europe as late as 2004, when we joined the European Union, but
> that our entry was just a topical statement that a small state in the
> heart of Europe belongs to it and that it actively participated in its
> "emergence", in the process of its growth, simply that our nation
> was at the roots of Europe since the beginning. (Vlk 2009)

The reign of Charles IV is, according to Vlk, a proof of the positive
impact of a close cooperation between the secular and spiritual spheres.
And this "important experience of our history" is what the Czechs can
offer Europe. Vlk spoke about Hus and Masaryk in more or less neutral
terms, though he went through the problematic periods of the Czech
past briefly. He pointed out that the Hussite period with its religious
wars foreshadowed European religious reform efforts and wars of the
following centuries, thus connecting the Czech experience to general
European trends. Reflecting on the role of Hus in the twentieth century,
he emphasized national aspects, together with the way Hus was used
by the Communist regime. The Czechs, unfortunately, were unable
to learn from the negative experiences of the totalitarian regime and
thus, according to Vlk, they can also offer Europe a negative example
of what happens when spiritual values are lacking in the life of a society.

Despite Vlk's careful phrasing, it is clear that the figure of Hus is still
somewhat problematic and divisive for the Czech Catholic Church.
In a short contribution on Hus, liberal Catholic priest Tomáš Halík
emphasizes that the time has come to overcome simplified ideological
templates of history, "a torn tradition", and open up for a new view
of Czech history that would acknowledge the right place to all great
personalities of the past without any exclusions:

Czech Catholicism cannot continue to perceive Hus as somebody who is outside its own tradition. Otherwise it will not be possible for many Czechs to be "Catholics without reservation" and for many Czech Catholics to be "Czechs without reservation" because Hus belongs to the great archetypes of the Czech nation and is one of the keys for the understanding of Czech spirituality (Halík 1995:312).

Hus indeed stands "among confessions, nations and centuries", and only an ecumenical, international and interdisciplinary dialogue can disclose a new path to a deeper knowledge of his personality and work, Halík concludes (1995: 312). These words seem symptomatic of the views of this leading representative of the Czech ecumenical movement and best-known Czech religious thinker, popular also among the broad public. Somewhat like Třeštík, Halík openly admits to being inspired by postmodernism. Unlike Třeštík, he seldom explicitly deals with Czech national identity (the quotes mentioned here represent rather striking exceptions) and is more interested in universal spiritual issues and the position of the Church in today's world than in specifically Czech questions (Halík 2004, 2009). It seems that for Halík, the Czechs' belonging to Europe is self-evident rather than a contested matter that has to be defended. He usually does not ask about the relationship between the Czechs and Europe, but between Europe (or Christianity) and the world, and argues for dialogue and "perspectivism".[7]

Yet, speaking of Eastern European experiences, Halík (n.d.) mentions that Czechs and Poles are suspicious of references to Pan-Slavism, which they see as a dangerous political instrument of Russian imperialism. When they hear "warnings against the corrupt West" from Church circles, Czechs are reminded of Communist propaganda. At the same time Halík points out "the enormous differences in the culture and religiosity of those countries"; for example, religiosity in the Czech lands is more like French religiosity than Slovak. He connects the differences to how successfully faith was incorporated in the national culture, life-style and thinking of the people. Like the secular intellectuals, Halík makes an effort to distinguish the Czechs from other Slavs, namely the Poles (and elsewhere the Russians), interestingly using references to Hussitism for this purpose:

> Unlike Polish history, Czech history has been marked by a painful tension between national identity and Catholicism. The tension,

which dates back to the Hussite wars and the violent re-Catholiciz-
ing of the seventeenth century, was intensified by the nationalism
of the last century. The already highly secularized Czechs seemed
ideal for a radically atheistic society. The goal of communism, a
town without God, seemed almost within reach in the Czech lands
(Halík 1996).

Religious intellectuals comment on a belief that because Eastern European
Churches had the good fortune to "sleep through the second Vatican
Council and the post-Vatican II developments", they will revitalize the
Church in the West. While Halík (n.d.) attributes this misconception to
traditionalist, conservative circles in the West, another liberal Catholic
intellectual, Martin Putna, who started to publish as an "angry young
man" in the early 1990s, ascribed this attitude to the Czech Catholic
Church itself. After the fall of Communism, representatives of the Czech
Catholic Church believed that the Czech Catholics have managed to
keep their faith uncorrupted, while the Church in the West is spoiled
by welfare and modernism, rationalism and moral decay. Therefore,
they came to the conclusion that, "we are the only true Catholics,
[and] the resurrection of the Church in the world will come from us"
(Putna 1994:25). This messianism, claims Putna, is of Eastern origin,
but is also widespread in Poland, which many Czech Catholics see as a
model. Putna, however, somewhat scornfully mentions that the Polish
model might fit Slovakia, but is completely unsuitable for the Czechs.

The views that Putna criticized in 1994 are echoed in 2009 by Petr
Hájek – journalist, writer, former spokesman and current vice-chan-
cellor of the Czech president Václav Klaus.[8] In an interview for a left-
wing newspaper, _Právo_, Hájek explained that while after the fall of
Communism, the Czechs have been painfully and slowly searching
for their identity, the Western European democracies are very quickly
losing theirs, as is Obama's America (Hájek 2009). Western nations
are distancing themselves from their roots and are thus "drying up".
The Czechs have been historically "saved by recatholicization" and, as
a result, they avoided German Protestantism. Today, they are not as
atheist as their left-wing elites present them, and (an interesting reference to the above-mentioned messianism) "are just somewhat sheep-
ishly carrying [their] cross". Hájek does not see Russia as a threat to
the Czech Republic. Russians are merely different, drawing from their
roots. "While in Western Europe Christianity is tired and decadent, for

Russian Orthodoxy, the defining image is resurrection and hope..." In this context, Hájek presented a different connection between religion and the nation – and its place in Europe – when he expressed his belief that the Czech Republic should leave the European Union.[9]

The more extreme conservative views on religion and the nation, little known to the general public and mostly not historically framed, are less relevant for the present context. One aspect worth mentioning here, though, is that they link religion, nationalism and attitudes towards Europe with gender.[10]

Approaching Gender After 1989

It is hardly surprising that conservative Catholic intellectuals attribute to women a traditional role in their interpretations of current Czech society and its history. More interestingly, the radical-liberal Putna, criticized in the 1990s for his sympathies towards the underground and non-conformist views (Gabriel 1993:4), went much further when he warned against the contemporary tendencies to emphasize "the feminine", be it feminist or related to the Marian cult. He considered these to be possibly "the last trap of the Devil" because the Marian cult can easily become a new non-Christian religion, worshipping an evil goddess who divides people and causes fanaticism and hatred (Putna 1994:77). In the same vein, Putna criticized feminism, making an intriguing parallel between feminists and Slovak nationalists, who both feel oppressed by another group, which despite its best efforts does not understand the complaint (1994:55).

The liberal Catholic Halík, open to a dialogue with other religions as well as non-believers and to inspiration from postmodernism, conspicuously avoids any references to gender. Judging from his works, he seems uninterested in the existence of women believers and in gender as a category of analysis, not to mention differences in sexual orientation. In Czech, with its clear grammatical gendering, Halík's consistent use of masculine forms, pronouns and references, though quite common among male – and some female – intellectuals, appears to be a statement, because the well-read Halík can hardly be unaware of the current literature on gender and religion or feminist theology.

Given the inclusiveness of his religious thought, Halík's omission is more surprising than the lack of attention paid to gender by other intellectuals, whether religious or secular. Rak (2006:95) briefly refers to women in the past, when he appreciates the foundation of a nineteenth-century women's association aiming to introduce American technical progress and a modern way of thinking among Czech women. Generally, however, mainstream historians are not interested in gender and often are explicitly antifeminist. The postmodernist Třeštík did not consider using his theoretical erudition and knowledge of medieval Czech history to bring new insights in the little-known gender relations in medieval Bohemia. Instead, he emphasized that historians in Central Europe had more important issues to study than women or homosexuals – namely to write national history in order to help the confused Czech society after 1989 find support in its past (presented, of course, by those who were not confused, i.e., the historians) (Třeštík 2005:171).

Much has been and more could be written on Czech antifeminism, prevailing even among well-known and respected intellectuals, and on the reasons why feminism has become a taboo subject that cannot be approached without a whole set of preconceptions (Havelková 1993; Šiklová 1993; Šmejkalová 2005). Here, the question is rather why gender does not play the role it used to from the nineteenth century up to at least the mid-twentieth century: why is it not used to make claims about the character of the Czech nation any more?

One of the possible answers could be found in the different way the Communist regime treated religion and gender. Although the Communists viewed Catholicism as more dangerous than the Czech Protestant Churches and appropriated Jan Hus and Hussitism for socialist propaganda, religion was generally suppressed rather than incorporated into the Communist rhetoric. In contrast, the regime claimed to have solved the woman question and women's (alleged) equality was used to show the achievements of the new Communist state. Dissidents did not pay any attention to gender issues, persuaded that the totalitarian regime oppressed women and men to the same extent or that the authoritarian character of the Communist state overshadowed the different consequences of the oppression on the lives of women and men.

This is also the case regarding Jiřina Šiklová, sociologist (graduate in history), dissident and later founder of the Czech gender studies in the early 1990s. In her famous defence, "Save these books", written when she was imprisoned in 1981, Šiklová did not comment on the gender aspects of the repressive regime. She emphasized that destroying books is particularly "alienating for our nation, which has always been proud of its struggle against the Counter-Reformation and the

Jesuits, a nation, whose traditions spring from the Enlightenment"
(2005:276), thus setting her arguments in the traditional paradigm
of Czech history.[11]

After 1989, allusions to women's rights, equality or representation
were interpreted as reminders of Communist propaganda or attempts
to bring back Communist practices. In efforts to find the Czechs'
place in Europe, religion could thus serve to distance the Czechs from
the Communist past, while references to women in history seemed to
tie them to the Communist heritage and/or open up the doors to the
feared and despised feminism.

Two groups of intellectuals defy this predicament: those striving
to establish gender studies in the Czech Republic and the historians
who write gender or women's history. Although there is an occasional
connection between the two groups, they do not tend to overlap: the
founders of gender studies who engaged in debates on feminism and
history particularly in the 1990s were not historians, while gender
analysis (or feminism) did not appear in historical research before
the late 1990s. Historians of the older generation, who were already
writing on Czech women's history in the 1990s, mostly made it clear
that their interest was purely academic: their works were completely
unrelated to contemporary issues and feminist theories, and did not
question the general paradigm of Czech history and historiography.

The founders of gender studies in the Czech Republic in the 1990s
were naturally more interested in current issues than the past, but they
also tried to base the new discipline in history. Historical references
fulfilled three aims. First, they were used to show that feminism had
Czech roots and a strong tradition in the Czech past, and was not a
post-1989 import from the West. For this purpose, the authors quoted
the achievements of nineteenth-century Czech women and the support the women's movement received from men in that century and
interwar Czechoslovakia (Hendrychová 1992:15, 1999:43–49; Šiklová
1992:24). Religion did not enter this debate, though early explorations
of feminist theology appeared in journals and edited volumes, alongside
other gender issues (Opočenská 1999).

Second, vis-à-vis Western feminism, representatives of gender studies
mentioned the shared experiences of women in post-Communist countries (particularly Poland and Hungary), in order to explain the specific
East (Central) European approach to feminism (Šiklová 1992:26–29,
1999:16; Havelková 1993:64–65). At the same time, however, they

also used historical references to emphasize the differences among the Eastern European countries (Havelková 1995:21) and the Czech peculiarities (Hendrychová 1999:48).

Third, gender debates reflected the acceptance of the myth of gender harmony created in the nineteenth century. Emphasizing the moderation of Czech women and the support of Czech men in history could serve to persuade the suspicious general public that promoting women's equality was "natural". It also reflected the genuine enthusiasm among the proponents of gender studies when they discovered the activities of their ancestors and learned about their cooperation with men in the nineteenth and early twentieth centuries (Hendrychová 1992, 1999; Šiklová 1992). Appreciating Masaryk's endorsement of the women's movement, Hendrychová (1999:48) pointed out that in accordance with Masaryk's "persuasion that the so-called woman question is a question of the whole society, Plamínková created a type of Czech feminism, which was not directed against men", but strove to base the relationship between man and woman on the freedom of both, mutual respect, and equal duties voluntarily taken upon oneself.

The works of the historians of gender and women grounded in feminist theories do not attract much attention among the general readership, but are worth noting due to the way they relate to the nineteenth-century master narrative. However, representatives of the younger generation who studied after 1989 seem less affected by the antifeminist stereotypes and are not afraid to research women's and gender history as topics related to feminism. They do not deal only with exceptional Czech women or details of nuns' lives, but also with conceptual questions of gender relations and the effects of the gender constructions on Czech society. In a paper on gender in the Catholic political culture, Petr Pabián (2008) mentioned that the Czech political culture was in all political camps constructed as masculine. He concluded by pointing out "an unintended proof of this fact" – the contributions at the workshop on heroism and cowardice in nineteenth and twentieth-century Czech political culture, which mainly understood heroism and cowardice as masculine categories: "In this way, contemporary Czech historiography not only mirrors, but also reproduces the political culture, which was and is gendered masculine" (2008: 122).

Denisa Nečasová, analysing Party documents from the 1950s, showed that Communism did not change the traditional prejudices against women. Gender stereotypes on women in politics, typical of the nine-teenth century, are deeply rooted in Czech society, she claimed, and are reproduced to this day with only minor changes:

> The 19th century did not only leave a trace in the present in the form of a small fragment without a major impact. It gave us a very broad path stepped by many pairs of shoes, which a person can only with difficulty avoid when looking for one's place in the world (Nečasová 2008: 490).

Occasionally, works on women and gender history display the continu-ing relevance of the myth of gender harmony in the early twenty-first century. Thus, for example, Marie Bahenská wrote in 2008:

> A specific feature of emancipation in our country is not only the undeniable cooperation with men, unique in Europe, but also a permanent regard for national interests, which are put before spe-cifically women's interests, and respect for the law in efforts to push through women's demands (Bahenská 2008:445).

We can also see a certain development in the views of those who have been studying the past and present of Czech gender relations since the 1990s, including efforts to conceptualize this past and attempts at a critical distance from the myths concerning Czech gender history (Havelková 2007). Generally, however, gender debates connected with history are rarer now than they were in the early or mid-1990s. Gender is addressed in response to the demands of the EU for gender equality and the related legislation, or other current issues. The question of Czech specificity in the treatment of women or gender relations does not appear among topics of public discourse in the early twenty-first century.

Concluding Reflections

So are the Czechs still entrapped in the perceptions constructed in the nineteenth century? The views of the intellectuals presented in this chapter show a striking continuity of the historiographical paradigm, starting with Palacký and up to the early twenty-first century. Hussitism, though criticized and challenged particularly by the Catholic participants in the debates over the meaning of Czech history, survives as the major defining phenomenon of the Czech national past. However, the role of religion in Czech historical discourse is rather pragmatic: religion is used to support the authors' views regarding the Czechs' place in Europe and their self-respect.

After 1989, the main division in the views on religion in the national past does not seem to run between secular and religious (Catholic) intellectuals. Both groups tend to base their views on the same historical consciousness, referring to the same myths and stories and often using them to the same effect. While secular historical discourse is strikingly rich in religious references, religious discourse can surprise us with its strong national framework. The national aspects often become evident in efforts to emphasize a Czech specificity, particularly compared to other post-Communist countries, common to both secular and religious intellectuals.

In contrast, gender is not used to support arguments about the Czechs' place in Europe and the world at the turn of the twentieth and twenty-first centuries, nor is it connected with the Czechs' understanding of their own past any more. Czech gender discourse is rather weak on history, and historical discourse is weak on gender. The connection between the fate of women and the nation, emphasized in the nineteenth and early twentieth centuries, was shortly revived in the debates around the emerging gender studies in the 1990s, but has little resonance among the general public today. The reasons are likely to be found in the Communists' use of women's equality (as opposed to their treatment of religion), though one might also consider the possibility that the myth of gender harmony and the achievements of the Czech nation manifested by women seems dated today.

More sophisticated descriptions of how nationalism connects with the past seem to fit the Czechs better, as suggested by the popularity of two quite different intellectuals, the Catholic priest Halík and the historian Třeštík. Despite all their differences, they both offer the Czechs a (post-)modern version of their past and present, which can make them feel part of contemporary (Christian, civilized) Europe, and yet preserves some of the traditional securities and values of Czech specificity.*

* I would like to thank Michal Pullmann for his comments on an earlier draft of this paper.

Notes

1 This refers to the volunteers fighting in the First World War on the side of the Allies who helped to secure their support for the creation of an independent Czechoslovakia. While occasionally referring to Czechoslovakia, the article leaves aside the construction of Slovak national history, which followed a different path.

2 The Czech version of his History of the Czech Nation in Bohemia and Moravia was published between 1848 and 1867.

3 First published in Chicago in 1907 and 1904, respectively.

4 In other contexts (p. 27), he suggested that Czech development was more progressive than that of the Poles.

5 This was represented by the prolific author of historical novels Alois Jirásek, whose books retained their popularity with the public well into the second half of the twentieth century.

6 I use the term religious intellectuals both broadly and narrowly, including writers who explicitly identify themselves as Catholics, yet leaving aside the no less interesting representatives of Protestant intellectuals, such as Zdeněk Bárta, Erazim Kohák or Jana Opočenská.

7 This means acknowledging that while I believe in my truth, I am only speaking from the perspective of my knowledge, place and experience, and cannot know God in His entirety.

8 Also of interest, though less known, are the views of Roman Joch, new advisor of Prime Minister Nečas, who refers to himself as a "papist", and connects his belief with that of the saints Václav, Vojtěch, Anežka, and of Charles IV. Both Joch and Hájek are considered to belong among extreme conservatives.

9 He emphasized that Václav Klaus does not agree with this view.

10 See e.g. Michal Semín: Brněnská mešita a blafující lidovci, www.semin.blog.ihned. cz, 28. 7. 2009 (accessed 20.9.2010).

11 Václav Havel (1990: 78–79), though confessing to know little about feminism (which, he admitted, might be more than an invention of some hysterical women, bored ladies or jilted mistresses) contributed to the Czech debates on gender by his often-quoted characterization of feminism as "dada". The label appeared in a description of how Czech dissident women refused to sign a petition on human rights presented as a women's manifesto because they were afraid that signing anything "as women" would make them appear funny. Havel considered the fear of being identified as feminist to be a part of the Czech and Central European scepticism towards pathos and sentimentalism (and the Czech sense of humour and irony).

References

Bahenská, Marie (2008): Pomalu, pozvolna, po špičkách. K chápání a reflexi pojmu emancipace v českých zemích v 19. a 20. století, in Milan Řepa (ed.): *19. století v nás. Modely, instituce a reprezentace, které přetrvaly*, Praha: Historický ústav.

Blom, Ida, Karen Hagemann and Catherine Hall (eds) (2000): *Gendered Nations. Nationalisms and Gender Order in the Long Nineteenth Century*, Oxford-New York: Berg.

Budil, Ivo (1992): Konec českého mesianismu?, *Prostor*, 5 (20): 17–18.

Epple, Angelika (2003): *Empfindsame Geschichtsschreibung. Eine Geschlechtergeschichte der Historiographie zwischen Aufklärung und Historismus*, Köln-Weimar-Wien: Böhlau Verlag.

Gabriel, Josef (1993): Pod zemí M.C. Putny. *Perspektivy. Příloha katolického týdeníku* 4 (6): 4.

Hájek, Petr (2009): Svobodný svět byla iluze, *Právo*, 12 December.

Halík, Tomáš (n.d.): *Christian Experience in Central and Eastern Europe During the First Decade After Communism*. [online]. Available at: <http://www.halik.cz/ja/christian_experience.php> (Accessed 17 August 2010).

Halík, Tomáš (1995): Hus a český katolicismus, in Jan Blahoslav Lášek (ed.): *Jan Hus mezi epochami, národy a konfesemi*, Praha: Česká křesťanská akademie.

Halík, Tomáš (1996): Post-Communism and its discontents, *First Things* 59 (January): 37–39.

Halík, Tomáš (2004): *Vzýván i nevzýván. Evropské přednášky k filozofii a sociologii dějin křesťanství*, Praha: Lidové noviny.

Halík, Tomáš (2009): *Stromu zbývá naděje. Krize jako šance*, Praha: Lidové noviny.

Hanka, Václav (1824): *Dějiny české v kamenopisně vyvedených obrazech*, Praha: Antonín Machek.

Havel, Václav (1990): Anatomie jedné zdrženlivosti, in Václav Havel: *Do různých stran. Eseje a články z let 1983–1989*, (arranged by Vilém Prečan), Praha: Lidové noviny.

Havelka, Miloš (1995): Spor o smysl českých dějin 1895–1938, in Miloš Havelka (ed.), *Spor o smysl českých dějin 1895–1938*, Praha: TORST.

Havelka, Miloš (2006): "Smysl", "pojetí" a "kritiky dějin"; historická "identita" a historické "legitimizace" (1938–1989), in Miloš Havelka (ed.), *Spor o smysl českých dějin 2, 1938–1989. Posuny a akcenty české otázky*, Praha: TORST.

Havelka, Miloš (2008): Esence, mýtus nebo hypotéza?! Pět fází diskuzí o smyslučeských dějiny (1895–1989), in Milan Řepa (ed.): *19. století v nás. Modely, instituce a reprezentace, které přetrvaly*, Praha: Historický ústav.

Havelková, Hana (1993): A Few Prefeminist Thoughts, in Nanette Funk and Magda Mueller (eds): *Gender Politics and Post-Communism. Reflections from Eastern Europe and the Former Soviet Union*, New York-London: Routledge.

Havelková, Hana (1995): Liberální historie ženské otázky v Českých zemích, in Hana Havelková (ed.): *Existuje středoevropský model manželství a rodiny?* Praha: Divadelní ústav.

Havelková, Hana (2007): Konec idyly? Možné konceptualizace postavení žen v moderní české historii, in Jana Cviková, Jana Juráňová and Ľubica Kobová (eds), *Histórie žien. Aspekty písania a čítania*, Bratislava: Aspekt.

Hendrychová, Soňa (1992): Z historie ženského hnutí v Československu, in Hana Havelková (ed.): *Lidská práva, ženy a společnost*, Praha: ESVLP.

Hendrychová, Soňa (1999): Z historie feminismu v českých zemích, in *Společnost žen a mužů z aspektu gender*, Praha: Open Society Fund.

Kennedy, James (2008): Religion, Nation and European Representations of the Past, in Stefan Berger and Chris Lorenz (eds): *The Contested Nation. Ethnicity, Religion, Class and Gender in National Histories*, Houndmills: Palgrave Macmillan.

Krásnohorská, Eliška (1881): *Ženská otázka česká*, Praha: Edv. Grégr.

McLaren, Anne (2002): Gender, Religion, and Early Modern Nationalism: Elizabeth I, Mary Queen of Scots, and the Genesis of English Anti-Catholicism, *The American Historical Review* 107 (3): 739–767.

Malečková, Jitka (2000): Nationalizing Women and Engendering the Nation. The Czech National Movement, in Ida Blom, Karen Hagemann and Catherine Hall (eds): *Gendered Nations. Nationalisms and Gender Order in the Long Nineteenth Century*, Oxford-New York: Berg.

Malečková, Jitka (2008): Where Are Women in National Histories? in Stefan Berger and Chris Lorenz (eds): *The Contested Nation: Ethnicity, Religion, Class and Gender in National Histories*, Houndmills: Palgrave Macmillan.

Marklík, Václav (2007): *Češi a Evropa. Sdílené dějiny*, Praha: Ideál.

Masaryk, Tomáš Garrigue (1929): Postavení ženy v rodině a ve veřejném životě, in Tomáš Garrigue Masaryk, *Americké přednášky*, Praha: Čin.

Masaryk, Tomáš Garrigue (1930): Moderní názor na ženu, in *Masaryk a ženy. Sborník k 80. narozeninám prvního presidenta Republiky československé T.G. Masaryka*, Praha: Ženská národní rada.

Masaryk, Tomáš Garrigue (2000): *Česká otázka. Naše nynější krize. Jan Hus*, Praha: Masarykův ústav AV ČR. (First published in 1895)

Mayer, Tamar (ed.) (2000): *Gender Ironies of Nationalism: Sexing the Nation*, London and New York: Routledge.

Nejedlý, Zdeněk (1947): *Komunisté – dědici velkých tradic českého národa*, Praha: OV KSČ.

Nečasová, Denisa (2008): Nadčasové stereotypy o ženách v politice, in Milan Řepa (ed.): *19. století v nás. Modely, instituce a reprezentace, které přetrvaly*, Praha: Historický ústav.

Opočenská, Jana (1999): Násilí a jeho překonávání, in *Společnost žen a mužů z aspektu gender*, Praha: Open Society Fund.

Ort, Alexandr (2008): *Češi a Evropa*, Praha: AgAkcent pro Dům Evropy (2nd edition).

Pabián, Petr (2008): Bojovníci Kristovi, ne bídní zbabělci! Gender v katolické politické kultuře, in Jan Randák and Petr Koura (eds): *Hrdinství a zbabělost v české politické kultuře 19. a 20. století*, Praha: FFUK 2008.

Palacký, František (1908): *Dějiny národu českého v Čechách a v Moravě*, Praha: B. Kočí.

Pekař, Josef (1929): *Smysl českých dějin. O nový názor na české dějiny*, Praha: Klub historický.

Petráň, Josef (2006): Spor o smysl dějin a dějepisu, in Miloš Havelka (ed.): *Spor o smysl českých dějin 2, 1938–1989. Posuny a akcenty české otázky*, Praha: TORST.

Plamínková, Franciska (1920): *Economic and Social Position of Women in the Czechoslovak Republic*, Praha: Politika.

Plamínková, Franciska (1930): Několik poznámek o práci československých žen in T.G. Masaryk, *O ženě. Se statí F.F. Plamínkové Několik poznámek o práci československých žen*, Praha: Čin.

Porciani, Ilaria and Mary O'Dowd (eds) (2004): History Women, special issue of *Storia della Storiografia* 46.

Prečan, Vilém (ed.) (2005): *Kočka, která nikdy nespí: Jiřině Šiklové k narozeninám/The Cat Who Never Sleeps: To Jiřina Šiklová on Her Birthday*, Praha: James H. Ottaway.

Putna, Martin C. (1994): *My poslední křesťané. Hněvivé eseje a vlídné kritiky*, Praha: Herrmann a synové.

Rak, Jiří (2006): *České evropanství. České národní dějiny v evropském kontextu/Czech Europeanism. The Czech National history in the European Context*, Praha: Národní galerie.

Reeves-Ellington, Barbara, Kathryn Kish Sklar and Shemo, Connie A. (eds) (2010): *Competing Kingdoms: Women, Mission, Nation, and the American Protestant Empire, 1812–1960*, Durham: Duke University Press.

Smith, Bonnie (1998): *The Gender of History: Men, Women, and Historical Practice*, Cambridge: Harvard University Press.

Special Eurobarometer 225 (2005): Social Values, Science and Technology. [online] Available at: <http://ec.europa.eu/public_opinion/archives/ebs/ebs_225_report_ en.pdf> (Accessed 2 September 2010).

Starkey, Pat (2006): Women Religious and Religious Women: Faith and Practice in Women's Lives, in Deborah Simonton (ed.): *The Routledge History of Women in Europe since 1700*, London and New York: Routledge.

Stloukal, Karel (1940): Žena v českých dějinách, in Karel Stloukal (ed.): *Královny, kněžny a velké ženy české*, Praha: Jos. R. Vilímek.

Šiklová, Jiřina (1992): Ženy a politika (Konfrontace se západním feminismem), *Prostor* 5 (20): 23–29.

Šiklová, Jiřina (1993): McDonalds, Terminators, Coca Cola Ads – and Feminism? Imports from the West, in Susanna Trnka and Laura Busheikin (eds): *Bodies of Bread and Butter. Reconfiguring Women's Lives in the Post-Communist Czech Republic*, Prague: Gender Studies Center.

Šiklová, Jiřina (1999): Gender Studies a feminismus na univerzitách ve světě a v České republice, in *Společnost žen a mužů z aspektu gender*, Praha: Open Society Fund.

Šmejkalová, Jiřina (2005): Framing the Difference: 'Feminism' and Plebeianism in Czech Media in the 1990s, in Jiřina Van Leeuwen-Turnovcová and Nicole Richter (eds): *Mediale Welten in Tschechien nach 1989: Genderprojektionen und Codes des Plebejismus*, München: O. Sagner.

Třeštík, Dušan (1999): *Češi. Jejich národ, stát, dějiny a pravdy v transformaci. Texty z let 1991–1998*, Brno: Doplněk.

Třeštík, Dušan (2005): *Češi a dějiny v postmoderním očistci*, Praha: Lidové noviny.

Vlk, Miloslav (2009): *Náš národ a kořeny Evropy* (14.5.2009). [online] Available at <http://www.kardinal.cz/index.php?cmd=article&articleID=345> (Accessed 18 August 2010).

Yuval-Davis, Nira (1997), *Gender and Nation*, London: Sage.

CHAPTER 3

Romania's Cultural Identity and the European Challenge

Convictions, Options, Illusions

Adrian Velicu

Milan Kundera's lament about a "kidnapped Europe" does not exactly match the cry of the "return to Europe" that has resounded through-out the former communist countries after 1989. Kundera had in mind Poland, Hungary, and Czechoslovakia, as it then was; those who wanted to return to Europe after the collapse of Communism, and considered themselves part of Europe too, were more numerous. Kundera meant an area that happened to end up behind the Iron Curtain, but one that had far more in common with Europe "proper" than with other areas that made up the transitory socialist camp (Kundera 1984:33–38). Some states in these other areas begged to differ.

Romania was one of those countries that regarded the return to Europe as a priority after the fall of the dictatorship. In so far as this is a question of being perceived as part of "civilized Europe", the issue turns largely on aspects of cultural identity. Two important components of the country's identity have been the Latin origin of its people as well as of its language, and the defining role of Christian Orthodoxy. Both the general aspiration of returning to Europe after 1989 and its more specific version of membership in the European Union have occasioned a number of references to these defining features of cultural identity. It could be argued that for the first time in the history of the coun-try the freedom to discuss such matters coexisted with the concrete intention to join specific European institutions. Such an option under these circumstances has compelled a fresh scrutiny of past and present convictions and illusions. This study examines the tension underlying the deployment of arguments based on the Latin legacy and Eastern Orthodoxy. In outlining some of the cultural implications of this tension, the present analysis points to ways in which aspects of national identity are at odds with one another, calling for a reassessment of the national self-perception.

A few words on the historical background are in order at this preliminary stage. The Romans occupied Dacia (the area roughly corresponding to today's Romania) for almost 170 years. In AD 271–72 the Roman Empire abandoned this province in order to consolidate its defences south of the Danube. At the time, it was customary for Roman army veterans to receive land and settle in an area of their choice, usually in the region where they were deployed when retiring from active service, and this was the case in Dacia as well. There is little evidence of what happened to the indigenous population in this abandoned Roman province. As for the Dacian language, it vanished with hardly a trace. The migrating populations that were beginning to settle in the area encountered an ethnic group that spoke a language derived from Latin, in time known as Romanian. Whether its speakers are descended from the Romans, or from a mixture of Romans and Dacians, or from an ethnic combination including Slavs along with other ethnic groups, is a moot point. Whether the Romanians have continuously dwelt in the same area or migrated elsewhere and then returned has again been difficult to establish beyond a shadow of doubt. The ebb and flow of imperial power and migratory pressures made for a turbulent age and a changed ethnic landscape. However, the Roman Empire's presence in the zone bequeathed a language and had an impact on the local ethnic configuration, amounting to what in time has been summed up as the Latin legacy.

As notions of cultural identity, civic aspirations and nationalist claims acquired an increased significance, particularly towards the latter eighteenth century, national minorities, and indeed nations, that needed to assert themselves scrutinized their past for suitable evidence. Against this background, a group of Romanian intellectuals in Transylvania, retrospectively known as the Transylvanian School, emphasized in their linguistic and historical works the Latin origins of the Romanian language and people in order to justify the claims to civic rights that Hungarians and Germans enjoyed but Romanians lacked in the Habsburg Empire and, after the 1860s, in the Austria-Hungary Double Monarchy. In a Herderian vein, the stress on this Latin cultural inheritance assumed that language carried formative cultural connotations and implied a sense of belonging to the Romance sphere of civilization, even if geographically the Romanians lived some distance away. Consequently, the intellectuals of the Transylvanian School set a pattern of using the cultural heritage as embodied in the language to make comprehensive claims about national identity. The concept of Latin legacy was thus in the process of acquiring an increasingly substantial content.

The arguments based on the Latin origins of the language and the people have over the years served to justify territorial claims and civic rights (not least questions of Romanian or Hungarian settling precedence in Transylvania), at times taking on an ideological dimension. Invoking the connection with other Latin nations has been an attempt to assert that in important cultural ways the Romanians are different from their neighbours. The recurring phrase "a Latin island in a Slavic sea" says it all. The strength of the conviction expressed by this commonplace has been such that it has preserved its currency under very different political systems. The implication of the island metaphor is that there is a Latin mainland to whose community the islanders properly belong.

Yet, Eastern Orthodoxy has firmly placed the Romanians within the Southeastern European cultural sphere. In the discussions about the Romanian cultural identity, the Orthodox religion has counted as a major contributing factor. The occasional extreme use to which it has been put appears in the succinct claim that "being Romanian means being Orthodox". This became one of the extreme right-wing slogans in the interwar years, circulating in intellectual as well as political circles. The return of this claim after 1989 shows the suspect connotations that have accompanied the return of religion to the public sphere. More importantly for the present analysis, the renewed circulation of this argument has clashed with the topical call to rejoin Europe.

The version of nationalist communism practised in Romania throughout the 1970s and 1980s proclaimed the importance of the Latin component, but silenced references to Orthodox Christianity. Once the communist dictatorship was gone, the cultural implications of Orthodoxy could again be discussed publicly, entering the soul-searching debates about national identity. One must distinguish between the institution of the Romanian Orthodox Church and the creed of Orthodoxy. The communist regime found a use for the institution, for instance in surveillance or public relations, but not for the creed. After 1989, unlike the Latin legacy, Orthodoxy therefore emerged unburdened by associations with national communism, even if burdened by its connection with the extreme Right in the 1920s and '30s. With political censorship gone, there was a long-awaited opportunity to disentangle historical evidence from tendentious claims in the nation's self-perception. These sporadic but recurring arguments need to be brought together and discussed as a consistent contrast relevant to the nature of Romania's European credentials.

One useful way to treat the present subject is by considering it in terms of the dynamics of cultural memory. In his attempt to define cultural memory, Jan Assmann outlines four areas featuring "external" aspects of memory: mimetic memory, the memory of things, communicative memory, and cultural memory (Assmann 1992: 21–22). The last one, that is, cultural memory, has a particular importance because it creates a space where the first three merge.[1]

The link between communicative and cultural memory is slightly different in a later work by Assmann. He starts with a distinction between episodic memory resulting from direct experience, and semantic memory derived from learning about a particular experience (Assmann 2006: 2). The semantic variety refers to memories that require the attribution of meaning in order to achieve coherence, a process that occurs in a social context. That is why Assmann finds it relevant to start from Maurice Halbwachs's view of memory as a social phenomenon; however, Assmann goes further and adds a cultural "basis" (Assmann 2006: 1, 8). As part of this strategy, he proposes the concepts of communicative memory and cultural memory. According to Jan Assmann, communicative memory is generational (synchronic), covering at most three generations, while cultural memory goes far back in time (diachronic), with the added important qualification that cultural memory is a "special case of communicative memory" (Assmann 2006: 8, 24; Assmann 2007: 56).

The crucial point here is that the meanings encapsulated by cultural memory (in sites, rituals, customs) are "handed down, learned, taught, researched, interpreted and practised" (Assmann 2007: 24). This clarifies the earlier statement that communicative memory subsumes the cultural one. Assmann insists that "[o]nly with the emergence of writing does cultural memory 'take off' and allow the horizon of symbolically stored memory to grow far beyond the framework of knowledge functionalized as bonding memory."[2] "Bonding memory" is for Assmann "the collective memory par excellence", which he contrasts with "learning memory". Forms of "writing-based cultural memory" that have the "status of a central, identity-creating, and in this sense 'connective' memory" (Assmann 2006: 29) indicate once more how cultural memory is ultimately a particular instance of communicative memory.

It is precisely such examples of "writing-based cultural memory" and their "identity-creating" role that define the present investigation. This is where the Romanian historian Lucian Boia's concepts become useful, as they focus on the particular circumstances of the Romanian cultural and historical outlook (Boia 1999: 357–359). One of these concepts is "the imaginary". As defined in this case, the imaginary supplies what is missing in the historical narrative, helping thus to ascribe meaning to an otherwise incomplete account. The other concept employed here is that of national "consciousness"; namely, that collective faculty of "identity-creating" through handing down a set of meanings that shape cultural identity as semantically acquired memories. The process of wrestling with matters of cultural identity by ascribing or reascribing meaning points to the manner in which illusions emerge, convictions materialize or options become available. The role of the imaginary in these undertakings and the extent of their mythical nature show how cultural memory hinges on the communicative one.

Before I pursue these issues by means of several illustrations, it is helpful to sketch the context in which these concrete examples occur. The wide framework of the analysis has to take into account Romania's first major attempt to enter Europe in the mid-nineteenth century, backed by historical and cultural justifications, even invoking pan-Latinism during a period when pan-Slavism and pan-Germanism circulated as mobilizing concepts (Boia 1999: 49; 2007: 216). The present discussion deals with the cultural dynamics of the second major attempt to "join" Europe which occurred after 1989 (Boia 1999: 49, 360–61). The post-1989 circumstances presented new specific problems and aims, but the earlier cultural justifications, by now part of a coherent national identity, continued to provide an overall meaning to the whole enterprise, beyond the technical aspect of concrete reforms.

The perception of Europe in Romania immediately after the fall of the communist dictatorship had little to do with becoming a member of the EU, a hardly realistic goal at the time; returning to Europe meant, in rather vague terms, a return to civilization. Soon enough, these vague aspirations took on increasingly concrete features as the debates driven by political interests tended to polarize the image of Europe. Referring to the early 1990s, an initiated social scientist has argued that "[i]n Romania during this period, 'Europe' meant, for its civil-society advocates, the sources of the political and economic forms Romania should adopt; for others, it meant a neoimperialist menace threatening Romania's independence" (Verdery 1999: 304).

When membership in the European Union began to appear as a more and more realistic proposition, the precise requirements for joining the Union called for specific measures, and the debaters addressed particular issues to do with economic, legal and political reforms. The campaign for the proper functioning of these mechanisms needed to prove Romania's suitability as a EU member is not the subject of the present discussion; numerous studies have examined the phenomenon, a comprehensive and critical analysis pointing out the ambiguous attitude towards the EU of a number of ruling or influential groups (Gallagher 2009: 3–12, 261–64, and passim). However, there have also been soul-searching arguments to do with national identity and its role in the process of "rejoining" Europe, which is the line of enquiry pursued here. The post-'89 freedom of expression, at a time when Romania needed once more to make its case as part of Europe, facilitated the use of a constellation of evidence and a type of self-scrutiny never quite encountered in this form before. References to a Latin heritage shared with other European states have recurred in justifying the modernization outlook since the late nineteenth century and have been underlying the post-1989 discourse as well. This argument has been persuasive enough to be accepted in rather sceptical European quarters. When the British periodical *The Economist* summed up the presence of the two fresh EU members by attempting to see matters from a Southeastern perspective, it adopted the Romanian (pro-Western) outlook, informing its readers that "whereas Bulgarians feel out of the mainstream, Romanians do not. They see themselves as a Latin outpost in a sea of Slavs. Their language is linked to Italian and French. Bulgarian is a Slavic tongue, as close to Russian as Danish is to Swedish" (*The Economist* 2007 [382]: 43–44). Thus, an argument launched in the philological and historical tomes of the Transylvanian School intellectuals was used approvingly by an important Western opinion-maker two centuries later. Possibly unaware of the whole picture, or unwilling to complicate matters, *The Economist* overlooked the contrast offered by the Orthodox element. Indeed, things have been quite different concerning the place of

Orthodoxy vis-à-vis (Western) Europe. For instance, a representative of the Romanian Orthodox Church who has worked for the World Council of Churches has expressed doubts about the values of Western modernity that might be passed to Eastern Europe: apart from values regarding the market economy and the profit motive, it is unclear for this author what the West has to offer (Bria 1995: 40–41). A majority of the Romanian Orthodox clergy, intellectuals and of the faithful in general have been sceptical about Romania joining the EU in particular, and about the allure of Europe in general (Banica 2006). True, the Orthodox Church's Patriarch, along with a predominantly younger minority of the clergy, have been in favour. The split is between a majority that is highly "circumspect" about the EU and a minority in charge of the institutional policy and possessing direct knowledge of the West (with exceptions such as Bria).

In singling out the tension between the Latin legacy and Orthodoxy, the present analysis suggests that the confrontation with the concrete conditions of rejoining Europe has revealed an uneasy juxtaposition in the Romanian cultural identity. In turn, this has imposed a fresh look at the cultural make-up of the nation. The contrast between choosing Western models (above all, France in the early stages of modernization, but also Belgium) and preferring strictly local values has frequently featured in the alternatives under consideration in Romania (Boia 1999: 59). Pondering on these options is as topical as ever; this time in an updated form, where the post-communist return of Orthodoxy – whether trendy or genuine – has a conspicuous role. It should be said in passing that, although this contrast may vaguely resemble the dispute between Slavophiles and Westerners in Russia, it is not quite the same thing. To take only one important distinction, the cultural affinities with the West, based on a supposedly shared Latin historical and cultural inheritance, differ from the kind of appeal the Western model has had for the Slavophiles.

One example of the recurring preoccupation with the specific national features and their significance for Romania's place in Europe is the reissue in 1995 of a book about the psychology of the Romanian people (Dumitru Draghicescu, *Din psihologia poporului român*) first published in 1907. An early work of ethnography relying mainly on French scholarship, the book seems seriously dated nowadays. However, it has been republished not as a quaint curiosity, but as an intervention in an ongoing debate. The author's chief point is that most imperfections in the Romanian psychology are due to the Turkish and Greek influence; the solution would be a national regeneration that would revive early values, many of them inherited from the Romans. Without necessarily being part of today's research in social sciences in Romania, this work does appear to be part of the overall cultural memory in a less than stringent but keen public debate. The fact that the distinguished intellectual Horia-Roman Patapievici has expressed admiration for this work, turning down the offer to write a preface and considering that the work deserves a proper expert, indirectly ascribes this book an importance and a scholarly value that shows what is at stake in reascribing meaning to supposedly historical evidence. Patapievici quotes approvingly a concise description of the Romanian nation that appears to explain some of the basic flaws in the local mentality: "A Western race with Oriental customs" (quoted in Patapievici 1990: 73). As seen below, various commentators return to this idea; some viewing it as a problematic tension, others as a successful compromise.

The recollection of the more exact interrelation between the Latin legacy and Orthodoxy has re-entered the post-1989 debates in other versions as well. In his critical scrutiny, Gabriel Andreescu, one of the few active opponents of the communist regime, has revived the interaction between the features derived from the Latin origins of the language and the people, on the one hand, and those derived from the formative influence of Eastern Orthodoxy, on the other. In fact, apart from anything else, he perpetuates the presence of these two cultural features in the contemporary discourse. A strong supporter of the European project, Andreescu offers an unusual way of handling past and present arguments in order to clarify the defining nature of the Latin and Orthodox features. In a brief but symptomatic reflection, he selects a couple of significant quotes from the late 1930s on the manner in which the Latin cultural inheritance and Orthodoxy complement one another; an idea which Andreescu in fact challenges by using Samuel Huntington's argument about the clash of civilizations.

The first quote belongs to the linguist and politician Sextil Puscariu, who remarked that "[t]his felicitous pairing of Latin blood and choice spiritual features derived from the East provides that combination of great and original qualities that elevate the quality of our [the Romanian] race" (quoted in Andreescu 1996: 174; my translation). It should be said that race is used here in the sense of people or nation. After this reference, which Andreescu characterizes as radical and extravagant, he turns to a theologian's view of the synthesis between the Latin and the Orthodox components. The theologian and priest Dumitru Staniloaie has argued that "[o]ur nation represents the perfect balance between these two poles, unlike other nations where the balance of this tension is disturbed in favour of one of them" (quoted in Andreescu 1996: 174; my translation). Qualifying this statement as "uncritical" and "ecstatic", Gabriel Andreescu has expressed his scepticism by means of a somewhat unexpected riposte. Faced with the argument of synthesis, Andreescu regretfully draws attention to the fact that if matters were to be judged by means of Samuel Huntington's thesis of the clash of civilizations, then there is a clear boundary between the Latin world and the Orthodox one; a fissure that mars Staniloaie's harmonious whole. A convinced pro-European and modernizer, Andreescu further refers in his notes to analyses published in the mid-1990s that use Huntington's mode of arguing in order to explain the cleavage between Eastern Europe and the rest of the continent. This is not the place to discuss whether the deployment of Huntington's theory in this case shows a proper understanding of its substance or whether it is valid at all. The relevant point is its very use to question the interweaving of the Latin and Orthodox features, or to stress the impossibility of such a synthesis due to the concept of boundary.

A more intriguing space for the synthesis between these two components appears in a reflection by Daniel Ciobotea, the Patriarch of the Romanian Orthodox Church. Writing in 2005 (when he was still Metropolitan of Moldavia and Bukovina) about the contribution of the Romanian Christian community to the European Union, Ciobotea explains that this contribution has been facilitated by "the cultural synthesis that Romania has long developed as a bridge between the East and the West. Such a synthesis is the Romanian Orthodox Church itself, uniting in its own identity the Eastern orthodox [sic] spirituality with the Western Latin spirituality" (Ciobotea 2008: 169). Thus, while Dumitru Staniloaie regards these two components in terms of a balance achieved through the nation, Daniel Ciobotea uses the stronger term of synthesis and places it within the institution of the Church. It is not without interest to mention here that Staniloaie was one of the teachers of Ciobotea and later supervisor of his doctoral thesis, defended at the Institute of Theology of Bucharest University, which was an extended version of the doctoral thesis presented at the University of Strasbourg. A "synthesis" within the Church appears more precise than the rather vague "balance" as represented by the nation. The references to "Western Latin spirituality" and its merging with Eastern Orthodoxy are somewhat unclear in the Patriarch's statement. One may interpret them as an explanation of how a particular Latin cultural legacy shared with the West has been accommodated within the identity of Romanian Orthodoxy. This way of understanding the Latin legacy may well throw additional light on the concept, but it is a view that differs from, or complements, the historical and linguistic, but non-religious, view of the Transylvanian School.

It has to be emphasized that the Orthodox and the Latin strands in the Romanian national identity as it positions itself in relation to Europe manifest themselves in different ways. Orthodoxy has had a conspicuous revival after 1989. The Latin strand has been present in a rather axiomatic manner in a continuous discourse, lacking the spectacular way in which Christian Orthodoxy has recently reasserted itself in Romania. Even if low-key in comparison with the new wave of Orthodoxy, the Latin element has never lost its basic significance concerning the foundation myth. Indeed, the very use of "myth" as a critical concept in this context can be a sensitive matter, as the storm of criticism and praise encountered by Lucian Boia's book *Istorie si mit în constiinta româneasca* has demonstrated.[3]

Boia's important and provocative contribution to the debates mentioned above contains three chief points: first, that a good deal of the arguments that have shaped Romania's national identity belong to myth (in the figurative sense of the concept) rather than to well-documented history; secondly, that the imaginary has played a considerable role in defining this identity; and thirdly, that the excessive emphasis on this self-definition sounds strident in a European context. As an expert in historiography, Boia questions the nationalist, indeed cavalier, use of the Latin cultural and historical components that have featured in history writing over the years. Far from denying the importance of the Latin element, however, Boia insists on a more detached examination of these matters which, in different ways, were ideologically fraught both before and during the Communist regime. Neither does his critical scrutiny spare the recent return of Orthodoxy to discussions about cultural identity. The presence of Orthodoxy once more in this context has unfortunate resonances. In the 1920s and 1930s the Iron Guard, the Romanian fascist movement, resorted heavily to religious symbols and justifications in its mystical nationalism. In a different manner but in the same spirit, some contemporary thinkers and university teachers along with their disciples leaning towards the extreme Right further cultivate the strong connection between nationalism and Orthodoxy in order to explain the nature of the Romanian cultural identity. The resumption of some of these arguments after the fall of Communism has added to that version of national identity which Lucian Boia criticizes. As a matter of fact, during the 1970s and the 1980s, Ceausescu attempted to tone down the "Roman pedigree" of the Romanian nation, favouring the local Dacian origin. After 1989 the argument of the Latin cultural (and ethnic) origin resumed its place along with the revived significance of the Orthodox thesis. A view of Romania's cultural identity that resorted once more to the Latin legacy, tacitly attempting to distance itself from the Slavic environment, meant that "the notion of the Balkans has remained loaded with pejorative connotations", as a Bulgarian scholar observed (Bechev 2006: 12). The extent to which the Latin and the Orthodox characteristics converge or separate points to the kind of options the debates contain, with the consequent impact on the self-image of the nation.

Boia's emphasis on Romania's two major attempts to "enter Europe" is of particular concern to the present analysis. Again, the first attempt was part of the early process of modernization that started in the 1830s and emphatically used the Latin historical background and its significance for the national identity to justify Romania's European claims. The second attempt, eventually successful in 2007, occurred after 1989. When Boia writes that the collapse of communism offers a new opportunity to join Europe that shouldn't be missed through shrill nationalism, he is aware of the two images of Europe in the Romanian debates of the early 1990s spelled out by Verdery (see above). One need stress once more that at this stage the references to Europe meant a general concept of civilization, as well as a type of political culture and a vague notion of market economy (approximately Kundera's Europe that included Central European countries but not those further east); these early debates did not refer to specific institutions such as the European Union, which Romania could hardly hope to join. The sceptical outlook towards Europe would reappear at the end of the 1990s when Romania's membership in the EU became an increasingly real possibility. Irrespective of the general or specific content in the stages of the discussions concerning Romania and Europe, Christian Orthodoxy preserved its privileged place as an identity marker that expresses clear reservations (if not downright opposition) towards European integration (Boia 2007: 191). The disclaimers of the Orthodox Church dignitaries and the attempts to accommodate the Latin element have raised problematic questions rather than reassured the public.

The significance of the Latin or of the Orthodox element has been circulating before in the context of cultural identity. Again, what is different about deploying these arguments after 1989 is their presence in the topical context of European integration. And that has revealed a number of anomalies and confusions.

As far as Orthodoxy is concerned, the Church has claimed a decisive role in shaping the national identity emerging in the nineteenth century (Stan & Turcescu 2007: 43–44). After 1918, in a Greater Romania forcefully asserting its identity under new political circumstances, the Orthodox Church appropriated the arguments based on the Roman cultural and ethnic bequest. Consequently, defining features for the national identity derived from Orthodoxy and the Latin legacy merged, but on the terms of the Orthodox Church, meaning that the affinities with other Latin nations in Europe, and hence with Catholicism, were toned down considerably. The process of handing down a set of meanings about the past underwent a clear change. When, in the 1920s and '30s, a number of influential philosophers and theologians discussed the specific virtues of Orthodoxy (Nae Ionescu, Nichifor Crainic, Lucian Blaga, Mircea Vulcanescu and later Dumitru Staniloaie, among others), they did it by contrasting them to Catholicism. After the collapse of communism, a popular student leader's statement that being Romanian meant being Orthodox echoed the arguments of at least one such interwar influential philosopher, namely Nae Ionescu.[4] Furthermore, the return after 1989, of a version of "neo-orthodoxism" has perpetuated the same claim, i.e. that Orthodoxy defines Romanian identity (Iordachi & Trencsényi 2003: 438). This emphatic association of Orthodoxy with the national image present during the interwar period, absent during the Communist years, and back after 1989 has not been confined only to intellectual disputes. As briefly discussed above, one concrete example of its wider impact has been the scepticism, if not downright opposition at grassroots level, of the Orthodox Church to Romania's EU membership.

When, two centuries earlier, the Romanian clergy of the Greek Catholic Church in Transylvania (then part of the Habsburg Empire) adopted the argument of the shared Latin legacy in its orientation towards Europe, the Orthodox Church in the Romanian Principalities (then part of the Ottoman Empire) showed scant interest. After the 1848 revolutions, this discourse of culturally attaching, if not integrating, the Romanian nation to Europe spread from Transylvania to the Romanian Principalities, starting a long tradition of close cultural links between Romania and France. Indeed, the Belgian Constitution served as the model for the new Romanian Constitution of 1866, when Prince Alexandru Ioan Cuza was removed in favour of Prince (later King) Carol I of the Hohenzollern family. The inspiration derived from the Western – predominantly Latin – models points to the emancipa tory meaning of the Latin legacy (at the time, the Belgian Constitution was regarded as one of the most progressive in Europe). Once the Orthodox Church took over this legacy in a united and much expanded Romanian state after 1918 (including Transylvania), there emerged an inward-looking use of the Latin legacy. While the earlier, outward-looking, emancipatory use of the Latin legacy meant aspiring to communion with civilized European regions, thus attenuating the nationalistic element, in a post-1918 newly assertive Romania it was the latter use of the Latin legacy that defined the nation's cultural identity.

In this context, the Latin-inspired nationalism developed a secular and a mystical version. The secular version has been associated with the historian Nicolae Iorga's Romantic nationalism, while the mystical one with the leader of the fascist Iron Guard Corneliu Codreanu's Orthodox version of nationalism. Indeed, scholars have pointed out the renewed "tensions between secular and mystical understandings of nationalism" after the collapse of communism (Dobrescu 2003: 409). Now, after 1989, we witness renewed tensions between these two concepts of nationalism. The original tensions of the interwar period – true, in a very different context – were far from a purely intellectual dispute. Nicolae Iorga became active in politics, serving even as prime minister for a short period. Sharing the fate of other Romanian politicians who opposed the extreme right-wing movements at the time, Iorga was murdered by members of the Iron Guard in 1940.

Thus, the uneasy juxtaposition of the Orthodox and Latin legacies as established after 1918, somewhat obscured during the communist dictatorship, and revived after 1989, has not found a clear place in the chain of recollections meant to enter cultural memory. Only a few years ago, a theologian admitted this tension, while trying to overcome it through a redefinition of the national identity: "[the] Romanians have the fortune to be a Latin people, a fact that ties us by blood with most people of the New Europe. At the same time, we are blessed to be Christian Orthodox. God purposely arranged for only one Latin people in Europe to retain the just faith and to avoid heresy. As Latin, we are not foreign to European mentalities. As Orthodox, we love God and other people, and have patience."[5] As an afterthought, this theologian concludes that "[the] Romanians will have to learn that 'I am Romanian' matters only if one can say 'I am European.'"

Despite the dose of the imaginary, mildly put, that colours these reflections, they amount to firm convictions in quite a few quarters, while dismissed by others as illusory, if not embarrassing. However, this is a sample of what Lucian Boia has called the "artificial maintenance and even amplification of certain historical and political myths" (Boia 1999: 47). Considered within Assmann's theoretical framework, these disputes constitute the moments of handing down the meanings that shape cultural memory. In fact, the Romanian historian admits that the resort to "myth" is inevitable, particular in cases where there is a dearth of historical evidence. However, as long as historical myths are recognized as such, they find a place in the accounts passed on to the subsequent generations in the process of shaping cultural memory. As Boia questions the convictions concerning cultural identity, he restates the kind of options that are available. Just as after 1918, when the Orthodox Church appropriated the Latin discourse, after 1989 Orthodoxy is faced with fresh choices as it faces the pressures of modernization and of the European integration.

A representative example where values and meanings are transmitted from one generation to another is the conversation between the priest and theologian Dumitru Staniloaie and Marian Munteanu, the legendary student leader of the early 1990s, subsequently politician and academic (Munteanu 1993). As seen above, this theologian has been influential over a long period of time, contributing to a significant strain of thought in the perception of contemporary Orthodoxy. Two important points need to be highlighted in this conversation of 1993: the relationship between Orthodoxy and modernity, and that between Orthodoxy and the Latin element.

At the time, Munteanu had started a political movement where religion featured prominently. In this conversation, he explains that the movement has argued that Orthodoxy is not a return to the past but "the only modern orientation". His interlocutor approves of it and finds a way of contrasting the modern orientation, in the sense of ascending higher spiritually, with the Westerners descending to lower levels. This concept of modernity may appear strained to a secular observer schooled in social sciences, but constitutes a useful piece of evidence for the intellectual historian who surveys the contemporary scene.

More controversial and eccentric is Staniloaie's view of the relationship between the Latin element and Orthodoxy; a view which Munteanu accepts in the spirit of an uncritical disciple. As the quotation above shows, the theologian does not dismiss the Latin legacy. But, while he regarded the presence of Latinity and Orthodoxy within the Romanian nation in the 1930s as "the perfect balance" between two poles, by the 1990s it is no longer a successful reconciliation of differences: the Latin component in the Romanian cultural make-up *preceded* Rome and along with the early Christianity shaped the Romanian people. It is true that Staniloaie advanced this opinion as "a strong probability" ("este foarte probabil"), but the reader of this conversation gathers that the young student leader unquestioningly absorbed this idea, facilitating its survival and diffusion. The "proto-Latinity" contemplated in this conversation comes unsettlingly close to the "protochronism" encouraged by the communist authorities in the 1970s and 1980s, according to which Romanian culture had anticipated important trends and elements in European civilization. This in itself points to worrying continuities after 1989 that compete with the modern European project. However, what is more relevant for the present line of argument is the claim that the Latin element is of an indigenous nature and together with Orthodoxy constitutes a cultural identity that firmly anchors the nation in Southeast Europe. This is a far cry from the way the Latin element was invoked by the Romanian intellectuals and clergymen in Transylvania at the end of the eighteenth and the beginning of the nineteenth century.

The limited evidence of this brief study ought to include, however, Teodor Baconsky's reflections on the "Latin nature of the Romanian Orthodoxy" (Baconsky 2006). The divergence of these two elements underlies the outlook of this intellectual and diplomat. He starts from the distinction between personalized and objective forms of governance, as characteristic of the Slavic and the Western (Latin) political systems respectively, where the term "Slav" is loosely employed as a synonym for "Orthodox". Further, Baconsky points out that the Romanian system is permeated by the Slavic outlook on governance (hence a way of looking upon truth as "personal" rather than "objective"), despite the Latin aspirations voiced throughout the centuries. The Romanians' Latin legacy has possibly functioned as a "defensive matrix or cultural alibi, but not as a real foundation of the political society" (Baconsky 2006). It should be said that there is a political agenda behind these cultural, historical and sociological reflections. Baconsky sees a solution in the return of Christian Democracy to the Romanian Parliament. However, it is significant that he focuses on this particular pair of cultural components in order to make a more general point concerning Romania's European integration. His argument goes on to claim that this proposal is the only way of stopping the tendency of a "quasi-Christian populism" to keep Romania away from the "intrinsic 'Latinity' of the European project". Thus, Baconsky argues in favour of a synthesis for the very reason suggested in his brief but substantial commentary that the Latin element and Orthodoxy pull in different directions.

What the arguments and counter-arguments mentioned above point to is a slow process of reassessing the significance of undeniable cultural components in terms of the nation's self-image, but also in terms of how this image is perceived from a distance. Some concepts are unstable; for instance, the Latin legacy is sometimes use interchangeably with Catholicism, although its content is basically cultural with ethnic connotations. Theoretical explanations jostle with nationalist rhetoric. It is a process that undermines the "bonding memory" which so far has expressed a consensus of the "collective memory", to use Jan Assmann's terms. At the same time, it is the kind of intellectual ferment that illustrates how the reascription of meaning to apparently established matters works as part of "identity-creation".

Returning to a relevant concept touched upon above, in so far as the present argument has outlined a cultural predicament stemming from questions of identity, the issue of boundaries is part of it. Since the establishment of an identity also points to what one is not, according to the principles of any definition, a boundary separates the specific features shared by the group from other features; asserting what an entity contains or is like involves a process of inclusion as well as one of exclusion. Klaus Eder's helpful terms of "hard" and "soft" boundaries, namely geographical and cultural (or identity-based), clarify some of these questions (Eder 2006: 255–271). The theoretical attempt to explain the "soft" borders as the result of "narrative construction" inadvertently supports the significance of the concepts of "communicative" and "cultural memory" for the present analysis. The suggestion that "drawing a boundary is embedded in a series of communicative acts which involve the circulation of stories" (Eder 2006: 257) expresses the role and the mechanism of communicative memory. Ultimately, these "communicative acts", which through their plausible narration contribute to the drawing of boundaries, consolidate the "cultural memory" that determines the overall identity.

By way of conclusion, I suggest that Romania's second attempt to enter Europe has been complicated by a version of the Latin legacy as appropriated by the Orthodox Church. In the first attempt of the 1830s to 1860s to join Europe, the Latin legacy carried the emancipatory connotations ascribed by the Greek Catholic Church. The second attempt of the 1990s and subsequent decade, this time much more successful, at least in a concrete institutional way, has occurred against an intellectual background where the Orthodox Church has appropriated "the Transylvanian Greek Catholics' nationalist discourse" based on the Latin legacy (Stan & Turcescu 2007: 43). This appropriation after 1918 has entailed the ascription of a modified set of meanings whereby the Latin legacy helped to emphasize a specific, regional self-image with vaguely mystical associations. A drastic reconsideration of the cultural memory, admitting the impact of the imaginary on what the identity-creation process chooses to preserve or to leave out, may well constitute a new manner of accommodating disparate legacies to confirm that the second entry into Europe has been more than just an institutional achievement.

Notes

1 "Das kulturelle Gedächtnis bildet einen Raum, in den alle drei vorgenannten Bereiche mehr oder weniger bruchlos übergehen" (Assmann [1992] 2007:21).
2 Assmann 2006:21. "Bonding memory" is for Assmann "the collective memory par excellence", which he contrasts with "learning memory" ("Writing, however, contains, latently at least … the possibility of transcending bonding memory, the collective memory par excellence, in favor of learning memory. Here we see opening up the further "memory spaces" of what might be thought of as an authentic "cultural" memory" (Assmann 2006: 20).
3 The second edition (1999) contains a new preface where the author answers his critics.
4 On Marian Munteanu's statement, see Shafir 1999: 22.
5 Quoted in Stan & Turcescu 2007: 208. Their reference in a note is to Marcel Radut Seliste, "Biserica Ortodoxa Romana si Noua Europa," *Rost,* 35 (2006), available at http://www.romfest.org/rost/apr_mai2004/oltenia.shtml.

References

Andreescu, Gabriel (1996): *Nationalisti, antinationalisti... O polemica in publicistica romaneasca,* Iasi: Polirom.

Assmann, Jan (2006): *Religion and Cultural Memory,* tr. Rodney Livingstone, Stanford, Ca.: Stanford University Press.

Baconsky, Teodor (2006): Crede si cerceteaza, *Dilema veche,* no. 122.

Banica, Mirel (2006): Despre Europa, altfel, *Dilema veche,* no. 149.

Bechev, Dimitar (2006): Constructing South East Europe. The Politics of Regional Identity in the Balkans, *Ramses2 Working Paper,* 1: 1–23.

Boia, Lucian (1999): *Istorie si mit in constiinta romaneasca,* Bucharest: Humanitas.

Boia, Lucian (2007): *Romania – tara de frontiera a Europei,* Bucharest: Humanitas.

Bria, Ion (1995): *Romania. Orthodox Identity at a Crossroads of Europe,* Geneva: WCC Publications.

Ciobotea, Daniel (2008): The Orthodox Church and the New Europe. Ecumenical Experience and Perspectives, in Wilhelm Danca (ed.): *Truth and Morality. The Role of Truth in Public Life,* Washington, D.C.: The Council for Research in Values and Philosophy.

Dobrescu, Caius (2003): Conflict and Diversity in East European Nationalism on the Basis of a Romanian Case Study, *East European Politics and Societies,* 17 (3): 393–414.

Eder, Klaus (2006): Europe's Borders. The Narrative Construction of the Boundaries of Europe, *European Journal of Social Theory,* 9 (2): 255–271.

Gallagher, Tom (2009): *Romania and the European Union. How the Weak Vanquished the Strong,* Manchester: Manchester University Press.

Iordachi, Constantin and Balász Trencsényi (2003): In Search of a Usable Past. The Question of National Identity in Romanian Studies, 1990–2000, *East European Politics and Societies,* 17, (3): 414–453.

Kundera, Milan(1984): The Tragedy of Central Europe, *The New York Review of Books,* 31 (7): 33–38.

Munteanu, Marian (2010): "Ortodoxia este viitorul omenirii". Sfaturi si indemnuri catre tineri adresate de Parintele Staniloaie intr-o convorbire cu Marian Munteanu, http://www.munteanu.ro/DialogStaniloaie.html (accessed on 26 October 2010).

The New Kids on the Block: The European Union's Two Newest Members, Bulgaria and Romania, are Both Economically and Politically Backward (2007): *The Economist,* 382 (8510): 43–44.

Patapievici, Horia-Roman (1990): *Politice,* Bucharest: Humanitas.

Shafir, Michael (1999): The Mind of the Romanian Radical Right, in Sabrina Ramet (ed.): *The Radical Right in Central and Eastern Europe since 1989* University Park, PA: Pennsylvania State University Press.

Stan, Lavinia and Lucian Turcescu (2007): *Religion and Politics in Post-Communist Romania,* Oxford: Oxford University Press.

Verdery, Katherine (1999): Civil Society or Nation? "Europe" in the Symbolism of Romania's Postsocialist Politics, in Ronald Grigor Suny and Michael D. Kennedy (eds): *Intellectuals and the Articulation of the Nation,* Ann Arbor: The University of Michigan Press.

CHAPTER 4

Cultural Religion or Religious Purism

Discourses on Orthodoxy, Authenticity and National Identity in Greece

Trine Stauning Willert

Purity is inherent in the Herderian conception of the national idea which builds on the myths of a pure and unadulterated national character. Purity is also articulated in terms like "authenticity", "genuineness" and "essence". Purity cannot be conceived without its antonym, which is not syncretism or synthesis, but pollution/contamination. In Greek cultural history the quest for purity has been driven by the fear of oriental pollution or, later, of modern Western pollution. As Bozatzis (2009: 438) notes, "oriental cultural pollution constitutes a representational resource deeply embedded in the history of narrating the modern Greek condition." Purity, of course, is not a real-world condition, but an ideal invoked in purist discourses. In analytical terms we can refer to purity, wholeness, authenticity and origin as powerful rhetorical markers[1] used by cultural actors to legitimize their claims for a specific true, pure version of collective identities.

Quests for cultural purity have been particularly intense in relation to Greece due to this nation's claim to be descendants of the ancient Greek civilization. All nations claim to have existed eternally since prehistoric times, but few other nations in the Western world have had a similarly imposing history to "live up to". The demand to prove an uninterrupted ancestry has imprinted itself upon most of modern Greek cultural history and identity politics. In 2005 a Sunday newspaper (*Apogevmatini tis Kyriakis*) reported a supposedly scientific result from a Stanford University study proving the 99.5% Caucasian DNA purity of the modern Greek population. The article, which keeps being reproduced on Greek nationalist blogs,[2] underlined several times that almost no traces of Slavic or Turkish DNA could be found in the DNA of contemporary Greeks. This shows how powerful the idea of purity and the fear of contamination have been and still are in modern Greek society. The fear of contamination inherent in the attempts to create a pure national Greek culture has been framed by two events, namely the linguistic creation of a purified national language, *Katharevousa* (literally meaning "the cleansed"), from the late eighteenth century onwards, and a theory, introduced during the 1830s by the Austrian historian and philologist Jakob Philipp Fallmerayer, suggesting that the people claiming to be (modern) Greeks had no relationship with the ancient Greek peoples, but more probably originated from incoming Slav or Albanian tribes (Skopetea 1997). Thus, during the nineteenth century the discussions about modern Greek identity were framed by these two theories regarding purity or contamination in the fields of language and race respectively. The nineteenth century saw the founding of a modern Greek identity as by and large built on the Greeks' ancient legacy and to a lesser extent on the Christian heritage of the Byzantine Empire. But political and historical events in the twentieth century challenged and questioned the conceptions of Greek national identity. In particular the Greek military defeat in Asia Minor in 1922, in Greek given the name "the Catastrophe", led to the end of the visionary irredentist political programme called "the Great Idea" (in Greek *Megáli Idéa*) projecting a greater Greece including Asia Minor and Constantinople/Istanbul. This defeat, together with the arrival of Modernism, was to influence Greek culture and identity politics immensely. During the first decades of the twentieth century a movement against the purified language had gained strength, and from the 1930s the vernacular linguistic idiom, Demotic, with many Turkish and Italian loanwords, dominated in the cultural progressive circles. The purified linguistic idiom remained, however, the official Greek language, taught in schools and used in state administration, until the fall of the Colonels' dictatorship in 1974.

The aim of this chapter is to show how various cultural discourses have used notions of purity and authenticity, and indirectly the fear of cultural or religious contamination, in negotiations about Greek national and religious identities and their position in relation to the West. The discourses examined have all attempted to promote an ever "truer", more authentic version of national or religious identity. The emergence of new tendencies in Greek theology since the late 1990s has highlighted a phenomenon in modern Greek cultural history, namely a back and forth movement of national or religious ideologies defined either by a search for the authentic national identity, rooted, among other elements, in the religious tradition of *Eastern* Christianity, or by a search for a pure Christian religious identity, partly inspired by theologies and religious patterns from *Western* Christianity. The dichotomies of pure/contaminated and East/West have guided this study because they characterize the ideals of the trends observed; not because they describe any objective truth. Since the emphasis of the chapter is on interpreting current developments in Greek theology, a recent thesis on the role of religion in late modernity is presented as a theoretical framework to add a contemporary global perspective to the local Greek phenomenon of fluctuation between East and West. Then the interchanging cultural and religious currents from the 1930s until the late twentieth century are presented; and finally, in a separate section, expressions of the new theological trend are analysed and its quest for the "pure religious" is interpreted in the light of contemporary cultural pluralism and late modern living conditions.

Religion and Purity in Late Modernity

Olivier Roy (2010) has recently diagnosed our age as the age of "religion without culture".[3] Roy formulates the thesis that, in a globalized world, religion thrives to the extent that it has cut off its ties with culture. Instead of a return to traditional religious worship, we are now, according to Roy, witnessing the individualization of faith and the disassociation of faith communities from ethnic and national identities. An extreme example of a religious practice detached from any cultural context is Pentecostalism, where God's word is transmitted through the faithful "speaking in tongues"; i.e., they speak in no known language with a cultural and historical rootedness, but in a language supposedly detached from culture and history. Pentecostalists thus overcome the problem of translation of the Bible as a historical and cultural text written in Hebrew, Greek and Aramaic (Roy 2010: 10). Roy suggests that the religions enjoying success today are those that accept "deculturation" and live by the myth of "the pure religious". However, his thesis applies in particular to fanatic and extreme versions of religious purification such as Protestant evangelicalism, Islamic Salafism, and Haredi Judaism, whereas he interprets Catholicism and Eastern Orthodoxy as too culturally integrated to follow this path of deculturation. Considering religion as having a pure essence independently of any historical or cultural context does not mean that the religious practice is not embodied in a given culture at a given time; it always refers to a transcendent order of truth and of the absolute, thus in essence remaining uncontaminated by earthly cultural traits. According to Roy (2010:28–29) culture may be viewed in three ways from the standpoint of "pure religion": as profane, i.e. antithetical to religion; as secular, i.e. as complementary to religion in a society; or as pagan, i.e. expressing its own kind of (lost) religion. It is the last way of viewing culture that is relevant for the analysis of the recent modern Greek theological proposal of a redefinition of Greek Orthodoxy freed from its relationship with what could be called the pagan culture of ethnophyletism.[4] A theory of individualization of faith seems relevant in examining religion in contemporary Greece, due to the tremendous changes that have happened in Greek society since the late 1980s. First of all, the general level of prosperity in the population has increased and urban centres have expanded, followed by a large entertainment and consumer industry. Second, Greece has become a country receiving rather than sending immigrants, and thus the composition of the population has changed from highly mono-cultural to multi-cultural. These new conditions have obliged the Orthodox Church and religious actors to invent new strategies to forward their agendas. In the 1990s and early 2000s, a traditional nationalist and community-oriented strategy was strengthened in particular through the Church leadership and certain influential religious intellectuals. As this chapter will show, this "traditional" strategy has recently been challenged by a new and more purely religious and individualistically oriented strategy, which can benefit from being analysed through Roy's more general thesis of religion in late modernity.

Orthodoxy and National Identity

Contemporary Orthodox Christianity is primarily known for its alliances with political power systems[5] and for its establishment in national or ethnic Churches, as is illustrated by the many autocephalous Orthodox Churches that have been established ever since nation-states began to emerge; from the Greek and Bulgarian national Churches in the nineteenth century to the Ukrainian, Montenegrin and Macedonian Churches in the late twentieth century. The continuing interest in establishing national Churches illustrates, on the one hand, the Orthodox tradition of expressing an ethnic or national affiliation, and, on the other, it exemplifies the enduring strength and importance attributed to religious symbolism in contemporary quests for national sovereignty. In Greece, where the "marriage" between Orthodox Christian and national identity is almost two centuries old, religion still plays a major role in the identity politics of the state and in the public debate on national identity and belonging. In the past twenty years Greece has experienced several national political crises where religion played a major role, and in each case Orthodox Christianity has been fiercely promoted by the Church and by nationalists as *the* unifying and distinguishing feature of Greek national identity. However, as this chapter will show, religion, and Orthodoxy in particular, has been used throughout Greece's modern cultural history as a tool for a great variety of cultural and religious ends. At times the religious identification and community has been in focus, and at other times the cultural uniqueness has been the aim. As the examples presented in the next section show, the concepts of *purity* and *authenticity* have been central in arguments for the right place and interpretation of Orthodoxy in the Greek national narrative.

What renders a retrospective view like this relevant today is the recent appearance and relative success of a new religious and theological discourse in the Greek public sphere. This new discourse has manifested itself in two spheres: (a) in the leadership of the Church, with the change of Archbishop from the nationalistic mobilization discourse of Christodoulos (1998–2008) to the moderate discourse of "controlled compromise" (Papastathis 2012) of Hieronymus (2008–), and (b) in the semi-private sphere of independent theology, where writers, theologians and intellectuals challenge and question the dominant theological paradigm, in particular through the theological journal *Synaxis*,[6] and the Academy for Theological Studies of the Holy Metropolis of Demetrias.[7] As Papastathis (ibid.) has shown, the new religious discourse of the Church leadership only superficially introduces a change of attitude; while as Willert (2012) suggests, the new theological discourse introduces a genuine break with the dominant strand of Greek Orthodox theology and its particular role in Greek national identity politics.

Quests for an Authentic Greek Identity in the Twentieth Century

The literary generation of the 1930s is a landmark in modern Greek literature. The authors and poets who published their first works in this decade became the architects of a revised Greek national identity after the military defeat in Asia Minor in 1922 and the subsequent population exchange of 1.5 million people. These traumatic events called for a complete redefinition of the Greek nation and of what it meant to be Greek. These authors, many of whom came from multicultural milieus in Asia Minor and Constantinople, found inspiration in a folkloric national identity, as opposed to bombastic, heroic national identities of previous times. Hence, cultural purity in the twentieth century was not predominantly sought in linguistic or racial purity, but in a new perception of the authentic modern Greek experience. The pure Greek culture was not to be found or dug out from under layers of contaminating foreign influence such as the Slav, Turkish or "Frankish". However, as a reaction to purist perceptions of language and racial descent, the profound change in Greek literature and art around the 1930s also led to its own purist perceptions. This generation was the first to attribute crucial importance to the term *Ellinikótita*, meaning Greekness, understood as a specific way of being in the world, which its proponents, such as Georgios Seferis, saw at one and the same time as the specific ethnicity of a historical experience embodied in the Greek nation and as a universal "state-of-mind"[8] applicable beyond the borders of the Greek nation-state. Gourgouris (1996: 213) notes that Seferis was ready to sacrifice "Greece" to Greekness, thus turning Greekness into an ideology.

In harsh times of human tragedy there is an intensified search for meaningful answers, which leaves room for actors proposing religion's simplified answers and promise of consolation. Therefore, it may be assumed that the traumatic experiences of the Second World War and the subsequent civil war may have led the artists who made their debut in the 1930s to rediscover folkloric Orthodoxy from the 1940s onwards as a source of the authentic Greekness they were seeking. These traumatic events may also be an explanation for the success of independent Orthodox religious organizations in the 1940s and '50s that cultivated a pietistic purist religiosity. Thus, after and parallel to the artists' cultural quest for an "ecumenical Greekness" from the 1930s onwards, there was a religious revival seeking religious piety and devoutness. The religious organizations became very influential, and according to the theologian and journal editor Thanasis Papathanasiou,[9] they may have attracted more active members than the actual institutional Church at some periods during the 1940s and '50s. The religious ideal of the members was to lead an ascetic, communal life, purified from contaminating cultural distraction. In this sense the organizations were inspired by Protestant piety and biblical fundamentalism, quite unlike the usual image of Orthodoxy as a version of Christianity which traditionally had left more room for earthly pleasure than Catholicism and Protestantism.

In the 1960s, the dominance of the religious organizations led several intellectuals, theologians and monks to protest against what they called the Protestantization of Orthodoxy, and they demanded a revival of Orthodoxy's specific cultural rootedness in an Eastern tradition. This revival was in its origin a theological project drawing inspiration from the Orthodox liturgy, the monastic tradition and from the writings of the Greek Church Fathers. In 1968 a periodical dedicated to patristic studies called *Klironomia* (Heritage) was founded, exemplifying the revival of patristic studies that the Neo-Orthodox paradigm introduced. However, in the early 1980s some charismatic persons from theological, monastic and artistic circles embraced the revival of Orthodox theology and turned it into a quite successful popular movement, often called the Neo-Orthodox movement (Makrides 1998). It is quite obvious that, in this case, the Orthodox religion was meant to serve as an identity marker providing people in Greece with a distinctive identity in the face of the country's entry into the European Community in 1981. The renewed interest in the Greek Church Fathers was an obvious chance to promote the specific Greekness of Orthodox Christianity. The revival of patristic studies also led to a rediscovery of Byzantium as the source and ideal of the living modern Greek Orthodox tradition. As European integration was intensified during the late 1980s and early 1990s, and as Greece remained the very poor relative in the European family, there was a lot of comfort to gain from the collective memory of past Byzantine glory. The 1990s was the decade that consolidated the new vision of a synthesis between Greek national identity and Orthodox religious identity. This period is, however, also characterized by an "Eastern" purism in its antipathy towards Western culture, which was seen as threatening to alienate the pure Orthodox Christian tradition. The theological philosopher Christos Yannaras is one of the key figures of this Neo-Orthodox movement, and he exemplifies the amalgamation of national and religious identity. In an interview with the younger theologian Stavros Yangazoglou (2002), he judged that his book *Modern Greek Identity* from 1978 had worked as a manifesto. The book proposed the Greek Orthodox ecclesiastic identity as the "genuine" and "authentic" Greek identity (Yannaras & Yangazoglou 2002: 124). In the interview Yannaras called other Greek identity markers "mimetic", "folkloristic or aesthetic", "rhetoric or psychological", while the true Greek identity, according to Yannaras, can be revealed: "beneath the rust of alienation" as the Greek way of perceiving and inducing meaning to reality, expressed through the Greek Orthodox theological tradition. In Yannaras' interpretation, this tradition is metaphysical and therefore precedes language and art in its authenticity. Later in the interview, Yannaras described the contribution of his generation as follows:

> During the '60s some people realized that the truly alive – and not just folkloric – element of Greekness, the cultural identity and historical specificity of a Greek person, is safeguarded in the ecclesiastic tradition, in Orthodoxy. (Yannaras & Yangazoglou 2002: 125)[10]

Even if Yannaras in this quotation specifically referred to "a Greek person", later in the interview he insisted that the Greek Orthodox tradition, rooted in a specific language, a specific geographic topos and time, may have universal applicability outside the borders of Greece, as long as it is kept pure and uncontaminated by Western influences. The quest for a universal Greekness is characteristic of both the theological and cultural trend of Neo-Orthodoxy and the literary generation of the 1930s. But the Neo-Orthodox rejected the authenticity that the literary generation drew from Greek folklore, and added instead a metaphysical religious dimension in order to render their proposal of Greekness even more authentic. The pietistic organizations in between these two quests for a Greek authenticity represent a different quest for authenticity; namely, the authentic or pure Christian belief expressed through a pious and unselfish life mode. The search for a pure religious identity is also the concern of the recent theological current, which will be discussed below.

Ecumenical Orthodoxy
– A Contemporary Theological Current

Yannaras' conceptualization of Greekness as a way of giving meaning to the world, rooted in the Greek Orthodox tradition, is contested by some contemporary theologians, who criticize his understanding of "Greekness" and Orthodoxy for being ethnocentric and exclusive rather than universal and inclusive. In November 2006 the centre-left newspaper *To Vima* devoted a special section to the relationship between the Orthodox Church and the Greek nation. Four of the five authors belong to an emerging progressive theological milieu. The titles of the articles all indicate the authors' view of the relationship between Church and nation as problematic: one title was "The misfortune of Orthodox Christianity" (Dodos 2006), another "How nationalism undermines both the Church and the nation" (Thermos 2006), and a third "The traumatic relationship between religion and national identity" (Karamouzis 2006), etc. These articles insisted that the Church of Greece must move away from its nationalistic rhetoric and instead turn its attention towards the existential and ethical dimension of life. Such criticism is not new, but what is different in the recent theological criticism is the fundamental change of self-understanding of the Orthodox Church that is advocated. A prime example of this changed self-understanding is the theologian and director of the Volos Academy for Theological Studies, Pantelis Kalaitzidis.[11] Just as Christos Yannaras may be pointed out as his generation's best-known advocate of the "Helleno-Orthodox" vision, Pantelis Kalaitzidis is the most distinct figure of his generation. Of course, in both generations there are many different voices and the reality is much more complex than the schematic picture presented here. However, for the limited space of this chapter it makes sense to concentrate on these two characteristic, and at the same time controversial, figures.

The central issue in Kalaitzidis' work so far has been criticism of the Church's abuse of its relationship with the Greek nation. At a seminar in 2004, Kalaitzidis said that the biggest problem for the re-evangelization of the Greeks is nationalism:

> Therefore, the adoption of an ecumenical ecclesiastic discourse, freed from constant references to the nation … is not just a demand for genuineness, authenticity and faithfulness towards the Orthodox

tradition, it is also an absolutely necessary … precondition for the Church to cross the threshold of this century instead of finding easy and comfortable refuge in past epochs. (Kalaitzidis 2005: 50–51)

Whereas the previous generation of theologians used the words "authentic" and "genuine" to refer to the Greekness of the Orthodox tradition, Kalaitzidis now uses these words to refer to an Orthodoxy freed from Greekness and from recourse to the national past. At a conference held in New York on the topic of Orthodoxy and Hellenism, Kalaitzidis explicitly addressed the issue of confusing national and religious identities:

> The Church, however, is paying a heavy price for forgetting its eschatological perspective and its supra-national mission … for confusing the national with the religious, and by becoming involved in a process of ethnogenesis and national competitions. (Kalaitzidis 2010: 376)

Kalaitzidis finds that the Church is paying a heavy price for its close ties with the nation, because he claims that it thereby loses its authentic mission which is supra-national. As a theologian and religious idealist, he believes in an essential authentic spirituality which can exist outside the human construction of (national) communities. This is indeed a purist and essentialist world view. Thus the new theological paradigm, here exemplified by Kalaitzidis, proposes a deconstruction of the essentialist fusion of national and religious identities, but the new identity paradigm proposed is itself essentialist and exclusive, just with another name.

At another international conference he even more explicitly addressed the damaging effect culture and the idea of national identity may have upon the authentic religious:

> Our Church ought urgently to decide what it defends and preaches: the unity of everything and the universal brotherhood of people or national particularity and fragmentation? Christian catholicity and ecumenicity or fragmentation and particularism, which is spiritual, theological and ecclesiastical provincialism? The first, via integration into the Church and progress in spiritual life, entails freedom and the gradual overcoming or the stultification of distinctions based on tribe, language, culture, origin, family bonds etc. The

> second takes us back to idolatry and to the worship of the nation
> and of the national identity, the sacralization of the land and its
> transformation into a metaphysical category, to "Judas' temptation"
> of ethnophyletism; it takes us back to a spiritual primitivism that
> subjugates us to the pagan infernal powers of the earth, the tribe
> and bloodlines. (Kalaitzidis 2011)

In this speech there is a clear distinction between what the speaker regards
as good and evil. In a hellfire-like discourse he indicates that all evil
("infernal powers") comes from human bonding in communities such
as "tribe, language, culture, origin and family", and it is the Church's
mission to supersede such communities and assist the believer in freeing
him- or herself from such bonds. There is almost a demonization of
cultural bonds which come from communities like the nation, with its
"sacralization of the land" that "subjugates us" (Christian believers or
all humans?) to "the pagan infernal powers of the earth, the tribe and
bloodlines". The reference to national culture as pagan corresponds to
Roy's analysis of the three ways in which culture can be seen from the
point of view of religion. In this case culture and cultural religion in,
for instance, nationalism is neither seen as secular or profane, but as
pagan and primitive; something backwards in comparison with pure
religion as it can be reached, according to Kalaitzidis, in the united
Christian Church.

It is interesting to note that an apparently moderate and progressive
discourse about the problems related to nationalism in this case is turned
into something resembling a hellfire sermon. In earlier speeches this
rejection of cultural bonds has been more moderate, as for instance in
the author's academic discourse on modernity. Kalaitzidis has suggested
a reconciliation of Orthodoxy with modernity because he sees it as a
necessary step in the continuous mission of the Christian Church. He
promotes the view that Orthodoxy should not reject the conditions
of modernity, but rather be open to dialogue, because "modernity and
post-modernity (or late modernity) and the framework they define constitute the broader historical, social and cultural environment within
which the Orthodox Church is called to live and carry out its mission"
(2008). By assuming this moderate stance, he distances himself from
fundamentalist and fanatic religious positions:

For in response to the challenge of globalisation, cosmopolitanism and internationalism, today the wind of traditionalism and fundamentalism is once again blowing violently through the life and theology of the Church. Whereas fundamentalism is a flight into the past of pre-modernity and involves turning back the course of history, eschatology is an active and demanding expectation of the coming Kingdom of God, the new world which we await; as such, it feeds into a dynamic commitment to the present, an affirmation and opening to the future of the Kingdom in which the fullness and identity of the Church is to be found. (Kalitzidis 2008)

Here, fundamentalism and traditionalism within the Church are labelled pre-modern in order to firmly situate the speaker and his theological position within modernity or even beyond it. In contrast to the "pre-modern" fundamentalists and traditionalists of Greek Orthodoxy, the new theology of eschatology presented by Kalaitzidis attributes a special quality to the present while it is at the same time future-oriented.[12] In an interesting way this theological discourse follows recent trends in psychological, therapeutic and communication discourses, where, in the paradigm of mindfulness, the power of the present is also given a very important place. Eschatology is not just the expectation of the Kingdom of God, but the believer is expected to perform "a dynamic commitment to the present". Therefore, Orthodoxy is a proposal that speaks directly to "the modern person" who should be freed from the past and especially from the bonds of the nation:

> To the modern person's thirst for life, the Orthodox Church can and ought to respond with its own proposal of life, with its "words of eternal life," and not with the continuous invocation of the past and its contribution to the struggles of the nation. (Kalaitzidis 2011)

The refusal to draw the meaning of religion from the past does not mean that Kalaitzidis rejects tradition as a concept. However, he understands the tradition of the Church as solely related to the divine and mythological aspect:

> In this perspective, Tradition is not identified with habits, customs, traditions or ideas or in general with historical inertia and stagnation, but with a person, Jesus Christ, the Lord of glory who is coming.

It does not relate chiefly to the past; or to put it differently, it is not bound by the patterns of the past, by events that have already happened. (Kalitzidis 2008)

This new theological position rejects viewing religion as a source of cultural memory. Orthodox Christianity should only care about the message of Jesus Christ and the expectation of the fulfilment of his mission with the Second Coming. History, "patterns of the past", created by humans should not be relevant to the Church.

In a way this theological position reflects the claim of the sociologist of religion Danièle Hervieu-Léger that religions in modern societies "have become sources of cultural heritage revered for their historical significance and their emblematic function, but to all intents and purposes poorly mobilized for the production of collective meaning" (2000: 90). Instead of analysing the interests at stake when modern actors put forward their versions of true and authentic memory and identity, Hervieu-Léger seems to imply that modern societies are in need of religion as production of collective meaning. Thus a theological project like that of Kalaitzidis would, from Hervieu-Legér's point of view, be necessary for religion to fulfil its role in late modern societies. However, this is a position that beforehand recognizes religion, especially moderate religion, as a "good thing", rather than analysing from a more neutral position the actual agendas that guide various actors to promote a religious world view. One way whereby theologians or advocates of religion in late modernity try to reinstate religion as a meaning-giving factor is to point out the "abuse" of religion within the modern "national era", and to make use of the openings given by the "era of globalization" for a new role for religion in late modernity. The intellectual, philologist, author and journal editor Stavros Zoumboulakis has also observed how "pure" faith has been replaced by memory as

> religion becomes an element in the ethnic or cultural identity of a people, a part of historical memory; it becomes tradition and culture, and ceases to be a way of life the basic characteristic of which is obedience to the will of God and the keeping of his commandments; it ceases to be a struggle of faith. (Zoumboulakis 1998, cited in Kalaitzidis 2008)

Zoumboulakis is part of the circle of theologians and intellectuals who work for a religious revival in Greek Orthodoxy and in particular, through his work as director of the foundation Artos Zoës (Bread of Life), which is dedicated to the publication of biblical studies, for its "return" to the original, authentic Christian texts from the Bible.

Kalaitzidis suggests that the change must come from the believers, who must start believing in the essence of their religion ("what they are supposed to believe in") and to reach its "essential core", which is freed from all historical relationships within that religion:

> This first significant and fundamental step has to be taken; church people need to show at least some rudimentary consistency with what they are supposed to believe; and there has to be an awareness that the Church is not identified with any period in history, any society, any given form, and the essential core of its truth cannot be confined to or exhausted by earlier examples of the relationship between world and Church. Only then can the Church address itself to the world and speak to the outside world and secular society or the community of citizens, to "those near and those far" from its faith, its experience and its tradition, in order to proclaim that "Jesus Christ is the same yesterday and today and for ever" (Heb. 13: 8). (Kalitzidis 2008)

Kalaitzidis also demands of the individual to make a conscious choice of faith instead of just accepting a cultural relationship with the Orthodox religion:

> Is our participation in the Orthodox faith, in other words, a custom, a part of a national folklore or a conscious and absolute personal choice with the proportional value? (Kalaitzidis 2011)

Seeing religion as a matter of individual consciousness is a very new idea in a country where slogans like "to be Greek is to be Orthodox" have been used widely in the media and by the Church hierarchy. According to the old religious paradigm, the majority of Greeks are "born Orthodox" and not "baptized Orthodox", while Kalaitzidis challenges this way of viewing religious identity as a cultural identity and suggests that a religious identity is not cultural, but existential and conscious. Such a focus on individual religiosity may be interpreted as a Protestant feature in his theology, or as an attempt at adjusting Orthodoxy to a globalized world and the living conditions of late modernity. In both ways Kalaitzidis exemplifies the global tendencies observed by Roy (2010), where faith rather than culture, individualism rather than community, are on the rise. Roy also discusses whether the changes in the religion market of late modernity have been brought about by the influence of mainstream culture or "the cultural predominance of the North-American model", i.e. of Christianity's or rather Protestantism's cultural hegemony (2010: 25), or whether it is more likely that the religions that define themselves as acultural are those which are spreading and flourishing. Roy thus asks whether a specific culture spreads a specific religion or whether a specific religion spreads because it is detached from any specific culture. He concludes that the first case is relevant for understanding the success of Evangelic Protestantism, i.e. as a side effect of global Americanization, while the second makes sense in the case of global Islam (2010: 24). It is possible, as we shall see later, to interpret the changes in Greek theology as to some extent provoked by societal and cultural changes in late modernity such as Americanization, but Kalaitzidis and other young theologians also continue a local tradition of Orthodox ecumenical theology and dialogue with Western theologies. Theologians like Nikos Nissiotis (1924–1986) and Savvas Agouridis (1921–2009) were founders of the tradition of ecumenical studies in modern Greek theology, and as advocates of the centrality of the Bible they were counter-voices to the Neo-Orthodox ethnocentric use of patristic texts already in the 1970s and 1980s. Thus the new generation's rejection of the relevance of the historical or cultural past also has to do with criticism first voiced by Agouridis and Nissiotis against the Neo-Orthodox paradigm. Kalaitzidis does not dismiss patristic texts as irrelevant, but he says that the focus on patristic studies and Byzantium as the ideal Orthodox society removes the focus from the real message of Christianity, which is the Bible. Therefore, a renewed interest in biblical studies and frequent use of Bible quotes is also characteristic of the new theological discourse. In previous generations the Bible had been neglected as a theological source in favour of patristic texts interpreting it. By reinstating the Bible in a central position in Greek Orthodoxy, contemporary Greek theologians and religious intellectuals envision a "return to Europe". Instead of considering Eastern Orthodoxy a demarcating feature of Greece vis-à-vis Europe, they advocate the common biblical heritage of Europe including Greece.

84

Stavros Zoumboulakis has proposed a reform of the religion class of Greek public education into a "biblical class", arguing that "today the European school absolutely needs the Bible, as it also needs ... Homer, Aeschylus, and Plato" (Zoumboulakis 2006). Criticizing the anti-European attitude of contemporary Greek Church hierarchs, he has also asked: "If Europe is not our socio-political reference then tell us what is" (Zoumboulakis 2002).

The "return to Europe" is moreover followed by a demand for Orthodoxy to come to terms with modernity through a *dialogical* stance towards the world without compromising its metaphysical dimension:

> We cannot stake Orthodoxy on an anti-modernist religious revival ... What we should be seeking is, on the one hand, an Orthodoxy rooted in the tradition and the Fathers, but an Orthodoxy that is open and in dialogue, conversing and understanding. An Orthodoxy that will not be subordinate to the social and cultural conditions at a given time, but will also not ignore or disregard and scorn societies and cultures or new cultural forms ... for in the final analysis everything is of God, everything bears ... breath of the Holy Spirit ... and is not restricted only to the Orthodox, to Greeks, to the Balkans or to the eastern Mediterranean. (Kalaitzidis 2007: 175–176)

This quotation, notably the statements "everything is of God" and about the Holy Spirit that is not restricted to any cultural or geographic specificity, shows the tendency towards pure and decultured religion that resembles Roy's analysis referred to earlier. This purist and religious world view makes a sharp contrast to the way this author positions himself as a modernizer in opposition to the "anti-modern" (or "pre-modern" in other quotations). It is also a paradox that this criticism of Orthodoxy is voiced from a position within the Church. Even if it is not at all appreciated by most members of the Church hierarchy, the Volos Academy is still closely related to the Holy Metropolis of Demetrias, and all its conferences and official lectures are welcomed by representatives of the Church hierarchy, in many cases bishops, and the activities are attended by Church officials. The new theological discourse gains strength from being in opposition and from positioning itself as progressive in contrast to the conservative strands of the Church. It proposes something new, and who is not thirsty for something new in today's Greece? But as we have seen in the quotations cited here, there is a strong international dimension in Kalaitzidis' academic activities, and up until now he has been very conscious not to address himself specifically to a limited Greek audience. When looking upon the new discourse through the lenses of Roy and the thesis of de-territorialization of religion, it seems plausible that it will have some success. However, when considering the economic crises in Europe and the tendencies towards re-nationalization (of economies, of border control, etc.), it is hard to imagine how long-suffering people in Greece will, at this moment, embrace a new way of believing. Another obstacle is the intellectualism of the new discourse. Assuming a progressive and academic profile makes it difficult to communicate its message to a broader public. The Neo-Orthodox movement, even if this current was also primarily rooted in elite milieus, could more easily find adherents among ordinary people because it referred to a well-known national past and aestheticism. For the argument of this paper, however, we have primarily been interested in the purist dimension of the discourses and, therefore, an examination of their endurance or success should be dealt with elsewhere.

Cultural Pluralism and Religious Purity

In order to understand the new development in Greek theology, it is helpful to look at the contemporary societal developments. There are at least two factors that have urged progressive or open-minded theologians and intellectuals to express their discontent and propose alternative interpretations of religious and cultural identity in this historical period. One crucial circumstance that brought the present generation of progressive theologians to formulate and intensify their criticism against the "nationalization" of the Church of Greece was the leadership of late Archbishop Christodoulos from 1998 to 2008. He fully exemplified the ethno-religious perception of the Orthodox Church that mixes the religious or sacred with the cultural or secular. During the decade of his tenure there was an open conflict between him and the voices from the theological opposition, meaning that they were unofficially banned from all Church-related media and other Church forums. The second factor has to do with the way religious values have been mobilized as responses to multi-culturalism and globalization.

Since the fall of the Iron Curtain, Greece has been receiving hund-reds of thousands of foreign workers, especially from Albania and other countries formerly under communist rule. The massive influx of immigrants supplying the country with cheap labour was one of the factors that enabled the Greek economy to thrive and considerably raise the standards of living for the first time since the Second World War. Also, a large amount of EU subsidies added to the thriving economy which in the 1990s led to an intense Americanization of Greek media, cultural life and lifestyles. Such rapid and deep societal changes have put new challenges to religious actors, who are urged to propose relevant answers to the new living conditions. The ethnic pluralization caused by immigration has challenged the mono-cultural and mono-religious self-understanding in Greek society, and the relativization of identities brought about by consumerism and Americanization has called for a stable, recognizable framework. The theological viewpoints that have been presented in this chapter reflect a way of taking up the challenges of the new living conditions and cultural pluralization.[13] The message of the contemporary progressive theologians seems to be that "we need not fear cultural diversity and unstable cultural identities, because there is one stable truth in which we may have confidence, and this truth itself advocates difference and otherness". This view has been developed by, among others, two progressive theologians, Stavros Yangazoglou and Thanasis Papathanasiou. Both attempt to develop a concept of "theology of otherness" (Yangazoglou 2006; Papathanasiou 2002). Such a theology does not compromise the Christian truth they believe in, but integrates it into a late modern world of cultural fuzziness and changing cultural identities. This religious "renewal" from Greece is an example of how the core values and "eternal" truths of religion are proposed as alternatives to the state of flux; of multiple, ever-changing identities in late modernity. Religious values are also presented as uni-versal moral values "uncontaminated" by fanaticism and especially by nationalism. Thus, engaging in progressive theology becomes a viable alternative for intellectuals who want to distance themselves from the nationalist discourse of their contemporary fellow-citizens. The critique of fundamentalist nationalism gives religious arguments a rational twist. Now the religious nationalists are depicted as irrational, intolerant and unenlightened, while the religious ecumenists present themselves as rational, tolerant, learned and progressive.

Contemporary theological arguments against a purist and essentialist perception of Greek history, culture and identity are similar to a trend since the 1990s among the so-called modernizers within secular academic circles.[14] This resemblance makes the theologians appear *rational*. The new irrational is nationalism, not religion or metaphysics. So, what is common among the secular and the religious intellectual elites is their disapproval of the unenlightened, emotional and ethnocentric masses or their demagogues. The theologians draw attention to the fatal error of their religion in becoming an ally of nationalism. Nationalism was (once) about finding (or inventing) the authentic, true, pure spirit of the national community. Now it has become a contaminating factor among secular as well as religious intellectual elites, who depict an image of a purely cosmopolitan or ecumenist community free from the self-deception of nationalism.

The debate about the role of Orthodoxy within national identity is still primarily to be observed in theological circles; and it may not even be termed a debate, since it is rather a certain group or strand of theologians proposing an alternative to the dominating perception of Orthodoxy and theology in Greece today. It is not yet a broad public discussion, since the views of these alternative voices are still mainly expressed in seminars and conferences organized within their own circles; for the most part they simply attract people of their own conviction. I have asked one of the key figures of the alternative Orthodox theology why he is not very visible in the public sphere, why he for instance does not attempt to spread his alternative views to lay people through newspaper articles or other means to reach a wider audience. He replied that he was hesitant to do so because he would not like to become a national public figure like Christos Yannaras, who for many years has had a weekly column in a major Sunday newspaper and in the 1990s also led a programme on television. For a progressive theologian today this would be unthinkable, because of his interpretation of the Orthodox ethos which is not directed towards any specific national community that could be reached through national media. But even if the prevalence of the new discourse in the public debate is rather limited, it receives a relatively large space within the Church of Greece because the local bishop at Volos, who is one of the most influential Greek bishops, supports the Volos Academy morally and financially. The late Archbishop Christodoulos was certainly not in favour of the Academy because it represented criticism of his way of leadership. Perhaps as a consequence of Greece's need for a conciliatory stance towards Europe and the EU in view of the economic crisis, the new Archbishop has chosen a different strategy of leading the Church. Instead of interfering with politics and attempting to lead the population with nationalist and isolationist rhetoric, as his predecessor did, he claims that his role is that of a spiritual guide and not a politician. In accordance with his moderate stance, he has also recognized the contribution of the Volos Academy to the Greek theological scene and the importance of its work by paying a visit to the Metropolis of Volos in May 2009 during an international conference on "Church and Culture" organized by the Volos Academy; and recently, in March 2011, by sending a representative to a conference also organized by the Academy on the controversial theologian Panayotis Trembelas.

Conclusion

This chapter has proposed an analysis of Greece's cultural history over the past eighty years as a continuous fluctuation between interpretations of Greek national and religious identity as either defined by a local Eastern (Byzantine) religious tradition or by a larger Western and/or ecumenical Christian tradition. In both cases, the idea of a pure, authentic and uncontaminated religious culture has been a guiding principle.

In the generation of the 1930s, and that of the 1960s to the '80s, there was a similar way of interpreting Greekness and Orthodoxy as two sides of the same coin. In both periods Greek culture and Orthodoxy were understood as unique cultural and religious traditions that, on the one hand, were exclusive and particular to the geographic area of (modern) Greece, but on the other hand also represented a universal alternative to Western (capitalist) culture. In the generation of the 1930s, which was not a religious but an artistic movement, Orthodoxy was seen as just one element of that unique Greek culture. In the 1960s and '80s, Orthodoxy was seen as *the* constituent feature of Greekness and the result was a *cultural religion*.

Likewise, some common features can be distinguished between the religious organizations in the 1940s and '50s and the progressive theological current of today. In both periods Orthodox Christianity was receptive to influence from the West and in both periods there has been a renewed interest in the Bible. In the case of the religious organizations, this influence (recognized or not) came from Protestant movements, i.e. from America and from Protestant missionaries, while the theological current today is opening up Orthodox theology towards other Christian dogmas as a way of dealing with modernization and globalization in general. In both periods the message of religion is central and culture is marginalized, and therefore these periods are characterized by *religious purism*.

Regarding the historical dynamics of national cultural religion versus religious purity, it is worth noting that it is the present generation of theologians, and in particular Pantelis Kalaitzidis (2008: 223–245, 257–271), who has interpreted the past literary and theological generations as harmful to the "true" character of Orthodoxy. It could therefore be said that it is the current generation's use and interpretation of the past that has highlighted the patterns in Greek cultural history that have been presented in this chapter. Of course, the significance of the notions of purity and mixture for the concept or invention of "Greekness" has been addressed before (Stewart 1994; Tsoukalas 2002); and without doubt they are intrinsically part of Greek cultural history. However, in this case we have seen how religious actors may set the agenda for a discussion on the "nature" of religion; hence, the focus upon religion's alienation by (national) culture is a choice on their part.

Apart from illustrating an inner logic of successive cultural and religious currents related to the history of modern Greece as a nation constructed along the ideational borders between "The East" and "The West", between Eastern and Western Christianity, this chapter has also interpreted the recent trends in Greek theology through the lens of Olivier Roy's thesis of "religion without culture" in the age of globalization. The global trend exemplified by Roy (2010) with a large variety of cases may work as one explanatory model for the developments observed in Greek theology today. The spatial and temporal cultural integration of Greek Orthodoxy cannot be disputed, and the religious tendencies that can be observed in Greece today are not "fanatic and extreme versions of religious purification" like those tendencies described by Roy. Yet, in a sense the contemporary theological current does illustrate a global phenomenon of claims to "uncultured religion". Claims of purity and authenticity are expressed indirectly as claims of cleansing a religious tradition from perceived foreign elements. In the case of progressive Greek theologians, nationalism and ethno-religiosity are seen as foreign to an authentic Christian tradition going back to the first Christian communities. As a defence against the insecurity and constant flux of identities in the living conditions of late modernity, *religious purism* should not only be interpreted as a local reaction to the phenomenon of cultural and nationalized religion, as is the case with Orthodoxy in Greece, but also as a broader global phenomenon where religion is reinstated as the absolute truth and a firm core identity unaffected by any culturally defined belonging.

Notes

1 I borrow the expressions regarding tradition and modernity as rhetorical markers from Sutton (1994), Argyrou (1996) and Herzfeld (2002).
2 Some posts from 2011: http://makedonia-is-greece.blogspot.com/2011/01/995-dna.html; http://www.ardin.gr/node/274; http://orthoboulos.blogspot.com/2011/07/995-dna.html; http://www.youtube.com/watch?v=55CIpVkEqvU. Blogs accessed 15 September 2011.
3 The expression "religion without culture" derives from the original French title of Roy's work: *La Sainte ignorance. Le temps de la religion sans culture* (2008). In the English translation the expression has been changed to "when religion and culture part ways".
4 Ethnophyletism was the term used by the Patriarch of Constantinople in the first half of the nineteenth century to condemn the establishment of autocephalous national churches. It designates the division of the Church, which according to one theological interpretation of the Bible should unite all nations and races; *ethnos* meaning nation and *phylon* meaning race.
5 This is seen in a fusion between religious and secular power as in the Byzantine Empire or in the case of Makarios (1913–1977), who was Archbishop of the Autocephalous Cypriot Orthodox Church (1950–1977) and also President of the Republic of Cyprus (1960–1977).
6 The journal *Synaxis* was founded in 1982 and served as a platform for a revival of modern Greek theology and the development of the Neo-Orthodox theological paradigm. Under the current editor-in-chief, Thanasis Papathanasiou, and since the early 2000s, the journal has, however, developed a critical view of the Neo-Orthodox impact on the Orthodox faith in Greece.
7 The Academy for Theological Studies of the Holy Metropolis of Demetrias was founded in 2000 by the local bishop under the direction of the theologian Pantelis Kalaitzidis. The Academy operates independently, but is supported financially by the Metropolis. Since 2000 it has organized debates and conferences on controversial issues in Greek theology, and in conservative circles the Academy is regarded as provocative and heretic (Ierotheos 2010), while in progressive theological and intellectual milieus it is welcomed as a daring and dialogic forum for revision of the traditionalist and conservative parts of Greek Orthodoxy (Bailis 2008; Zoumboulakis 2007).
8 Gourgouris (1996:214) quotes the following from Seferis' diary: "Hellenism means Humanism".
9 Interview, February 2008.
10 This and all subsequent quotations in Greek are translated into English by the author.

11 See note 7.

12 The first collective volume published by the Volos Academy for Theological Studies was devoted to eschatology (Kalaitzidis ed. 2003).

13 This is also an obvious tendency in the field of education within the discussion regarding the religion class in primary and secondary school. The class is taught by theologians, but a group of progressive teachers have proposed a reform of the class which aims at embracing all pupils regardless of their ethnic or religious background. They envision the religion class as a unifying and integrating element in a pluralistic and ideologically blurred society, providing the pupils with a religious perspective without the national exclusion discourse inherent in the current curricula (Willert, forthcoming).

14 Examples of such constructivist approaches to Greek national identity and the national narrative are Frangoudaki and Dragonas (eds) 1997 and Avdela 1998.

References

Argyrou, Vassos (1996): *Tradition and Modernity in the Mediterranean. The Wedding as Symbolic Struggle*, Cambridge: Cambridge University Press.

Avdela, Efi (1996): *Istoría kai scholeío* [History and the School], Athens: Nisos.

Bailis, Panos (2008): Sto diálogo den ypárchei... ávaton [In Dialogue There is no... Inaccessibility], *Eleftheros Tipos tis Kyriakis*, 24 February.

Bozatzis, Nikos (2009): Occidentalism and Accountability. Constructing Culture and Cultural Difference in Majority Greek Talk about the Minority in Western Thrace, *Discourse & Society* 20: 431–453.

Dodos, Nikos (2006): I symforá tis Orthodoxías [The Misfortune of Orthodoxy], *To Vima*, 26 November.

Frangoudaki, Anna and Thaleia Dragonas (1997): *Ti ein' i Patrida mas? Ethnokentrismós stin ekpaídefsi* [What is our Fatherland? Ethnocentrism in Education], Athens: Alexandreia.

Yannaras, Christos and Stavros Yangazoglou (2002): Ellinikótita os nóima víou. Synéntefksi [Greekness as Meaning of Life. Interview], *Indiktos*, 16: 124–129.

Gourgouris, Stathis (1996): *Dream Nation. Enlightenment, Colonization, and the Institution of Modern Greece*, Stanford: Stanford University Press.

Hervieu-Léger, Danièle (2000): *Religion as a Chain of Memory*, Cambridge: Polity Press.

Herzfeld, Michael (2002): Cultural Fundamentalism and the Regimentation of Identity. The Embodiment of Orthodox Values in a Modernist Setting, in Ulf Hedetoft and Mette Hjort (eds), *The Postnational Self. Belonging and Identity*, Minneapolis and London: University of Minnesota Press.

Ierotheos (2010): Diati apoteloún diéresi i metapateriki-neopateriki 'theología', enó eínai nárki eis ta themélia tis Orthodóksou theologías [Why the Metapatristic-Neopatristic "Theology" is Heretic, while it is Undermining the Foundations of Orthodox Theology], *Orthodox Tipos*, 12 December.

Kalaitzidis, Pantelis (ed.) (2003): *Ekklisía kai Eschatología* [Church and Eschatology], Athens: Kastaniotis Publications.

Kalaitzidis, Pantelis (2005): O ethnikismós kai i progonolatreía: dyo embodia gia ton epanevangelismoú tou simerinoú Ellina [Nationalism and Worship of the Forefathers. Two Obstacles for the Re-evangelization of the Contemporary Greek], Paper published in *The Young of Our Age. A Youth Conference on the Re-Evangelization of the Greeks*, Published by Youth Educational Society of Syros.

Kalaitzidis, Pantelis (2007): *Orthodoxía kai neoterikótita. Prolegómena* [Orthodoxy and Modernity. Prolegomena], Athens: Indiktos Publications.

Kalaitzidis, Pantelis (2008): Did Orthodox Christianity Come to a Halt before Modernity? The Need for a New Incarnation of the Word and the Eschatological Understanding of Tradition and of the Church-World Relationship, School of Theology, Catholic University of Linz, Austria, May 15. Unpublished paper.

Kalaitzidis, Pantelis (2010): Orthodoxy and Hellenism in Contemporary Greece, *St Vladimir's Theological Quarterly*, 54 (3–4): 365–420.

Kalaitzidis, Pantelis (2011): Nationalism as cause of division and conflicts in the Orthodox World, Paper for the Workshop "The Role of the Orthodox Church in Peace-building" organized in the framework of the International Ecumenical Peace Convocation, Kingston, Jamaica, 21 May. Paper: http://www.acadimia.gr/images/stories/2011/kalaitzidis_workshop_the_orthodox_church_in_war_and_conflict_jamaica_revised.pdf (Accessed on 26 May 2011).

Karamouzis, Polykarpos (2006): I travmatikí schési thriskeías ke ethnikís taftótitas [The Traumatic Relationship between Religion and National Identity], *To Vima*, 26 November.

Makrides, Vasilios (1998): Byzantium in Contemporary Greece. The Neo-Orthodox Current of Ideas, in David Ricks and Paul Magdalino (eds), *Byzantium and the Modern Greek Identity*, Publications for the Centre for Hellenic Studies, King's College London, Vol. 4, Aldershot: Ashgate.

Papastathis, Kostas (2012): From Mobilization to a Controlled Compromise. The Shift of Ecclesiastical Strategy under Archbishop Hieronymus, in Trine Stauning Willert and Lina Molokotos Liederman (eds), *Innovation in the Orthodox Christian Tradition? The Question of Change in Greek Orthodox Thought and Practice*, Farnham: Ashgate.

Papathanasiou, Thanasis (2002): *O theós mou o allodapós. Keímena gia mia alítheia pou eínei tou drómou* [My God the Foreigner. Texts of a Truth which is "of the Street"], Athens: Akritas.

Roy, Olivier (2010): *Holy Ignorance. When Religion and Culture Part Ways*, London: Hurst and Company.

Roy, Olivier (2008) : *La sainte ignorance. Le temps de la religion sans culture*. Paris: Seuil.

Skopetea, Elli (1997): *Fallmerayer. Technasmata tou antipalou deous* [Fallmerayer: Devices of the Opposing Belief], Athens: Themelio.

Stewart, Charles (1994): Syncretism as a Dimension of Nationalist Discourse in Greece, in Charles Stewart and Rosalind Shaw (eds), *Syncretism/Anti-syncretism. The Politics of Religious Synthesis*, London: Routledge.

Sutton, David E. (1994): Tradition and Modernity. Kalymnian Constructions of Identity and Otherness, *Journal of Modern Greek Studies*, 12: 239–60.

Thermos, Vasileios (2006): Pos o ethnikismós yposkáptei kai tin Ekklisía kai to ethnos [How Nationalism Undermines both the Church and the Nation], *To Vima*, 26 November.

Willert, Trine Stauning (Forthcoming): Religious, National, European or Inter-Cultural Awareness: Religious Education as Cultural Battlefield in Greece, in Ruy Blanes and José Mapril (eds), *Sites and Politics of Religious Diversity in Southern Europe*, Leiden: Brill.

Willert, Trine Stauning (2012): A New Role for Religion in Greece? Theologians Challenging the Ethno-religious Understanding of Orthodoxy and Greekness, in Trine Stauning Willert and Lina Molokotos Liederman (eds), *Innovation in the Orthodox Christian Tradition? The Question of Change in Greek Orthodox Thought and Practice*, Farnham: Ashgate.

Yangazoglou, Stavros (2006): Prósopo kai eterótita. Dokímio gia mia theología tis eterótitas [Person and Otherness. Essay on a Theology of Otherness], *Indiktos*, 21: 87–125.

Zoumboulakis, Stavros (2002): O fóvos kai i echthrótita pros tisképsi [Fear and Hostility towards Thinking], in *God in the City. Essays on Religion and Politics*, Athens: Estia Publications.

Zoumboulakis, Stavros (2006): Ta thriskeftiká os vivlikó máthima [The Religion Class as a Biblical Class], in *Religious Education and Contemporary Society*, Athens: En Plo Publications.

Zoumboulakis, Stavros (2007): To ananeotikó engcheírima tis Akadimías Theologikón Spoudón [The Renovating Enterprise of the Academy for Theological Studies], *Nea Estia*, 1805: 1024–1029.

RELIGION AND NATIONAL HERITAGE

IN CENTRAL EUROPE

CHAPTER 5

Duke Widukind and Charlemagne in Twentieth-Century Germany

Myths of Origin and Constructs of National Identity

Peter Lambert

Controversy in a "Totalitarian" Society – Identity-Politics and History in the Third Reich

> It is a wonderful thing to turn the word *Volksgemeinschaft* [community of the people / race] into a reality. ... Sometimes we are overcome by the feeling that ... the hand of the Lord had to strike us to make us ready for this, the greatest inner good fortune there is, the good fortune of mutual understanding within one's own people.

With these words, in a speech delivered in Saarbrücken in March 1935, Hitler welcomed the Saarland into the Third Reich. He seemed to promise not only a future, but a present free of internal strife (Domarus 1992: 645). In fact, even if one were to leave the radicalizing persecution of German Jews out of the equation, Hitler's divination of a condition of "mutual understanding" among Germans was of course short of the truth. True, general support for the Nazi regime was indeed increasing, while the campaign of terror mounted against the German Left in 1933 and 1934 was on the wane, its task substantially complete. Yet pressure on the Christian Churches and persecution of uncounted individual priests was on the rise, and did not go unnoticed in the public sphere of Nazi Germany, increasingly cowed and distorted though it was. The onslaught on the Churches was connected with one decidedly curious anomaly within a "totalitarian" society. Totalitarian societies, by definition, should have been free of open controversy. Yet an intense, polarized and very public debate was held in the early years of Nazi rule in Germany. It was a debate about history, and in particular about the origins of the Germans. Stories of origin are invariably associated with constructs of identity. In this case, the religious character of Germany and its relationship to the Roman Empire, its state and its civilization, were at stake. In light of the twentieth-century European fashion for "medievalism" and the habit of using medieval motifs to frame commemorations of events even in the very recent past (Evans & Marchal 2012), its subject matter gave it added piquancy.

By any standards, the contest was extraordinary. In a retrospective written in 1938, Rudolf Buchner reflected that "For two years, the quarrel over Karl and Widukind kept the German people in suspense, holding its breath, as perhaps no quarrel over matters historical had ever done before." (Buchner 1938:244) The years in question were 1934 and 1935; "Karl" was Charlemagne (Karl der Große) and Widukind the leader of Saxon resistance to his rule. Which of these was a hero of German history, and which a villain? Nobody appeared to doubt that answering the question was of vital importance for an understanding of Germany's past and a means of mapping out its future. Was Charlemagne's long and ultimately successful war of subjugation of the Saxons essentially a foreign invasion of German territory, or was it on the contrary the essential precondition for the emergence of a German nation and state?

And there were other, more general questions which were tenaciously pursued in the course of the debate. Were "great men", capable of instrumentalizing the power of the state, the makers of German history, or was the appropriate perspective that offered by *Volksgeschichte*? The first of these theories of history posited only the state and its leaders as agents, whereas the second tended to view "the people" (defined overwhelmingly in racial terms) as the motor of history. The older, "statist" view still predominated in the Third Reich's universities, but *Volksgeschichte* was certainly a rising force (Oberkrome 1993). Events of the late eighth and early ninth century took on a degree of relevance to twentieth-century Germans that made them seem immediate, tangible. The controversy was further coloured by various protagonists' appeals to *Heimat*. This concept is untranslatable, but has connotations of local or regional patriotism, and is associable with a vision of the nation as a sort of patchwork quilt of individual localities and identities. Its advocates – the *Heimatler* – constituted a diverse movement from the nineteenth century onward; they commanded a repertoire of "heritage" and folkloric symbols, and celebrated local landscapes and nature as much as they did the local traditions and dialects (Applegate 1990; Boa & Palfreyman 2000). Malleable and ambiguous, *Heimat* could serve as a comfort-zone, an imagined refuge from Nazi rule. In other hands, it became an element of Nazi ideology and an instrument of Nazi propaganda.

It seems surprising in light of the way in which it engaged contemporaries that there should as yet be no full-scale study of the Widukind *versus* Charlemagne controversy. German historians have, however, addressed it sporadically over the last half-century, so that it has not altogether fallen out of historiographical awareness (cf. esp. Werner 1967; Kühn 1986; Kuhlmann 2010).

The origins of Charlemagne's war on the Saxons no doubt lay in raids and acts of retribution for them, and were perhaps structurally determined by the proximity of the very loosely allied Saxon tribes to the highly organized Frankish territories. (The account which follows is based on Becher 2003: 59–79, and Kuhlmann 2010: 13–30.) The commencement of the war itself is conventionally dated to 772, when Charlemagne led a significant incursion into what is now Lower Saxony, took a major fortification (the Eresburg), and destroyed the Irminsul – a tree-trunk (or more likely several tree-trunks) venerated by the Saxons. In 774 and 776, Saxon uprisings occurred; in the course of Charlemagne's suppression of the second of these, the Eresburg was re-taken, and the greater part of the Saxon aristocracy surrendered at Lippspringe. Mass conversions of Saxons followed and, in 777, Charlemagne held a diet at Paderborn – within Saxon territory. The Saxon aristocracy attended to render homage to Charlemagne, but one of their number, Widukind, "one of the great men of Westphalia" according to the Frankish Einhard Chronicle, absented himself, fleeing to the court of King Siegfried of Denmark. From 777 to 785, Carolingian sources repeatedly identified Widukind as the leader in fermenting rebellion among the Saxons. After a Frankish counter-offensive launched in 780 had reached the river Elbe, a further wave of mass conversions ensued. The Carolingian success was marked and solidified at a further diet, in Lippspringe in 782. All the Saxon chieftains attended – with the sole exception of Widukind – as the Frankish administrative system, led by counts, was extended to Saxon territories.

RETHINKING THE SPACE FOR RELIGION

In the same year, a Frankish army marching against Slavic forces was confronted by Saxon rebels and defeated in a battle on the Süntel: two royal officials, four counts and twenty other Frankish nobles were reported to have been killed. Frankish retaliation for the shock defeat appears to have been swift and brutal. Again according to Frankish sources, Charlemagne had 4,500 Saxon hostages executed at Verden an der Aller. In 784–785 Frankish victories followed, and Widukind's resistance was finally broken. Widukind surrendered, swore an oath of allegiance to Charlemagne, and then converted to Christianity – probably with Charlemagne himself serving as godfather. Widukind was granted lands around Enger – and then vanished from the Frankish record. Confined to the north-eastern regions of Saxony, and seemingly leaderless, a Saxon resistance nevertheless continued until around 803/4.

On one side of the arguments about how to make sense of those distant events and their relatively sparse traces in the contemporary documentary record, there assembled an array of Hitler's principal lieutenants. Foremost among them were Alfred Rosenberg, Heinrich Himmler, R. Walther Darré, and Baldur von Schirach. Alongside them gathered: the Hitler Youth and the SS; schoolteachers and the authors of school textbooks; playwrights and novelists; Nazi journalists and amateur historians; archaeologists and "heritage industry" professionals obsessed with the Germanic tribes; anti-Christian polemicists and neo-pagans who were self-styled advocates of a "Germanic religiosity". For these, Charlemagne was not "the Great" at all, but a brutal and greedy despot. At worst, he was "the butcher of the Saxons" – the most tenacious lovers of freedom and *Heimat* of all the Germanic tribes. He was the destroyer of a centuries-long Germanic culture and its religion – a religion of "nature" identifiable with ancestor-worship. He imposed on the Saxons an utterly alien belief-system. For some, that belief-system was wrong because it was a "romanized" Christianity: cosmopolitan and dogmatic. For others, Christianity itself was inadmissible: "oriental" and (of course) "Jewish". And, with consequences at least as dreadful to contemplate, Charlemagne had entered into alliances with Slavs and introduced Jews into German territory. All this could only have been the work of a man who had lost all sense of his own Germanic identity, who was degenerate and therefore infinitely more French than German. The *Reich* he had built had, in a thousand-year-long pursuit of "universalist" goals incompatible with German national interests, drained the blood of brave but hapless and misled Germans who had fought and died for this rootless monstrosity. Widukind, on the other hand, was the personification of Germanic honour and faithfulness; a warrior-hero and simultaneously a political *Führer* who would himself have created a *Reich* (and a genuinely German one!) had not the overwhelming might of Charlemagne's forces combined with the treachery of the bulk of the Saxon nobility to destroy his dream.

If these Nazis and neo-pagans had expected to have it all their own way in the repressive climate of the Third Reich, they were to be disappointed. Too many Germans felt their interests, and their national or religious identity to be under threat for them quietly to relinquish Charlemagne or accept the revisionist programme propounded by authoritative representatives and organs of the new regime. In January 1934, Ferdinand Thürmer complained that

> Strange allies have come together in order repeatedly to emphasize the outstanding services to Germany rendered by Karl der Große and to defend them against the growing recognition of the true facts of the case. First, the Christian confessions appear on the field of battle. Holders of high office in the Catholic Church strain themselves ... to prove that our Germanic ancestors had no culture. Then, whether openly or covertly, they seek to draw the logical consequence: that it was only Christianity that brought some light into the sorry existence of this pitiable people. Press articles appear in the Protestant Christian press. They characterize the attempt at shedding light on the pre-Christian history of the Germanic people as a new heathenism.

> These belligerent priests are joined by individual representatives of the universities, who interpret the "Karl der Große" problem from altogether different perspectives. Some emphasize the national point of view, and protest that it would surely be self-defeating to reject this important ruler. Alternatively, they even assert that to do so would be damaging to Germandom since it would advance the French ambitions to interpret Charlemagne as a representative of their people, as the real founder of the French *Reich*, and above all as guiding their later policies regarding the Rhine. Other historians again declare that it was only through the subjugation of the Saxons that the subsequent foundation of the German *Reich* on a Germanic basis became possible at all. In particular, they stress that

it was only through main force that the Saxons could be brought to a higher statist consciousness. (Thürmer 1934: 241)

If, to return to the optimistic appraisal Hitler had offered in March 1935, Germans had arrived at a genuine mutual understanding, then in this particular context they understood chiefly that they had mutually irreconcilable understandings of what it meant to be German. Thürmer had identified his opponents and their arguments perfectly accurately. But understanding did not lead to tolerance. Thürmer's metaphorical allusion to the debate as a "battlefield" was apt.

Foremost among the "belligerent priests" of whom Thürmer had complained was surely Cardinal Michael von Faulhaber. In a New Year's Eve sermon which galvanized many German Roman Catholics who noisily displayed their emotions (Krebs 2011: 216), Faulhaber sought to defend Christianity from what he certainly saw as a mounting neo-pagan onslaught. Not that it was religion alone that was at issue: the religious future of Germany was bound up with its national destiny. Any "backsliding from Christianity and relapse into paganism would be the beginning of the end of the Germany people", and a defence of Christianity even offered, Faulhaber argued, a defence of the Germanic people (Faulhaber 1934: 103). Left to their own devices, the Germanic tribes had slaughtered one another. Tacitus's *Germania* had arrived at a tally of fifty Germanic peoples, which he had described as being permanently at war with one another; the bulk of them, Faulhaber warned, had "vanished from history." It was, he asserted, "an historical fact that this agglomeration of peoples was brought together into a settled entity and a *unitary Volk* only through conversion to Christianity." Tacitus himself had hoped on Rome's behalf that "mutual loathing" would continue to infect the Germanic tribes; Christianity had "turned that curse … into a blessing", into "mutual love. And no greater happiness can come to us than the harmony of our *Volk*" (Faulhaber 1934: 113). The immediate responsibility for securing the unification of the German tribes under Christian auspices had of course been borne by Charlemagne. His *forced* conversion of the Saxons was, Faulhaber acknowledged, wholly unjustifiable from a theological point of view. However, it was perfectly defensible from a secular, German nationalist standpoint. Charlemagne had combined the partially forced conversion of the Saxons with their political subjugation "because he knew that the political unity of these tribal peoples

would be impossible to attain without [their] religious unification."
(Faulhaber 1934: 112)

Thürmer's polemical article was one early response; another came
from Johann von Leers, an amateur historian with a background in
the neo-pagan "German Faith Movement", whose career in the Third
Reich was to take him via SS membership to a full professorial chair
in "Racial History" at the University of Jena. The exchange between
Faulhaber and von Leers involved a curious instance of role- reversal.
Faulhaber had built his case on Tacitus's *Germania*, and so angered
many Nazis for whom that text had acquired a sacral status (Krebs 2011:
214–244). Von Leers, however, criticized him on the very reasonable
ground that he had drawn upon no other authority, and that Tacitus
had known Germanic lands only at second hand (von Leers 1934:
11). For the rest, however, his tract was typical of the anti-Christian
movement, and strikingly similar to Thürmer's.

Von Leers advocated a religiosity grounded in what he imagined as a
racial and cultural Germanic heritage, not a literal revival of a defunct
pagan belief-system. He depicted that religious heritage as rooted in
the soil of the *Heimat* and characterized by ancestor-worship, un-
doctrinaire, never prone to be the source of civil wars (unlike Christianity, of course!) and free of proselytizing tendencies. Accordingly, he
disavowed any intent to assault Christianity or the Roman Catholic
Church. It was, he insinuated, the Church that was trying to deprive
believers in a German Faith of their rights, but to "force them onto a
road to Palestine" and threaten them with "the danger of Jewification
of the soul". That was precisely what Christian missionaries among
the Germanic tribes had done. From St. Boniface onward, they had
exhibited "boundless contempt for indigenous piety" in the "violence
of their methods of conversion". Von Leers, by contrast, claimed to
entertain a modest and peaceable ambition: the securing of religious
toleration within the Nazi *Volksgemeinschaft* (von Leers 1934: 49,
59–60). Yet, "for the great numbers among our *Volk* who are Nordic
in their orientation, these 'ancestors of Christianity', the patriarchs of
the Old Testament, are unbearable." Old Testament stories were tales
of immorality "repugnant to the sensibility of these Germans", and if
any one of their characters was sympathetic, then it was the "Pharaoh
who keeps the Jews at work until he finally gets rid of them – gets them
out of his country" (von Leers 1934: 56). Similarly, Thürmer inveighed
against teaching the Old Testament in German schools – against

"people who have no sense" that the story of Cain and Abel "is a matter of Jewish crime statistics which has nothing to do with the belief of German children". Why, he asked, was it considered legitimate for Germans to study the histories of "Egyptians, Babylonians, Sumarians, Greeks and the old Romans", but not the "cultic arrangements of the pre-Christian Germanic peoples"? "One would think", he continued,

> that the faith of our Germanic ancestors would be more important to us than stories of the Cain and Abel sort. Moreover, this instance of fratricide also lies long before the beginning of the Christian tradition. Why then is the engagement with this base act not neo-paganism? Perhaps because it is Jewish? We must at long last develop a habit of viewing early German history from a perspective other than that of Jewry, Christianity or the *Imperium Romanum*, or of the Middle Eastern cultures (Thürmer 1934: 242–243).

The sole proper vantage-point from which to appraise German history was naturally that of "the north German territory with the inhabitants who had been indigenous to it since ancient times" (Thürmer 1934: 242–243).

Charlemagne, in whom secular and religious motives had been inextricably intermingled, according to von Leers, had "broken a living people at its root. The Saxon *Volk*" which he had injured "were no barbarians or depraved heathens, but a distinguished farming people" (von Leers 1934: 49). For Thürmer, they were likewise "a *Volk* of high peasant culture" (Thürmer 1934: 245). Charlemagne's war on them had been "planned and conducted" as a "war of annihilation" from the first. It had duly been characterized by a sequence of war crimes: "unheard of devastation, mass murders" and the forced eviction of the surviving population. And that was entirely in keeping with an already firmly established Frankish tradition. For the "history of the war-mongering Franks" had already "for centuries consisted of faithlessness, treachery and worse" (Thürmer 1934: 246). Thoroughly contaminated by Roman and Christian influences, the Franks' ties with their Germanic origins had, "with the exception of the East Franks on German soil", become so tenuous by Charlemagne's time that they could "scarcely be described as Germanic any more"; their moral decay had consequently been complete from top to bottom of their social hierarchy (Thürmer 1934: 244). While the Franks' territorial expansionism had been inspired by greed and alien ideas, that of the Saxons had been determined by their natural and objective need for "*Lebensraum*" (Thürmer 1934: 245). The employment of that keyword in the Nazi vocabulary was not an isolated or chance occurrence in Thürmer's narrative. In the face of the Frankish invasion, any Saxon brutality was legitimate:

> Everything is permitted to a *Volk* which is fighting for its life. To meet enemy armies of occupation faithfully and with well-meaning attention to their welfare is surely just as much of an impossibility for decent people today. (Thürmer 1934: 246)

In particular, Thürmer denied that there was anything "Germanic" about the "world empire" Charlemagne had forged (Thürmer 1934: 245). His wars had been fought against the "common foe of the romanized West Franks and of the Catholic Church, the Germanic tribes as such." What else was to be expected of the Catholic Franks? Had they not already treacherously ruined one attempt "to unite all the Germanic *Reichs* into one Germanic world-*Reich*?" Thus, under Theoderich, "The might of the Germanic armies had destroyed the *Imperium Romanum*. But Romandom triumphed on a spiritual level because of the Franks' breakaway from the common Germanic front" (Thürmer 1934: 244).

Widukind himself was at best incidental to von Leers' view, which seemed almost to implicate him in a general treason of the Saxon aristocracy: "First under Widukind, and then alone, deserted by its upper echelons, the Saxon peasants resisted almost to the point of [their own] annihilation": a "tough and courageous *Volk*" defending "*Heimat*, folklore and its own quiet piety against the coercion of the soul" (von Leers 1934: 50). Thürmer went further. "The Saxon leadership, *including Widukind* [my emphasis], had failed in the final analysis. The resistance was carried by the peasantry as such", since Charlemagne had been successful "in partially buying the nobility" (Thürmer 1934: 248).

This was *Volksgeschichte* – with a vengeance. The anonymous collective *Volk* was the hero, and only through its survival did enough Germanic stock and spirit survive to make possible the eventual coming of the Third Reich. And the Saxons had exhibited precisely the values of the Nazi *Volksgemeinschaft*. Whereas the Saxon "peasant Republic" had acted according to the precept "that a larger share of the common soil brought with it an obligation to greater achievements", the Franks had "a legal concept of land and soil that was already almost one of individual property rights" (Thürmer 1934: 248). This unmistakeably alluded to the Nazi definitions of "Socialism" and "capitalism": the former alluded to a responsible use of private property for the greater good of the *Volkgemeinschaft*; the latter to an abuse of private property for egotistical gain at the expense of the *Volkgemeinschaft*. Finally, Thürmer imputed to the Franks a strategy which, in the course of the Second World War, was to become a Nazi one. He suggested that, cleverly, Charlemagne had elected to murder not the Saxons' military elite, but their *intellectual* elite (Thürmer 1934: 248). When the Nazis set about the programmatic murder of the Polish intelligentsia in 1939 (Burleigh 1988: 189), they acted according to the same logic: destroy the intellectual head, and the body will die. Nazi "intellectuals" had a habit of imputing to their opponents, whether past or present, thought-processes and actions which were in fact the Third Reich's own. It was as if, in attributing the authorship of a crime to an enemy, they felt justified in committing the crime themselves.

The practical and contemporary relevance of Charlemagne was just as evident to von Leers. To defend Charlemagne – and with him the forced conversion of the Saxons – was to transgress against "the *Führer's* work of political unification" and against the "unity of blood and soil", before whose demands all religions were bound to give way (von Leers 1934: 58). Besides, it was perfectly reasonable that the Swastika itself, "the old sign of returning light", should "suffice" for a good German "if he should find religious values in it" (von Leers 1934: 59).

While Faulhaber's and von Leers' position-statements used the Saxon wars as pivots in an argument, the figures of Widukind and Charlemagne came increasingly to occupy centre-stage in the course of 1934. In June, Rosenberg and his allies in the Nazi leadership toured Lower Saxony. Rosenberg delivered a sequence of set-piece speeches in the context of highly ritualistic rallies. The Saxon wars were declared to have been "Germany's first Thirty Years War"; Widukind's defeat "in the ninth century" was to be lamented; however, "in the twentieth [century], he triumphs in the person of Adolf Hitler". For a thousand years between Widukind's defeat and Hitler's victory, German heroes had necessarily been "rebels against the *Reich*" – and the Third Reich viewed itself as fulfilling those "rebels'" project, not as the successor to the Holy Roman Empire. Rosenberg and the SS combined to create a "Saxon Grove" to commemorate 4,500 Saxons allegedly murdered on Charlemagne's instructions near the site of the Grove at Verden an der

Aller. Each of the Saxon victims was represented by a stone, and the stones were then arranged in a pseudo-prehistoric rectangular alignment interspersed with mock-dolmens and with stone circles. The Grove, Rosenberg declared, was sacred, just as every clod of German soil on which German blood had been spilled was sacred. But the Nazis were not content with the construction of new neo-pagan monuments. Even as Rosenberg denied any ambition to remove crosses from churches – so long as the Nazi Party's own sites of ritual performance in turn be free of Church interference – he temporarily took over churches for his own rallies.[1]

As Thürmer had noted, there was no shortage of anxious Christian responses. Not only Roman Catholic, but also Protestant polemicists reacted to the Nazi initiatives. For them, Widukind was also a hero – but precisely for the reason that gave many of his neo-pagan Nazi hero-worshippers some trouble, namely his own conversion (Mensing 1934; Koch 1935; Schaller 1935). Historians felt themselves equally called upon to contest Rosenberg's version of the German past. They did not like to have to debate with rank amateurs, and felt Rosenberg's utterances to be an affront to their professional values. Johannes Haller, a medievalist recently retired from a Chair at Tübingen University, entered the lists early with a newspaper article (Haller 1934)

> in order to tell a shameless ignoramus what's what. For that, I re-
> ceived a number of expressions of thanks from strangers, whom
> my "brave, manly pronouncement" (sic!) had pleased. So we really
> have reached the point at which a snotty-nosed brat can slap the
> discipline in the face, and if a professional contradicts him, it is a
> hazardous enterprise which causes surprise.[2]

Haller's wrath was aroused chiefly because he really did not distinguish between the *Volk* and the common herd. In his highly politically conservative interpretation of history, great men using the coercive apparatus of the state had always been necessary to mould Germans into a nation, while Germanic tribal warriors like Arminius had tried to buy into the Roman Empire, not to destroy it (Haller 1922; idem 1934). In 1935, eight academics (of whom seven were historians) joined in a ringing endorsement of Charlemagne's claims to be seen as a positive figure in German national history. At least two of them, Karl Hampe and Martin Lintzel, could claim genuine expertise in the subject (Hampe et al. 1935;

Reichert 2009: 271–276). Though several of the contributions bore the marks of the influence of the fashion for Germanic tribal virtues and the overall tenor of the volume was profoundly nationalistic, they received mixed reviews from the Nazi press, including one so hostile as to make sense of the flattering comments about his courage Haller had received (Reichert 2009: 276).

But it was in the theatre and around ceremonial occasions that the debate spilled over into really raucous confrontations in early 1935. In Hagen, a performance of a "Widukind-drama" by Edmund Kiß was disrupted by angry Roman Catholics; in Aachen, the annual *Karls-fest* in the Cathedral, though uniformed Nazis were involved in the Church ritual and an SA band provided some of the entertainment, was disturbed by a Hitler Youth demonstration parading up and down immediately outside and making "rough music" (Gadberry 2004; Strobl 2007: 142–143; Lambert, forthcoming 2013).

Kiß's play had caused such consternation that it was performed in public only three times. Undeterred, he went on to write a novel on the same theme, with the same basic structure and adopting very much the same tone. In his variation on the Widukind theme, racial and religious motifs were thoroughly intertwined, and both were connected in turn with *Heimat*. Kiß made Alcuin, the Northumbrian priest and teacher at Charlemagne's court, a pivotal figure. He depicted Alcuin as an Anglo-Saxon simultaneously proud of his Germanic ancestry and incapable of reconciling it with his Christian faith. The crisis of identity came to a head as he rode with a small troop of Frankish warriors into Saxon lands to negotiate with Widukind on Charlemagne's behalf. The call of the Germanic forest made Alcuin and his party uneasy:

> here, in ancient groves of the Germanic peoples, the breeze carried the breath of an intractable will to resist all intruders of alien blood; here, every giant tree spoke of a high song of freedom; here, every low, straw-covered timber-framed farmhouse, every lonely block-hut told of the deep ties between the inhabitants and divine nature. As brothers and relatives of the deity, the hardy farmers of the Weser-land had their seats here: above them the regulated path of the stars and beneath them the faithful soil ... (Kiß 1935:117–118).

Alcuin felt the call of the forest to his Germanic blood, but his Christian training overcame it after a struggle, and he "throttled" his own instinct:

"He wanted to remain what he was! A soldier of Christ struggling for the rule of the Jew-god on the earth." (Kiß 1935: 117–118).

The story, as Kiß refashioned it, did not deny Widukind's conversion. It offered an explanation. A shame-faced Alcuin, acting as Charlemagne's emissary again, had threatened that, were Widukind not to surrender and convert, Charlemagne would have 60,000 captive "Saxon maidens" raped by the assortment of Jews, Slavs and the scum of his own army whom he had incarcerated in a string of camps along the Rhine. Henceforth, racially alien children would populate the Saxon forests. A further condition of the acceptance of his surrender was that Widukind was sworn to silence as to the terms Charlemagne had offered. Appearing to have accepted a bribe of lands and titles, Widukind had to sacrifice his own honour for the preservation of his *Volk*. If there was not one shred of evidence for any of this, then it was simply because the sources at historians' disposal had all been written by Charlemagne's servants. They were a "victors' history" grounded in programmatic mendacity (Kiß 1935:288–295).

Hitler's Intervention – The State as Manufacturer of the People

The tenor of the debate was significantly altered in the space of a few days in September 1935 when Hitler himself chose the occasion of the Nuremberg Rally to intervene. Didactic to the point of being schoolmasterly, Hitler delivered what was in effect a lecture on the origins of Germany and on the Nazi interpretation of history (Hitler 1935: 71–78). Nor was it only Hitler's subject-matter and use of language that might strike us now as being more appropriate to the lectern and the lecture theatre than to a Nuremberg rally: Hitler's arguments precisely reflected those advanced by the academic historians so recently abused in some of the Nazi media. Hitler did not go so far as to give Rosenberg a public dressing-down. He actually named neither Charlemagne nor Widukind. He did not refer directly to the destruction of the Irminsul or to the "Bloodbath of Verden". He did not even mention the Saxons. Yet his meaning was nevertheless clear to many, and it amounted to a cocktail of bitter medicines for Rosenberg and his allies to swallow. First, Hitler insisted "that the unification of the members of the German tribes ... was attainable not by means of a conscious ... *process of becoming a people* [*Volkwerdung*], but only by means of *state-formation* which was aspired to as a result of other intentions." Those German tribes had indeed belonged together by virtue of their shared blood. Crucially, however, they had not been conscious of the fact. Sporadically, and only when some "foreign threat" was at hand, might an individual have perceived an underlying commonality determined by blood. Yet *"recognition of what was natural* and therefore *necessary* about the *collective whole"* was, Hitler emphasized, "as good as completely absent." In the context of the first millennium AD, Hitler thus attached agency not to the *Volk* but to the state, which not only predated the German people, but had actually brought it into existence. There had been no other feasible means of doing so than through acts of brutality aimed at destroying tribal identities. Thus, "the consolidation of German people into a state could only be arrived at through the rape of the particular popular life [*des volklichen Einzellebens*] of the individual German tribes." The result, inevitably, was that "there also appeared a contradiction between the organization of the state and a particular people which endured until the Germans, from having been conscious members of their tribes, became conscious members of one nation. That was a hard process, and for many centuries a painful one."

Hitler's train of thought led him to advance further, equally difficult homilies to his adherents. They were introduced as the ineluctably logical consequences of the path to German unity he had mapped out. It was "therefore also wrong to bewail the sacrifices of particular religions and states which this path towards becoming a people demanded. *What happened in these centuries had to happen."* Hitler accepted that the scale of suffering Germanic tribes had endured had been vast. "Countless individual capacities and symbols" had been "sacrificed"; it was "perhaps possible to regret them individually, but one should never condemn history on the ground that the path from dozens of German tribes to one single German nation led ... through tens of thousands of the often very valuable fallen, and through lost traditions."

Where Edmund Kiß had sought to shock his audience and readers out of any residual sympathy with Charlemagne in his lurid fantasies of the Frankish king's threat to orchestrate the mass rape of "German maidens", Hitler contended that the "more or less cruel act of rape" actually perpetrated against the "German" tribes should simply and dutifully be accepted: as a heavy price paid for a greater good. Nor was Hitler in the least perturbed by what had most offended the defenders of Germanic tribal virtue, civilization and pagan belief, namely Charlemagne's motives. Whoever tried "to analyse the inner motives of those who come into our view as the creators of the first larger and great German states" was wrong. "Who would lay bare for us … the inner soul, with its thoughts and driving forces, of those great Germanic emperors who strove for a greater unity of Germans, with hard swords and careless of the destinies of the individual tribes!" At this point, Hitler legitimated his position with reference to the intervention in human affairs of a divine hand: "Providence, desiring that *the German tribes should become a German Volk*, made use of those [emperors] in order to accomplish the making of this *Volk*" (Hitler 1935: 73). Hitler frequently justified his own policies and actions by asserting that they were determined by "Providence"; "Providence", as Rainer Bucher has argued, was indeed an indispensable factor in Hitler's "world-view", since it also underpinned Hitler's whole view of history and made sense of the otherwise inexplicable (Bucher 2011: 49–57). The Christian origins and connotations of the "Providence" Hitler invoked could scarcely have escaped any but the most obdurately and wilfully deaf of his hearers in light of what he immediately went on to say about the emperors' collaborators and models involved in the processes of state-formation and nation-building. For it was

> again through an act of Providence that two helpers offered themselves. Without them, the Germanic foundation of states and so the precondition of the making of the German People would certainly either not have succeeded at all, or at least not within this relatively short time-span. After all, the peoples step into our historical field of vision when they set themselves the task of attaining the zenith of their power, of their urge for life and of the impact of their life, and do so as *organized entities*. … *Had one's gaze not been directed towards the antique states of ancient times, and but for the assistance of Christianity, no Germanic states could have been imaginable at that time* (Hitler 1935: 73–74, emphasis in original).

The contribution of Christianity had been to confront "the exclusively divergent tendencies of the individual tribes with the first consciously felt and emphatic *community* [*Gemeinsamkeit*]." It took the form of a religious world-view which was the base on which the construction of a state organization became possible. It was not and could not have been of a tribally unitary character. Yet this path was historically necessary if a German *Volk* were finally to emerge at all out of the countless German tribes. For it was only on this platform, created at first only for purposes of religion and of the state though it was, that the exclusivist tribal peculiarities could be worn down and overcome. (Hitler 1935: 74)

Thus, anybody who still entertained a residual hankering after some other course of German history than the one actually taken would have not only "to accuse History", but also "Providence" – for its inability "to find a better means of advancing and attaining the very result that we, the accusers, had ourselves desired". Certainly, the long-term effects on conditions within the *Reich* created problems, yet Hitler was not disposed to characterize them in Rosenberg's spirit – as some dreadful deviation from the path of German history. Rather, "The *contradiction between the idea of the state and the goal of the state on the one hand and the people on the other*" was simply "unavoidable in this period of the Germans becoming a people. That was regrettable, but necessary". And, ultimately, the founders and leaders of the medieval *Reich*, "those men who were the historical executors in this process", had done precisely what Hitler had loudly and often proclaimed that he himself was doing: they had "acted on behalf of a Providence which desired that we Germans become a *Volk.*" Thus far, Hitler's analysis amounted to a re-affirmation of the statist interpretation of history: "It was on this level that, through many centuries, the statist – that is to say the external and organizational – integration of the German tribes occurred."

This argument was congruent not only with the orthodoxy among academic historians, but also with Faulhaber's position – at least as far as the eighth and ninth centuries were concerned. But there were important lines of argument apparently inherent in the case mounted by each that neither was prepared to extend into the twentieth century. Faulhaber had been at pains to make it clear that the Jews he had lauded were the Jews of the Old Testament and those of the New Testament who became Christ's followers. With Christ's coming, Jews had ceased to hold a special relationship with God (Faulhaber 1935). Theologically, this was of course perfectly orthodox. In the context of the Third Reich, however, the distinction Faulhaber had insisted on should surely have made very plain to his readers what the limits of his dispute with Nazi ideology were. Yet some contemporaries did not understand him. They ranged from the Nazis who tried to assassinate him to a Jew who wrote to congratulate him on his courage (Krebs 2011: 215). Oddly, Hitler's defence of the Roman Catholic Church's role bore a marked resemblance to Faulhaber's of the Jews: it, too, was time-bound and contingent. Since the Reformation, Hitler argued, Christianity had diminished in its significance, while the state modelled on classical antiquity had come to dominate; finding a final expression in the absolutist monarchy of the eighteenth century, only to be destroyed by the ideas of the French Revolution. The Christian Churches, however, had subsequently "demeaned" themselves through active participation in parliamentary democracy. For, regardless of his intentions, whoever participated in politics "on the level of that anarchic struggle" became a *de facto* "ally of international Marxism" and an accessory to the destruction of the German state the Church had once helped to found. In rehabilitating the eighth- and ninth-century Church, then, Hitler was emphatically offering very limited real succour to the twentieth-century Churches. They had betrayed their own heritage. Similarly, the lifeline he appeared to hold out to professional historians still steeped in a statist conception of history emphatically did not reach into the present. Since Germans were now a *Volk*, in respect of all epochs since their having become one, history should be viewed from the perspective of the *Volk* (Hitler 1935: 75, 77).

The End of the Debate?

Hitler's speech had been delivered shortly after he had received a copy of Charlemagne's sword in the course of the same Nuremberg rally. Crestfallen and shocked, Rosenberg was doubly plagued by the determination of Josef Terboven, *Gauleiter* of Essen and *Oberpräsident* of the Rhineland Province, to point out to him the "diametrical opposition" between Hitler's view and "all that you have hitherto preached as the Final Revelation of National Socialism". Rosenberg began to rein himself in – protesting all the while that he had never gone so far as to call Charlemagne the "butcher of Saxons" – but was unable to get Hitler to intercede on his behalf with Terboven, even though the latter is supposed to have said that he had taken measures to keep Rosenberg out of the Rhineland (Bollmus 2006: 195–196). Himmler began to seek alternative heroes of German history, looking first to Henry the Lion and then settling on Henry the Fowler (Longerich 2012: 269–274). Their critics heaved sighs of relief. "*Karl der Große* – we are allowed to say that again", one German *Gymnasium* teacher had written to another just before the 1935 Nazi *Parteitag*. On hearing (or reading) Hitler's speech, his colleague replied with tongue firmly in cheek as he likened the authority of Hitler's utterances to those of the word of God:

> Concerning Carolum Magnum: now the most powerful man – his sayings are as infallible as any revelatory statement emanating from the Holy Ghost in the Bible – has rehabilitated him in all due form in his "great" speech about the development of Germanness. Who can have inspired him to do so? Was it ultimately the 8 professors who have together brought out the little book ... "*Karl d[er] Gr[oße] oder Charlemagne?*" (a camouflaged title!)?[3]

There is no evidence of Hitler's having read the work in question, but that such influence should have been attributed to it is telling. And Hitler's intervention should no doubt have been the end of the controversy. One recent biographer of Charlemagne evidently thinks that it was. The debate concerning Karl and Widukind was indeed "halted by Hitler himself" (Becher 2003: 148). The biographer of the historian Karl Hampe agrees: Hitler's was "the last word, i.e. a word of power" in the controversy, and a vindication of Hampe and his colleagues as much as of Charlemagne (Reichert 2009: 277). But in fact the arguments rumbled on – without quite achieving the kind of public profile they had had in 1934–1935. The sheer volume of publication of newspaper and journal articles on the question did diminish rapidly. There were no further public disturbances like those in Hagen and Aachen in 1935. Aachen authorities were palpably relieved to be able to report that the 1936 celebration of Charlemagne in the Cathedral passed off without incident (Vollmer 1957: 357).

Nevertheless, old wounds were sporadically reopened. Martin Lintzel, who had made genuinely important and scholarly contributions to the vindication of Charlemagne at the height of the controversy, continued to suffer consequences thereafter. Nazi students at the University of Kiel – to which he had just been appointed with SS support – mounted attacks on his scholarship which were so abusive as to encourage him rapidly to quit his new job (Zöllner 1975: 33–35). In 1936 Goebbels found himself obliged to re-enforce Hitler's message. Before making a public utterance, Goebbels had confided to his diary all his anxieties about the "nonsense of racial materialism which looks not at behaviour or character, but at bottle-blond ... In the end, all that will be left of our history is Widukind, Henry the Lion and Rosenberg. That is rather little."[4] Months later, he issued an instruction to the media:

> It will not do to judge the whole of German history and its heroes by the yardsticks of National Socialism and to examine whether they had acted like good National Socialists. With the exception of the period from 1918 to 1933, which can only be regarded as criminal, it is not to be borne that everything should be measured by the yardsticks of the present day ... *Karl der Große* was nothing less than the creator of the concept of the German *Reich*. This "jumble sale of German history" does not lie in the spirit or the interest of National Socialist popular enlightenment.

The outcome of such a bargain sale of German history would, Goebbels continued, "be an unparalleled impoverishment and degeneration of cultural life".[5]

Again, academic historians at least were glad of his support. "Goebbels has rehabilitated Charlemagne", one senior medievalist wrote to another.[6] Also in 1936, Käthe Papke, a longstanding Protestant activist and author (Papke 2001), published a novel which, while celebrating Widukind's love of *Heimat* and liberty, nevertheless depicted his struggle first and foremost as inspired by paganism. His own military defeats gradually undermined his religious faith, and his eventual route to surrender to Charlemagne was bound up with a Damascene conversion. Finally, Widukind, slayer of so many priests, heeded a call he had often dimly heard before but never answered:

> Christ, the God of the Franks, stood there, brightly shining before his spiritual inner eye. – "Come unto Me" he heard again as he had done before, but now His voice was earnest, warning, urgent. As if in a picture, he saw his devastated *Heimat* blossom anew under the mild regiment of this gracious God, saw his people gather around the Cross for which the Franks, brave unto death, had fought. No: the new faith did not make men into slaves and did not weaken them. How else would so many adherents of this Christ joyfully have endured death for His sake? He, Widukind, had after all had all too many opportunities to witness them himself.

"Christ has triumphed; there is only this one God; He alone is the
true, the eternal, the giver of life eternal." That became an insuper-
able certainty for Widukind in these hours; the certainty to which
he now at last gave full space within his life (Papke 1936: 157).

Where Kiß's Alkuin had found his soul tortured and torn apart by the
competing claims of Germanic blood and forests on the one hand and
his Christian training on the other, Widukind's new-found "certainty"
was bound to win through in a comparable contest. "After all, it had
long, long struggled for mastery in his soul." To his astonishment,
Papke's Widukind discovered that his wife and his most loyal follower
had already accepted Christianity (Papke 1936: 156–157).

Alone of the "Widukind"-novels first published in the pre-war Third
Reich, Papke's did not go into a second edition. It fell foul of censorship
(Westenfelder 1989: 252). Yet, among those published after Hitler's
1935 address, it stood out also because it most clearly echoed Hitler's
own view that Christianization had been essential to nation-building (Papke 1936: 168). In 1937 and 1938, two further "Widukind"
novels appeared. They diverged in their interpretations of Charlemagne, but two of them condemned the conversion of the Saxon tribes
while the third viewed their Christianization as a temporary expe-
dient.

Margot Boger's Widukind, like Kiß's, inhabited a proto-Nazi Saxony
where "*Volksgenossen*" ("comrades of the *Volk*") lived in an organic "*Volksgemeinschaft*"; Widukind only *pretended* to convert, having understood
that the survival of the Saxons was more important than freedom or
honour. His nephew Ramwolt, however, at first held out, foreseeing
a miserable future even once Charlemagne's "tower of Babylon" had
collapsed: for eight centuries the old Germanic peoples would be torn
apart by petty princelings, and the *Volk* itself would probably forget its
blood-ties, its originary "*Volksgemeinschaft*", as "*Volksgenossen*" fought
one another "to pursue the meaningless feuds of their lords". A moment
later, a prophetic vision came to Ramwolt, allowing him finally to come
to terms with his defeat:

Yet one day the time will come in which the *Volk* will remember
its roots! The fragmented tribes will find their way back together.
Powerfully will they stand side by side! And then perhaps the
laws of our free *Volk*-communities [*Volksgemeinden*] will return to

honour and respect! Even if a thousand years should pass! (Boger 1937: 288–289)

Fritz Vater's 1938 novel *Weking* appeared with the imprimatur of the Nazi Party's own publishing house. Its Postscript dutifully followed where Hitler had led. There could "no longer be any doubt that the years 772–785 were of the utmost importance for the whole course of subsequent German history since, as we can now be certain," – and here Vater quoted Hitler directly – "'it finally came into being, that Germanic *Reich* of the German nation'." According to Vater, Charlemagne had in fact never intended to force conversion upon an unwilling Widukind. His motives and goals had ultimately been secular. And indeed Widukind surrendered politically and militarily but kept his pagan religiosity intact. Devious Roman Catholic prelates, however, had sought to blackmail Charlemagne into converting Widukind nevertheless. The uneasy compromise Charlemagne reached was to allow the Church to proclaim that its old foe had indeed accepted Christ. The very name "Widukind" was thus a Christian invention, and "Weking" had never accepted nor been given it in life (Vater 1938: 364ff). A further novel, by Kurt Pastenaci, had first been published in 1920, but appeared in a new edition in 1939. Perhaps surprisingly, its text remained substantially unaltered. Both editions end with Charlemagne deep in thought about Widukind, "his greatest opponent". Between wakefulness and sleep, Charlemagne was confronted by a disquieting vision based on a new understanding of his old enemy:

> Undefeated in war, Widukind has sacrificed himself to the future and was not without effect.
>
> Harsh as the light of the torch that fell from the heavens, the recognition blinds Karl's heart and his senses. The Duke had triumphed even as he had surrendered. His work grew. A new *Volk* was setting out on its path and, though scarcely born, was proving itself in battle … Will this *Volk* be stronger than the *Reich* which he had forged? Does the future belong to Widukind's work? …
>
> The emperor's thoughts relapse into confusion and finally succumb to sleep. (Pastenaci 1920: 277, idem 1939: 318).

A similar resolution to the Charlemagne – Widukind conflict was suggested in the final novel dedicated to Widukind to appear in the

Third Reich, and the only one first published during the Second World War. Its author was Heinar Schilling, a former Leftist and Expressionist who had turned to *völkisch* politics and an interest in the Germanic tribes in the course of the 1920s (Wesolowski 2009). His "Widukind" ended with its hero and Charlemagne each recognizing that the other had been pursuing a political goal they in fact shared. Widukind had been the first to see their underlying commonality of purpose – and had decided to surrender as soon as the insight had come upon him. Without relinquishing his own pagan faith, he witnessed first-hand the potential of Christianity to serve political purposes. Standing cloaked and unobserved by the door of the church at Bardowieck, where Charlemagne had set up his winter quarters, Widukind watched as the king and his warriors listened to a sermon. The pagan found himself deeply impressed by the "new, mild teaching" of the priest which had a "secret power to soften antagonistic feelings and to reconcile mutually hostile spirits. So it would lend itself to making the Saxons and Franks into one people. And that was enough to justify it for this period of transition." In the wake of Widukind's surrender, Charlemagne realized that his old enemy "could have been his best friend and helper, so pronounced was the resemblance between their thoughts and plans." For Widukind's aspiration, as Charlemagne now understood, was "also one united *Volk*, one unified *Reich* – only he sees the world from the North and not from the Maas, from the West". The last word rested with Widukind:

> There is only one thing that I fear for your *Reich*, King! You extend your borders too far, to alien peoples, alien blood. Have you forgotten how many Nordic peoples bled to death in the South? Here, by the holy graves of our ancestors, there stood also the cradle of your *Volk*. Here is the source of your power. And if, defeated by your sword, I now bend my head to the alien belief from the South, then I nevertheless know this: the old Gods are only sleeping. And one day they will rise again, watching over our grandsons. For here is the heart of your *Reich*, and that is why I bow to you, King. (Schilling 1941: 205–206, quotations 207–208)

In all these three novels, Widukind's surrender gave way to a deeper victory, and his vision of a German *Reich* – racially pristine, Saxon-led and anti-Christian – outlasted Charlemagne's.

In 1942, with the Third Reich at the height of its territorial extent, a celebratory ritual performance, reminiscent of Rosenberg's carefully orchestrated and grandly conceived historicizing rallies in Lower Saxony, was held in Aachen. It was proclaimed as marking *"the Starting-point for the Making of the German* Volk." Josef Grohé, the *Gauleiter* of Cologne-Aachen, toed Hitler's 1935 line in all material respects. Before the late eighth century, there had been "no such thing as a German *Volk* in the sense that we understand the words today." True, Germanic tribes had already "accomplished great historic achievements" in earlier periods. They had demonstrated "the creative force and the worth of Germanic people in high degree". Yet they had "formed no unified whole." The roles of a Roman model and of Christianity were duly acknowledged as having provided the remedy. And Grohé went one step further, making explicit what Hitler had left as a merely implicit reference-point: he identified the "great Germanic man" who had "united the Germanic tribes together, uniting them in a single mighty Reich" by name: *Karl der Große* (*Westdeutscher Beobachter* 3 April 1942).

Not the least among the tasks of the SS Security Service was the compilation of round-up reports on civilian morale. These national surveys, based on local reports sent in by up to 80,000 Security Service functionaries, were intended for the eyes of the regime's power-elite only. At this moment, they took time off from documenting attitudes to the Nazi armies' fortunes on the Eastern Front to register responses to the heroization of Charlemagne. Not only popular pleasure, but also surprise and even sharp criticism of the regime's evident confusions and contradictions were noted. How could it be, people had been heard asking, that "only a few years ago one had counted as an un-reliable National Socialist if one left *Karl der Große* with so much as a single unblemished feature and not spoken ... in tones of loathing of the 'butcher of Saxons' and 'the lacky of the Pope and the bishops'"?[7] Hitler's 1935 intervention had clearly not had a decisive impact. Would its re-enforcement in 1942 establish a consensus? The circumstances were certainly more auspicious. The Third Reich's moment of hubris had coincided with the twelve-hundredth anniversary of Charlemagne's birth; the Third Reich's expansionism was capable of connection with that of the First. Within a matter of months, of course, and especially in the wake of defeat at Stalingrad, the Nazi regime was bound to suffer from such comparisons with Charlemagne. Even in 1942 itself, however, there were still dissonant voices to be heard within the Nazi chorus.

While the historian Gerhard Krüger was faithful to the new Party line in celebrating Charlemagne in 1942, the basis on which he did so was a kind of synthesis of Rosenberg's and of Hitler's views on the relationship between Germanic tribal and German national history. Nevertheless, Krüger's stance was closer in essentials to Rosenberg's than to Hitler's version of the relationship between Germanic and German history. It was, he insisted, "not the case that – as is so often asserted – it was only a Roman model and the Christian Church that awakened the *Reich-* and state-formative power within the Germanic people" (Krüger 1942b: 94).

This was represented as a riposte to the Austrian historian Heinrich von Srbik's characterization of the *Reich* as a kind of synthesis of "universalist" Roman and above all Christian with Germanic elements (Srbik 1941: 458–459; cf. Krüger 1942a: 457–470). At the same time, it was manifestly also incommensurable with Hitler's 1935 declaration that it was a matter of "irrefutable fact", first, that "*Christianity* gave this first Germanic state formation – that is, this first gathering of all the German tribes within a higher entity – its shared religious world-view and morality", and that Christianity had "toppled that which fell – because it had to fall if our *Volk* wanted to rise out of the chaos and confusion of those petty tribal existences and to achieve the clarity and force of a greater state entity and so also of unity as a people." Second, "*Monarchy*" had been "inspired by the idea of the antique state", had brought "a more suitable organization" than Germanic ducal authority had been capable of achieving, and "above all" had secured "the stable *maintenance of what had been achieved.*" Hitler's relatively pithy summary of his position had plainly been intended to guard against any possibility of going unheard or of being misunderstood by his own party-faithful (Hitler 1935: 74–75; emphasis as per the original).

The *Reich* Charlemagne had created was, in Krüger's revisionist polemic, *not* the beginning of the tragic millennium Rosenberg had imagined. His view diverged from Rosenberg's here because, Krüger argued, the Carolingian *Reich* had, for all its more superficially than really significant assimilation of Christian and Roman ideas, in fact been "Germanic at its core" and rested on a "Germanic concept of the *Reich*" at the moment of its foundation (Krüger 1941b: 84). The ideal of a unified Germanic people and state had, he argued in another passage which was again clearly at odds with Hitler's publicly stated opinion, *predated* Christian influence: the continental European Germanic peoples were *already* "on the path toward unity" before Charlemagne's intervention. Charlemagne stood "in a line of pan-Germanic endeavours on behalf of the *Reich*"which reached back as far as Arminius (Krüger 1942b: 85). From this perspective, "the danger of one-sided partisanship" was therefore to be avoided in any evaluation of the Saxon wars. The problem was that the Saxons had been caught in the midst of an inevitable process of transcending "internal contradictions" when Charlemagne's invasion began. Widukind's "heroic fight for freedom" provided "proof" that, but for the Frankish onslaught, "the Saxons certainly would have had the capacity to bring the process of the natural reformation of the state to a positive conclusion". Echoing Schilling's fictionalized account, Krüger implied that the Franks and Saxons had in effect competed in a race to secure Germanic unification (Krüger 1942b: 91). And both accounts implied also that, had the Saxons crossed the finishing-line first, the Germans would have been spared Roman Catholicism and political entanglements that were a legacy of the Roman Empire.

Krüger's image of a quintessentially and consciously Germanic Charlemagne outbid that even of the most extreme advocates of the same position in 1935. Charlemagne was of "purely Frankish-German" origin, stemmed from a family rooted in "the purely Germanic part of the *Reich*" and maintained that "blood-anchorage" through his own dynastic marriage-politics; he had "certainly regarded the *Germanen* within his Reich as a single *völkisch* entity"; no minion of the papacy, he had fought "ultramontane" politics; no promoter of Jewish immigration into Germanic territories, he had "protected the *Volk* from Jewish usury and profiteering" (Krüger 1942b:83–84, 86, 89, 92).

The "Europeanization" of Charlemagne

In a survey of the German historiography of the politics of the medieval *Kaiser* published in the same year as Krüger's ambivalent article on Charlemagne, Friedrich Schneider had declared the old controversies concerning Widukind to be definitively at an end – at least as far as professional historians were concerned. He could now be generally lauded as "the Father of Europe" (Schneider 1942: 26–27, 178 note 28). It was clearly not without reason, however, that Krüger could depict himself as a contributor to a controversy which, far from having been brought to a close in 1935, was still continuing. The debate, "which has been occupying the spirits for years", was itself worth celebrating. It was "proof of how lively our Volk's engagement with the historical process of becoming has become". But all previous positions had to be revised from the perspective of 1942, "a point in time which is creating the foundations for a re-making and a new order of the *Reich* and of Europe" (Krüger 1942b: 82).

Hitler had already highlighted Charlemagne's significance beyond Germany in his 1935 speech, declaring that, had it not been for German state-formation with all its classical models and Christian influences, "the fate of Europe, and of the rest of the world as far as the white race is concerned, would be inscrutable, and certainly impossible to imagine today" (Hitler 1935: 74). In 1942, the European dimension overwhelmed older concerns with *Heimat*. After 1945, the dominant image of Charlemagne in Germany was still chiefly a European one, but shorn of course of its associations with dreams of German domination (Pape 2000, 2003). The "father of Europe" was recycled both within and beyond Germany as a model first for the EEC, then for the European Union (Laughland 1997: 137; Story 2003: 1–4). While Franco–German antagonisms had long been expressed in relation to various nationalist interpretations of Charlemagne, he has latterly been paraded as a figure of Franco–German reconciliation. Yet whether Charlemagne has or is likely to acquire a genuinely popular appeal in Europe or even simply in Germany is less evident (Kerner 2000: 273–277; Drost 2010).

Widukind remains a regional hero in Lower Saxony and – like Charlemagne – a sort of unofficial saint. Both Widukind and the Saxon fallen of Verden an der Aller have recently been commemorated also by neo-Nazi neo-pagans like Patrick Agte and the late Jürgen Rieger (Agte 2001; Rieger 2002). But a fully-fledged national Widukind cult seems highly unlikely to return. Like a number of other German traditions, the Widukind myth is simply too closely associated with Nazism to have any foreseeable prospect of a German rebirth. And the Widukind cult had been genuinely national only for a fleeting two years at the beginning of the Third Reich. Ironically, the question "Widukind or *Karl der Große?*", which had been so hotly contested in the closed society of the Third Reich, has never been a matter of public debate in the open society of the Federal Republic of Germany.[8]

Notes

1 Kurt Teserich, "Herzog Widukind unterlag im IX. Jahrhundert. Im XX. hat er in Adolf Hitler gesiegt. Alfred Rosenberg auf dem Niedersachsentag in Enger, Verden, Wildeshausen und Braunschweig", *Völkischer Beobachter*, North German ed., 26. 6. 1934; anon., "Widukind für immer das Symbol des heldenhaften

Widertandes. Reichsleiter Alfred Rosenberg weiht den Ehrenhain am Leutfeld an der Aller", ibid., 24/25. 6. 1934. For a more detailed discussion, see Lambert, forthcoming 2013.

2 Bundesarchiv Koblenz: Johannes Haller Papers no. 29, Haller to Heinrich Dannenbauer, 1. 7. 1934.

3 Otto Schulmann to Martin Havenstein, 16.8.1935, and Havenstein to Schulmann, 16.10.1935 (Hammerstein 1988: 40, 93).

4 Goebbels's diary entry for 24. 6. 1936 (Fröhlich 1987: 632).

5 Goebbels's instruction to the media, 17. 10. 1936 (Hagemann 1948: 99).

6 Bundesarchiv, Koblenz: Haller Papers no. 19. Professor Heinrich Dannenbauer to Professor Johannes Haller, 13. 12. 1936.

7 SS Security Service report of 9. 4. 1942 (Boberach 19: 3600; cf. also Lambert 2007: 537–538).

8 I am grateful to R. Gerald Hughes and Catharina Raudvere for their comments on an earlier version of this text.

References

Agte, Patrick (2001): *Der Sachsenhain bei Verden. Naturdenkmal für 4500 durch Karl den Großen getötete Sachsen*, Pluwig: Munin Verlag.

Applegate, Celia (1990): *A Nation of Provincials. The German Idea of Heimat*, Berkeley: University of California Press.

Becher, Matthias (2003): *Charlemagne*, New Haven: Yale University Press.

Boa, Elizabeth and Rachel Palfrey (2000): *Heimat. A German Dream. Regional Loyalties and National Identity in German Culture 1890–1990*, Oxford: Oxford University Press.

Boberach, Heinz (ed.) (1984): *Meldungen aus dem Reich. Die geheimen Lageberichte des Sicherheitsdienstes der SS 1938–1945*, vol. 10, Herrsching: Pawlak Verlag.

Boger, Margot (1937): *Der Gödowolf*, Gütersloh: C. Bertelsmann.

Bollmus, Reinhard (1969): 2nd ed. 2006. *Das Amt Rosenberg und seine Gegener. Studien zum Machtkampf im nationalsozialistischen Herrschaftssytem*, Munich: Oldenbourg.

Bucher, Rainer (2011) *Hitler's Theology. A Study in Political Religion*, London and New York: Continuum.

Buchner, Rudolf (1938): Das Blutbad von Verden – ein Mißverständnis? Zur Beurteilung Karls und Widukinds, *Deutscher Glaube*, 5: 244–250.

Burleigh, Michael (1988): *Germany Turns Eastwards. A Study of Ostforschung in the Third Reich*, Cambridge: Cambridge University Press.

Domarus, Max (ed.) (1992): *Hitler. Speeches and Proclamations*, London: I. B. Tauris.

Evans, R. J. W. and Guy P. Marchal (eds) (2010): *The Uses of the Middle Ages in Modern European States. History, Nationhood and the Search for Origins*, Basingstoke: Palgrave.

Dost, Bianca (2010): *Karl der Große – ein deutscher Erinnerungsort? Die Bedeutung des Frankenkaisers für die deutsche Erinnerungskultur*, Saarbrücken: DVM Verlag.

Faulhaber, Kardinal (1934): *Judentum. Christentum Germanentum. Adventspredigten gehalten in St. Michael zu München 1933*, Munich: A. Huber.

Fröhlich, Elke (1987): *Die Tagebücher von Josef Goebbels. Sämtliche Fragmente Teil I: Aufzeichnungen 1924–1941*, vol. 2, Munich, New York, London & Paris: Saur.

Gadberry, Glen W. (2004): An "Ancient German Rediscovered". The Nazi Widukind Plays of Forster and Kiß, in Hellmut Hal Rennert (ed.), *Essays on Twentieth-

Century German Drama and Theater. An American Reception 1977–1999, New York: Peter Lang.

Hagemann, Walter (1948): *Publizistik im Dritten Reich. Ein Beitrag zur Methodik der Massenführung*, Hamburg: Hansischer Gildenverlag.

Haller, Johannes (1922): *Die Epochen der deutschen Geschichte*, Stuttgart: J. G. Cottasche Buchhandlung Nachfolger.

– (1934a): Widukind und Karl der Große, *Süddeutsche Zeitung* 170, 1934.

– (1934b): Der Eintritt der Germanen in die Geschichte, in *idem: Reden und Aufsätze zur Geshcichte und Politik*, Stuttgart: J. G. Cotta'sche Buchhandlung Nachfolger.

Hammerstein, Notker (ed.) (1988): *Deutsche Bildung? Briefwechsel zweier Schulmänner 1930–1944*, Frankfurt a. M.: Insel.

Hampe, Karl et al. (1935): *Karl der Große oder Charlemagne? Acht Antworten deutscher Geschichtsforscher*, Berlin: E. S. Mittler und Sohn.

Hitler, Adolf (1935): *Die Reden Hitlers am Parteitag der Freiheit*, Munich: Franz Eher.

Kerner, Max (2000): *Karl der Große. Entschleierung eines Mythos*, Cologne: Böhlau.

Koch, Karl (1935): *Widukind. Heide und Heiliger*, Cologne: J. P. Bachem.

Krebs, Christopher B. (2011): *A Most Dangerous Book. Tacitus's* Germania from the Roman Empire to the Third Reich, New York and London: Norton.

Kiß, Edmund (1935): *Witlekind der Große*, Landsberg / Wathe: Verlagsgesellschaft Max Völkow.

Krogel, Wolfgang (1997): Widukind. Ein historischer Mythos und Chance für die Stadtentwicklung, in Stefan Brakensieck (ed.), *Widukind. Forschungen zu einem Mythos*. Bielefeld: Regionalgeschichte Verlag.

Krüger, Gerhard (1942a): Um den Reichsgedanken, *Historische Zeitschrift*, 165 (3): 457–471.

– (1942b): Die Stellung Karls des Großen in der deutschen und europäischen Geschichte. Zum 1200. Geburtstage des Kaisers am 2. April, *Vergangenheit und Gegenwart*, 32 (3): 81–102.

Kühn, Rolf (1986): Kirchenfeindliche und antichristliche Mittelalter-Rezeption im völkisch-nationalsozialistischen Geschichtsbild, in Peter Wapnewski (ed.), *Mittelalter-Rezeption. Ein Symposium*, Stuttgart: J. B. Metzler.

Kuhlmann, Sabine (2010): *Der Streit um Karl den Großen, Widukind und den "Tag von Verden" in der NS-Zeit*, Stade: Landschaftsverband der ehemaligen Herzogtümer Bremen und Verden.

Lambert, Peter (2007): Heroisation and Demonisation in the Third Reich. The Consensus-building Value of a Nazi Pantheon of Heroes, *Totalitarian Movements and Political Religions*, 8 (3–4): 523–546.

– (2013 – forthcoming): "Widukind or Karl der Große"? Perspectives on historical culture and memory in the Third Reich and post-war West Germany, in Peter Lambert et al. (eds), *Mass Dictatorship as Ever-Present Past*, Basingstoke: Palgrave.

Laughland, John (1997): *The Tainted Source. The Undemocratic Origins of the European Idea*, London: Little, Brown and Company.

Leers, Johann von (1934): *Der Kardinal und die Germanen*, Hamburg: Hanseatische Verlagsanstalt.

Longerich, Peter (2012): *Heinrich Himmler*, Oxford: Oxford University Press.

Mensing, Karl (1934): *Karl und Widukind und die Bekehrung der Deutschen*, Dresden: Bekenntnisgemeischaft der Ev.-luth. Kirche in Sachsen.

Oberkrome, Willi (1993): *Volksgeschichte. Methodische Innovation und völkische Ideolisierung in der deutschen Geschichtswissenschaft 1918–1945*, Göttingen: Vandenhoeck and Ruprecht.

Pape, Matthias (2000): Der Karlskult an den Wendepunkten der neueren deutschen Geschichte, *Historisches Jahrbuch*, 12: 138–181.

– (2003): Franke? Deutscher? oder Europäer?, *Jahrbuch für europäische Geschichte*, 4: 243–254.

Papke, Käthe (1936): *Fürst Widukind der Sachsenführer*, Neumünster i. Holst: Christopherus Verlag.

– (2001): *Aus meinem Leben. Erinnerungen*, Stuttgart: Edition Anker.

Pastenaci, Kurt (1920): *Der Herzog und die Könige. Ein Roman um Widukind, Karl und Göttrik*, Karlsbad: Adam Kraft.

Pastenaci, Kurt (1939): *Der Herzog und die Könige. Ein Roman um Widukind, Karl und Göttrik*, Berlin: Büchergilde.

Reichert, Folker (2009): *Gelehrtes Leben. Karl Hampe, das Mittlealter und die Geschichte der Deutschen*, Göttingen: Vanenhoeck & Ruprecht.

Rieger, Jürgen (2002): *Sachsenmord und Sachsenhain in Verden*, 2nd ed., Hamburg: Die Artgemeinschaft.

Schaller, Theo (1935): *Karl und Widukind. Geschichtliche Wirklichkeit gegen Widerchristliche Legendenbildung*, Berlin: Kranz-Verlag.

Schilling, Heinar (1941): *Widukind. Eine Historie*, Berlin: Widukind-Verlag.

Schneider, Friedrich (1942): *Die neueren Anschuungen der deutschen Historiker über die Kaiserpolitik des Mittelalters*, Weimar: Böhlau.

Srbik, Heinrich Ritter von (1941): Die Reichsidee und das Werden deutscher Einheit, *Historische Zeitschrift* 164 (3): 457–471.

Story, Joanna (ed.) (2005): *Charlemagne. Empire and Society*, Manchester: Manchester University Press.

Strobl, Gerwin (2007): *The Swastika and the Stage. German Theatre and Society, 1933–1945*, Cambridge: Cambridge University Press.

Thürmer, Ferdinand (1934): Karl der Große – Charlemagne – Karl der Sachsenschlächter, *Hammer. Blätter für deutschen Sinn* 33 (1): 240–249.

Vallery, Helmut (1980): *Führer, Volk und Charisma. Der nationalsozialistische historische Roman*, Köln: Pahl-Rugenstein.

Vater, Fritz (1938): *Weking. Die Sage vom Heldenkampf der Niedersachsen*, Munich: Franz Eher Nachf.

Vollmer, Bernhard (ed.) (1957): *Volksopposition im Polizeistaat. Gestapo und Regierungsberichte 1934–1936*, Stuttgart: Deutsche Verlags-Anstalt.

Werner, Karl Ferdinand (1967): *Das NS-Geschichtsbild und die deutsche Geschichtswissenschaft*, Stuttgart: Kohlhammer.

Wesolowski, Tilmann (2009): Der Expressionist und Nationalsozialist Heinrich (Heinar) Schilling. Bruch und Kontinuität einer Biografie, *Zeitschrift für Geschichtswissenschaft*, 57 (9): 702–722.

Westenfelder, Frank (1989): *Genese, Problematik und Wirkung nationalsozialistischer Literatur am Beispiel des historischen Romans zwischen 1890 und 1945*, Frankfurt, Bern, New York, Paris: Peter Lang.

Wolnik, Gordon (2004): *Mittelalter und NS-Propaganda. Mittelalterbilder in den Print-, Ton- und Bildmedien des Dritten Reiches*, Münster: Lit Verlag.

Zöllner, Walter (1975): *Karl oder Widukind? Martin Lintzel und die NS-"Geschichtsdeutung" in den anfangsjahren der faschistischen Diktatur*, Halle: Martin-Luther-Universität.

CHAPTER 6

Myth of Victimhood and Cult of Authenticity

Sacralizing the Nation in Estonia and Poland

Jörg Hackmann & Marko Lehti

Introduction

Even two decades after the end of communist rule, the national past has remained a highly politicized and delicate issue in Estonia and Poland, and it still easily generates strong emotions and exaggerated political reactions, in particular if someone is seen to profane or disregard national dignity. It seems as if the echoes of the Second World War have not yet silenced in Estonia and Poland, but on the contrary have gained new resonance through public performance of national identity. Polish and Estonian national narratives are firmly anchored in the Second World War as a crucial turning point between legal and illegitimate, natural and abnormal (Stukuls Eglitis 2002: 70–72). Another tentative observation is that the national past is still more visible than in Northern and Western Europe, and that seemingly there is a vigorous need to perform the past.

In Estonia and Poland the myth of victimhood – mainly concerning victims of the occupations during the Second World War and the era of Communism – has played a crucial role as an anchorage of national self-esteem during the last few decades, after the Soviet-type heroization of the fight against fascism had been dismissed as a legitimization of Soviet hegemony. Victimhood has been attached to the commemoration of victims of murder, deportations and persecutions, who are presented like saints of a nation: those who sacrificed their lives to a nation so that others could live. This narrative of salvation has obvious biblical roots. Those who have given their lives for the nation, be they patriotic heroes or unknown victims of war or genocide, are the glorious dead commemorated in public whose dedication and fate sanctify the nation. Profaning their memory would desecrate the nation as well (Smith 2003: 230).

Victimhood also legitimized the recovered sovereignty in Eastern Europe. It has served as the main argument to justify the return to Europe. Because the West had abandoned Eastern Europe after the Second World War, a dominating argument since the 1990s was that the Western nations have the moral obligation to admit the Eastern nations to their natural home, but this function was lost after the EU and NATO enlargements. Nevertheless, victimhood is problematic as a source of national pride as it involves a certain passivity that contradicts claims for subjectivity. It also conflicts with other – in particular international – narratives of the Holocaust (Hackmann 2009). Therefore it seems obvious that the previously uncontested myth of victimhood has been turning more problematic, but nevertheless it is present in new narratives, which will be studied in this chapter.

If one examines the development during the first decade of the twenty-first century in Estonia and Poland, it seems that the determination with which victimhood has been celebrated has decreased, but simultaneously public performances of the past have been given more exaggerated and blatant expressions. Are these observations true? Do the war memorials really constitute a dominant platform for performing the nation at the beginning of the second millennium in Estonia and Poland?

In the Estonian case, the Bronze Soldier incident in 2007 serves as an example of how the question of victimhood still matters and touches the whole nation. How is it possible that such strong political emotions can be focused on a single war memorial, and that its removal from the city centre to a cemetery generated violent riots in the streets of Tallinn and a diplomatic conflict between Estonia and Russia? In Poland, the debates following the deaths of the Polish delegation on their way to a memorial ceremony in Katyń in April 2010 reached a new climax with regard to issues of national victimhood and recognition in internal as well as external – i.e. mainly in relation to Russia – discourses.

In this chapter we intend to study how in a post-Cold War context a sacred communion of people is recreated, and in particular how this sacred core is performed and thus shared and secured. The myth of victimhood has played a crucial role on the national and international scenes and has been anchored to national self-esteem; it has thus been a vulnerable target of any challenges. Further, we argue that monuments and public performances have regained an important role in establishing and legitimizing a new national trajectory, and thus letting public ceremonies point to the true self of a nation and sacralize the nation. This also explains why such a constellation has been more vulnerable to political conflicts within the country and has also a specific international dimension, first of all with regard to Russia, in both cases dealt with here.

Recent Estonian and Polish public performances of the national past are highly interesting examples that offer an opportunity to study the cult of a nation in the early twenty-first century. The European division into a civilized West and a barbarian East, of course, is far too simplistic. Still, Estonia and Poland are struggling partly with other challenges than countries to the west, but that does not yet tell anything about their position in Europe. In order to interpret what is going on in Estonia and Poland and why performing the past has gained such importance, we need to carefully scrutinize the role of history, on the one hand, and the necessity to perform identity, on the other, and then ask what role and forms these aspects have acquired in the early twenty-first century. Nationalism studies have concentrated more on the founding years of national Europe in the nineteenth and early twentieth centuries than on the issue of how national identity is re-narrated and upheld in the twenty-first century.

Our aim is to show how the narrative of victims and heroes as well as how the cherishing of national history, which was more familiar in previous centuries, fits into the era of late modernity. In contrast to Western European countries, national space had to be reconstructed in the Eastern European countries and in particular in the former Soviet Republics in the 1990s. This new formative moment obviously explains certain similarities to the classical era of nationalism. That being said, it does not offer a thorough and exhaustive explanation, and in particular does not explain at all why performing the national past has been even more blatantly expressed in the early twenty-first century. Introducing two separate cases, we intend to outline a comparison of Estonia and Poland that tries to explain whether or not there is a larger regularity of development.

The Cult of Authenticity and Performing the Past – Seeking Self-Esteem

Each particular nation demands to be represented as a unique, particular and privileged entity (Greenfeld 1995: 487–488). This requires *national trajectories* in which crucial symbols and metaphors are nationalized and presented as particular and exclusive. As Jens Bartelson (2006: 33) writes, "states and nations could hardly be understood other than as outcomes of long historical processes. Each state or nation had its own temporal trajectory." This trajectory is presented as a natural, logical and solid narrative. Sometimes the telling of a/the national trajectory requires travelling over decades or centuries, but temporal distance is rendered insignificant. Forgetting, or national amnesia, is an essential part of the national drama: ill-fitting elements and unnecessary diversity are simply deleted (Bartelson 2006; Roshwald 2006: 58). Ernest Renan underlined long ago that the construction of modern nations is based on forgetting. Memory does not exist without forgetting, but following Paul Ricoeur (2004), there is a difference between passive and active forgetting, between amnesia and amnesty, or forgetting and forgiving. Most important in that context are the moral and political implications of forgetting.

Anthony D. Smith (2003: 218) calls the national trajectory "the drama of the nation", which according to him "has three climactic moments, each of them glorious: its golden age, its ultimate national destiny, and the sacrifice of its members". Discovering a true self would "be difficult, if not impossible" without the idea of a national golden age (ibid., 190). While the ultimate destiny remains uncertain, the points of certainty, and thus nodal points of the drama of the nation, are upholding, remembering and celebrating the commitment and self-sacrifice of members of the nation. "What we might term 'destiny through sacrifice', therefore, forms the final sacred foundation of national identity" (ibid., 218). Although the ideal of noble self-sacrifice has varied greatly, it has always required heroes and messiahs of the past to offer a guide to how to follow national geniuses and to fulfil heroic virtues in the present (ibid., 40, 223–224).

Commemorating the national heroes is essential for upholding the ideal of noble self-sacrifice, but heroes and forms of celebrations have varied. In the early phase of an elite nationalism, the middle-class "focussed primarily on representations of the virtuous actions of charismatic individuals and groups" mainly from the field of art, music and literature. These were treated as "the exemplary qualities", and the authenticity of a nation was performed in artistic virtues. Mass nationalism, however, has looked more for heroes and heroines, and thus "the focus shifts to rites and ceremonies performed in an orchestrated mass choreography at specific sites, purveyed in monumental sculpture and architecture and by means of secular liturgies and secret emblems" (Smith 2003: 223–224).

The most sacred heroes and heroines are the fallen patriot heroes – the glorious dead – as they have sacrificed even their lives for the nation so that the nation would flourish. According to Smith (2003: 246–253), the nationalistic cult of the glorious dead merges the Greek-Roman tradition of dignifying patriotic virtue and Judeo-Christian-Islamic tradition of dedicating a certain place to the memory of sacred persons. Ritual mourning and glorifying of the dead requires a holy place, a monument that enables collective commemoration. However, the sites commemorating the glorious dead and forms of performance have varied greatly during past two centuries of the era of modern nationalism. The cult of the great man was characteristic of the nineteenth century, while the Tomb of the Unknown Soldier reflected non-heroic horrors of the First World War. Collective mourning of innocent victims of genocide is associated mostly with the Holocaust, which has received its own memorials. Public celebration of national heroes has been replaced by private mourning of unnamed victims at public sites. Still, in many societies, "memorials and ceremonies continue to have a national, as well as personal, significance" (ibid., 251).

Depicting the national Other, oppression and achieving one's freedom are also essential elements of the drama of the nation. As Aviel Roshwald (2006: 88) reminds us, "The memory of what others have done to the nation helps define the meaning and value of liberty and highlight the necessity of shaking off foreign yokes or of fighting to maintain independence and security." The national plot is usually based on the classic narrative of the struggle between good and evil, in which only two alternative frames are available: that of heroic epic or that of glorifying tragedy. The latter is often attached to the myth of victimhood. Being a victim transformed a tragedy – a massacre, a genocide or a fatal defeat – into an acceptable element in the drama of the nation and even as a source of national self-esteem. It is still relevant to ask with Pascal Bruckner (2010: 105) whether a nation could "forever identify with its torturers, its traitors, and its hoodlums, or sanctify its citizens who were defeated, shot, or martyred. It must first of all celebrate its heroes and heroines who, at the most critical moment, dared to resist and allowed a people to recover and move forward with their heads held high. It is their example of which we have to show ourselves worthy."

Furthermore, pursuing the national destiny is impossible without self-respect, and this points at national dignity as the sacred nucleus of a nation. Liah Greenfeld (1995: 491) defines national identity as "a matter of dignity" and adds that nationalism is frequently driven by the vanity of a community, which is always trying to legitimize its position, protect what has been achieved, or trying to move towards a new, enhanced position. According to Richard Ned Lebow (2008: 61–64), spirit as a fundamental motivation or emotion of human activity is undermined in social sciences, and thus the premise has been forgotten that "people, individually and collectively, seek self-esteem" and "self-esteem is a subjective sense of one's honor and standing". The nucleus of national self-esteem and thus the heart of a nationalist belief-system is the quest for the true self and the cult of authenticity. "Authenticity functions as the nationalist equivalent of the idea of holiness in so many religions" (Smith 2003: 37–38).

The search for self-esteem, subjectivity and recognition is important for all national movements, but has particular resonance if it is inter-twined with notions of marginality and liminality. This becomes clear when comparing self-esteem (how we regard ourselves) and esteem (how we are regarded by others). These are not synonyms even if they are closely related. Self-esteem always requires a certain recognition from others, and particularly the self-esteem of marginal and small nations depends on this connection and is thus more vulnerable to their disjunction. As Roshwald (2006: 122) argues, national dignity is intertwined with security and thus guides political decisions. "Indeed, perceived threats to collective dignity and national well-being often include both challenges to official myths of violation and overt acts of violation, oppression, or exploitation. The cult of past martyrdoms and the awareness of contemporary dangers to national honour, sovereignty, and/or security are commonly intertwined in a dynamic, ever-changing relationship."

Performative Identity and Collective Memory

If the nation is presented as "a sacred communion of the people", a separate public cult is needed for uniting "its adherents into a single moral community of the faithful" (Smith 2003: 32). Pointing out the sacred and rites of salvation are essential for any nationalism and nation. According to Smith (2003: 42), "a sacred communion of the people; the elevation of the voice of the people; the return to nature and to roots; the cult of authenticity; and the sacrificial virtues of heroes and prophets ... are the main themes and beliefs of the belief-system of nationalism, or what we may term a new *religion of the people*." This "religion of the people" has borrowed its core narrative of salvation and its quest for authenticity, as well as many of its performative habits, from Christian tradition.

One's own nation is "usually represented as serving the cause of justice" and thus God is seen to be on our side (Lorenz 2010: 78–79). Therefore, nationalism can also be interpreted as nationalization of Christianity. Essential to national trajectories are a linear timeline and an idea of progress: in the future there will a promised land waiting for a nation. Simultaneously, a cyclical timeline may emphasize the return to the original sacred homeland. Following Smith (2003: 137), one should distinguish between two kinds of sacred homelands: "one is the promised land, the land of destination; the other the ancestral homeland, the land of birth". These two may overlap, but can also be conceived separately. Both of them, however, present a nation in spatial terms and attach it to a certain sacred landscape and territory.

To analyse expressions of the cult of authenticity, we need to examine the changing relationship between history and collective memory as well as new forms of performing identity. Who is narrating national trajectories and participating in their renewal in the twenty-first century? How do people attach their personal experiences and memory to the drama of a nation? What kind of cults of authenticity resonate with the demands of people in our late-modernity? To answer these questions we need to scrutinize the relationship between history and memory and how they become attached to (national) narratives.

The relationship between history and memory is complicated. In principle, history is memory seen through and criticized with documents of many kinds, while memory is history seen through affect, but both overlap in many respects. Modern scholarly historiography developed hand in hand with emerging national ideas in the nineteenth century; thus the core agent, unchallenged for a long time, in history-writing was the nation(-state). Historians, however, lost their monopoly on narrating a drama of the nation a long time ago, if they ever had a monopoly on that. A variety of actors contribute to the national trajectory, and besides written representation other, mainly visual, forms of representation have become more powerful. Apart from documented arguments by historians, emotions raised by fictional narratives of the past shape people's interpretation of the past. In practice, Lorenz (2010: 90) argues that we are living in the era of "presentism" which is shaped by a new kind of relationship with the past and future. Instead of national history, key terms are now memory and heritage, which can be seen as "a sign not of continuity between the present and the past, but as a sign of rupture and of discontinuity due to the acceleration of change". The past has to be experienced and it is treated as a commodity.

Jay Winter (2010: 15) tries to escape the dichotomy between history and memory by introducing the notion of "historical remembrance" that both combines and distinguishes it from familial remembrance. Through historical remembrance the performative nature of national identity is emphasized. Following Jay Winter, "the performative act of remembrance is an essential way in which collective identities are formed and reiterated". The performative act is understood in this case in a broad sense: "The performance of memory is a set of acts, some embodied in speech, others in movement and gestures, others in art, others still in bodily form. The performative act rehearses and recharges the emotion which gave the initial memory or story imbedded in it its sticking power, its resistance to erasure or oblivion" (Winter 2010: 12).

As Jan Assmann (1995: 129) says, each nation has fixed points of national trajectory that are "fateful events of the past, whose memory is maintained through cultural formation (texts, rites, monuments) and institutional communication." Visual symbols associated with various public performances and festivities strengthen collective memories and prevent forgetting. Cyclically repeated celebrations like an independence day "serve to concretize the sense of a transcendent national experience that bridges awkward historical chasms" (Roshwald 2006: 63). In the cult of authenticity it is more important how the drama of nations is performed than how it is told, because that serves as a key to how individuals can attach themselves to nations. According to Smith (2003: 223–224), the public imagery of national communion includes "the public ceremonies of celebration and commemoration with which the citizenry could identify and in which they could, eventually, participate".

Another aspect is important with regard to the performance of memory: the relation between memory and space, which forms the basis of the notion of *lieux de mémoire*. This connection between space and memory is not confined to intentionally erected monuments, as well known already from ancient cultures. As a kind of anthropological constant, it seems fit for adaptation to modern societies. According to Nora (1996), the preservation of collective identity can only be achieved by keeping alive fragmented memories connected to national symbols. What is important to remember is that the site itself does not matter, but rather how it is attached to collective memory through a performative act and thus receives its significance for identification (Koselleck 2000: 275–284).

The ways in which Nora's notion was transferred to and adopted by other regions and nations in Europe during the last decade show a great variety of terms, definitions and notions. This refers to the understanding of "lieux", where we also see "sites" or "realms" (Judt 1998); as well as to memory, where we see "Erinnerung" vs. "Gedächtnis" in German, "memory" vs. "commemoration" in English; while the Polish ("pamięć") and Estonian discussions ("mälu, mälupaik"), for instance, are less encumbered with the difference between remembering and memory. Although there is not much disagreement that "places" do not necessarily need to be spatially concrete and may also be conceived as metaphorical ones, the spatial dimension obviously remains pivotal in all these approaches.

Concluding this theoretical framework, we must confess that scrutinizing recent developments is more difficult than analysing the formative years of nationalism. All in all, the notion of fragmenting the approach towards collective commemoration of the past matches another element of the memory paradigm, highlighted by Dan Diner (2007). According to him, diversity, not homogeneity, is the signature of memory, and the aim of this study is to study multiple ways of expressing the authenticity of a nation and methods of performing national identity that could be regarded as essential elements of vivid nationalism. Therefore it seems to be relevant to study how national memory is performed and to focus on performances that have gained wider popularity and/ or express juxtapositions. By examining new public forms of performing the nation, we may highlight how the authenticity of a nation is presented. For that purpose we have chosen on the one hand to look at new national museums of occupation and resistance, and on recent debates centred on the Bronze Soldier conflict in Estonia, and on the other the commemoration of Katyń in Poland. They may be regarded as sites of experience of a traumatic past but also as performances of the past that challenge or exclude other interpretations.

Poland after Smolensk

Strengthening the Polish nation in internal and external discourses has been a major topic within the project of a "Fourth Republic", which has been first of all connected to the government led by the Kaczyński brothers' party PiS (Prawo i Sprawiedlowość – Law and Justice) from 2005 to 2007. The notion of the "Fourth Republic" emerged around the year 2000 amidst growing discontent with political compromises under the preceding Liberal and post-communist governments. According to Paweł Śpiewak (2003), who suggested the term in a newspaper article, the political system that emerged in 1989 had degenerated to bargaining for bribes and cronyism and could only be overcome by a radical break.

The PiS government then introduced clear claims for national self-esteem and respect in internal and external politics. Notably, President Lech Kaczyński cancelled a meeting of the "Weimar Triangle" in 2006, obviously due to a satirical text in a German newspaper which compared the Polish president with a potato. This absurd episode also reflected challenges to national identity that accompanied Poland's EU accession. One of the Kaczyński brothers' major fields of activity was history politics (Brier 2009), conceived as a reaction to the concept of *gruba kreska* (i.e. drawing a thick line under the history of the People's Republic) and replacing it with a rigid lustration of all former elites during socialism. Moreover, PiS history politics tended to respond to the challenges to national self-esteem as posed by the debate on the murder of Jews in Jedwabne and the expulsion of the Germans after the Second World War (Kicz patriotyczny).

The effects of this policy are probably most visible in the broadened and partly highly politicized activities of the Institute of National Memory (IPN), which developed large publication activities, dealing first of all with repressions during the socialist period (Machcewicz

2007). Besides using the IPN as an agency to "de-communize" Polish society, the Museum of the Warsaw Uprising, which – after the official inauguration on 31 July – opened for the public in autumn 2004, was the second major issue of Polish history politics in recent years. As if this had not been a sufficient starting point for an inquiry into recent discourses on victimhood and heroism, the fatal crash of the presidential plane at Smolensk, when Lech Kaczyński was on his way with a high-ranking delegation of politicians, officials and military officers to a commemoration ceremony at Katyń on 10 April 2010, has added even more relevance to the topic (Niżyńska 2010).

In many of the public reactions, the crash, with its almost 100 victims from political and military elites, has been regarded as another specific Polish national tragedy, and not as an unfortunate chain of mishaps – such as the delay of the departure from Warsaw, bad weather conditions at Smolensk airport, pilots' mistakes, and insecurity or incapability among the Russian personnel at the airport to give precise advice to the aeroplane – nor as a result of the president's determination to arrive right on time for the memorial ceremony despite information about weather conditions not allowing a safe landing. The national dimension of the catastrophe was also enhanced by the fact that this commemoration was planned as an exclusively Polish ceremony, in contrast to the Polish-Russian one attended by the prime ministers Tusk and Putin three days earlier. The coining of a "second Katyń", which emerged in the Polish public immediately after the crash, underlined once again the Polish self-image of being a victim of foreign powers, and for many it included allegations of Russian responsibility for the accident. The dominant language in many media was about the president's sacrifice for the nation and his death on duty like a soldier. Attempts to give meaning to the accident emerged immediately and were ubiquitous; they referred first of all to a reconstruction of national unity and also to reconciliation with Russia. Particularly in the first weeks after the crash, voices that tried to blame Russia for another murder of the Polish elite had been overlaid by the recognition of official Russian sympathy, which was understood as supporting Polish claims for respect. Only after some weeks of moderation and after his defeat in the presidential elections did Jarosław Kaczyński start to utter allegations against Russia based on conspiracy theory, which still has a broad base in the Polish public. As the commemoration of the first anniversary shows, however, public opinion and also public performances of commemoration are split, as they had been before the accident: PiS claims to represent the true core of the Polish nation, whereas the majority of society seems to be fed up already with such national rhetoric.

The religious dimension of the accident did not only appear in the performances of public mourning (as with the cross erected by scouts in Warsaw, which later on had been fiercely defended against its translocation to a church), but also in the decision of the Polish Catholic Church (actually by the Archbishop of Kraków, Cardinal Dziwisz) to agree to a burial of the presidential couple in the crypt of the cathedral on Wawel Hill in Kraków, which functions as a sanctuary of the Polish nation with the tombs of Polish kings and national heroes. Thus Lech Kaczyński became the first president to be honoured with a funeral there after General Pilsudski, the first head of state of the restored Polish Republic after the First World War, in 1935. Although Cardinal Dziwisz explained his decision with a request from the family (which would imply from Jarosław Kaczyński), he also argued that the president had died "as a hero" on his way to Katyń and hence had acquired the honour of resting beside the Polish national heroes. Jadwiga Staniszkis (2010), a sociologist closely connected to Polish dissent in the 1970s and 1980s, highlighted that the burial on Wawel Hill is justified rather due to the fact of the tragic death than the president's role as a national victor. Other voices, such as the conservative historian Andrzej Nowak (2010), explained that the president died on duty and that his death contains the meaning of overcoming the long-lasting Polish–Russian conflict, or that the president's death in symbolic circumstances requires a symbol denoting national unity (Zdort 2010). And the Primate Henryk Muszyński underlined that the president's death finally crowned his attempts to reinstall national self-esteem under the banner of "God, Honour, Fatherland" (Forecki, 2012).

The Sejm Marshal and interim president Komorowski's speech at the funeral ceremony obviously tried to actively promote national unity and consolidate a political programme: "Today the ring of Zygmunt's bell reminds us all that the death of 96 Polish women and men, the death of the Polish president and his wife was not a futile sacrifice. That the feeling of community in the mourning for the pilgrims of the Polish cause who died tragically will bring good fruits. That we immersed in mourning will be able to stand together on the side of freedom, solidarity and truth. It calls us to reconciliation with the

Russian nation in order to overcome the drama of Katyń" (*Gazeta Wyborcza* 19 April 2010: 4).

The whole funeral ceremony showed a close linkage between the president's death and the national trauma of Katyń. An urn with soil from Katyń had already been placed near the sarcophagus of Pilsudski, and the act of placing Kaczyński next to him was thus also read as homage to the victims of Katyń. However, the decision about a funeral on the Wawel was also publicly criticized as being inappropriate – for instance by Andrzej Wajda, director of the film *Katyń* from 2007, Adam Michnik, editor of the largest Polish daily *Gazeta Wyborcza*, and Władysław Bartoszewski, former Minister of Foreign Affairs and a combatant in the Warsaw Uprising of 1944.

Apart from the official ceremony, spontaneous collective mourning in front of the president's palace and at other public places in Warsaw and elsewhere reflected the close relation between national identity and religion. The symbolic centre of this phenomenon became a wooden cross provisionally erected by a group of scouts in Warsaw. Against this background, the documentary film *Solidarni 2010* by Ewa Stankiewicz and Jan Pospieszalski, was made and shown on public television as early as two weeks after the plane crash. It displayed a broad criticism of the media which were harshly accused of profaning the nation, whereas the film in contrast allegedly gave a platform to what was presented as the authentic voice of the nation. This authenticity of the ordinary people was, however, a blatant construction based on suggestive questions as well as on the unmentioned participation of actors and politicians. Although the film spread another message of conspiracy theory, that the crash could not have occurred by accident, the more important message was the presentation of *vox populi*, of the national people, who wanted to express their authentic bond with the president and the nation (Forecki 2012). Unlike what this film was asserting, the presented performance of national authenticity was not so spontaneous and the authors of the film were reprimanded for violating the standards of good journalism. Thus the film's message continued the political struggle preceding the crash.

The wooden cross then became the source of a dispute about the role of religion in the public. The newly elected successor as president, Bronisław Komorowski, declared it a symbol of the period of national mourning, which afterwards should be relocated to a church. After violent protests to keep the cross as a national monument at its original site, it was first temporarily removed to the chapel of the president's palace, and finally transferred to St. Anne's Church in Warsaw on the eve of the national holiday of 11 November 2010.

Religion and Nation in Poland

In order to frame the performance of national authenticity after the plane crash, one should at least briefly look at the role of religion in national discourses in Poland. The religious national discourse has a strong tradition in Polish history, reaching back to the wars against the Ottoman Empire, the Swedish Empire and finally also against the Russian Empire. The idea of "antemurale christianitatis" from the fights with the Ottoman Empire was subsequently transformed into an identification of Polish national identity (in the sense of the Noble-men's Republic) with Catholicism. After the defence of the monastery on Jasna Góra against the Swedes during the "Deluge" in 1655, the Virgin Mary was symbolically crowned Queen of Poland – expressing both the victimhood and the heroism of the nation.

The blending of religion and national identity received a new dimen-sion during the nineteenth century with the notion of Polish messian-ism, promoted not least by Adam Mickiewicz and Juliusz Słowacki after the defeat of the 1830 uprising (Walicki 1978). This idea was initially conceived as being "transnational" – as it presented Poland as sacrifice for the freedom of the European nations, but later during the nineteenth century messianism became confined to Catholicism and to the nation – referring now to the Polish nation and not to the others (Porter 2000).

Furthermore relevant is the question of when and how national and religious discourses in Poland merged after 1945. The Catholic Church tried to continue a national stance also under socialist rule, for instance in the practical acquisition of the new territories in the west. The Church was also an agent of national identity in the 1960s, when the millen-nium of Polish statehood and Christianization was commemorated. Decisive for recent debates, however, is the merging of religious and dissent discourses in the protest movement. In the debates after the strikes of 1970/71 national unification among the opposition against the regime became an important issue, because former protests in the 1960s by leftist intellectuals and students, as well as by workers in 1970 and 1976, had been defeated by the regime. Hence the idea of broad societal cooperation emerged, between workers and intellectuals as well as between Catholic and leftist intellectuals. The main protagonist of this idea has been Adam Michnik, one of the leaders of the students' protests in 1968 (Michnik 1987, 1993; see also Stala, this volume).

The effects became visible in Gdańsk during the protests in August 1980, which led to the foundation of Solidarność. Whereas the shipyard worker protest did not initially have a religious component, its impact has steadily increased after the strike in Gdańsk: there were holy masses at the shipyard, and the Gdańsk monument to the dead workers of 1970 was not only a monument commemorating the dead (as in Szczecin), but combined national and religious elements into a new quality. This monument did not occur all of a sudden; instead, one may note that the commemoration of those shot in December 1970 subsequently changed its forms during the 1970s. After the introduction of martial law in December 1981 and the dissolution of Solidarność, the religious victim discourse was among the dominating forms of protest, as churches and monasteries as well as religious practices were save havens from state interference. Finally, the murder of the priest Popiełuszko by the secret service in 1984 added another national martyr to the opposition against the socialist regime, followed by a cult of commemoration in his parish church in Warsaw.

Katyń and the Warsaw Uprising as Core Elements of Polish Martyrology

A particular place in this trajectory of sacrifice during the twentieth century took Katyń as a symbol for the execution of more than 20,000 Polish prisoners of war by the NKVD in 1940. In fact, thousands of Soviet prisoners were murdered there too (Cienciala et al. 2007). In contrast to the commemoration of German crimes in Poland, Katyń became a mythical place, which was not only due to the extent of the murders, but also to the fact that the Soviet Union spread untruths and denied responsibility. Therefore, this issue could not be frankly addressed in socialist Poland and thus occupied a specific place in national martyrology. In the 1980s the commemoration of Katyń became partly public – in churches, for instance. Public disputes emerged when an official monument blaming the Germans for Katyń was erected in 1985 in the military cemetery at Powązki in Warsaw, with the inscription: "To the Polish soldiers resting on the land of Katyń as victims of Hitlerite fascism – 1941". After 1989, the official day of commemoration became 17 September, the day of the Soviet attack on Poland in 1939, which thus links the specific crime to a larger context: to Soviet occupation and subsequent annexation of the Polish eastern territories. In that way, Katyń created a kind of foundational myth of a society after socialism – it represented Soviet occupation and domination as well as socialist untruths.

Although the Russian policy of declaring responsibility for Katyń had been introduced by Boris Yeltsin during his struggle for the dissolution of the Soviet Union, Russian authorities under Putin reverted to being hesitant about confirming this position until 2010. The meeting between the prime ministers Tusk and Putin showed that Russia now seems willing to revise former positions denying responsibility for the murders in Katyń. The crash in Smolensk, however, concealed the fact that the second commemoration, to which Kaczyński and the Polish delegation were headed, was designed as a solely national Polish one, not a Polish-Russian one (Niżyńska 2010). This may also explain why Lech Kaczyński underlined the relevance of his visit in distinction from the prime minister's visit three days earlier. It was meant as a confirmation of Polish self-esteem, not as a contribution to national reconciliation between Poland and Russia.

As a similar case with regard to national authenticity one may see the commemoration of the Warsaw Uprising, which began on 1 August 1944 and ended with the almost total destruction of Warsaw after the defeat in October. Although it had been the largest uprising against German occupation in the Second World War, its commemoration had been highly contested since the end of the war (Borodziej 2001; Bömelburg 2011). On the one hand, there were debates about the strategy and beginning of the uprising as well as about its victims among combatants and the civil population; an argument previously put forward by Czesław Miłosz in his "Rodzinna Europa" ("Native realm: a search for self-definition") in 1958. Besides this, the uprising's alleged anti-Soviet motivation was criticized in official discourses in socialist Poland. On the other hand, supporters of the uprising stressed its psycho-political impact on the Polish nation (Bömelburg 2011). The public discourse about the strategy of the uprising, as well as about the role of the Allies with the Red Army arriving on the right bank of the Vistula in August 1944, was largely confined by the *raison d'état* of the People's Republic. Thus the uprising was part of the general public heroization of resistance as it was manifested in the monument of Nike, symbolizing the heroes of Warsaw (erected in 1964).

Unlike the monument for the Warsaw Ghetto uprising of 1943, erected in 1948 (Kobylarz 2009), no monument was established for the 1944 uprising until 1989. The image of a heroic though vain fight against a superior enemy, however, was a subject of literature and films from the late 1950s (as in Wajda's film *Kanał*). This memory was clearly shaped by features of martyrology – sacrifice for the Polish nation, heroism and vicitimization – as the monument of the "Little Insurgent", erected in 1983, reveals, followed by the monument for the heroes of the Warsaw Uprising in 1989. Both monuments had been projected much earlier, but could only be realized at the end of the socialist regime. With regard to the monument of 1989 and subsequent plans for a museum, Barbara Szacka (2006: 180) has spoken of "regained memory" after 1989.

History Politics and the Museum of the Warsaw Uprising

When Lech Kaczyński became mayor of Warsaw in 2002, he declared the realization of long-existing plans for a museum of the Warsaw Uprising one of his main tasks, to be completed on the eve of the sixtieth anniversary of the uprising on 31 July 2004 (Borkowicz 2004; Loew 2008). The museum has been located in a building from tsarist times – a tram power station – which thus had survived the destruction of the city after the uprising; however, it was not directly linked to fightings (Żychlińska 2009: 104). According to the official guide, the power station was remodelled into a "patriotic temple" by introducing a "commemoration wall" and a "freedom park" (Jasiński & Ukielski 2007: 9). The exhibition is arranged by the days of the uprising, with calendar sheets to tear off and collect, and is intended first all to put visitors (and also children) into the role of Polish combatants by displaying a canal, ruins and also an Allied aircraft. Right from the beginning, the museum gained the status of being on the agenda of official programmes for state guests. After three months it had already been visited by 100,000 people, with numbers for later periods being similar.

In official presentations of the museum, the oppression of the combatants and falsification of the image of the uprising during the People's Republic has been highlighted; furthermore, the delay in presenting the "true" image after 1989 was criticized. Thus it was conceived as correcting a hitherto prevailing image that was not predominantly shaped by national pride. Dariusz Gawin, deputy director of the museum and one of the active supporters of the Kaczyńskis' history politics, men-

The Museum of the Warsaw Uprising, established 2004 in the former building of the tram powerstation. Photo: Jörg Hackmann.

tioned the aspiration for respect or authenticity as a major goal of the museum. The museum clearly aims at evoking emotions and reviving the uprising by displaying calendar sheets or presenting accounts by participants as phone calls on pre-war telephones.

The exhibition and the catalogue refer to a clearly defined "we" – the Polish nation – whereas German occupation is referred to as the "Germans" and not to German soldiers, the SS or other combatants. One of the museum's further ideas was to present a new image of the "Armia Krajowa" (the Polish Underground Army, the largest resistance movement during the Second World War) as a group repressed in socialist Poland and thus requiring a new presentation as national heroes. All in all, the museum is part of a representation of Polish agency, which is more national but also more concrete than the previous commemoration of the fight against fascism during the socialist period. In that respect, one may speak of a "re-heroization" that attempts to highlight the "victory of the soul" (Kurz 2007), but does not refer to the politics of the uprising. In addition, the museum complex comprises also a sacral element with the wall of commemoration displaying the names of the dead fighters of the uprising (Żychlińska 2009: 94–95).

This staging of the past, which transforms the visitors into re-performers of the uprising, is accompanied by rock concerts and scenic plays, and may be described as forms of "prosthetic memory" (Landsberg 2004). It seems to be one of major changes in the collective commemoration of the Second World War in Poland in recent years. In fact, the acceptance of the museum seems to be particularly widespread among the young generation, who find this living history more appealing than critical reflection (Kicz patriotyczny). Against criticism of displaying patriotic kitsch and presenting the combatants as heroes, and by the same token remodelling the defeat into a moral victory (Loew 2008), Gawin has stressed that the intention was not heroization or martyrology, but claiming respect for the Polish nation, which also shapes the discourse of the many associations of combatants of the uprising.

Criticism of the museum refers in particular to the fact of exposing first of all the fighters in the uprising, but keeping the civil population out of commemoration, although they made up 90 per cent of casualties during the uprising (Bömelburg 2011). This at least may indicate that such an extension of national martyrology from the Second World War to 2010 has not been generally accepted among the Polish public. Szacka (2006) is surely right in noting a general change from heroization to victimization in Polish commemoration of the Second World War, but the museum actually combines both threads into an image of the sacrifice of the youth for the nation. Such discourses have been called victimhood nationalism (Lim 2010).

Although one might state that recent Polish debates reveal that the national martyrology has been deeply contested, staging the past and making claims for national respect, nevertheless, are shaping debates even beyond the initial scope of the history politics of PiS. However, ongoing museum projects such as that about the Second World War in Gdańsk (Machcewicz Pac 2011) and about the protest movements under socialism might contribute to different ways of defining and performing collective identity. Nevertheless, the relevance of national self-esteem is still high, also among the younger generation, and will also shape further projects, even beyond the end of the history politics of the Fourth Republic.

Estonia and the War on Monuments

In the Estonian case, the "war on monuments" has received a lot of attention in (international) media as well as in research literature (Burch & Smith 2007; Brüggemann & Kasekamp 2008; Lehti, Jokisipilä & Jutila 2010; Brüggemann 2010). Many of the actions connected to this event were indeed highly performative. It all started in the small provincial town of Lihula in September 2004, when the Ministry of Interior had a memorial honouring those Estonians who fought on the German side against the Red Army during the Second World War removed from a public place. The decision to intervene was not justified by denying the historical significance of the monument but primarily to salvage Estonia's international reputation – the esteem of a nation. The erection of this privately funded monument was noticed not just by Russian media but also by international ones. Cherishing soldiers in Nazi German uniform as national heroes was not understood elsewhere, and while the historical context was missing the monument was linked to extreme-right movements. However, the support for and significance of the memorial as a national symbol should not be overestimated. The man behind the memorial can obviously be regarded as an extremist, but still some thousands of German Army veterans as well as local people participated in the unveiling ceremony. During the Soviet years it was not allowed to commemorate publicly those Estonians who served in the German Army or in the Waffen-SS, they were simply treated as traitors and Nazis; while Estonians in the Red Army were regarded as heroes of the people. In the early years of independence this constellation was turned upside down, and for many it was a question of recognition of their own and their parents' memories (Brüggemann & Kasekamp 2008).

The intervention of the Estonian government was followed by a series of acts trying to profane Red Army memorials around Estonia. Monuments were painted red and graffiti messages were left (Burch & Smith 2007). There were still over 100 war memorials that remained more or less untouched after the regaining of independence in 1991, and with a few exceptions they have remained mostly invisible till these days (Kattago 2010). In the early years of independence the nationalization of space concentrated mostly on Lenin statues, which were comprehended as major symbols of foreign occupation. The Red Army memorials cherishing the Great Patriotic War turned into sites of a struggle for national esteem only in the twenty-first century as part of a wider debate about the Second World War. The most visible, and thus from the Estonian point of view most disturbing, was the Red Army memorial in the very centre of Tallinn, in front of the National Library. Performative actions of Estonians and the Russian-speaking minority on the site in spring 2007 marked a new benchmark in the symbolic struggle over history, the authenticity of the nation and the place of memory.

The original memorial had been unveiled in September 1947 and dedicated to the Liberators of Tallinn, commemorating the Red Army soldiers who had conquered the city three years earlier. The soldier himself is anonymous but has a specific and recognizable uniform. Recently there has been a debate in Estonia about who served as a model for the statute, with some voices claiming and other denying that it was the Estonian Olympic medallist Kristjan Palusalu, a national hero (Lehti, Jokisipilä & Jutila 2010: 35). Re-burying soldiers at the site transformed the monument into a memorial, and the addition of an eternal flame in 1964 further strengthened the sacredness of the place. In the Soviet era the monument legitimized Soviet rule and obliged the citizens to build up the new Soviet Estonia for which these glorious dead had sacrificed their lives (Brüggemann & Kasekamp 2008).

For the Estonians the statue initially symbolized their national tragedy. Celebrating the memory of a Red Army soldier – the organizer of deportations, a war criminal, a murderer – profaned the Estonian nation, an interpretation still widely held. The memorial has been an embarrassing relic cherishing false history, according to the Estonians, and thus soon after regaining independence the Estonian government tried to soften the symbolism of the monument, as its message was completely contradictory to the new narrative of Estonians as victims of the cruel occupation by the Soviet Union. However, in the early years of independence the measures were still rather cautious. The monument was renamed and the eternal flame put out. In an act of de-Sovietization it was rededicated to all who fell in the Second World War, thus making it fit to serve the prevailing myth of victimhood. However, the soldier still had his distinct uniform and the monument was a central site for the revived Victory Day celebrations of the Russian Estonians on 9 May. For the Russian-speaking minority the monument offers a site to oppose the government, and it symbolized a counter-narrative to the Estonian national one and cherished the victory of their "grandfathers and parents" over fascism. Therefore, it was symbolically important to try to protect the monument.

After the Lihula incident the site of the Bronze Soldier witnessed ritualized performances of collective memory, with one group trying to guard their symbols and others aiming to defile them and eventually erase them completely from memory. The Estonian government made crucial decisions in the spring of 2007. The criminalization of Soviet symbols and the removal of Soviet memorials were for a long time a hot issue in the Estonian political debate. Legal decisions by parliament made the removal of the statue possible in spring 2007, and this was finally accomplished on the night of 26–27 April 2007. The statue was relocated from its original location in the city centre to the more remote Estonian Defence Forces cemetery (Lehti, Jokipisipilä & Jutila 2010: 20–22).

This operation triggered violent riots in the streets of Tallinn, diplomatic conflict between Estonia and Russia, and an aggressive but theatrical performance organized by the Russian youth organization "Nashi" (Ours). The one-night riots in this peaceful Northern European country were a shock for Estonians, but should perhaps be seen more as a result of frustration on the part of the Russian-speaking minority and thus equivalent to riots among young migrant populations in West European urban centres. But they were also associated with strong national symbolism. Moscow's interests and references to Russian national memories obviously gave extra colour to the incident. Still, the riots were also read in domestic media as an expression of serious failures in integration policy but simultaneously as an impudent effort by Russia to intervene in Estonian internal affairs. They were even compared with the failed communist coup in Tallinn in 1924 (Astrov 2008). Thus, it was insinuated that national sovereignty was under threat. In the end, however, the operation seems to have been rather successful and the removal also marked the end of the war on monuments. The new and more marginal place of the Bronze Soldier has been partly accepted by the Russian-speaking minority, and simultaneously the memorial has lost much of its symbolic power as a counter-narrative that contests the dominant Estonian one.

The Estonian government attempted to emphasize the shift from Soviet to Western European tradition by introducing an official honorary visit to lay wreaths at the Holocaust memorial at Klooga, the monument to the Unknown Soldier (previously the Bronze Soldier) and the Maarjamäe memorial complex on 8 May as a day of commemorating the victims of the Second World War, in contrast to 9 May as Victory Day in the Soviet tradition. It is obvious that the new official ceremony on 8 May was created to prove Estonia's Europeanness, and its main audience was not a national but an international one. Thus, what was performed was the quest for the justified esteem of Estonia. However, it seems that, after the removal of the Bronze Soldier, Estonian self-esteem as a source of national dignity was no longer attached to these war memorials, and as they lost their performative power to celebrate the nation these memorials ceased to be sites for expressing authenticity of the nation.

The Museum of Occupation and the Fight for Freedom

During the era of the Singing Revolutions after the mid-1980s and in the first decade of Estonia's independence, the Soviet era was interpreted exclusively in terms of suffering and resistance, and thus a denial or collective amnesia of the whole period became a pivotal feature of the Estonian national narrative. A myth of victimhood was created by explaining away the Soviet era: the suffering Estonians were presented as innocent victims who still had not lost their belief in the nation.

Hence a connection between the lost past and the new future was required. By performing the past and expressing the nation's authenticity, a continuity between new and old independence was imagined. Restoring the old monuments and heritage sites was the most visible tool with which to perform the nation in the first phase of national reawakening during the 1980s. This was followed and accompanied by the collection of memories and data of the victims of deportations. Since the late 1980s, *Eesti Muinsuskaitse Selts* (the Estonian Conservation Society) has been a prime channel to recreate national history and to perform the national past destroyed by the Soviet regime. Its activities concentrate on the restoration of monuments commemorating the Estonian War of Independence from the 1920s and 1930s that were destroyed in the Soviet era. The break in history was to be bridged by creating continuity over the Soviet era.

For many Estonians the public commemoration of civilian victims combines the historical memory of the nation and family remembrance; participation in the nation is thus a highly emotional act. Still, even though the deported have their own official day of commemoration (14 June) they lack a major public monument. Only the statue of Linda on Toompea Hill, depicting the wife of the epic hero Kalev mourning the loss of her husband, serves as a forum of commemoration. During the Soviet era the statue, which was created in 1880 but erected on Toompea Hill only in 1920, became an unofficial memorial to the victims of Stalin's terror, today acknowledged by the plaque text "to remember the ones taken away." Regardless of its political meaning, the statue has remained a site of personal mourning free of state-centric heroism (Lehti, Jokisipilä & Jutila 2010: 30).

During the past decade the mourning of civilian victims has been replaced by the dignification of resilience. Instead of forgetting the Soviet period and mourning the families' fate, new generations are now requested not to forget the suffering of the nation and to glorify national bravery. The Museum of Occupation, founded in Tallinn in 2003 and located just one block from the original site of the Bronze Soldier, was intended as a site to experience national memories (Feest 2007). Interestingly, the official name of the museum is "Museum of Occupations" (in the plural), although the museum is often referred to simply as the museum of occupation and for a while also as the "Museum of Occupation and the Fight for Freedom". This first museum building in Estonia of the post-1991 era was initiated and financed by a private institution in the United States, the Kistler-Ritso Foundation (Velmet 2011). Its director Heiko Ahonen was imprisoned in Soviet times for political reasons and was one of the activists in the independence movement.

The museum's objectives are "to document the catastrophes and cataclysms which took place during the last fifty years and to find detailed proof about the past based on facts and analysis." Even if the museum refers also to "Russians, Germans, Jews, Swedes and other minorities under the totalitarian regime" (Velmet 2011: 191), its main focus is without doubt on ethnic Estonians: "The aim of our activities is to seek and find answers to essential questions about the recent history of Estonia: Who are our heroes? Who are our friends? Who are our enemies? The main directions are: to help determine an identity, to determine and consolidate a national consciousness and to teach our small nation the value of its independent statehood." The museum is presented not just as a museum but as a preliminary sanctuary for commemorating "those who did not return to their homeland", and a memorial complex that "would be a tombstone for the thousands of countrymen buried in anonymous graves. Our dead will remain unburied until the memoirs of those that perished are immortalized."[1]

The Estonian Museum of Occupations in Tallinn which was established 2003, has the sculpture "Trains" by Leo Lapin in its main hall. Photo: Jörg Hackmann.

The exhibition consists mainly of various Soviet relics, which are not only connected to occupation or repression but also display everyday life (such as cars, radio sets, a telephone booth, etc.). The large ground floor hall, however, has an obvious element of staging the Soviet occupation: on the one side there is refugee boat with a mine close by, which represents the escape over the Baltic Sea from Soviet repression; on the opposite side a collection of Soviet prison doors is displayed. The way between the refugee boat and the prison doors leads past a sculpture by Leo Lapin called "Trains", showing two almost colliding locomotives with swastika and hammer and sickle; thus alluding to the "gate of hell" the visitor has to pass. In the basement of the museum some disposed Soviet monuments are exhibited. Besides this dramatization, the museum intends to portray "history as it was" – thus without the overdone dramatization as in the Polish case. Nevertheless, beyond "objectified" history an obvious drama is told with minimalistic dramatization. Visualized narratives of the periods of Soviet rule (the "first red year", "war and German years", "the Stalin era", "the era of Stalinism", "the sixties", "the period of stagnation", "the liberation") with the presentation of various relics contributes to the narration of the national drama; that is, first of all exposing the experience of deportation and life under two occupations. It is an ethnic Estonian elite's view that dominates the documentary films covering the period from 1940 to 1991 and provides a narrative that is shaped by dramatic historical film sequences and a calm and distanced scholarly presentation, which paradoxically enhances the message of a dramatic national struggle for independence. It is also revealing to consider what is told and shown in the exhibition and what is left out. The Holocaust, as an American scholar noticed, is "almost completely absent", and the camp at Klooga is called a "labour camp" (Velmet 2011: 197). Furthermore, the declaration of Estonian towns as "Judenfrei" by the Nazi occupiers (Weiss-Wendt 2009: 126) is not mentioned at all.

The dominating purpose of the exhibition is to present the Estonian nation as a victim of the Second World War and to legitimize its position with regard to domestic as well as foreign visitors. The museum offers a narrative without frictions and without alternatives – it is an either/or drama in which you either obey national virtues or you are an enemy. The museum creates a "myth of descent" and a "special dignity" that "endows the Estonian nation with a sense of entitlement, as well as a special uniqueness" (Velmet 2011: 197; Smith 1984: 105–107) and thus points at the sacred core of the nation. It is like a canonized text and ritual that should be just taken and believed in, but not doubted.

The museum refers, as outlined above, to an important discourse among the Estonian population: remembering their own fate as experienced under Soviet rule; but in a certain way it also aims to connect the message to the international debate on the Holocaust in the Baltic region during the Second World War. The first exhibition sign states that "the Museum reflects the struggle between the preservationist responses of the people and the destructive impetus of the occupations"; that is, efforts to save the pure Estonian culture from the savage intruders trying to demolish it. The expressions of Estonianness in the Soviet era are reduced simply to people "yearning for freedom" and "never losing hope". In this ethnicized narrative, resistance is the only true Estonian virtue and all else represents alien Russian culture. The active role of ethnic Estonians in politics and culture is silenced, as well as the deportation of ethnic Russians, too, during the first Soviet occupation. As Li Bennich-Björkman (2009) reminds us, in Estonia a national civic society existed even during the communist era and in practice made a rather smooth transformation to independence possible. Paradoxically, while any influence of the Soviet era on Estonian culture is disputed, it is at the same time needed to dramatize the national narrative. The very name The Occupation Museum articulates both the original drama of oppression and the emerging new heroic epic deifying those who fought for Estonian independence.

In contrast to earlier narratives, the Estonians are not presented purely as victims, but by emphasizing the role of dissent, a certain amount of agency is revived in the form of active resistance. Self-esteem and the expression of the authenticity of the nation is not primarily grounded on the myth of victimhood but anchored more deeply in the resilient nature of Estonians under the pressure of Sovietization. Thus, what is to be proven is the claim that Estonians did not lose their authenticity during the Soviet era and to explain why occupation and resistance are underlined, whereas everyday experience and expressions of Estonian culture in the Soviet era, although displayed in the exhibitions, are marginalized, while unconditional resistance is celebrated as a mark of the authenticity of the nation.

New Sites of Estonian Heroism

In recent years new sites of commemoration have been established in Estonia, which reveal a striking difference from earlier sites. First, these new memorials and monuments can be counted as official or semi-official, as they are usually financed and supported by prominent political actors (such as the state president) and erected in public spaces. Second, they commemorate Estonian (military) heroes instead of civilian victims who were the glorious dead in the earlier narrative of victimhood. In similar terms, if the fixed point of history was previously the destruction of Estonian independence and civic community by the Soviets, the new sites now commemorate the struggle for freedom and a sovereign state after the First World War.

In recent years the War of Independence of 1918/19 has been represented as a fixed point of the Estonian drama that declares the true authenticity of the nation. A new narrative cherishes once again the Estonian struggle for freedom instead of the previously dominant mourning of civilian victims. On 3 January 2008, at an anniversary ceremony for the War of Independence, the Estonian Defence Minister

The Freedom Cross by Rainer Sternfeld et al. erected in 2009 on the Freedom Square in Tallinn. Photo: Jörg Hackmann.

Jan Aaviksoo urged people to "commemorate those who were and are willing to take up arms to protect Estonia's freedom … After having exhausted all other means, we are also willing to take up arms to protect our freedom."[2] Five days later he opened an exhibition about General Johan Laidoner at the Estonian War Museum, emphasizing that "the heroes of the War of Independence have a fundamental importance today and even more so for the future. Only an individual willing to give up everything in the name of his or her future can be free in the real sense of the word."[3]

The new rhetoric of the War of Independence is connected to the most striking recent example of performing the past: the huge Freedom Cross in the very heart of Tallinn.[4] The square close to which the Freedom Cross stands was formerly a site for symbolic struggle of ownership. There, the monument to Peter I, celebrating the 200th anniversary of Russian rule, was erected in 1910. This was removed in 1922 during the first years of independence, but it was only in 1933 that the square was renamed Vabaduse Väljäk (Freedom Square). A competition was held for a monument to freedom, but plans could not be realized before the loss of independence in 1940. The submitted architectural proposals mostly depicted modernist tall pillars, and the shape of the monument erected seventy years later resembled these earlier plans, although much more traditional in its symbolism (Tamm & Haala 2008).

The unfinished plans for the Freedom Monument were revived in the political debate in the late 1990s, but only in 2005 was it finally decided that the monument should be located at Freedom Square and thus be completed as the true monumental centre for the independence of Estonia. In October 2005 the future location of the monument was marked temporarily by a stone, in order to confirm the erection of the Freedom Monument. The winning competition entry was a 23.5 metre high pillar consisting of 143 glass plates and with the Cross of Liberty, Estonia's most distinguished award established in 1919, on top of it.[5] At the opening ceremony on 22 June 2009, President Ilves recalled that Estonians strove for freedom for two centuries, starting with the abolition of serfdom and culminating in the War of Independence. The president invited "everybody tomorrow to take flowers to the closest Monument to the War of Independence in your parish, in your neighbourhood", because "only then will we understand that the men and women who brought freedom to the people of Estonia came from the very soil, the very place, you come from yourself".[6]

In the Freedom Cross, Christian symbolism is strikingly and somehow surprisingly present. Traditionally, Churches and nationalism have remained separate in Estonia. The roots of this distance can be dated all the way back to the nineteenth century, when the Estonians identified the Protestant Church as a German institution (and the Orthodox Church as a Russian one) and thus as symbols of foreign rule. Religious symbolism was not part of national performances in the years of the Singing Revolution or the first decade of independence, but things have changed. The official Estonia now refers to Christian symbolism as the Freedom Cross itself. A telling example is President Ilves' Independence Day greeting card from 2011 presented on his website. In the picture, central objects are the Freedom Cross, the Church of St John and a young (Estonian) couple. All traditional elements of conservative national thinking – patria, God and family – are centrally present and combined. Religious symbolism is used for sacralizing the nation and offering salvation – a hope for the future. The struggle for freedom is presented as a God-given mission and thus as a sacred nucleus of national self-esteem offering a safe and secure future for young Estonian couples.[7] In the end, Estonia is presented as a state guarded by God and dignified through its brave struggle for freedom in the past.

The new sites that commemorate Estonian heroism are better fitted to sacralize the state, and they are not as easily compatible with family remembrance as was the case with the myth of victimhood. Therefore, an interesting question, to which we do not have any definite answer, is whether the new sites and monuments offer ordinary Estonians a real opportunity to perform their own national identity.

An interesting example, showing that such tendencies to sacralize the nation are contested and meet counter-narratives, is Kristina Norman's art performance "After War", which seeks to blur the hegemonic modernist and nationalist narrative. Norman is a young Estonian visual artist and documentary filmmaker who made a provocative gesture on Victory Day on 9 May 2009 by (re)locating a gold-painted papier-mâché replica of the statue at the original site of the Bronze Soldier. A video documentation then became part of the "After War" installation in the Estonian Pavilion at the International Art Exhibition of Venice, 2009. Norman herself interprets the message of her performance as follows: "If 'after-party' [the riots in Tallinn] is something that follows the 'official event' [the removal of the statue], then AfterWar is an art research project, a participatory experiment and an intervention through which I am trying to create a possibility for more tolerant approaches to history between official historical writings. By not choosing a historical 'truth' from either of the confrontational 'memory collectives', I am asking uncomfortable questions regarding democracy, tolerance, xenophobia and fear."[8] Kristina Norman's art performance stands as evidence that an era of uniform national narratives has come to an end and more diversified and tolerant narratives are needed to contest narratives of victimhood.

Conclusions

This chapter has tried to identify a shift in national trajectories from the emphasis on victimhood and sacrifice to heroism in Poland and Estonia. Comparison of these two cases is not an easy task as differences between Estonian and Polish trajectories are clearly visible, but simultaneously common developmental trends are also recognizable. However, earlier studies have shown with regard to collective commemoration of the Second World War that there are – despite differing historical legacies – similar challenges and discourses, in particular referring to the connection between commemorating the Holocaust and the political endeavour to enter NATO and the EU (Hackmann 2009).

Trajectories of victimhood have a long tradition in both societies. They have cherished religious kinds of rituals and practices: canonical narratives, good/evil juxtaposition, looking for salvation. Seeing oneself as a victim can be used simultaneously for cultivating the myth of authenticity. Self-esteem has been grounded on the narrative that, despite hard times (of occupation, genocide, etc.), national virtues survived and flourished.

In Poland those trajectories have been closely connected first of all to the Catholic Church, and one may note an ongoing sacralization of politics ever since the Great Strike of 1980, whereas in Estonia this connection to church institutions is absent. However, in Poland the role of the Catholic Church in sacralizing (as well as influencing) politics has become increasingly contested, as debates about the burial of President Kaczyński in April 2010 show. The dispute about the role of religion among the public became even more contested with the struggle for the permanent place of the wooden cross commemorating the dead of the plane crash on a public spot versus a sacral space. Conversely, the religious symbolism has recently become more visible in Estonia, as the Freedom Cross proves. In both cases simplified narratives of victimhood have been challenged in public debates.

Obviously, after having established their positions in the EU and NATO, the pre-accession constellation has changed in Estonia and Poland. Nevertheless, one may note a twofold agenda in both these nations – an internal self-assurance, and external claims of defending the nation's dignity and interests first of all towards Russia (and Germany in the Polish case) or towards Europe. The problematic and traumatic Russian relationship has continuously invigorated victimhood narratives, but simultaneously the need to return to Europe has been slowly replaced by challenges towards the old Europe and the need to define one's own new Europe and one's position in it (Lehti 2007). Therefore victimhood has also been losing its importance, while the image of passive victims does not correspond to the new, more active role Estonia and Poland have tried to achieve in recent years. This significant shift has also affected national trajectories and generated new demands to perform national self-esteem.

However, the victimhood narratives have proven to be surprisingly resilient. One may explain the history politics of the Kaczyński brothers partly as a reaction to the challenge Jedwabne posed to national self-esteem. In similar way in Estonia, the war on the monuments can be explained as a reaction to the challenge to the narrative of Estonian victimhood and national dignity. As the legitimacy of victimhood has been challenged from outside as well as from inside in Poland as well as in Estonia, it has gradually been transformed into a contested issue but also proved to be resilient in nature. It seems obvious that national narratives are not only contested but divergent, and thus national authenticity and self-esteem do not depend on one uniform narrative.

In recent years new heroic elements have been introduced to the drama of a nation in Estonia and Poland, and the most visible public performances of nation nowadays include a celebration of heroism. As we have argued, trajectories of victimhood have a long tradition in both societies, and they offered a source of national self-esteem during formative years after the regaining of independence (Estonia) or after Communist rule (Poland). It is, however, obvious that victimhood no longer offers the sole foundation for the drama of the nation, and self-esteem is sought from another direction.

This change raises several questions:

First, can victimhood and heroism coexist and be complementary elements, or are they necessarily contradicting narratives? Our analysis of the Museum of Occupation in Tallinn and the Museum of the Warsaw Uprising shows how victimhood and sacrifice can be intertwined with a need to narrate an active resistance into the drama of the nation. Both museums are examples of the effort to construct a new kind of sanctuary for a nation that offers the people a possibility to experience the drama of the nation. Public acceptance shows that obvious elements of staging – reliving the Warsaw Uprising day by day, or standing in front of prison doors or entering the "gates of hell" in the Estonian

Museum of Occupation – have an impact on both societies. A major difference may be seen in the presentation of everyday objects: in the Estonian case they underline Soviet repression (and by the same token Estonian victimhood); in the Polish case they are displayed in order to underline Polish agency and heroism.

Second, how is the whole drama of the nation being transformed, and how is the cult of authenticity expressed? The Freedom Cross in Estonia represents another trend in which, instead of civilian sacrifice, soldiers and their fight for the sovereignty of the nation-state are commemorated. The nodal point is no longer to pinpoint the resilience of national authenticity under a foreign yoke, but to highlight how the nation has struggled for freedom and sovereignty. While the myth of victimhood mourns civilian victims, a heroic narrative commemorates soldiers, and thus the focus of national cults and the performance of national authenticity has slowly been shifting from the citizen to the state. Performing authenticity is attached to formative moments of creating and defending the state, whereas previously the resilience of civic society under foreign occupation was the dominant narrative. Even if the Freedom Cross displays Christian symbolism, it represents not so much a spiritual or Christian mythology of salvation and sacrifice, but rather embodies the shift from civic to state-centric drama and from salvation to sovereignty.

The question of how powerful new monumental expressions of past heroism really are, and whether they have been more visible while being debated but not yet physically present, has to remain partly open. In Estonia the Freedom Cross is located in the very heart of Tallinn, but it could be seriously questioned whether it offers a real object for Estonians to perform their identity and a site of collective memory. Does it really express the authenticity of Estonians as most Estonians feel it, or was it just a counter-reaction to the war on monuments, and was the target of its blatant symbolism solely Moscow? Still, as long as its symbolism is used as part of official discourse, it has not become invisible. Referring to Poland in this context, the issue of new monuments after Smolensk is still to come; what is obvious, however, is that the performance of national unity when commemorating the dead has come rather quickly to an end after the presidential election in June 2010, giving way to party struggle, in particular regarding relations to Russia before the accident.

The last question concerns how we regard this change in a wider

European perspective. These recent developments are not directly dependent on the impact of 1989/91, and thus they can not be explained solely
as a result of the end of socialism. Nor do they constitute a linear and
irreversible process – as the Polish debates after Smolensk show. One
should therefore take into account that they are connected to national
paths with longer traditions – national discourses of heroes and victims
in Poland and those of a small nation in Estonia. Besides, we see similar
tendencies to sacralize the nation and stress victimhood vs. heroism elsewhere in Europe. These processes are also connected to a shifting emphasis
based on changes in the international framework, as national narratives
are trying to react in order to secure self-esteem. Further, in both cases
the political consensus characteristic to the formative years after the end
of Communist rule has given way to more multiple voices. Apart from
the obvious need to perform national self-esteem in international forums,
these multiple voices, including the existing option for national indifference, have on the one hand transformed public expressions of national
identity into monumental and ceremonial manifestations, but on the
other hand new museums simultaneously offer people "playgrounds of
history" in which they experience and relive the national tragedy. Thus
simple explanation schemes of East vs. West or postmodern vs. modern
do not apply. Rather, we see an overlapping and condensation of different trends – performing memory, focus on the Holocaust, promoting
victimhood, nationalism, and competition with rival national narratives.
The latter point may be seen as one based on politics after socialism –
claiming respect for the prolonged suffering after 1945.

Notes

1 www.okupatsioon.ee/en/who-we-are. Accessed on 26 August 2011.
2 Anniversary of the Estonian War of Independence ceasefire commemorated at
   Tallinn Reaalkool, 3 January 2008, Estonian Ministry of Defence, www.mod.gov.
   ee. Accessed on 24.1.2008.
3 General Laidoner exhibition opens at Estonian War Museum, 8 January 2008,
   Estonian Ministry of Defence, www.mod.gov.ee. Accessed on 24 January 2008.
4 The statue of liberty of the War of Independence receives its revamp, 19 November
   2007, Estonian Ministry of Defence, www.mod.gov.ee. Accessed on 24 January
   2008. See also Vabaduse Monument www.vabadusemonument.ee. Accessed on
   26 August 2011.
5 vabadusemonument.ee/; see Pihlak et al. 2009.
6 The President of the Republic at the unveiling of the Monument to the War of
   Independence, 22 June 2009, www.president.ee.
7 Opening page, http://www.president.ee/. Accessed on 15 March 2011.

8 Kristina Norman, http://www.re-title.com/artists/Kristina-Norman.asp; Mark Nash on Kristina Norman, http://works-and-places.appartement22.com/spip. php?article67. Accessed on 28 August 2011.

References

Astrov, Aleksandr (2008): Monumentaalne kriis. "Natsid", "okkupnadid" ja teised hinilisted, in Marek Tamm and Pille Peetersoo (eds): *Monumentaalne Konflikt: mälu, politiika ja identiteet tänäpäevä Eestis*, Tallinn: Varak.

Bartelson, Jens (2006): We Could Remember It for You Wholesale. Myths, Monuments and the Constitution of National Memories, in Duncan Bell (ed.): *Memory, Trauma and World Politics. Reflections on the Relationship between Past and Present*, Basingstoke: Palgrave Macmillan.

Bennich-Björkman, Li (2009): The Communist Past. Party Formation and Elites in the Baltic States, *Baltic Worlds*, 2 (3–4), 29–36.

Bömelburg, Hans-Jürgen (ed.) (2011): *Der Warschauer Aufstand 1944. Ereignis und Wahrnehmung in Polen und Deutschland*, Paderborn: Schöningh.

Borkowicz, Jacek (2004): Muzeum Powstania w rękach trzydziestolatków, *Więź*, 8–9, 4–5.

Borodziej, Włodzimierz (2004): *Der Warschauer Aufstand 1944*, Frankfurt am Main: Fischer-Taschenbuch-Verl.

Brier, Robert (2009): The Roots of the "Fourth Republic". Solidarity's Cultural Legacy to Polish Politics, *East European Politics and Societies*, 23 (1), 63–85.

Bruckner, Pascal (2010): *The Tyranny of Guilt. An Essay on Western Masochism*, Princeton: Princeton University Press, French original 2006.

Brüggeman, Karsten and Andres Kasekamp (2008): Ajaloopolitiika ja "monumentide sóda" Eestis, in Pille Petersoo and Marek Tamm (eds): *Monumentaalne konflikt. Mälu, politiika ja indentiteet tänäpäevä Eestis*, Varrak.

Brüggemann, Karsten (2010): Geteilte Geschichte als transnationales Schlachtfeld. Der estnische Denkmalstreit und das sowjetische Erbe in der Geschichtspolitik Russlands und der baltischen Staaten, in Birgit Hofmann et al. (eds): *Diktaturüberwindung in Europa 2010*, Heidelberg: Winter, 210–225.

Brüggemann, Karsten and Andres Kasekamp (2008): The Politics of History and the "War of Monuments" in Estonia, *Nationalities Papers* 36 (3), 426–448.

Burch, Stuart and David J. Smith (2007): Empty Spaces and the Value of Symbols. Estonia's "War of Monuments" from Another Angle, *Europe-Asia Studies*, 59 (6), 913–936.

Cienciala, Anna M., Natalia S. Lebedeva and Wojciech Materski (eds) (2007): *Katyn. A Crime without Punishment*, New Haven: Yale University Press.

Diner, Din (2007): From Society to Memory. Reflections on a Paradigm Shift, in Doran Mendels (ed.): *On Memory. An Interdisciplinary Approach,* Bern, New York: Lang.

Dreifelds, Juris (1996): *Latvia in Transition*, Cambridge: Cambridge University Press.

Feest, David (2007): Histories of Violence. National Identity and Public Memory of Occupation and Terror in Estonia, in Tsypylma Darieva and Wolfgang Kaschuba (eds): *Representations on the Margins of Europe. Politics and Identities in the Baltic and South Caucasian States*, Frankfurt and New York: Campus.

Forecki, Piotr (2012): Gräber und Erinnerung. Die Auseinandersetzungen um die Begräbnisstätten von Lech Kaczyński und Czesław Miłosz in Dieter Bingen, Maria Jarosz and Peter Oliver Loew (eds): *Legitimation und Protest. Gesellschaftliche Unruhe in Polen, Ostdeutschland und anderen Transformationsländern nach 1989*, Wiesbaden: Harrassowitz.

Hackmann, Joerg (2009): From National Victims to Transnational Bystanders? The Changing Commemoration of World War II in Central and Eastern Europe, *Constellations*, 16, 167–181.

Greenfeld, Liah (1992): *Nationalism. Five Roads to Modernity*, Cambridge, Mass.: Harvard University Press.

Jasiński, Grzegorz and Paweł Ukielski (2007): *Przewodnik po Muzeum Powstania Warszawskiego*, Warszawa: Muzeum Powstania Warszawskiego.

Judt, Tony (1998): A la Recherche du Temps Perdu. Review of "Realms of Memory: The Construction of the French Past" edited by Pierre Nora, 3 vols., Columbia University Press, *The New York Review of Books, 45*.

Kattago, Siobhan (2010): Commemorating Liberation and Occupation. War Memorials along the Road to Narva, in Jörg Hackmann and Marko Lehti (eds): *Contested and Shared Places of Memory. History and Politics in North Eastern Europe*, London: Routledge.

Kicz patriotyczny, *Gazeta Wyborcza*, 6, 7 January 2006.

Kobylarz, Renata (2009): *Walka o pamięc. Polityczne aspekty obchodów rocznicy powstania w getcie warszavskim 1944–1989*, Warszawa: IPN.

Kończal, Kornelia (2007): *Europäische Debatten über "les lieux de mémoire"*, Berlin: Centrum Badań Historycznych PAN.

Koselleck, Reinhart (2000): *Zeitschichten. Studien zur Historik*, Frankfurt am Main: Suhrkamp.

Kurz, Iwona (2007): Przepisywanie pamięci: przypadek Muzeum Powstania Warszaw-skiego, *Kultura Współczsna*, 33, 150–162.

Kuus, Merje (2007): *Geopolitics Reframed. Security and Identity in Europe's Eastern Enlargement*, New York: Palgrave.

Landsberg, Alison (2004): *Prosthetic Memory. The Transformation of American Remem-brance in the Age of Mass Culture*, New York: Columbia University Press.

Lebow, Richard N. (2008): *A Cultural Theory of International Relations*, Cambridge: Cambridge University Press.

Lehti, Marko, Markku Jokisipilä and Matti Jutila (2010): Never Ending Second World War. Public Performances of National Dignity and Drama of Bronze Soldier, in Jörg Hackmann and Marko Lehti (eds): *Contested and Shared Places of Memory. History and Politics in North Eastern Europe*. London: Routledge.

Lehti, Marko (2007): Protégé or Go-between. The Role of the Baltic States after 9/11 in EU–US Relations, *Journal of Baltic Studies*, 38(2), 127–151.

Lim, Hie-Jyun (2010): Wszyscy chcą być ofiarami?, *Więź*, 53 (2–3), 22–34.

Loew, Peter Oliver (2008): Helden oder Opfer? Erinnerungskulturen in Polen nach 1989, *Osteuropa*, 58, (6), 85–102

Lorenz, Chris (2010): Unstuck in Time. Or: the Sudden Presence of the Past, in Karin Tillmans, Frank van Free and Jay Winter (eds): *Performing the Past. Memory, History, and Identity in Modern Europe*, Amsterdam: Amsterdam University Press.

Machcewicz, Paweł (2007): *Poland's Way of Coming to Terms with the Legacy of Communism*, www.eurhitxx.de/spip.php%3Farticle40&lang=en.html. Accessed on 29.5.2012.

Machcewicz, Paweł and Grzegorz Pac (2011): Muzeum ofiar i bohater. Rozmowa, *Wiez*, 54 (2–3), 80–91.

Michnik, Adam (1987): *Letters from Prison and Other Essays*. Berkeley: University of California Press.

Michnik, Adam (1993): *The Church and the Left*, Chicago: University of Chicago Press.

Niżyńska, Joanna (2010): The Politics of Mourning and the Crisis of Poland's Symbolic Language after April 10, *East European Politics and Societies* 24, 467–479.

Nora, Pierre (ed.) (1996): *Realms of Memory*, 2 vols., New York: Columbia University Press.

Nowak, Andrzej (2010): Wyjątkowy urząd, wyjątkowa śmierć. Stąd Wawel, *Gazeta Wyborcza*, 88, 15 April.

Pihlak, Jaak, Alo Lõhmus, Lauri Vahtre, Rainer Sternfeld and Andri Laidre (2009): *Vabadussõjast võidusambani*, Tallinn: Valgus.

Po co polityka historyczna, *Gazeta Wyborcza*, 229, 1 October 2005.

Porter, Brian (2000): *When Nationalism Began to Hate. Imagining Modern Politics in Nineteenth-Century Poland*, New York: Oxford University Press.

Ricoeur, Paul (2004): *Memory, History, Forgetting*, Chicago: University of Chicago Press.

Roshwald, Aviel (2006): *The Endurance of Nationalism*, Cambridge: Cambridge University Press.

Salo, Vello, Ülo Ennuste, Erast Parmasto, Enn Tarvel and Peep Varju (eds) (2005): *The White Book. Losses Inflicted on the Estonian Nation by Occupation Regimes 1940–1991*, Tallinn: Estonia Encyclopaedia.

Smith, Anthony D. (2003): *Chosen Peoples. Sacred Sources of National Identity*, Oxford: Oxford University Press.

Staniszkis, Jadwiga (2010): Na Wawelu nie leżą sami zwycięzcy, *Gazeta Wyborcza*, 88, 15 April.

Stukuls Eglitis, Daina (2002): *Imagining the Nation. History, Modernity, and Revolution in Latvia*, University Park, PA: The Pennsylvania State University Press.

Szacka, Barbara (2006): *Czas przeszły – pamięć – mit*, Warszawa: Scholar.

Tamm, Marek and Saale Halla (2008): Ajalugu, politiika ja identiteet. Eesti Monumentaalsest mälumaastikust, in Pill Petersoo and Marek Tamm (eds): *Monumentaalne konflikt. Mälu, politiika ja indentiteet tänäpäevä Eestis*, Tallinn: Varrak.

Velmet, Aro (2011): Occupied Identities. National Narratives in Baltic Museums of Occupations, *Journal of Baltic Studies*, 42 (2), 189–211.

Vesilind, Priit (2008): *The Singing Revolution. How Culture Saved a Nation*, Tallinn: Varrak.

Wszyscy chcą być ofiarami?, *Więź*, 53 (2–3), 2010.

Walicki, Andrzej (1978): Polish Romantic Messianism in Comparative Perspective, *Slavic Studies*, 22, 1–15.

Weiss-Wendt, Anton (2009): *Murder without Hatred. Estonians and the Holocaust*, Syracuse: Syracuse University Press.

Winter, Jay (2010): Introduction. The Performance of the Past: Memory, History, Identity, in Karin Tillmans, Frank van Free and Jay Winter (eds): *Performing the Past. Memory, History, and Identity in Modern Europe*, Amsterdam: Amsterdam University Press.

Zdort, Dominik (2010): Akt historycznej sprawiedliwości, *Rzeczpospolita*, 15 April.

Żychlińska, Monika (2009): Muzeum Powstania Warszawskiego jako wehikuł polskiej pamięci zbiorowej, *Kultura i Społeczeństwo* 53(3), 89–113.

CHAPTER 7

Open Catholicism vs. Theocratic Impulses

The Polish Catholic Church as a Source of Liberal Democratic Values or a Hegemonic Structure?

Krzysztof Stala

On the eve of Poland's entrance into the European Union, José Casanova, author of the influential book *Public Religions in the Modern World*, recalled the splendid era of Polish Catholicism. It was a time when the Polish Church was struggling jointly, hand-in-hand, with Polish workers and intellectuals for democracy, human rights and freedom. Accentuating the productive, challenging, and mobilizing role of the Polish Church during the Solidarity period, Casanova reflects hopefully on the future of Polish Catholicism in the new democratic Poland soon to enter the European Union. He summarizes as follows:

> Obviously, only the future will tell whether Polish Catholicism will be up to the opportunity, the challenge, and the task presented by European integration. But, the repeatedly demonstrated power of renewal of Polish Catholicism, a capacity that should not be confused simply with the preservation of a residual and recessive tradition, has confounded skeptics and critics before. It could happen again. (Casanova 2003)

According to Casanova, the democratic potential dwelling in religion became evident in the peaceful revolutions at the end of the twentieth century: in Spain, in Eastern Europe, in South America. The concept of modern public religion (mainly Christianity) being involved in politics, contributing to democratization, was a pivot in Casanova's vision of a peaceful, benevolent return of engaged Christianity into the modern world. These cases would have strengthened the argument against de-privatization of religion, and reveal the positive potential of renewal inherent in Christianity. It is in this context that Casanova praises the positive, crucial impact the Polish Church exerted in the transition to democracy in the 1980s. One may wonder how much of that "power of renewal" remains in the new millennium, especially in the case of Poland. Has the potential for change and for rejuvenation, so admired by Casanova and others, been fulfilled? Or it is rather true that the other pole, "the preservation of a residual and recessive tradition", has dominated the outlook of the past two decades?

In surveys and analyses of the new democratic Poland, the power and significance of religion, epitomized by the Catholic Church, has frequently been emphasized. The role the Church plays in the modern public discourse in Poland, in informing democratic attitudes and the values of an open society, is nevertheless perceived as ambivalent, if not counter-productive. On the other hand, in the majority of trans-formational agendas – the economy, the consolidation of democratic institutions and praxis – and in the sphere of education, the positive changes are perceived, even praised, by impartial observers. Poland's amazing ability to face the challenges of catching up with Western Europe, for rapid economic development and structural changes, is generally recognized, even admired. The major source of discontent consists in the slow pace of transformation in civilizatory attitudes, slow dissemination of the ideas of the open society: tolerance, plural-ism, respect for diversity of lifestyles and views. The institution often blamed for blocking the mental transformation is the Polish Catholic Church and its teachings.

In their diagnoses of the impact the Catholic Church exerts on Polish society, politics and mentality, Polish and Western observers note the transformation of its attitudes after 1989. The chain of events and arguments from the 1990s, sometimes called "the cultural wars", epi-tomized the new hegemonic position for which the Catholic Church strove at the beginning of the democratic transition. The controversial abortion law, consequences of the Concordat, and quarrels about the preamble to the Polish Constitution, interference in party politics and the elections in the early 1990s, the national-populist and anti-Semitic propaganda stemming from *Radio Maryja*, *Nasz Dziennik* and other Catholic media, mark the milestones of the conservative turn the Polish

Church has undergone during the first years of democracy in Poland. The Polish sociologist Zdzisław Mach summarizes the development thus:

> it seems that the Roman Catholic Church finds it difficult to respond to new challenges which arise from the development of democracy in Eastern Europe and of the desire of those countries to join European institutions. The Church still uses the discourse of conflict, inherited from communist times, when the Church built its unique position, at least in the Catholic countries like Poland. Moral monopoly and direct influence on the state and the law are still its main aims. ... Consequently the Church is losing its popular support and its influence, and often relies on the old methods of ideological polarization and the discourse of conflict to win its cause. (Mach 2000: 15)

Other authors draw similar conclusions. Timothy Byrnes (2008) writes about the consolidation of power, and "complex navigating" of the Church in the realm of the modern liberal democracy, while Peter Barker states cautiously that "imposing Catholic values was not always conducive to democracy", and that the Church in modern Poland remains "a persisting symbol of nationhood". (Barker 2008: 107–108). Sabrina Ramet (1995) proposes the most radical interpretation, when writing on "the theocratic impulses" in the outlook of the Catholic Church in the 1990s, while Mirella Eberts recognizes the "Return to the interwar model ... to the nationalist and intolerant Catholicism, where the *Polak-katolik* mentality could reign supreme and the Church would be prominent in the public sphere" (Eberts 1998: 136). These verdicts are truly severe, and do not leave space for the hope expressed by Casanova.

The discrepancy between Casanova's enthusiasm and the harsh verdicts of the other scholars can be explained in two ways. Either the Catholic Church in Poland has dramatically shifted its position: from the clearly pro-democratic and pro-liberal stance in the last years of communism towards a hard-line position against the democratic-liberal ideals surfacing in the transition period (1990s–2000s). Or, the pro-democratic, progressive image of the Church from the 1970s and 1980s seems to be exaggerated or overstated, and both Casanova and the Polish intellectual elites have been deluded, or even seduced by that embellished vision.

In order to explicate the contradictory role the Church played in the public sphere in Poland, one should look closer at the formation that has contributed to the constructive image, namely, the phenomenon of Open Catholicism, and scrutinize its impact, agents, ideas and transformations.

In the Communist period, especially in the 1970s and 1980s, some segments of the official Church, together with lay intellectuals, promoted a renewed, modern image of Catholicism. The following reconstruction of the history and the discourse of that formation will help us in understanding the contemporary tensions and ambivalences.

Open Catholicism – The Religious Resurgence in Poland in the 1970s and 1980s

In order to explain the "power of enchantment" exercised by the Polish Church in contemporary Poland, it is not sufficient to point out the durable historical bond between the Catholic Church and the Polish nation. The transformations of traditional, popular Catholicism in post-war Poland, its complex strategy against the Communist regime (between dialogue and resistance), towards the dissident intellectuals, towards Western Europe and the processes of modernization, have been analysed and scrutinized by a number of scholars. The period immediately after the war (1940s and 1950s) has often been described as the defensive era, when the Church attempted to survive the massive persecutions, forced secularization, and anti-clerical official propaganda. The strategy of survival consisted in retreat to pure confessional values, in withdrawing from the public sphere into the crypt of practising religious rituals, maintaining churches and monastic orders, and blocking the communists' efforts at ideological penetration (secret agents, spies, secessionists).

The signs of change in the strategy of the Catholic Church appeared already in the late 1960s. This conservative institution, hitherto sticking to its clerical, solely confessional values, now opened up to the real world, towards Poland's social and human miseries, towards their potential partners in the struggle for human dignity and freedom. Casanova, in his book on *Public Religions in the Modern World*, emphasized this change and defined it as the gradual shift from the principle of religious resistance, through the principle of national resistance, into the final principle of civil resistance. In other words, with its growing self-confidence and feeling of increasing national support, the Polish

Church broadened its spheres of involvement, eventually becoming the major institution of resistance against the inhuman totalitarian system:

> Having established its own right to defend both religious rights and the rights of the nation, the Church slowly began to expand its protection into new areas of human rights, civil rights, and worker rights. At first, these new rights were defended in connection with the rights of the nation, as if to imply that civil rights were derived from national rights or, at least, that the duty of the Polish Church to protect human and civil rights was derived from its role as the nation's keeper. Progressively, however, the Church began to use a new language of universal rights, detached from any particular religious or national tradition. Furthermore, the right and duty of the Polish Church to defend those rights was no longer grounded on the national character of the Polish Catholic Church but, rather, on the universal mission of the Church of Christ. (Casanova 1994: 100)

The impulses for this renewal come both from the centre and from the peripheries. The process of rethinking within the Catholic Church, *aggioramento*, had its sources in the Second Vatican Council. The vision of a renewed Church, open to modernity, to pluralism, to civil rights, and dialogue, began gradually to affect even the traditional Polish Catholicism. The eminent Polish bishop, Karol Wojtyła, one of the intellectual architects of Vatican II,[1] argued in the early 1970s for reforms in the Polish Church and encouraged new forms of religious activity, especially among the youth and intelligentsia. Cardinal Wyszynski, the Polish Primate, through Episcopal letters and sermons, encouraged the Polish people to maintain their historical memory and identity, and to continue their non-violent resistance to the totalitarian regime. On the grassroots level, there was a growing number of organizations and institutions attempting to find new forms and a new language of commitment and religiosity. The Clubs of Catholic Intelligentsia,[2] active in the main Polish cities, organized discussions, seminars, and meetings on the topics of human rights, the philosophy of personalism,[3] and the teaching of Vatican II. Catholic newspapers and magazines such as *Znak*, *Więź* and *Tygodnik Powszechny* promoted modern theological and philosophical currents from abroad, such as personalism, phenomenology, philosophy of dialogue and existentialism. The developing sense of ecumenism resulted in a growing awareness of the complexity of Jewish–Polish relations, interest in Protestant Churches and theology, and in Orthodox Christianity. There were, however, two significant events that accelerated these processes: the establishment in 1976 of an organized opposition, The Workers' Defence Committee,[4] and the election of Karol Wojtyła to the papal throne in 1978. The Committee was eventually supported by a part of the clergy.[5] Both events strengthened the sense of unity between the institutional Church and society, and accelerated processes of rapid change in the self-confidence of the Poles, in their will to transform the political reality, their eagerness to recognize the Church and religion as an important ally in the struggle for human rights and a modern society. The growing political and civic concern in the Church and religion anticipated an intellectual awakening towards Christianity, its theology, symbols and concepts. The Catholic Church was now perceived not only as a dogmatic, tradition-keeping institution. In its history and thought, inspiration and tools could be found that were useful in understanding modern tensions and problems.

It is essential to discern four dimensions in that process of religious resurgence. The first aspect, already mentioned, consisted in the implementation of the post-conciliar changes within the realm of the Polish Church. Karol Wojtyła, the bishop of Kraków, was a pivotal actor in this process, and Casanova is right in describing him as "the main force behind the movement for post-Council reform in Poland". He continues as follows:

> Himself an intellectual, he found it easier than Cardinal Wyszynski to develop close ties with reform-minded Catholic intellectuals, particularly with the Znak group, which often internalized the Council's message sooner and deeper that did much of the Polish hierarchy. As cardinal of Krakow he had promoted the "Oasis" or "Light-Life" Movement, the first revivalist-evangelical movement within Polish Catholicism. As pope he is the sign of the mutual influences, interdependencies, and contradictions between the Roman Catholic Church and Polish Catholicism. (Casanova 1994: 103–104).

Both Casanova and Michel[6] admit, however, that the modernizing reforms in the Polish Church proceeded rather slowly and encountered significant resistance in the mainstream of clergy. It was mainly the lay intellectuals from the above-mentioned Catholic circles who advocated the changes. The mainstream of the institutional Church remained relatively untouched by these processes, and held on to the traditional clerical values.

Another important dimension of the revival was undoubtedly expressed by the increasingly active participation of the Church in the public sphere. The history of the shift towards a growing involvement of the Church in the "principle of civil resistance" has been marked by the chain of interventions and commentaries concerning the current political issues. In the pastoral letter from 1963 the bishops highlighted some "civil" issues: social justice, brotherhood of nations and races, "the personal dignity of rational beings"; all that signalled an attempt to find a neutral language, such as the human rights discourse, compatible with left-wing humanism, and even with Marxism. The controversial "Letter to German Bishops", dated 1965, indicated an entrance into the realm of international relations: the Polish bishops, twenty years after the end of the Second World War, called for reconciliation between both nations, for (mutual) humility and respect. The letter marked the beginning of a long conciliatory process between Poland and Germany. There were important references in the letter to the multicultural (also German) legacy in the Polish culture.

In 1968 the Church sided with the persecuted students and intellectuals following the revolt of the same year. The key words were freedom of science and education, and human rights. The Church, however, did not utter a single condemnation of anti-Semitism, dominating in the Communist Party's reaction to the events.

The idea of human rights as a remedy against the totalitarian oppression was further developed by the Polish Primate in his publicly held sermons in the Holy Cross Church in Warsaw in 1974. He interpreted human rights in the light of Christian personalism; as the universal, inviolable right to freedom, to life in dignity, to free choice of lifestyle (including a Christian way of life). The idea of freedom of choice was a new element in the Catholic post-conciliar teaching, and soon turned into praxis. The Church extended sympathy and support for the workers' strikes in 1976; in subsequent years some support was given to the dissident Workers' Defence Committee (KOR). The supportive outlook increased substantially during the "Solidarity revolution" (1980), and afterwards, especially under martial law (1981–84), the Church became the main actor/patron in the independent cultural and political semi-underground movement. This position dominated throughout the 1980s.

This issue is closely related to the third one namely the Church's alliance with dissident intellectuals. The Polish intelligentsia, in its mainstream predominantly liberal and progressive, had been flirting with Communism in its beginnings, explicitly in the 1940s and 1950s. After failed efforts to reform the Communist system through its democratization and liberalization in 1956, leading Polish intellectuals were growing more and more disillusioned with the potential of the Marxism-inspired, socialist emancipatory project. The intellectual efforts to overcome the deficiencies and wrongdoings of Communism, epitomized by the so-called Humanist Revisionism, were met with growing disapproval by the Party. Consequently, the Polish intelligentsia felt an urgent need for a re-orientation of their ideological principles. The reformed, post-conciliar Catholicism seemed to offer a solution. In order to challenge the de-humanizing praxis of the communist regime, Polish intellectuals turned (cautiously) towards Christianity.

The breakthrough came in 1976, when an organized dissident movement appeared on the political scene. The Workers' Defence Committee, KOR, established in Warsaw, was fighting for broader support from society in its struggle for democracy and freedom. The kernels of independent civil society had gradually emerged in different layers of. Polish society. In the same year Adam Michnik, the former revisionist, and now dissident, one of the KOR's leaders, published a remarkable book: *The Church and the Left* (Michnik 1993). In it he argued for a close alliance between intellectuals and the Church in the struggle for democracy, for respect for human rights, and freedom. As Casanova remarks:

> In *The Church and the Left* Michnik correctly argues that the Pastoral Letters of the Polish bishops and the pronouncements of the pope provided religious legitimation for the model of a modern, differentiated, pluralistic, and self-regulated society. He notes, of course, that this is also the model of society pursued by the secular left and seems to be struck by the fact that the Church appears to have assumed some of the central norms and values of modernity and the Enlightenment. ... According to Michnik, it was only in the course of their involvement in the political opposition that secular intellectuals "far removed from the Church", "were discovering that

the Church was itself a source of democratic and humane values."
(Casanova 1994: 101–102)

By reinterpreting the role of Polish Catholic Church, Michnik, together
with a growing faction of the liberal Polish intelligentsia, was able to
rediscover the Christian source of the universal human values. The
concepts of responsibility, civil courage, the dignity of the human, the
freedom of speech, constitutive for the vocabulary of liberal humanism,
can be traced, according to Michnik and his intellectual master, Leszek
Kołakowski, to the legacy of Western European Christianity. Michnik
establishes in his book that the ascending current of Open Catholicism, with its philosophy of dialogue, personalism, existentialism and
recognition of human rights and diversity of "ways to God", uses the
language of values shared even by a liberal humanist. Only through the
language of fixed, absolute and universal values is one able to contest the
totalitarian practice of dissolving values, dissolving morality, dissolving
truth, through the harmful Newspeak of dialectical materialism and
communist propaganda.

Consequently, the religious "awakening" of the liberal Polish intelligentsia resulted in a radically transformed attitude to the Church. The
growing confidence in the institutional Church was manifested by mass
participation in important anniversary masses (3 May, 11 November: the
symbolic days of the Polish Constitution and acquired independence,
celebrated in pre-war Poland, officially downplayed and forbidden under
communist rule), as well as in diverse activities in churches, organized
by politically engaged priests and intellectuals both before and during
the Solidarity period (with the participation of actors, dissident writers,
charismatic priests). That rising participation was not necessarily of a
strictly religious nature; the Church offered a shelter, a secure public
space for a manifestation of authenticity and freedom of expression.

Polish sociologists have also noted an essential shift in the intelligentsia's attitude towards the Church. While in 1978 the group of believers and strong believers in the highly educated part of the population
amounted to 53.9%, five years later, in 1983 the declared religious
commitment reached 87.7%: an increase of 34% (Darczewska 1989).

The intelligentsia, as a "community of interpretation", resting on
the old tradition of informing the public sphere, was an important
actor in creating the culture of trust. The growing legitimacy of the
Polish intelligentsia in the 1970s and 1980s coincides with the religious

revival and intensified dialogue between the lay intellectuals and the Church/Christianity. The outcome of that dialogue was a proliferation of texts, debate articles, films, and performances inspired by religious values, symbols, and thoughts. Polish culture, both the official and the underground, gradually rediscovered the heritage of Christian theology, metaphysics, and modern trends in religion-inspired European philosophy, such as (Christian) existentialism, hermeneutics, or the philosophy of dialogue. They even rediscovered their own Polish tradition of intellectual absorbance of Christian thought, epitomized by nineteenth-century Polish artists and thinkers such as Cyprian Kamil Norwid, or the Christian Positivists.

That growing national awareness of religion and Christian heritage coincided with the shift in the outlook of religious faith during the late '70s and '80s. Patrick Michel summarizes that transformation in the following items:

> Indifference to religion is increasingly being counterbalanced by a deepening of faith, the main characteristics of which are described by Polish sociologists as follows
> 1. a more intellectual and individual approach to religion;
> 2. an increasingly widespread need of spiritual living and religious experience;
> 3. a growing turning to the Church as a community (frequently found in young people and intelligentsia);
> 4. a developing orientation towards a "socialized" Church, that is to say, a Church committed to the creation of social order based on strong ethical values, ensuring respect for the human person, the emancipation of the individual and of society through work and public life under the influence of the spirit of Vatican II, the personalist philosophy, the progress of the modern national consciousness. (Michel 1992: 99)

Rediscovery and reintegration of the Christian discourse into the mainstream of culture was a significant element of that transformation. The Open Catholicism, initially a current within a narrow strand of the progressive Catholic intellectuals gathered around a few Catholic magazines and the Clubs of Catholic Intelligentsia, was now transformed into the civic/cultural movement absorbing a great part of the intellectuals. In the 1980s it became an official image of Polish

Catholicism. The process shaping the phenomenon of the Open Church was multifaceted and consisted of several layers. To some extent it may be called "a minor Reformation", a profound redefinition of the key ideas inherent in religious thinking. It has both international (Vatican II, the secularization process in the West) and local dimensions.

In order to elucidate that trend it is necessary to reconstruct the intellectual field of the discussions about religion, its place in society, culture and politics that went on in the 1970s and early 1980s and consequently created the thought-world and thought-style of the Open Church. The key terms of the dissident programme were: strong moral values, life in truth, and free human agency (*podmiotowość*) as preconditions for authentic life. Facing the dehumanizing practices of Communist rule, the dissidents felt a need for a solid ground for their vision of humanity, freedom and justice. Modern, post-conciliar Catholicism, with its stress on human dignity and indispensable human rights for all people, irrespective of their race, status, ideology or faith, constituted a genuine counterbalance to the ideology of collectivism, class struggle and relativism launched by the Communist Party. The upsurge of moralism that appeared in the public discourse in the period anticipating and following the Solidarity movement was a product of assimilation of certain Christian values into the discourse of the dissident liberal intelligentsia. The concept of human agency, central to Adam Michnik's writings from these years, has both secular and religious roots. The contemporary Polish-American scholar Elzbieta Matynia interprets that concept in the following way:

> The essential semantic ingredient of *podmiotowość*, that of dignity, made Michnik's often-anonymous message understood and welcomed, and then it gradually spread beyond the circles of the secular intelligentsia to churchgoers and workers. Its performative power made the sense of *self*, and of subject, extend beyond the private. A large collective self saw itself physically during the new Pope's first visit to Poland in 1979, and heard together in his memorable "Do not fear." New voices articulated themselves, and the construction of social communication on a large scale had begun.
>
> Agency, as Michnik saw it, was above all an attribute of society, more specifically of a civil society, expressed "by building up self-determination in civil society, by creating associations from below and avoiding the intermediary role of the state institutions

in public life" The categories of agency and civil society helped to verbalize, and therefore to discover, and then to implement the new competence of individuals and communities to perform, to act vis-à-vis the structures of the party-state. ... "Freedom is identical with self-creation. I will sculpt my life on my own," Michnik wrote while in prison in 1982. (Matynia 2009: 57–58)

There was a strong element of a quest for emancipation in this new trend of moral revival. Life in truth, life in authenticity, courageously contesting the conformism of the average Pole (thinking in one way but acting in another) was depicted and striven for not only in the articles of the opinion-makers like Józef Tischner, Adam Michnik or Leszek Kołakowski, but was also expressed in popular culture, in films and novels. The trend in Polish cinema prevailing in the 1970s and early 1980s has been called *the cinema of moral discontent* (*Kino moralnego niepokoju*) because of its strong ethical involvement. Films of Andrzej Wajda, Krzysztof Zanussi, Krzysztof Kieślowski and others promoted non-conformist attitudes, expressed yearning for authentic life. Direct religious inspirations, however, are not in fact discernible in these films, perhaps with the exception of Zanussi's early production, for instance *Illumination* from 1972. The celebrated *Decalogue* by Kieślowski from the 1980s is probably the most significant artistic achievement in that moralizing trend. By setting his narrations inspired by the Ten Commandments in the modern, urban world (Warsaw of the 1980s), Kieślowski reveals tensions between the strong moral obligation of Christian law and the real conditions of modern life. The characters in these films are torn apart between their desires, false gods, individual life-strategies and the strong moral claims represented by the Christian codex. The answers emerging from those films are highly ambiguous: the Ten Commandments are still an important normative codex in modern Western civilization; they are nevertheless a moral source open to critical reflection and rethinking.

The debate about universal, absolute values was an essential part of that Christian–liberal exchange of ideas. It appears already in Michnik's book from 1976. In order to create a stable ethical platform for contesting the moral nihilism of the Communist system, one needs, according to Michnik, "an absolute sanction". The legacy of European culture, including Christianity, is the ultimate source for such a canon. "This sanction is both human and meta-human. Human, because humans created it; meta-human, because the eradication of that canon would mean annihilation of all contents of human existence, worth to live and die for" (Michnik 1993: 217).

One is able to recognize influences here stemming from Michnik's intellectual master, the philosopher Leszek Kołakowski, to whom I shall return later.

Another powerful impulse in the reorientation of the religious discourse consisted in strengthening the social concerns, mentioned by Patrick Michel as a "developing orientation towards a socialized Church" (Michel 1992: 99). Both the circles of progressive Catholics, grouped around *Znak, Więź* and *Tygodnik Powszechny,* and Cardinal Wyszyński himself developed, already in the 1960s, a language of social sensibility, understood as Catholic-inspired responsibility for the poor and marginalized people. Nevertheless, the first systematic attempt to formulate a Christian-based philosophy of inter-human relations and responsibility for the Other appeared in the 1980s, in the wake of the Solidarity revolution. The main protagonist of this philosophy was the Catholic thinker Józef Tischner, an intellectual, a close friend of Karol Wojtyła, and a prominent figure in the movement of Open Catholicism in Poland. In his sermons directed to the striking workers, in his homilies in the Wawel Cathedral for the members of Solidarity, he developed his vision of the Ethics of Solidarity.

A contemporary American acolyte of Tischner's thought explains the main ideas of the solidarity ethics in the following words:

> According to Tischner, one cannot be in solidarity with a person who has severely blunted his or her conscience. However, hope in the human person allows us to believe that even those who have deformed their conscience can restore it if they truly desire. In his view, a person cannot irrevocably destroy his or her conscience; even the most depraved can still undergo conversion. ... In Tischner's words, "solidarity is directed towards everyone and against no one. In solidarity, people engage in dialogue with those who betrayed them in the hope that the latter will look in the mirror, see themselves as they are, and undergo transformation. This hopeful anthropology, which, to reiterate, recognizes the gravity of human

evil, is the foundation of Solidarity's commitment to social change through nonviolence. (Beyer 2007: 212)

In order to exemplify the subsequent tendency of reoriented attitudes towards religion, consisting in a need for spirituality and religious or metaphysical reflection, one has to mention the poet and essayist Czesław Miłosz, a Nobel Prize Laureate in 1981. Miłosz, an exile writer and scholar who spent his adult years in America, had always declared his ambivalent, cautious attitude to Catholicism. Contesting in his earlier works all forms of aggressive or messianic Polish nationalism, expressing his contempt for pre-war alliances between the Polish Church and the ideologies of organic nationalism (National Democracy), the writer refers, in his poems and articles from the '70s, to the religious metaphysics and Christian symbols. The turning point in his intellectual journey is the essay book from 1976, *The Land of Ulro* (Miłosz 1984). The spiritual landscape of modern man presented in the book is essentially pessimistic, leaving almost no hope. Miłosz depicts the spiritual desert produced by Western civilization on the threshold of the third millennium. He traces the origins of that process, and recalls the Cassandric thinkers and artists who tried to avert the danger, to reverse the process, and warn humankind of the fast-approaching disaster. The past two hundred years of European culture represent, according to Miłosz, a period of rapid disintegration of values, of a civilizatory breakdown. The nineteenth century has created a myth of rational humanitarian progress. In the twentieth century, with all its calamities, that myth was gradually deconstructed. The disintegration has many reasons, argues Miłosz, and all of them are rooted in the heart of the civilizatory process that has affected the Western world during the last 200 years. That process is nowadays called the Enlightenment project, or simply – Modernity.

Poetry, elevated to the status of modern religion, constitutes, according to Miłosz, the remedy for the spiritual desert we dwell in. Such a post-religious poetry is capable of restoring the vertical dimension of our existence, is able to re-establish trust in human nature, unique and irreplaceable, to awaken the metaphysical yearnings. In his conservative humanism, Miłosz resembles some conservative American thinkers such as Daniel Bell, Gertrude Himmelfarb, or Charles Taylor.

The formation of Open Catholicism has often been called dialogical. The idea of dialogue appears in the many titles of books and essays, such as the previously mentioned "The Church, the Left, the Dia-logue" by Michnik (the original Polish title), or Tischner's "The Polish Shape of Dialogue" from 1979. With its roots and inspirations in the ecumenical "disclosure" after the Second Council, the Polish version of openness attempted to break up with the exclusivist interpretation of Polishness and Catholicism. The Catholic intellectuals launched a conciliatory discourse with atheists, with the secular world, with Germans, Russians and Jews. Particularly, the Polish–Jewish dialogue got its initial drive from the milieus around Open Catholicism (Steinlauf 2007; Irwin-Zarecka 1990).

After many years of oblivion and non-existence of Jewish topics in Polish public discourse, one could observe in the early 1970s a growing awareness of "things Jewish" expressed in the Catholic magazines and the Clubs of Catholic Intelligentsia. The "Weeks of Jewish Culture", started by *Więź* in 1974, and the publications of Polish–Jewish litera-ture on the Holocaust by the Catholic publishing house *Znak*, mark important milestones in that conciliatory dialogue. Regardless of the ecumenical trends in universal Catholicism, the Polish version of dia-logue with Jews had its local dimension. As Irwin-Zarecka concludes, "if the universal Church's rapprochement with Judaism has meant a dialogue of faiths, that of Polish Catholic intellectuals is a dialogue with the Jew, both past and present." She interprets that dialogical turn as a sign of their reorientation of the attitude to the meaning of Polishness:

> Maybe paradoxically, these very Catholic Poles are also open to the idea of non-Catholic Poles. Theirs is a highly demanding, highly questioning Catholicism, a basis for moral, not national, integrity. In other words, it is a Catholicism which welcomes – at least in principle – the presence of people with different if not opposite views of the world. It is a Catholicism that leaves room for rationalism and agnosticism in discussions it generates. It is a Catholicism that also makes room for the Jew (literary, too, by inviting Jewish writers to publish under the auspices of the Church, for example). In short, it is a Catholicism which guarantees at least a debate on the notion of "Pole=Catholic". (Irwin-Zarecka 1990: 91)

The process of Polish–Jewish rapprochement went on in the 1980s and 1990s and significantly contributed to the phenomenon of the reconstructed and regained memory (described by Steinlauf in his book *Bondage to the Dead*, from 1997). What has been "reconstructed and regained" is, however, not only the memory of the Holocaust, but also the memory of Jewish presence, history and contributions to Polish culture, the painful topics of the Polish past and the present anti-Semitism. The debates in *Tygodnik Powszechny*, especially in the "Jewish" issues of *Znak* and *Więź* from the 1980s, exhibitions and publication of numerous books on these topics, contributed to a Jewish boom in the public sphere in the late 1980s and 1990s. The Open Catholic circles played a great part in that rapidly growing curiosity, empathy and commitment to "things Jewish".

In the reconstruction of the various threads of the Polish intelligentsia's reorientation towards religion, one cannot overlook the work and thought of Leszek Kołakowski. Already in his early, famous article "The Priest and the Jester" from the 1950s (Kołakowski 2004), he traces Christian inspirations in the history of European philosophy. Our modern concepts of human integrity and freedom, of a universal moral code, of progress, have developed in dialogue with Christian theology, claims Kołakowski. The dynamics in culture between the conservative and the innovative forces, represented by the tension between the Priest and the Jester, constitute its indispensable pivot, declares the writer. In his early text, Kołakowski adopts the position of the Jester, of a critical sceptic who undermines the official doctrines and Grand Narratives.

Kołakowski's thought developed from the orthodox Marxism of the 1950s, through the Marxist revisionism of the 1960s, and finally arrived at the critical inquiry of the totalitarian tendencies inherent in the ideology of Communism. The disclosure of the contradictions and blind spots of Marxism was fully expressed in his fundamental *Main Currents of Marxism*, from the 1970s. Kołakowski uncovered the quasi-religious elements in the messianic eagerness of Marxism. That quasi-religious ideology had its High Priests, its Guardians of the Purity, its heretics, eschatology and vision of salvation. Paradoxically, the uncovering of the quasi-religious elements in the Marxist doctrine led Kołakowski to the recognition of religion, in particular Christianity, as a remedy for the incurable deficiencies of human existence, for the discontents of Modernity. It was by no means an apologetic acceptance; his vision of Christianity and its significance was infringed by numerous doubts and critical thoughts. It is, however, apparent that Kołakowski the philosopher gradually moved from the position of Jester towards the role of the Priest. His book from 1982, *Modernity on Endless Trial*, became the turning point in that development. As Roger Scruton remarks:

In particular, he emphasized the great loss, as he saw it, which has ensued with the disappearance of the sacred from the worldview of Western intellectuals. "With the disappearance of the sacred," he wrote, "arises one of the most dangerous illusions of our civilization – the illusion that there are no limits to the changes that human life can undergo, that society is 'in principle' an endlessly flexible thing, and that to deny this flexibility and this perfectibility is to deny man's total autonomy and thus to deny man himself." (Scruton 2009)

And John Gray summarizes Kołakowski's significance in the following words:

> There are some philosophers for whom the only place for religion in philosophical inquiry is that of a bogey, a specter of irrationality that must be exposed and expelled so that philosophy can be an entirely secular discipline. As Kołakowski has argued, however, a good deal of secular thought has been shaped by Western religion. Exorcising religion is harder than it seems. Under the influence of the analytical movements of the last century, it has come to be widely accepted that questions that seem in principle unanswerable can scarcely be worth asking. Kołakowski represents a different view, the view of Pascal and Montaigne, which sees asking unanswerable questions as essential if we are to learn the limitations of human understanding. This is the modern tradition of skeptical fideism that Kołakowski continues today. ... in showing how philosophy and religion have been and should continue to be linked, Kołakowski's work is exemplary and indispensable. (Gray 2008)

This tradition of "skeptical fideism", represented by Kołakowski, was concordant with the other concepts of Open Catholicism and its partners in Poland. That explains why Kołakowski became a major intellectual mentor for generations of Polish intellectuals, as the many admiring articles after his death in 2009 have confirmed.

The specific style of thought that emerged amongst the Polish intelligentsia during the 1980s was thus highly influenced by the dialogue with Open Catholicism. The set of values inherent in that thought style was a fusion of liberal, emancipatory ideas such as personal freedom and responsibility, ideas of social commitment, a tendency to a dialogical, civic concept of national identity, with a conviction of the importance of a Christian, European legacy for the true Polish identity, and trust in absolute moral values preserved through tradition. The elite of the Polish intelligentsia – Czesław Miłosz, Leszek Kołakowski, Andrzej Wajda, Jozef Tischner, Krzysztof Kieślowski, Adam Michnik, and many others – defined themselves as adherents of the Open Catholicism formation; as modern, reflective believers, or at least sympathizers with vaguely/broadly defined Christian values.

On the eve of the emergence of an independent democratic Poland in 1989, it seemed that the progressive religious sources, together with the democratic values, would influence the new democracy. With Tadeusz Mazowiecki[7] as prime minister, and members of the lay Catholic faction in the first government, one could easily presume that the formation of the enlightened Catholicism would soon gain more and more adherents and would inform the direction of post-communist Polish transformation. With the growing public presence of the main protagonists of Open Catholicism, such as Józef Tischner, Jerzy Turowicz, Adam Boniecki and Leszek Kołakowski, now entering the public media, it was almost apparent that the formation of Open Catholicism had won the struggle for the modern Polish identity, for "the Polish soul". Polish intellectual elites, influenced by the modern outlook of Open Catholicism, full of respect for the Polish pope as the highest moral authority, launched the concept of universal Christian values as the foundations of culture, politics and mentality. The vision of authenticity, human agency and dignity, a communitarian collectivity (the ultimate idea of solidarity) would act as the remedy for the "dead", disarmed ideologies of both socialism and nationalism.

Open Catholicism in Decline in the Period of Transition

Twenty years on, the situation is radically different. The discourse of Open Catholicism has almost disappeared from the public scene. The dominant image of Polish Catholicism has become that of the soft hegemony. The vigorous intellectual discourse, pregnant with new ideas and reinterpretations, has been replaced by unreflective cultural religion. The insightful potential (power of renewal, religious impulse of reshaping mentality, essential for the debates of the 1970s) has diminished or become marginalized; the real and symbolic power of the Church has increased. Instead of productive debates about the limits of freedom, the importance of dialogue, on Christian responsibility for the world, on the Christian legacy in modern culture and thought, we encounter an endless fixation on sexual ethics (abortion, in vitro fertilization, homosexuality), and a ceremonial expression and consolidation of Polish-Catholic collective identity. The dialogical, open outlook has been replaced by the complex of the besieged fortress, governing the strategy and policy of the official Church. The politics of suspicion, exclusion and condemnation has substituted the previous policy of public education for democracy and freedom, exercised in the 1980s and early 1990s by Józef Tischner, Jacek Kuroń and Leszek Kołakowski, argues Tadeusz Bartoś, the voice of a new generation of dissident priests (Szostkiewicz 2007).

Such a radical shift raises a number of questions. It appears that certain elements of the transitional process have contributed towards the stagnation of the religious discourse. The Polish intellectuals contested, or tried to contest, the trend towards a growing hegemony of the Church, but they were not successful in their resistance. The vision of an all-embracing Open Church with *open channels (paths)* into democracy, emancipation, dialogue and freedom has eventually collapsed.

One of the crucial reasons lies apparently in the change of the strategy of the Church as an institution. As mentioned at the beginning of this chapter, the temptation of a triumphant and hegemonic position won the hearts of the Polish bishops in the early 1990s. They attempted to maintain their monopolistic position in a new, changing, post-communist reality. That reality, however, proved to be out of control: the diversity of ideas, attitudes, and discourses appearing in the post-communist Poland after 1989 transgressed the horizons of the traditional thought-forms. As Zdzisław Mach remarked:

> The pluralistic world, relativism and tolerance, acceptance of differences and readiness to establish different platforms of interaction with people and groups of different world-views, was for the Church a new world. It seemed easier to try and apply totalitarian methods, the old, familiar language of struggle rather than competition. Even some prominent members of the Church hierarchy were aware of that. ... The Church – the major agent of the anti-communist opposition, largely responsible for its destruction in Central Europe – found it difficult to accept the consequence of

the fall of communism, the birth of democracy and the development of open and pluralistic civil society, in which all institutions,
including the Church, must compete for influence. (Mach 2000)

The first traces of cracks in the Open Catholicism formation appeared
already in the early 1990s. A number of leading intellectuals, hitherto
sympathetic to the Church, began to express their caution and wor-
ries about the growing triumphalism of the Polish Catholic Church.
The most profound critical analyses were expressed in the books and
essays of Józef Tischner, the main protagonist of the Open Catholicism
formation. Tischner argued that the Polish Church in the 1990s was
no longer capable of coping with the realm of freedom, as the title of
his most famous book from that period explicitly indicates: *Nieszczęsny
dar wolności* (A hapless gift of freedom). The mentality of the besieged
fortress, the fear of the modern world, fearfulness in the face of a pluralistic society – all these blunders deteriorate the dialogical potential of
the Polish Church and draw Catholicism back into the authoritarian
position. The cardinal sin of the Church, according to Tischner, was
its "fundamental incapability to lead a meaningful dialogue" with the
challenging world and changing society (Tischner 1993).

The Catholic Church's attempts to monopolize the moral, ideological and political landscape in post-Communist Poland triggered
opposition among the lay intellectuals from the Open Catholicism
camp. Adam Michnik, Leszek Kołakowski, and Czesław Miłosz were
early in articulating their reservations about the hegemonic ambitions
discernible in the new strategy of the Church. They all expressed fore-
warnings against the prospects of a "theocratic state" in Poland, while
still acknowledging the indispensability of the Catholic framework in
the national identity of the Polish people. As Michnik put it, there
was still some hope: "the idea of dialogue between lay liberals and
Christianity about the democratic values is still worthy of concern."

The diversification of ideological discourses went on, however, and
resulted in the much more pluralistic intellectual and political public
scene in the late 1990s. After the "cold religious wars" about the abortion
law, the Concordat and Constitution of the 1990s, a variety of political
parties, ideological think tanks, NGOs, independent associations and
institutions emerged in the public sphere. The anti-totalitarian common
platform of ideas and dialogue, inclusive and all-embracing (religion,
ethics, philosophy, life-world, identity, social teaching), dominating

in the era of Open Catholicism has disseminated into the manifold small circles, groups, and individuals, each of them performing its own reinterpretation of the Christian legacy and Catholic values. On the other hand, the number of organizations and groups openly criticizing the Church and its alleged hegemony increased: "The New Left", feminists, dissident priests.

The centre of gravity in using religion for a political purpose moved however from the "liberals" to the political right. The right-wing intellectuals "kidnapped" the Catholic ideas and translated them into modern conservative politics. Magazines such as *Teologia Polityczna*, *Arcana*, *Fronda* and *Christianitas* gathered the Christian intellectuals who were attempting to establish a conservative political discourse by linking *homo politicus* with *homo religiosus*. Their political and cultural conservatism developed from both secular and religious inspirations: the teaching of John Paul II and St Thomas coexists with Roger Scruton, Carl Schmitt and Robert Weigel.

The scope of ideas produced and reclaimed by the conservatives is extremely wide: maintenance of the Christian legacy of Europe, the struggle against the nihilism of post-modern culture, defending family values and promoting pro-life attitudes, reclaiming the obsolete gentry-republican tradition as a possible ideal for modern Poland, the rehabilitation of the organic model for Polish nationalism, and so on (Nowak 2011). The real impact of these intellectuals is rather narrow: some of them were, however, included in the circle of advisors to the late Polish President, Lech Kaczynski. The popular conservatism is much more perceptible in broader, less refined Catholic media: *Radio Maryja* broadcasting, *Nasz Dziennik, Niedziela*.

There exists nevertheless a faction of "Open Catholics" in the Polish contemporary public sphere. Magazines like *Tygodnik Powszechny*, *Więź* and *Znak* still attempt to preserve an open attitude towards the modern world, to promote ecumenism and tolerance, to criticize the conservative stance of the official Church. New initiatives appear, such as the dynamic Center for Culture and Dialogue, led by the Jesuits in Kraków, or the new modern Catholic television channel Religia.pl., Paradoxically, those Catholic intellectuals who remain true followers of the Open Church spirit are no longer members of the official church. During the preceding years the most prominent clerical protagonists of the open attitude broke with the institutional Church. They formed a group of "dissidents"; still Catholics, but outside the official structures.

In books and articles they openly struggle against the "soft hegemony" and conservatism of the Episcopate. The titles of their recent books say a lot: Tadeusz Bartoś' "The End of the Absolute Truth" (*Koniec prawdy absolutnej*), Sławomir Obirek's "Religion: The Shelter or the Prison?" (*Religia: Schronienie czy wiezienie?*) and "The Liberated Mind: In Search of the Mature Catholicism" (*Umysł wyzwolony: W poszukiwaniu dojrzałego katolicyzmu*). The significance of that faction is nevertheless declining; the centre of intellectualized Catholicism has definitely shifted to the right.

Why the Experiment of Open Catholicism Failed – Conclusions

The essence of the Open Church experiment consisted in a historic alliance between the Polish liberal intelligentsia and the institution and teaching of the Catholic Church. The latest development (1990s and 2000s) bears nevertheless witness to the gradual dissolution of that alliance. There is no trace of the "power of renewal" so hopefully proclaimed by Casanova in his articles on the democratic potential of the Polish Church. From the current, more distant perspective one may attempt to identify the reasons and conditions for that dissolving.

Firstly, the Church's position as an institution changed dramatically on the eve of the democratic era. It is no longer the "Church of catacombs", acting as defender of the poor and weak, as a courageous, heroic opponent to the totalitarian regime. Its role has been normalized in the democratic Poland, and the Church has gradually achieved a soft-hegemonic status in the public sphere. In the new reality, the enemy was no longer the communist regime but the liberal order, secularization and other "diseases" of modernity. The liberal intellectuals could not be seen as partners in that new struggle; they were rather considered as opponents.

The Vatican context was significant as well: the Polish Pope, and then Benedict XIV, both the former "architects" behind the reform movement in the Catholic Church in the 1960s, have gradually abandoned the modernizing trends of the Second Vatican Council. The 1990s and 2000s bear witness to the Vatican's growing criticism, almost crusade, against the nihilism, materialism and immoralism of (post) modern Western civilization. This led to the strengthening of the conservative wing in the Polish clergy, and resulted in the gradual fading of the ideas of Open Catholicism. Its protagonists disappeared from the public scene (Tischner, Kołakowski, Miłosz, Turowicz died in the 2000s, Michnik being almost "mute"); a new generation of younger Catholic progressive intellectuals (Obirek, Bartoś, Węcławski) broke with the official Church.

The liberal intelligentsia, the former ally of Open Catholicism, has gradually realized that the alliance with the Church is no longer achievable and productive. That process was painful, the disillusion was traumatic. The intellectuals slowly became aware that, in their enthusiastic response to the Open Church in the 1970s and 1980s, they often mistook their own idealized image of Christianity for the reality of the (Polish) Church as an institution. It was clear now that the reinterpretation of Christianity undertaken in the 1970s and 1980s by the Polish intelligentsia never touched the average members of the clergy, neither the theologians nor the educational institutions within the Church. The Polish Church has always been traditional and con-servative as the whole. The image of the progressive religion, opening paths into dialogue, pluralism, and modern values, has turned out to be a delusion; a marginal faction of a few passionate priests and theo-logians who never won full recognition, neither in society nor among the high ranks of the Polish institutional Church.

That disillusion nevertheless occured rather slowly, and this can explain the soft criticism of the Church undertaken by the intelligentsia in the 1990s. In spite of the growing politicization and cultural and moral hegemony the Church gained in the period, the intellectuals' responses were rather moderate and still somewhat hopeful. They still conceived the development after 1989 through the lens of their image of Open Catholicism, and that contributed to their myopia. It was only in the 2000s that the intellectuals "opened their eyes" and realized that the other discourses – liberal, feminist, Left or socialist – are incompatible with the old-fashioned discourse of the official Church. As Zdzisław Mach summarizes in his already mentioned article:

> It became evident, even before the conflict over abortion law, that the Roman Catholic Church was not prepared to function in a democratic society which emerged from post-communist Eastern Europe. The Church – powerful, strictly centralised, and in its in-ternal organisation a very non-democratic institution – developed mechanisms of surviving and achieving success in a totalitarian

system. In particular, the Church was very skilled in mobilising people's energy and action in a centralised, authoritarian state, ideologically and politically polarised, in which all contributors to debate taking place in the public sphere used the symbolic discourse of black-and-white, polarised world, picturing opponents as enemies and accumulating categories of value-loaded classifications. (Mach 2000)

The geopolitical shift Poland has undergone during the past few decades constitutes the broadest context for the analysed processes. Under Communism, the "kidnapped Poland" and its elites identified their main enemy, significant other, as the East: the Communist Soviet Union. In this period the reformed Catholicism could serve as the common platform of resistance against totalitarian rule, and was able to unify the Church, intelligentsia, and "the people" (*naród*) against the monopolistic Communist Party. Thus, Catholicism represented the broken links to Western Europe, acted as the shield against radical Sovietization, as the guardian of human rights and of the continuity of the Polish Western legacy. The reinterpretation of Catholicism, accomplished by leading intellectuals and part of the clergy, and facilitated through a "constructed" image of an Open Church, contributed to a broad acceptance of the Catholic frame, even in the circles of Polish liberal elites that have traditionally been opposed to that institution. Catholicism became a symbolic link to the West, and seemed to embrace all the constructive values of democracy, pluralism, and open society.

After the reorientation of the geopolitical framework in 1989–1991, the East, as represented by the Soviet domination, gradually ceased to play the role of the "significant enemy" in Polish politics. Opening towards the West, the "return to Europe" contributed to a more sophisticated political map,[8] in which the image of the West became more multivalent, even ambiguous. The West was now conceived both a promise and a threat, as an ally in the democratization process but also a cradle of moral nihilism, or a source of homogenizing globalization. For some Poles the significant other moved from Moscow to Brussels, to the centre of Euro-bureaucracy, while for others the Vatican became the epitome of backwardness, especially after the death of John Paul II. The new task was now to redefine or reclaim Polish identity against a Western European, or simply European background: as partner or peripheral actor, as imitator or cohabitant.

In these new conditions, Polish Catholicism was no longer able to serve as the common frame for national identity. Differentiation of attitudes, multifaceted identities, and the polarization between various groups of interests made the existence of a unifying Catholic platform virtually impossible. The Church has managed to keep its position on the public scene as a significant agency, but is no longer an all-important actor. And the formation of the Open Church appears more and more as an illusory construction of a group of "seduced" intellectuals.

Notes

1 Beginning in October 1962, Bishop Wojtyła took part in the Second Vatican Council (1962–1965), where he made contributions to two of the most historic and influential products of the Council: the Decree on Religious Freedom (in Latin, Dignitatis Humanae) and the Pastoral Constitution on the Church in the Modern World (Gaudium et Spes).

2 Clubs of Catholic Intelligentsia (Kluby Inteligencji Katolickiej) were founded after Gomułka's Thaw (1956), evolving into a mild Catholic-centre opposition group in communist Poland. The Clubs were the only independent civil movements in the country, with no Party control and a relatively free position towards the official Church.

3 Christian personalism was developed in the twentieth century, in France, by the philosopher Emmanuel Mounier (1905–1950), who was the leading proponent of personalism, around which he founded the review L'Esprit. The Polish philosopher Karol Wojtyła (later Pope John Paul II) further developed the idea of personalism. In his work Love and Responsibility (1960, eng. ed. 1981) Wojtyła proposed what he termed "the personalistic norm": "This norm, in its negative aspect, states that the person is the kind of good which does not admit of use and cannot be treated as an object of use and as such the means to an end. In its positive form the personalistic norm confirms this: the person is a good towards which the only proper and adequate attitude is love."

4 The Workers' Defence Committee (Komitet Obrony Robotników, KOR) was a Polish civil society group, consisting mainly of prominent intellectuals and students, that emerged under communist rule to give aid to prisoners detained after labour strikes in 1976, and to their families. KOR was an example of successful organization related to specific issues relevant in the public's daily lives; a precursor and a source of inspiration to the Solidarity movement a few years later.

5 One of the founding members of the Committee was a Catholic priest, J. Zieja.

6 In his book Politics and Religion in Eastern Europe: Catholicism in Hungary, Poland and Czechoslovakia (1992), Patrick Michels compares the impact the local Churches had on the political transformations in Central Europe.

7 A Polish author, journalist, and Christian Democrat politician, one of the leaders of the Solidarity movement. He was one of the founding members of the Catholic Intelligentsia Club, which was established in 1957. In 1958, Mazowiecki established the monthly Więź and became its editor-in-chief. In 1989 he became

the first non-communist prime minister in Central and Eastern Europe after the Second World War.

8 "The collapse of the Soviet Bloc and gradual re-integration of Poland, and other countries of the region, into the Western system of institutions, political and economic space, made the West the main point of reference for political, academic and cultural debates. In effect, the attitude toward the West ... became the main factor defining the fundamental cleavage of Polish politics." (Zarycki 2011: 83)

References

Barker, Philip W. (2008): *Religious Nationalisms in Modern Europe. If God Be for Us,* London: Routledge.

Berger, Peter L. (2001): Reflections on the Sociology of Religion Today, *Sociology of Religion,* 62 (4): 443–454.

Beyer, Gerald J. (2007): A Theoretical Appreciation of the Ethics of Solidarity in Poland Twenty-five Years After, *Journal of Religious Ethics,* 35: 207–232.

Byrnes, Timothy A. (2002): The Challenge of Pluralism. The Catholic Church in Democratic Poland, in Ted G. Jelen and Clyde Wilcox (eds): *Religion and Politics in Comparative Perspective. The One, the Few, and the Many,* Cambridge: Cambridge University Press.

Casanova, José (1994): *Public Religions in the Modern World,* Chicago: University of Chicago Press.

Casanova, José (2003): Catholic Poland in Post-Christian Europe, *Tr@nsit online,* no. 25/2003.

Casanova, José (2004): Religion, European Secular Identities, and European Integration, http://www.eurozine.com/articles/2004-07-29-casanova-en.html (Accessed 7 June 2009).

Darczewska, Krystyna (1989): *Katolicyzm we współczesnym społeczeństwie polskim,* Warszawa: Ossolineum.

Demerath, Nicholas Jay (2003): *Crossing the Gods. World Religions and World Politics,* New Brunswick, NJ: Rutgers University Press.

Eberts, Mirella (1998): The Roman Catholic Church and Democracy in Poland, *Europe-Asia Studies,* 50(5).

Gowin, Jaroslaw (1995): *Kościół po komunizmie,* Kraków: Znak.

Gray, John (2008): A Rescue of Religion, *New York Review of Books,* 9 October, 2008.

Irwin-Zarecka, Iwona (1990): *Neutralizing Memory. The Jew in Contemporary Poland,* New Brunswick: Transaction Publishers.

Kołakowski, Leszek (2004): The Priest and the Yester, in Kołakowski, Leszek: *The Two Eyes of Spinoza,* Chicago: St. Augustine Press.

Kosela, Krzysztof (2003): *Polak/Katolik. Splątana tożsamość,* Warszawa: IFiS PAN.

Mach, Zdzisław (2000): *Polish National Culture and its Shifting Centres,* Centre for European Studies, Jagiellonian University, available at http://www.ces.uj.edu.pl/mach/national.htm (accessed 7 June 2009).

Mandes, Sławomir (2004): Formy religijności w społeczeństwie polskim, in Jasińska-Kania, Aleksandra and Marody, Mirosława (eds): *Polacy wśród Europejczyków,* Warszawa: Scholar.

Marody, Mirosława (2004): Przemiany religijności Polaków, in Jasińska-Kania, Aleksandra and Marody, Mirosława (eds): *Polacy wśród Europejczyków,* Warszawa: Scholar.

Martin, David (2006): Religia, świeckość, sekularyzm i integracja europejska, *Res Publica Nowa*, 1/2006.

Matynia, Elżbieta (2009): *Performative Democracy*, London: Paradigm Publishers.

Michel, Patrick (1992): *Politics and Religion in Eastern Europe. Catholicism in Hungary, Poland and Czechoslovakia*, Cambridge: Polity Press.

Michnik, Adam (1993): *The Church and the Left*, Chicago: University of Chicago Press (Polish original: *Kościół, lewica, dialog*, Warszawa, 1976).

Miłosz, Czesław (1984): *The Land of Ulro*, New York: Farrar, Straus, Giroux.

Nowak, Mattias (2011): The Polish Christian Right and the Idea of the West, in Barbara Törnquist-Plewa and Krzysztof Stala (eds): *Eastern Europe in Focus. Social and Cultural Transformation after Communism*, Lund: Nordic Academic Press.

Porter, Brian (2001): The Catholic Nation. Religion, Identity, and the Narratives of Polish History, *Slavic and East European Journal*, 45 (2): 289–99.

Ramet, Sabrina (1997): *Whose Democracy? Nationalism, Religion, and the Doctrine of Collective Rights in Post-1989 Eastern Europe*. Oxford: Rowman & Littlefield.

Scruton, Roger (2009): Leszek Kołakowski: Thinker for Our Time, *Open Democracy*, 29 July 2009, http://www.opendemocracy.net/article/leszek-Kołakowski-thinker-for-our-time-0.

Steinlauf, Michael C. (1997): *Bondage to the Dead. Poland and the Memory of the Holocaust*, Syracuse, New York: Syracuse University Press.

Szawiel, Tadeusz (2005): Społeczne podstawy konserwatyzmu w Polsce, *Europa*, 45 (6).

Szostkiewicz, Adam (2007): Głosy Kościoła, *Polityka*, 24.

Taylor, Charles (2000): Religion Today, *Transit online*, 19/2000.

Tischner, Józef (1984): *The Spirit of Solidarity* (Polish original 1981), San Francisco: Harper and Row.

Tischner, Józef (1993): Smugi cienia, czyli wiara religijna po komunizmie, *Tygodnik Powszechny*, 3 January 1993.

Tischner, Józef (2002): *Polski kształt dialogu*, Kraków: Znak.

Zarycki, Tomasz (2011): From Soviet to Western Oriented Political Scene. The Context of Evolution of the Images of Polish Political Mentalities in the Post-communist Period, in Barbara Törnquist-Plewa and Krzysztof Stala (eds): *Eastern Europe in Focus. Social and Cultural Transformation after Communism*, Lund: Nordic Academic Press.

RELIGIOUS STRATEGIES
IN A POST-1989 PERSPECTIVE

CHAPTER 8

Remembering the New Martyrs and Confessors of Russia

Karin Hyldal Christensen

The Russian Orthodox Church has become a strong symbol of traditional values in post-Soviet Russian society. Although the church has only limited political influence, it has successfully built a relationship with the state that allows it to advance its own agenda within Russian society and to propagate its values and ideals of human behaviour.[1]

This ideal is embodied in the saints. Veneration of saints was an integral part of pre-revolutionary Russian culture, and a popular form of this seems to have found its way back into mainstream culture and to extend beyond the relatively small circle of Orthodox Christians, who attend church services regularly, observe fasts, pray regularly and in general meet the recommendations of the Church as regards personal piety.[2] Icons of saints (particularly the patron saint of travellers, Saint Nicholas) hang in the windows of buses and cars to protect the driver and passengers, and lines of people wait in front of churches to kiss famous relics of saints. From the highest authority in the Church, the ideal of the saints is propagated as an inherited part of the national identity, which is, however, challenged by modern society. The patriarch of the Russian Orthodox Church, Kirill, said during a meeting with the Japanese ambassador in April 2011:

> For many centuries, Orthodoxy has formed the moral values of Russia's peoples. For many years the common ideal has been sanctity, and not success, wealth or creative talents .... Our country has been called Holy Rus' not because everybody in it was a saint, but because sanctity was the ideal and the purpose of life. This is why it is so important to protect the traditional moral values,

which the modern secularized society challenges on a daily basis (The communication service of the Department of Inter-Christian relations 2011).

The Church has not only propagated the "old" saints of the ancient Church and the Middle Ages. It has also activated the long-dormant tradition of making saints by canonizing almost two thousand so-called new martyrs and confessors of Russia who were subject to Soviet religious persecutions. By canonizing the new martyrs and confessors, and by propagating their saintly ideal, the Church inevitably takes part in the debate about Soviet repression.[3]

This chapter analyses the saintly ideal of the new martyrs and confessors and reflects on their significance in contemporary Russia. The first section of the chapter provides a brief history of canonizations in Russia. The second section analyses the saintly ideal of the new martyrs and confessors, as construed and propagated by the Church today. The ideal is exemplified and communicated by the Church through saints' lives (hagiographies), icons, frescoes, sermons, hymns, commemoration sites, architecture, autobiographies, films and more. It is not the intention of this chapter to analyse the communication of the saintly ideal through these art forms and activities, but to analyse it as it is formulated explicitly by leading figures in the Church today. The third section of the chapter discusses how the Russian Orthodox Church interprets the Soviet anti-religious persecutions and takes part in the memory debate about Soviet repression. The topic of Soviet repression has been largely ignored both in public debate and in the agenda of the post-Soviet Russian state. The Russian Orthodox Church is one of the few organizations in contemporary Russia dealing with the question at all.

A Brief History of Russian Canonizations of Saints

When Rus' was Christianized in 988, the newly established Church inherited a multitude of ancient saints and medieval Byzantine saints of various types: martyrs, confessors, blessed bishops, saintly princes, righteous monks and nuns, and "fools in Christ". The first Russian saints, the sufferers Boris and Gleb, were canonized in Kiev Rus' at the beginning of the eleventh century, only a few decades after the country was Christianized. In the beginning, most saints were canonized in single dioceses by the local bishop of the diocese, or even more locally at separate monasteries. In 1547–51 the Metropolitan Makariy organized a series of local church councils.[4] In one of these it was decided to canonize nine new saints and elevate a large number of local saints to national sainthood. During the local councils of 1547 and 1549 a total of 39 saints became national saints (Golubinskiy 1903: 107).

Throughout the history of the Russian Orthodox Church, the veneration of some saints has faded away; the saints have been forgotten, the only evidence of their existence remaining an equally forgotten and abandoned manuscript in a distant monastery. In other cases the veneration of saints has grown; lives of the saints have been copied and rewritten, and a steady stream of icons depicting the saints has been produced. Sometimes the veneration of a saint has grown as a grassroots movement, "from below", locally, and only after a long time the Church has canonized the saint. In other cases the veneration has been generated "from above", by the hierarchs of the Church, and then spread "downwards". Even when a saint had been canonized, there was no guarantee that the saint would actually be popularly venerated.

In the eighteenth century, canonizations of saints in the Russian Orthodox Church became rare. The patriarch Nikon's liturgical reforms from the 1650s had caused a schism in the Church as the "Old Believers" (*staroobryadtsy*, literally translated "Old Ritualists") fiercely objected to his reforms and in return were persecuted severely by the Church and the state.[5]

The schism weakened the Church and broke its authority. This circumstance allowed the emperor Peter the Great to restrict the power of the Church and, in effect, to subordinate the Church to the state. When the patriarch Adrian died in 1700, Peter hindered the election of another patriarch, and in 1721 he passed a Spiritual Regulation which abolished the Patriarchate altogether and replaced it with an institution called the Holy Synod. The leading authority of the Holy Synod was a lay official, a procurator, who was appointed directly by the emperor, and the supreme power of the Church was thus de facto in the hands of the state. The ideal of *symphonia*, a "symphonic" cooperation between Church and state where the state was occupied with the citizens' earthly needs and the Church took care of their spiritual needs, was superseded by a new order inspired by the Church regulations of Protestant countries. This new order did not encourage the canonization of saints.

Throughout the nineteenth century a new religious, and patriotic, consciousness revived the interest in the Russian saints of the past, and a larger number of saints were actually canonized towards the end of the century during the reign of Nicholas II (1896–1917). In the entire period of 175 years from the introduction of the Spiritual Regulation to the coronation of Nicholas II in 1896, only four canonizations were carried into effect, whereas seven saints were canonized during Nicolas's reign of twenty-one years (Semenko-Basin 2010: 21). However, the Church could not decide alone who to canonize. It was still the emperor who had the final word.

"The Reign of the Godless"

The incipient tendency to revive the practice of canonization was put to an end with the coming of the Russian Revolution. The February Revolution in 1917 initially granted more liberty to the Russian Orthodox Church; when Nicholas II abdicated on 15 March 1917, he ceased to be the head of the Church, and it was free to hold the first local church council in over two hundred years. The council had been planned in the Church since the beginning of the century, but was postponed again and again by the procurator (i.e. the emperor) due to the instability of the times. The position of the procurator, Konstantin Pobedonostsev, who was known to be very conservative, is well expressed in a letter he wrote in March 1905: "Today, our times are such that one should not undertake anything new. God give that we can preserve the old" (Orekhanov 2002: 67).

The first session of the local church council opened on 15 August 1917 and the last of the council's three sessions was closed on 20 September 1918. The most important decision of the council was to reinstall the Patriarchate, and already in 1917 the revered and well-respected metropolitan Tikhon was elected the first Russian patriarch since 1700. Many questions had accumulated during the period of 200 years since the last local church council was held, and the partipicants of the three sessions took many decisions and worked out guidelines for the future work of the Church. However, as the sessions went on in an increasingly gloomy atmosphere, it became clear that the Church had fallen out of the frying pan into the fire. On 31 October, while the council was in the midst of its first session, a report of a murdered priest reached the members of the council (Semenko-Basin 2010: 49), and it was followed by other reports. The persecutions during the civil war were chaotic and random, and most often no trial preceded the execution of a clergyman. The newly elected patriarch Tikhon described the conditions in an encyclical of 19 January 1918, criticizing the brutality of the Bolsheviks:

> Nobody feels safe. Everyone lives under the constant threat of search, robbery, eviction, arrest, execution. Hundreds of defenceless are grabbed, persecuted for months in prisons, sentenced to death, often without any investigation or trial. (Lobanov 2008: 239)

The founding conceptions of the new martyrs and confessors of Russia were outlined during the council of 1917–1918, seventy years before the canonization of the new martyrs was made possible. The first bishop to be killed by the Bolsheviks was the metropolitan of Kiev, Vladimir Bogoyavlenskiy. In March 1918, the council chose the date of his death, 25 January, as the commemoration date for all Orthodox victims of the persecutions. In 1992, when the first new martyrs were canonized, this date was to become the official commemoration date of the new martyrs and confessors of Russia (Semenko-Basin 2010: 49).

Soviet Man Replacing the Saints

In the Soviet Union, active cultural forgetting was an important part of the attempt to construct communism. Working in the field of cultural memory studies, the German Egyptologist Aleida Assmann underlines the importance of cultural forgetting. She differentiates between passive and active cultural forgetting. Whereas passive cultural forgetting is unintended – we often unwittingly hide, disperse or abandon things – active cultural forgetting implies actions of censuring, throwing out or destroying (Assmann 2008:100). Active cultural forgetting in the Soviet Union was brought into force on many different levels. The urban landscape changed: monuments to previous rulers, the tsars, were removed, and many signs of the religious past disappeared. Church buildings were torn down and monasteries were closed. Church property was confiscated, icons were destroyed, and church bells were melted down. Church literature was destroyed, and in 1929 a new resolution "On religious associations" made religious propaganda illegal (Zubov 2009: 78). The state actively supported schisms within the Church,

Archaeological excavations carried out on the Butovo Polygon in 1997 revealed that it was a place of execution and mass burial. The ground was filled with human bones, clothes, boots and bullets. Photo: The parish of the Butovo Polygon.

closed seminaries for educating priests and, most importantly, persecuted priests and laymen.

Members of the Church were not the only social group to be persecuted. Aleida Assmann expresses the viewpoint that acts of cultural forgetting may contribute constructively to healthy societal transformations if they are not directed against foreign cultures or persecuted minorities. It would hardly be an exaggeration to claim that, taken together, the persecutions of different demographic groups in Soviet society constitute an act of cultural forgetting directed at a persecuted majority of the population. A new human ideal of "Soviet Man" was introduced to replace the old ideal of the saint; atheistic propaganda was reinforced. Interestingly, only the most important part of worship was officially allowed namely the right to hold the service of the Liturgy and administer the Holy Communion.

In spite of intense efforts to eliminate religion, by the mid-1930s there were still many Orthodox believers in Russia. According to a Soviet census carried out in 1937, 56% of the population identified themselves as believers (Knox 2005: 5). New intensified persecutions of priests, bishops, monks and laymen were initiated in 1937–38 during Stalin's "Great Terror", when at least 700,000 Soviet citizens were killed (Nérard 2009: 3). According to statistics from the Governmental Commission on the Rehabilitation of Victims of Political Repressions, instituted by the Presidency of the Russian Federation, the state executed at least 85,300 priests in 1937, and 21,500 in 1938 (Zubov 2009: 964). During the Second World War (The Great Patriotic War as it is called in a Soviet or Russian context) the conditions of the Church improved, partly because the state now needed the Church to strengthen the morale of the Soviet population, and partly because the Germans reopened churches in the occupied territories and the Soviet government therefore was forced to do the same.

Although the persecutions were never again to reach the magnitude of the Great Terror, they continued after the Second World War. Under Khrushchev (1953–64), the repression was reinforced, but the methods were different and less violent. However, the aim of the anti-religious policy was clear: eliminate religion. As late as 1986, during the last Soviet atheistic campaign, initiated by Mikhail Gorbachev, a textbook on the atheistic education of school pupils stated that "atheist education must be initiated from the first grade regardless of the family the child is raised in, whether atheists or believers. It is necessary that the child gets a positive attitude to atheists and their activities from the very beginning of its school attendance, and that it gets a negative attitude to religion" (Rogova 1986: 3).

In 1986, the same year as the last atheistic campaign was launched, Mikhail Gorbachev introduced a much more successful initiative; namely, the reform programme which was to become known all over the world as *perestroika* (restructuring) and *glasnost* (openness). Glasnost finally made possible an open discussion of Soviet repression. Millions of Russians had family members who had been liquidated in the Soviet period, and there was an urge in society to talk about it (Bogumil 2010: 4). A human rights organization named the Memorial Society was founded during the period of perestroika as a community of local organizations in different regions of today's Russia, Ukraine, Kazakhstan, Latvia and Georgia. The organization describes its main task during the years of perestroika as "the awakening and preservation of the societal memory of the severe political persecutions in the recent past of the Soviet Union" (Memorial 2011). At the beginning of the 1990s the Memorial Society initiated both the construction of commemoration sites for the victims

Every year, the Russian Orthodox Church conducts a Liturgy in the open above the mass graves of the Butovo Polygon. Here, a bishop communicates the Eucharist during the Liturgy in May 2011. Photo: Karin Hyldal Christensen.

of political repression and an official remembrance day for them on 30 October. Today, the Memorial Society has extended its mandate to observe human rights in contemporary society – notably in the Northern Caucasus – and to protest against abuses.

In 1988, two years after the last atheistic campaign and the launching of perestroika and glasnost, the Church celebrated its Millennium Jubilee. This was a turning point for the Church, perhaps even more dramatic than the fall of the Soviet Union three years later. At the Jubilee even representatives of the state participated in the celebration. The Church founded a Synodal Commission on the Canonization of Saints of the Russian Orthodox Church (hereafter the Canonization Commission) in 1989; later the same year it canonized Patriarch Tikhon; and in 1992, one year after the collapse of the Soviet Union, it canonized the first new martyrs. Another five canonizations of new martyrs followed during the 1990s, but it wasn't until the new millennium that the canonizations became a mass phenomenon. At the Archbishop's Council in August 2000, the Church canonized as many as 1,097 saints, 860 of whom were new martyrs and confessors of the Soviet religious persecutions. At a lecture held at the council, the chairman of the Canonization Commission at that time, Metropolitan Yuvenaliy of Krutitsk and Kolomna, linked the canonization of the new martyrs and confessors and the work of the Local Church Council of 1917–18:

> Completing this canonization we continue the work of our brothers who gathered in the local church council in 1917–1918, and who, already then, started the churchly veneration of the martyrs, killed for their faith in Christ. (The Moscow Patriarchate 2001: 90)

The establishment of a Synodal Canonization Commission in 1989 was a novelty in the Russian Orthodox Church, though it was presented as a continuation of the work accomplished during the local council in 1917–18 and thereby legitimized as a structure rooted in the pre-Soviet history.

The Making of the New Martyrs and Confessors of Russia

What, then, is the work that contemporary theologians of the Russian Orthodox Church have continued? What is the saintly ideal that the Church propagates in Russia today and what are the criteria for canonization?

Saints – Imitators of Christ and Salt of the Earth

One of the important functions of saints is to be a role model for other Christians. The saints imitate Christ and are thus imitable themselves. According to Metropolitan Yuvenaliy, the new martyrs and confessors fill this purpose of being role models; in the lives of the new martyrs, "Orthodox Christians find an image of faith, an example of the sacrificial love to God and one's neighbour" (The Moscow Patriarchate 2001: 70). The secretary of the Canonization Commission, hegumen Damaskin (Orlovskiy),[6] describes the new martyrs and confessors as "the salt of the Gospel" (Damaskin 2009a), i.e. the salt of the earth, further described as "light" and given the commandment (Matthew 5:13–16) to "shine before men, that they may see your good works, and glorify your Father who is in heaven".

According to the Commission member and theology professor Archi-mandrite Iannuariy (Ivliev), God is the source of sanctity: "Everything else – people, things, actions, places, times – becomes holy only when God makes it His and thus sanctifies it" (Iannuariy 2011: 9). Express-ing the same understanding, Damaskin states that "when the Church celebrates the saints, it celebrates God's actions in the world" (Dam-askin 2009a). Sainthood is described by Iannuariy as closely connected with the conception of salvation. Salvation, he argues, is two-sided and depends on both God and humans (Iannuariy 2011: 14). This "joint effort" of God and humans in the pursuit of salvation is often referred to, in Orthodox theology, as *synergia*. In this understanding, all Christians are called to be saints and to be saved, and the saints are those who most fully realize this synergetic relationship with God, as reflected both in their inner life and in their actions. Damaskin argues that "the Holy Spirit may live in a human being, if the human being has provided space for It; has purified himself from the passions of the body and the soul; and if his soul, with all its passions, sins and pride, sets itself aside" (Damaskin 2009a). What the Church canonizes in its saints, he continues, is their dislike of glory, wealth and earthly ameni-ties. The ideal of the saint is an ideal of humility:

> The ideal of the saint, whether he be canonized as a righteous or as a martyr, is a self-belittling of the holy person, a self-abasement and a self-annulment, which contemporary man most often does not agree with, because he loves and values his "I" more than anything else. (Damaskin 2009a)

There are very few examples of martyrs in earlier Russian Church history. The two Varangians John and Fyodor, who were killed while working as missionaries in Russia before the Christianization of the country, were the first martyrs of the Russian Orthodox Church (however, they were canonized after the first Russian saints, the sufferers Boris and Gleb). Apart from them, only a few persons who were killed during the Mongol occupation have been canonized as martyrs: Mikhail Chernigovskiy († 1246), his boyar[7] Fedor (†1246) (Golubinskiy 1903: 62), and Merkuriy Smolenskiy († 1238) (Malakhova 2010: 375). However, as is made clear from Damaskin's phrase – "whether he be canonized as a righteous or as a martyr" – the virtues of martyrs and other types of saints are considered to be similar, regardless of whether the saint is an ascetic, a confessor or

To mark the seventieth anniversary of Stalin's Great Terror, Vladimir Putin surprisingly visited the Butovo Polygon on 30 October 2007 together with patriarch Aleksiy II. The priest of the Butovo parish, father Kirill Kaleda, shows them the territory. Kirill Kaleda's own grandfather was among the victims. Photo: The parish of the Butovo Polygon.

a martyr. According to Damaskin, "one of the most important criteria is the piety of the person, his pursuit of a complete fulfilment of Christ's commands" (Demidov 2010: 2). Just as the saintly ideal is similar for all types of saints, Damaskin believes that the ideal does not change with time (Demidov 2010: 4). The world – the spirit of the time – may change, but the saintly ideal is to remain the same. But still, the "time-less" saintly ideal of humility, self-abasement, self-sacrifice, purity and mercifulness needs to be exemplified and personalized for it to fulfil the purpose of being imitable.

Investigating the Lives of the Saints – Principles and Criteria for Canonization

The investigation carried out by the Canonization Commission was initiated both by inquiries "from below" – from the "people of the Church" (*tserkovny narod*) – and by inquiries from the Synod or the patriarch. The Canonization Commission itself has no mandate to canonize a saint (Maksimov 2008).

Hagiography[8] serves a double purpose. Besides communicating the saintly ideal, it serves as a "justifying document". Today, as in ancient times, a hagiography has to be written before the canonization (Golubinskiy 1903: 41). Lenhoff defines a *vita* – a hagiography – as "an account of events in the life of a person who imitates the example of Christ to a degree regarded as in some way exceptional. The events of the subject's real life are selected and combined so as to demonstrate that he or she is worthy of veneration" (Lenhoff 1989: 27). Lenhoff thus defines hagiography as a kind of apology for canonizing a particular saint. The compiler – the hagiographer – wishes to see "his" saint canonized, and writes the hagiography as a praise of that person to convince the Church authorities of the qualifications of the saint. In the case of the new martyrs and confessors the procedure is often different, because the hagiographies of the new martyrs may have been written not by a propagator for a particular saint but rather by an investigator who has no particular interest in one saint rather than another.

The most active investigator of potential saints' lives, and by far the most productive compiler of hagiographies in post-Soviet Russia, is the previously introduced member of the Canonization Commission, hegumen Damaskin (Orlovskiy), who became secretary of the Commission in July 2011. His methods of investigation have influenced the approach of the Church to the investigation process since the fall of the Soviet Union. As early as the 1970s he led a working group which secretly collected oral testimonies from witnesses to the lives of the potential saints (Foundation 2010). In 1997, with the blessing of Patriarch Aleksiy II, Abbot Damaskin formed the "Regional Public Foundation in Memory of the New Martyrs and Confessors of Russia" (hereafter the Foundation of the New Martyrs).

The Foundation of the New Martyrs has published hundreds of hagiographies – most of them compiled by Abbot Damaskin – which are also available on the Foundation's website: fond.ru. Damaskin became

The official icon of the Assembly of the New Martyrs of Butovo. The wooden church, the cross and the graves are clear features on the icon.

a member of the Canonization Commission in the late 1990s, and the Foundation of the New Martyrs is therefore closely connected with the Canonization Commission. Hegumen Damaskin divides his investigative work into two periods: before 1991 and after. Prior to 1991 he and his assistants were occupied with finding witnesses and receiving their testimonies. He describes this work as having been difficult, but he believes that "the Lord Himself showed us His servants, those He thought necessary, He Himself spoke in their hearts, so that they could talk about the shrines kept in their memory" (Anon 2011a: 16). After 1991, the national and regional archives were opened for investigation, and, as described on the website of the Foundation of the New Martyrs, "the trustworthiness of the facts given in the oral testimonies was verified through an examination of the archive sources"[9] (Foundation 2010).

Damaskin describes his methods as source-critical and historical, requiring objectivity of the researcher. The investigator, he believes, must consider all the information available to him about the actions of the saint *in spe*. Canonizing a person unworthy of canonization based on an unjustified personal – or political – wish to have him canonized is considered a sin that will harm the Church and delude the people. Current investigation consists almost entirely of archive work:

> If we talk about the collection of oral testimonies, then it has stopped for the present, because those who carried the memory have almost all left for the other world, and today we encounter myths and legends which reflect contemporary people's impression of the past rather than trustworthy facts. (Anon 2011a: 16)

Elsewhere, he writes that oral testimonies have to be verified, because the witnesses, whether by mistake or intention, may make mythical images of the potential saint, and these may conform only to their own subjective conceptions of what a saint is. Moreover, the remembered events often happened many years earlier, and the memories may therefore be distorted (Damaskin 2009b: 24). In the opinion of Damaskin, just as the saintly ideal is considered to be unchangeable, the "criteria for canonization are themselves unchanging" (Demidov 2010: 2). However, the lives of the saints are still exemplified differently in different historical periods. The living circumstances of saints in early Christianity were quite different from those of the twentieth century's saints.

The persecutions of the ancient Church, he argues, were not as consistent as the persecutions of the Russian Orthodox Church in the Soviet period. In the Roman Empire there were peaceful periods in between the brief periods of persecution, whereas in the Soviet Union the persecutions went on during the entire Soviet period of about seventy years. Damaskin divides the Soviet persecutions into two main periods: that "of martyrdom, which started in 1918 and went on until 1939, and the following period of the Confessors" (Damaskin 2010: 8).[10] Moreover, the persecutions were not necessarily equally harsh in all parts of the Roman Empire at the same time. Christians could flee to remote places in the empire untouched by persecutions. In the Soviet Union, by contrast, there was nowhere to flee: "The persecutions were all-pervasive, incessant, and there was no place in the country where a

Christian could hide" (Damaskin 2010: 2). The Roman Empire openly considered Christianity to be a threat to the state. The Soviet Union officially proclaimed freedom of conscience and therefore had to find other official charges than religious affiliation. The most commonly used one was "anti-Soviet propaganda".

This means that the situation of the new martyrs differed notably from that of the "classical" martyrs, whose lives could be spared if they renounced their faith. Metropolitan Yuvenaliy discussed this condition during a lecture in 1995. Whereas in the Roman Empire the renunciation of the faith could spare the life of the apostate, he argues, the new martyrs hardly had any such possibility:

> The Russian new martyrs normally had no such clear, classical choice. They were killed without trial, and when they were actually condemned to death by a court, most of the time the accusations directed against them were not directly related to their confession of Christ. During the mass persecutions of the 1930s even the renunciation of the Christian faith made by a bishop, a priest or a layman would hardly have spared the victim from repression or execution. Therefore, it would be wrong to consider all those who were killed, priests as well as laymen, martyrs solely because they were murdered. It is necessary for the canonization to carry out a serious investigation of the circumstances of the death and the life of the victims. (The Russian Orthodox Church's Commission on the Canonization of Saints 1999: 172)

A "serious investigation" means that various archive files from different periods are studied and compared. In many cases a person was arrested several times and acted throughout all interrogations in a manner to be expected from a saint, except on the last interrogation: "It happened that those who resisted the persecutions in the 1920s fell in the 1930s, and those who stood out through both of these periods acted in a cowardly way in the 1940s" (Damaskin 2009a). According to Damaskin, this is often not evident from the files themselves, but may be deduced from the fact that a group of believers was arrested and only one person in the group was released. The only way this could be possible was if the person agreed to become an informer and make false accusations about the fellow arrestees. This, however, did not prevent the communists from arresting and shooting this person later, but it should, argues

Damaskin, inhibit the Church from canonizing him. Therefore, "the fact of violent death doesn't play any defining role, but it is important what life – a Christian or an anti-Christian life – the person lived" (Damaskin 2009b: 18). Since the fact of violent death is not sufficient for a person to become a martyr, and since it is a complicated process to analyse the chain of actions in any life, Damaskin believes that it is important to clarify the religious-moral motivation of the person; the "inner condition" of his soul, his "life position" (Damaskin 2009b: 17).

To become a martyr, the person had to act irreproachably during the interrogation. He shouldn't inform against others nor make false testimonies about others or himself. The former secretary of the Commission (until July 2011), the priest Maksim Maksimov, describes the qualities of the new martyrs' actions during their imprisonment in an interview in *Komsomolskaya Pravda*, 14 January 2011:

> When they imprisoned you with criminals, when they starved you, beat you and demanded unclear things of you, and your Christian conscience was not shaded: You hadn't denounced God, you hadn't made false testimonies (Mat 19:18) about your neighbour or people unknown to you. This is the deed of the new martyrs: that they didn't break. (Ovchinnikov 2011)

Maksim Maksimov listed the main formal criteria for canonizing saints in a lecture about the activity of the Commission in 2003: "A righteous life, immaculate Orthodoxy, popular veneration, miracles, and, if they exist, incorruptible relics" (Maksimov 2003). However, it is questionable whether all of the criteria are in fact applied. In the contemporary canonization practice of the Russian Orthodox Church, a "righteous life" and "immaculate Orthodoxy" seem to be favoured over the others. Firstly, the existence of miracles, performed by the saints in their lifetime or at their graves, is not obligatory when the saints are martyrs. In the interview quoted above, Maksimov himself points out that "miracles are not necessary criteria for canonizing a martyr" (Ovchinnikov 2011). Secondly, there has never been a strict demand in the Russian Orthodox Church that the relics must be incorruptible (Greene 2010: 20) and, concerning the new martyrs, their earthly remains are often buried either in unknown places or in mass graves. Thirdly, martyrs little known to the public have been canonized in many cases, and the initiative to canonize specific new martyrs has often come from the Synod or the patriarch, and not as a result of popular veneration (Maksimov 2003).

The Commission on Canonization Challenged from both Inside and Outside

Today, the Canonization Commission is challenged both from the outside and the inside. The most serious challenge coming from the outside is that the archives, opened to the Church after the fall of the Soviet Union, are less accessible than they were just a few years ago. Patriarch Kirill treats this as a serious problem in his speech at the Archbishops' Council in January 2011: "In the past years state organs have passed new laws that hinder the research in the archives into the new martyrs." This means in reality that the canonization process of more new martyrs has stopped. He continues:

> Only a full insight into the material of the archives may clarify whether he was an informant, whether he witnessed falsely against himself or his neighbour. Without a clarification of these questions it is impossible to decide a canonization, which cannot be carried through solely on the basis of the violent execution performed by the godless persecutors. (The information service of the Archbishops' Council 2011)

From the inside, the work of the Canonization Commission is (perhaps increasingly?) challenged by representatives of the people of the Church. The Patriarch noted this challenge during the Council:

> One of the ills of our time is the increase in the veneration of persons who cannot be canonized. Such persons have their hagiographies and akathists[11] written, and signatures in favour of a canonization are collected. The misled people ask: "Why is this person not canonized?" Some have misunderstood the canonizations of recent years as "posthumous rewards for their labour". (The information service of the Archbishops' Council 2011)

A famous example of this is an old dispute about the canonization of the soldier Evgeniy Rodionov, who was killed in Chechnya in 1996 because he allegedly refused to take off his cross and convert to Islam, even though it could have saved his life (Bodin 2009: 135). In this respect, his story is more that of a "classical" martyr than is the story of the new martyrs. The dispute blazed up again in January 2011, after the earlier mentioned interview with the former secretary of the Canonization Commission, Maksim Maksimov, in *Komsomolskaya Pravda*. Maksimov stated that Evgeniy Rodionov could not be canonized because there was a lack of documentation about the circumstances of his death and no trustworthy oral testimonies. Those who agitated for the canonization of Rodionov were misled. This comment provoked, among others, the right-wing journalist Viktor Saulkin, who represents the movement "Russkaya Narodnaya Liniya" (The Russian People's Line). When he was interviewed on the Orthodox radio station Radonezh a few days later, he expressed the viewpoint that Maksim Maksimov did not respect public veneration. The election of a new secretary of the Commission may have been a consequence of the controversy.

It is not only right-wing extremists who see a martyr in Evgeniy Rodionov. The popular preacher and head of the Synodal Department for Cooperation with the Armed Forces and Law Enforcement Agencies, Father Dmitriy Smirnov, has led several requiems for Evgeniy Rodionov on his commemoration date, 23 May (he was killed on his nineteenth birthday). Smirnov believes that Evgeniy Rodionov will be canonized eventually, although it may be in a remote future. In an interview from 2004 he stated: "I believe and confess that Evgeniy Rodionov committed an act which is fully worthy of canonization. And that's it! I hold on to that! ... But a canonization, that is something else. It could be in 600 years! Dmitriy Ivanovich Donskoy[12] was canonized after 600 years" (Arendarenko 2004). It became clear during the debate about the statements of Maksim Maksimov in *Komsomolskaya Pravda* that Dmitriy Smirnov still believes Evgeniy Rodionov will be canonized in the future (Krayniy 2011).

For many people, not least Russian soldiers, the veneration of Evgeniy Rodionov is appealing because young soldiers can relate to him as "one of us", and their mothers can identify with his mother's sorrow. Rodionov lived even closer to our time than did the new martyrs, and the Russian soldiers today can easily imagine that they could be captured by Chechen rebels in a similar way. How would they react? Moreover, the persecutor is well-defined as the "other". The young Russian soldier Evgeniy was killed by Chechens, a traditional "enemy" of Russians, which makes a clear division between "us" and "them" easy to maintain. As we will see in the last section of this chapter, the interpretation of the Soviet persecutions is more ambiguous. The veneration of Evgeniy Rodionov has clear political, nationalistic undertones, and an eventual canonization could have troublesome implications for the Russian Orthodox Church. Even if the Canonization Commission found evidence that Rodionov was truly a martyr and decided to recommend canonization, it would still be highly controversial to do so and could create tensions between the Russian Orthodox Church and representatives of the large Muslim minority in Russia.[13] This might partly explain why the popular veneration of Evgeniy Rodionov has not so far served as an argument for his canonization.

An example of an equally controversial canonization proposal, which ended with an actual canonization concerns the last emperor, Nicholas II and his family, who were canonized in 2000 together with the Assembly of New Martyrs and Confessors. The most persistent advocates for the canonization belonged to the same group of Orthodox nationalists who promote the canonization of Evgeniy Rodionov. They published unofficial hagiographies and akathists praising the imperial family as martyrs, and circulated mass-produced icons of the family even before the canonization, which is against the canon of the Orthodox Church. After hefty debates both in the Russian Orthodox Church and in Russian society as a whole, the members of the imperial family were canonized – not as martyrs killed for Christ, but as "sufferers" (*strastoterptsy*) killed *in* Christ, i.e. in a Christ-like manner like the first Russian saints Boris and Gleb, meekly and forgivingly accepting their bitter fate, as it were. Nevertheless, the members of the imperial family continue to be commonly venerated as martyrs.

There were strong opponents to a canonization of the imperial family among leading hierarchs of the Church and in Russian society as a whole, and the canonization of Nicholas II and his family might have been to a high degree on the grounds of Church policy, as it was a necessary condition for the reunion of the Russian Orthodox Church with the Russian Orthodox Church Abroad which was finally carried through in 2007.[14] Today, the Church still demonstrates an ambiguous attitude towards the saintly status of the imperial family. On the one hand, it is depicted centrally on the icon of the new martyrs and confessors revealed to the world during the Archbishops' Jubilee Council in 2000. On the other hand, an official hagiography has yet to be written about the lives of the imperial family. As "sufferers", their hagiography is not included in the *cheti miney* of the new martyrs and confessors of Russia – the collection of hagiographies organized by the month and published by the Foundation of the New Martyrs.

The ideal of the new martyrs and confessors of Russia does not appear to be particularly deeply rooted in post-Soviet Russian society. According to Irina Papkova, the secular media in Russia have paid little attention to the new martyrs and confessors of Russia. Therefore, they are mostly unknown to broader society (Papkova 2008: 68). Kathy Rousselet's field-work at Butovo Polygon[15] did not convince her that a large-scale pilgrimage culture had been established yet (Rousselet 2007: 55). But this does not mean that the phenomenon is insignificant. The new martyrs and confessors play a crucial role in the self-perception of the Russian Orthodox Church today. As formulated by Bodin, suffering and the thought of suffering have become a significant part of Orthodox identity in today's Russia (Bodin 2007: 231). The number of hagiographies, icons, hymns and biographies that have been produced is immense, and the popular veneration of the new martyrs that does exist is strongly supported by the leadership of the Church.

"For Our Sins" – Memory Actors of the Soviet Repression

By agitating for the new martyrs and confessors, the Russian Orthodox Church offers its own interpretation of Soviet repression. The Church deals implicitly with Soviet repression whilst bringing forth the ideal of the new martyrs and confessors and venerating them at its publicly accessible religious commemoration sites. Thereby the Church inevitably participates in the post-Soviet debate about the totalitarian past.

According to Veronika Dorman, the efforts to establish a memory of the Gulag past culminated during perestroika and glasnost and continued in the 1990s. But from the middle of the 1990s, what she calls the "memorial enthusiasm" had already started to fade away. Today, in her view, only a small group of people are occupied with restoring the memory of the repression, either relatives of the repressed or "memory experts" (Dorman 2010: 328). Suzanna Bogumil refers to the "memorial enthusiasm" of the late perestroika days in terms of a Bakhtinian carnival of the Gulag memory. It lived a short life of freedom by its own rules and then died out; unlike the medieval carnivals treated by Bakhtin, however, it didn't acquire any cyclical character but happened only once. Bogumil ascribes the loss of interest in the Gulag to the social and economic problems of the early 1990s, which supplanted the need for engaging in the memory of a terrifying past. The present was bad enough as it was, and surviving in the present became the first priority.

With the fall of the Soviet Union, the system responsible for the persecutions no longer existed. Formally, the Russian Federation was the successor of the Soviet Union, but it may be discussed whether the new federation was responsible for the persecutions carried out by the Soviet state. With the fall of the Soviet Union, Russia was thrown into a veritable national identity crisis. In the words of the Danish historian Hans Bagger, the Russians now asked themselves: "If we are not Soviet people anymore, what are we?" (Bagger 2008: 185). There was a general "longing for history" (*toska po istorii*), for pre-Soviet history, that is (Bagger 2007: 110); an appetite for reopening the pages of history that were forcefully forgotten in the Soviet system. But other pages of the more recent history were thereby forgotten. People were tired of the Soviet reality, and in particular the darker chapters of its history. The Gulag was not spoken of anymore. Persistent activists of the Memorial Society had become irritating reminders of the Soviet past. In the opinion of Alexander Etkind, Russian society has not yet come to terms with the history of the Soviet repression. The lack of attention towards the Soviet Terror creates a kind of post-Soviet "hauntology", where society is "haunted by the unburied past" (Etkind 2009:182).

The Church represents, in Bogumil's phrase, one of the "persecution discourses" of the Soviet repression in Russia today, whereas the other main persecution discourse, she believes, is articulated by the Memorial Society. Likewise, Dorman identifies two categories of Gulag activists: secular and religious. Rousselet refers to the driving force behind the efforts of these activists as a commemorative and a religious logic. In my opinion, a third logic, a "political logic", is represented by the state (of course, the secular and religious activists do not lack a political logic, either). I identify three main actors in the commemoration of the Gulag: human rights organizations like the Memorial Society, the Russian Orthodox Church,[16] and the Russian state. Each of these participants has its own agenda, or "persecution discourse". Roughly speaking, the human rights organizations – often consisting of relatives of the repressed – wish to assign responsibility; the Church wishes to strengthen the veneration of the new martyrs while the state aims to do as little as possible but is nevertheless obliged to commemorate the repression in some situations. Sometimes these parties interact with each other as allies, sometimes as antagonists.

The Butovo Polygon – the shooting range at Butovo – where the Soviet state executed 20,760 people in 1937–38, has in a way come to serve as a stage for the commemoration of Soviet repression, where the three actors – the Memorial Society, the Church and the state – perform the memory of the Soviet repression. In the following, let us first analyse how the commemoration site and former shooting range of Butovo is used by the Church as a space of veneration. Then we will see how the Butovo Polygon has come to function as a stage or perhaps even a kind of battlefield for the memory of Soviet repression.

Commemoration Sites as Local Places for Veneration

The veneration of the new martyrs and confessors is closely connected with specific places. Although most of the new martyrs have been canonized nationwide, they mainly appear to be venerated on a local basis. For example, the parish of the Church of the Nativity of the Theotokos (Mother of God) in the Moscow suburb of Krylatskoe, where the priest-martyr Zosima Pepenin (locally referred to as Zosima Krilatskiy) used to serve as a priest, celebrates him on his yearly commemoration date and has an icon depicting him in the church (The Church of the Nativity of the Theotokos 2012). In the village of Pezhma, the new martyr Apollinariya is considered to be a patroness of the restoration of the Transfiguration Church, in which she used to be an active parishioner (Mordasheva 2011: 34). The convent of John the Baptist in Moscow venerates the priest-martyr Aleksey Skorbtsov, a deacon for twenty years and a priest for ten in the convent (Golovkova 2005: 77ff.). The monastery in Optina Pustyn' has published a collection of hagiographies of "their" new martyrs (Optina Monastery & Damaskin 2008).

Another example of the local veneration of new martyrs and confessors is the veneration of the new martyrs in the Butyrskaya prison. Many of them were inmates there in the 1930s. They were imprisoned, interrogated, maybe tortured, and then either released, sent to a Gulag camp or executed. The prison is still a functioning prison and one of the prison chaplains, Father Konstantin Kobelev, explains in an interview published in the Moscow Patriarchate's journal for prison ministry, *Mir vsem* (Peace to all), how at least 216 former inmates have been canonized as new martyrs. Among them are several bishops. So far,

75 icons of these local new martyrs embellish the walls of the prison church (Anon 2011b: 4–5).

A few commemoration sites of the new martyrs have become national symbols of the anti-religious persecutions as well as Soviet repression in general. According to Dorman, the Transfiguration monastery in the Solovki archipelago is the main symbol of the Gulag. Founded in the fifteenth century, it was used as a Gulag camp from 1923 to 1939 and partially given back to the Church in 1990. Dorman believes that Butovo Polygon is gradually gaining significance as the second "Russian Golgotha" in Russia today (Dorman 2010: 330).

The Butovo Polygon was established as a commemoration site on the basis of documents which were taken from an old political archive. In 1991, a former prisoner of the Kolyma Gulag camp in the Russian Far East, Mikhail Mindlin, obtained a collection of documents from the local KGB archive in the Moscow area. They were "shooting books"; transcripts from the execution protocols containing the names of 20,760 victims all shot at the same execution site between August 1937 and October 1938. To hand over such documents was not the usual procedure for the KGB, but it was possible thanks to the personal goodwill of the local head of department in the KGB (Demina 2011: 27). In 1992, the location of the execution site was discovered; it was the Butovo Polygon in a southern suburb of Moscow (Rousselet 2007: 57). Archaeological excavations carried out in 1997 confirmed that the Butovo Polygon was a mass burial site. Thanks to the "shooting books", it was possible to identify the victims, unlike those shot at similar places all over Russia in 1937–38, whose names are either lost or still hide in the depth of secret archives.

The mass terror of 1937–38 caused practical problems for the NKVD. It was difficult to get rid of the bodies of inmates shot in the prisons, and therefore the Butovo Polygon started to serve as a combination of execution site and mass grave. It was remote enough from Moscow not to attract too much attention and close enough not to cause logistical problems. People in the nearby village of Butovo possibly heard the screams and wondered why so many delivery vans with the sign "Bread" on them entered the deserted shooting range, but the neighbours were most likely too afraid to ask any questions. In reality, the delivery vans contained prisoners who were taken from their cells to the Butovo Polygon for execution. On each prisoner the NKVD officers received a file dossier with a photograph. The photograph served to identify the victim and to make sure that the right person was shot. Years later, when the Church started investigating the files, the photographs were found in them and some were then used by icon painters to create the image of the saint. The shootings did not stop in October 1938, but no lists establishing the identities of victims shot from 1939 until Stalin's death in 1953 have been found in any archives, and therefore the total number of people executed at the shooting range remains unknown (Rousselet 2007:56; Golovkova 2007: 59ff.).

When a handful of victims' relatives first gained access to the Butovo Polygon in 1993, the area was covered with giant hogweeds and in the years to come underwent a transformation. A continual fight was waged with the weeds, and commemorative signs were gradually put in place. In 1993, a memory plaque was placed there on the initiative of the Memorial Society; in 1994, a wooden cross was erected on the shooting site on the initiative of the director of the Saint Tikhon University of Humanities, Vladimir Vorob'ev, and in 1996, a small wooden church, named after the new martyrs, was built there. Eleven years later, in 2007, a large stone church was consecrated next to the shooting ground, also named after the new martyrs. The priest in charge of the parish, Father Kirill Kaleda, has been a driving force in the growth of the parish since the 1990s, he himself being a grandson of a canonized new martyr buried in the mass graves of Butovo, Vladimir Ambartsumov (1892–1937) (Kaleda 2007: 131).

Up until the present day, the Russian Orthodox Church has canonizd 330 new martyrs from the Butovo Polygon. Butovo has been highly prioritized by the Church authorities since the canonization of the Assembly of the new martyrs and confessors in 2000. Each year from 2000 until his death in 2008, Patriarch Aleksiy II conducted an outdoor liturgy on Butovo Polygon along with several bishops, hundreds of priests and a couple of thousand churchgoers on the commemoration date of the new martyrs of Butovo, the fourth Saturday after Easter. Patriarch Kirill has continued this tradition since his enthronement in 2009. In 2002, members of the parish church in Butovo founded the Memorial Centre "Butovo", with the aim of establishing a memorial complex for all the victims buried in the mass graves and providing groups of relatives, pilgrims and other visitors from Russia and abroad with information about the victims.

Many of the commemoration sites of the new martyrs are connected to one another. For example, several new martyrs were imprisoned in the Butyrskaya prison and later shot at the Butovo Polygon. They are now venerated in both places. Others were kept in the Solovetsk Gulag camp and later shot in Butovo. A current project of the Memorial Centre "Butovo" tries to establish connections between Butovo and parishes of the churches where the new martyrs of Butovo served, in order to increase the knowledge about the new martyrs and create a network of interrelated places of veneration.

Commemoration Sites as Battlefields for the Memory of Soviet Repression

An important fact concerning the Butovo Polygon is that it is owned by the Russian Orthodox Church. While it seemed "natural" that the territory of the Solovetsk monastery was – at least partly – given back to the Church after the fall of the Soviet Union, it was more accidental that Butovo Polygon was to become an "Orthodox place". The special interest of the Russian Orthodox Church in the Butovo Polygon is due to the high proportion of clergymen among the victims executed there. One of the volunteers who helped to preserve and catalogue the "shooting books" at the beginning of the 1990s, Kseniya Lyubimova, discovered that a large number of priests and bishops were among the victims, and she made a separate list of this specific group and handed it to Patriarch Aleksey II (Demina 2011: 29).

Although the Butovo Polygon is owned and administered by the Church, its significance is not only religious. Butovo is at the same time a shrine for the veneration of new martyrs and a commemoration site for all victims of the Soviet repression. Rousselet has studied the double function of the Butovo Polygon and has come to the conclusion that the coexistence of the two functions sometimes becomes a source of conflict between the commemorative and religious logic. The presence of the Russian Orthodox Church in Butovo is accompanied by a religious valorization of the place and may cause offence to those for whom the commemoration is secular.

Almost all the commemoration signs at Butovo are indeed of a religious – Orthodox Christian – character, apart from the previously mentioned commemoration stone raised by the Memorial Society in 1993, and a stone commemorating Korean victims, likewise raised at the beginning of the 1990s. A problem with this course is that although baptized Orthodox Christians represent the majority of the victims

buried in the mass graves of the Butovo Polygon, there are representatives of other religions and confessions too: Jews, Muslims, Buddhists,
as well as Roman Catholics and Protestants, not to mention atheists.
Victims of over sixty different nationalities are buried in the soil of
Butovo. Some would have preferred the Butovo Polygon to be exclusively a non-denominational cemetery. Others would have preferred the
commemoration site to "fully respect the plurality of opinions and the
confessions of the victims" (Rousselet 2007: 67).

The parish does, as a matter of fact, make a point of commemorating all the victims in a non-religious way. The memorial complex
aims to be a non-religious memorial for all victims alike. But the
parish also commemorates all the victims in a religious way through
requiems (*panikhidy*) held on the shooting range for those killed on
a particular date; for example, a "requiem for the 294 killed on this
place" on 26 September, or a "requiem for the 194 killed on this place"
on 3 November. Some strict believers might protest that the Church
should pray only for Orthodox victims, not for the others. However,
such objections can be ignored at this site, where there seems to be
an understanding that all the victims – whether Orthodox Christians,
Jews, Muslims, Roman Catholics, Protestants, or even atheists – are
united in the grave through their sacrifice. The parish welcomes other
religious communities to commemorate their dead in accordance with
their own religious rituals on the Butovo Polygon and even in the
church building. However, the other religious communities are not
allowed to erect their own monuments. Butovo is first of all an Orthodox Christian "sacred place", and next a joint commemoration site for
all the victims; it is not a multi-religious commemoration site and the
architecture does not reflect the diverse confessional affiliations of the
victims. Rousselet quotes Alexander Agadyanyan calling the pluralism
of Butovo a "limited and hierarchical pluralism" (Rousselet 2007: 68).

The Role of the State in the Post-Soviet
Memory of Soviet Repression

The status of the Butovo Polygon as a national Gulag symbol was
underlined in 2007 in connection with the 70th anniversary of the
Great Terror. As Dorman puts it, "to everybody's surprise" Vladimir
Putin visited the Butovo Polygon on the secular commemoration
date for the victims of Soviet repression, on 30 October. The parish

of Butovo was of course gratified by this sign of attention from the president. The Memorial Society, however, was not impressed. While it would have been indecent of Putin to ignore the anniversary, the organization called his visit a "minimal political act", as he chose to visit the commemoration site of the Church rather than the Solovetsk stone in Lyubyanka Square,[17] where the Memorial Society's activists gather on 30 October and read the names of thousands of victims out loud (Dorman 2010: 338).

In Alexander Etkind's opinion, the Russian state, unlike post-Nazi Germany, has failed to recognize the repression in terms of facilitating and constructing what he calls hard memory: monuments. The absence of monuments to the Soviet repression makes the soft memory – the texts, debates and public opinions – vulnerable to denial and revisionism. Moreover, Russia hasn't had any "Nuremberg trials". The only attempt (so far) to judge the Communist Party at a trial in 1992 failed. The trial was won by the lawyers of the Communist Party who argued that the communist organization could not be blamed for the repression, even though it organized it, because "the communists suffered more than others". It was unclear who was to blame; a tendency which Etkind traces back to Nikita Khrushchev's de-Stalinization campaign in 1956, when Khrushchev used the depersonalized concept of "unjustified repression", lacking any specified agency, as an expression for arrests, deportations and executions (Etkind 2009: 184). The parish of Butovo equally criticizes the state for its lack of interest in building the "hard memory". Dorman quotes Father Kirill Kaleda saying that the state stays in the shadow, and that it should have been the state and not the parish in Butovo which carried out the organization of the commemoration site (Dorman 2010: 339).

The Interrelation of the Memorial Actors

The inactivity of the state has left an empty space. According to Dorman, the mass canonization of the martyrs in recent years has been followed by a gradual transfer of the functions of preserving the Gulag memory from the state to the Russian Orthodox Church. This has, in its turn, led to a particularization of the Gulag memory. Out of the millions of victims, those who died for their faith have been distinguished from the others. Not only do the names of the new martyrs and confessors appear in church services and activities of religious communities, they also have a central place in the general representations of the Gulag. In mixed memorials like the Butovo Polygon, they are more broadly represented and, according to Dorman, the religious commemoration supplants other kinds of commemoration. She quotes secular activists saying that they perceive it as dangerous that the Church takes control over national history (Dorman 2010: 340).

However, this opinion is not shared by all secular activists. The chairman of the Memorial Society's representation in Moscow, Arseniy Roginskiy, is only partly critical of the role of the Church in the Gulag memory. He was interviewed in the *New York Times* when the Church of the Resurrection of Christ and the new martyrs and confessors of Butovo was consecrated in May 2007. Since the victims buried at the shooting range are of different nationalities and confessions, and even religions, he finds it strange that the shooting range is an "Orthodox place", and would have preferred it to be a multi-confessional site. Nevertheless, he believes that an Orthodox commemoration site is better than no commemoration site: "If the state is not ready to help understand the meaning of terror in its history, the role of terror in its history, it's not so bad that the Orthodox Church has taken it upon itself" (Kishkovsky 2007).

Secular and religious activists sometimes work together as allies. Rousselet describes how the local representations of the Memorial Society have various views on religion. Locally, there are close ties between the Memorial Society and the Russian Orthodox Church (Rousselet 2007: 67).[18] In light of the general lack of attention towards Soviet repression in contemporary Russian society, the memory discourse of the Russian Orthodox Church and that of the Memorial Society generally share the same interest. The two organizations have a common interest in remembering the victims of the Soviet persecutions, and even though they remember differently, they still have in common the fact that at least they remember.

Every year at the Orthodox celebration of *radonitsa*,[19] a requiem is held at Butovo Polygon. The celebration is co-arranged by the parish of Butovo and the Memorial Society. On *radonitsa* in May 2011, six buses with descendants of the victims of the Soviet repression arrived. During a speech after the requiem, a representative of the Moscow branch of the Memorial Society, Valeriya Dunaeva, said that she was tired of the lack of attention from the state: "There are no dignified monuments, no dignified graves, nothing dignified" (Dunaeva 2011). In reply to

Valeriya Dunaeva, the director of the Memorial Centre "Butovo", Igor Garkavy, said: "It is necessary to fight for memory. Memory is not given to us by itself. Memory is hard work. Memory is a struggle. Memory is effort. If we don't make an effort in our organizations, it will actually be forgotten" (Garkavy 2011). Talking about "our organizations", he referred to the Memorial Society and to either the Memorial Centre "Butovo" specifically or the Russian Orthodox Church in general. Either way Garkavy saw the Memorial Society and the (parish of the) Russian Orthodox Church as two distinct organizations which share a common aim and purpose.

Taking a closer look at the relationship between the Church, the state and the Memorial Society, a general trend seems to be that the Church has come to function as a connecting link between the three actors. The Church maintains a relationship with both the state and the Memorial Society, while there is only sparse contact between the state and the Memorial Society. As mentioned above, the state chose to commemorate the 70th anniversary of Soviet repression by Putin's visit to the Butovo Polygon. Putin participated in a requiem for the victims of the repression, conducted by Patriarch Aleksiy II, and Father Kirill Kaleda took him on a private tour of the territory of the Butovo Polygon together with the patriarch. It is doubtless more acceptable for the state to be associated with the Church than with the Memorial Society. The explanation for this might be sought not in the past but in the present. A considerable part of the Memorial Society's activities, as mentioned earlier, involves keeping track of current events in the Northern Caucasus.[20] The Church, on the other hand, has a Synodal Department for Cooperation with the Armed Forces and Law Enforcement Agencies, and sends army chaplains to the Northern Caucasus (it could be argued here that the Church does so for the benefit of the soldiers rather than the state).

Bogumil points to another reason why the Church's discourse has become the dominant "persecution discourse", preferred by the state over secular persecutions discourses: the discourse of the Memorial Society criticizes the Soviet state and refrains from giving any explanation for the seemingly meaningless repression, whereas the discourse of the Russian Orthodox Church, she argues, is fundamentally a positive one. The Church explains the repression as meaningful, since the sacrifices made by those who suffered from the repression were valuable and necessary for the rebirth of the faith. To continue Bogumil's line of thought, we may say that the discourse of the Church therefore contributes to positive nation-building; although the country lived through terrible repression, there was a meaning to the suffering. Bogumil goes further and identifies the Church and the state as close allies opposed to the secular organizations, rather than separate institutions having two distinct spheres of interests. She argues that the Soviet repression has been included in the – apparently still functioning – sixteenth-century ideology of "Moscow the third Rome".[21] According to this ideology, co-constructed by the Church and the state, the repression is, in Bogumil's view, valued as confirmation of the Russian people as a chosen people of heroes rather than victims (Bogumil 2010: 9). Bogumil refers to unspecified "Orthodox theologians" who believe that the death of the new martyrs has given the Church the possibility of growth and development and thereby of building a better future for the Russian people (Bogumil 2010: 9).

Indeed, the interpretation of the Soviet persecutions made by the Orthodox theologians in the sources treated in this chapter reflects a strong tendency in the Russian Orthodox Church to interpret them triumphantly. In accordance with a Christian world view, the glory of the new martyrs does not exclude a focus on their suffering, but the glory outshines the suffering. The double focus on both the glory and the suffering and their implicit hierarchy is clearly expressed in the architecture – and in the name – of the Church of the Resurrection of Christ and the new martyrs and confessors of Russia in Butovo. The ground floor of the church is dedicated to the suffering of the new martyrs. Quite unusually for an Orthodox church, photographs of people – victims of the persecutions – hang on the walls of the porch. These are some of the previously mentioned photographs from the execution files. Some of the victims' belongings, found in the mass graves, are likewise displayed in glass cases as in a museum, and the walls of the ground floor are embellished with icons of the new martyrs of Butovo arranged by their commemoration date, i.e. the day of their execution.

The second floor of the church is dedicated to the resurrection, to the overcoming of the suffering, and is ornamented with frescos depicting the lives of Patriarch Tikhon, the new martyrs and confessors and, centrally, the Resurrection of Christ. In a booklet published and sold by the church, the symbolism of the churches on each floor is explained in the following way: "If the lower church symbolizes Holy Week, then the upper church symbolizes Easter" (The Church of the new martyrs and confessors of Russia: 47). Although both the suffering and the glory are represented, the main focus is nevertheless on the overcoming of the suffering; on the Resurrection rather than on the Crucifixion. It is the most important upper church which is dedicated to the Resurrection. The same priority was expressed in Patriarch Aleksiy's opening speech at the Archbishops' Jubilee Council in August 2000: "Our Church lived through dreadful trials, suffering, persecution, but was adorned and strengthened by the blood of the martyrs" (The Moscow Patriarchate 2001:15).

In his lecture at the Archbishops' Jubilee Council, Metropolitan Yuvenaliy does in effect value the sacrifices of the new martyrs as a foundation for the rebirth of the Church, as suggested by Bogumil. He calls the assembly of the new martyrs and confessors an "abundant fruit of the seed of Salvation", and continues: "From the first centuries of Christianity the Church has grown from the seed of the martyrs' blood. And today, reborn, it reaps the fruits of this Divine seeding" (The Moscow Patriarchate 2001: 69). Finally, he concludes that the canonization of the new martyrs and confessors of Russia "is the greatest spiritual occasion in the history of our Church" (The Moscow Patriarchate 2001: 89). In fact, as Bogumil indicates in her reference to the role of the Russian people as a chosen people, a global mission may be traced in comments like the following, given by Father Kirill Kaleda, the priest of the parish of Butovo. He writes about the Russian Orthodox Church that "it has witnessed for the whole world, more and more secularized, further and further removing itself from God, that for many of its members the values of the spiritual world are higher than the values of the material world" (Kaleda 2011:18).

However, this triumphant interpretation does not stand alone. There is one other important aspect to the Church's "persecution discourse", namely that of repentance. It does not exclude the triumphant interpretation. The two interpretations rather coexist. In the repentant interpretation, the persecutions are understood as a consequence of the sins of the Russian people, in particular what Yuvenaliy calls the "sin of apostasy from God" (The Moscow Patriarchate 2001: 90). According to Damaskin, before the Revolution many people who formally served as priests in the Church did so not out of a wish to serve God but because the conditions for clerics, modest as they were, were still better than the living conditions of the peasants. They served the Church for bread:

> This is the source of the unreligious, and often anti-religious, mood of the students at the theological seminaries, the revolts at the seminaries in the years preceding the revolution, the mass departures of the graduates from the seminaries to secular universities ... and in general the leaving from the Church. (Damaskin 2009b:19)

So, before the Revolution only a few members of the Church were actually the salt of the Gospel: "If this hadn't been the case, then Russia wouldn't have fallen into the power of the godless at the beginning of the twentieth century, and the Church wouldn't have been subject to such embittered persecutions" (Damaskin 2009a). It is worth mentioning that the greatest persecutor of the Russian Orthodox Church in the twentieth century, Joseph Stalin, studied at a theological seminary in his youth.

The repentant interpretation does not offer an image of a Russian people chosen by God to facilitate the salvation of all peoples, but of a people that has fallen so deep that the only possible salvation for them is to be "purified" through the persecutions, as Damaskin points out:

> We would have been left completely without holy ideals, without ascetics, without torches of the spirit, had it not been for the persecutions, during which a multitude of confessors were glorified by their martyrdom for Christ, preferring as they were Christ's way rather than all the amenities of earthly life. (Demidov 2010)

Maybe the aspect of repentance is one of the reasons why the question of the Soviet repression has been ignored in Russia both in public debate and by the state. Today, there are descendants of both executioners and victims of the Soviet repression in Russia. Unlike in the story of Evgeniy Rodionov, the "enemy" is less clearly defined. Someone who was your friend yesterday could be an informer against you today, just as yesterday's executioner could be today's victim. In Etkind's view, the Soviet repression is reminiscent of a suicide (Etkind 2009: 184).

While the Russian Orthodox Church acknowledges that some priests, bishops, monks, nuns and Orthodox lay people cooperated with the Soviet system – indeed, the canonization criteria reflect a thorough understanding of this – the Church has not "repented" as an institution for the Moscow Patriarchate's toleration of the Soviet regime. The history of the Russian Orthodox Church underground and diaspora is complex, and this is not the place for a thorough analysis of the historical conditions leading to various schisms and their subdivisions. In the 1927 declaration of loyalty to the Soviet state, signed by the *locum tenens* of the Patriarch, Metropolitan Sergiy, it was declared that "we want to be Orthodox and at the same time recognize the Soviet Union as our civic motherland. Her joys and successes are our joys and successes, her misfortunes are our misfortunes" (Pospielovsky 1998: 251). The declaration of loyalty had an enormous negative impact on the authority of the Moscow Patriarchate, and led to the "schism from the right" where leading hierarchs of the Church diaspora broke the Eucharistic unity with the Moscow Patriarchate and created the "Synodal Church", also to be known as the Russian Orthodox Church Abroad, whereas other parts of the Russian diaspora were to find shelter under the wing of the Constantinopolitan patriarchate. In the Soviet Union, underground movements like The True Orthodox Church and the True Orthodox Christians founded their own "catacomb" structures independently of the Moscow Patriarchate. The extent to which the Church was subordinated to the Soviet state is cruelly displayed in a publication of the Moscow Patriarchate from the 1950s (the exact year of publication is unknown), "The Russian Orthodox Church, Organization, Situation, Activity", not least in the chapter "The Church and the Soviet State". Here, the consequences of the Soviet Government's decree "on the freedom of conscience and the separation of the Church from the State" from 23 January 1918 are described in the following way:

> Some believers too could not grasp the meaning of freedom of conscience. They interpreted the separation of the Church from the State as the persecution of religion, while elements hostile to the new regime spread false reports abroad that the Church in Russia was not able to function freely and was being harassed in all kinds of ways by the authorities.
>
> Of course, these separate tendencies of isolated individuals and small groups were drowned in the ocean of popular devotion to the Soviet power, for which the people were fighting on all fronts at that time. (Moscow Patriarchate 1950s: 9)

Nevertheless, one may discuss whether it was not exactly this position of the Church leadership that allowed the Russian Orthodox Church to survive as a legal institution, and whether the hierarchs of the Russian Orthodox Church Abroad were fair in criticizing their archiepiscopal colleagues in the Soviet Union from their own much cosier corner of Europe.

Some of the twentieth century's schisms have been "healed". The Russian Orthodox Church was reunited with the Russian Orthodox Church Abroad in 2007, and the new martyrs have to some extent become a symbol of this reunion. The canonization of the new martyrs – and the imperial family – was a precondition for the reunion, and one of the first liturgies held by the reunited parties of the Russian Orthodox Church was celebrated in the then recently constructed Church of the Resurrection of Christ and the New Martyrs and Confessors of Russia in Butovo. However, some parishes of the Russian Orthodox Church Abroad refused to reunite with the "patriarchal church", and underground churches such as the True Orthodox Church (The True Orthodox Church 2012), which, although marginalized, still exist.

With the propaganda for the new martyrs and confessors, the Russian Orthodox Church stands forth not as a fellow traveller of the Soviet regime but as a persecuted Church, with bishops, priests and lay people strong enough in their faith to resist the pressure from the Soviet regime. This in its turn strengthens the legitimacy of the Church in post-Soviet Russia.

Conclusion

The ideal of the new martyrs is propagated by the Russian Orthodox Church as an eternal ideal above history and time-spirit. The Christian ideal cannot be changed. As claimed by Damaskin, all *kinds* of saints share the saintly ideal of humility, purity, self-sacrifice and mercifulness, no matter whether they are martyrs, confessors, blessed bishops or other types of saints. However, the theologians quoted in this chapter tend to compare the new martyrs with the ancient martyrs rather than with Old Russian saints, because the nature of their sainthood presumably has more in common with that of the ancient martyrs than with that of other kinds of saints: their stories are comparable. Here again, the qualitative core of their martyrdom is presented as – essentially – the same: like the ancient Christian martyrs, the God-fearing new martyrs did not leave the Church out of fear for their lives or attachment to earthly amenities. At the same time, the historical setting for their martyrdom, their "place in life" (*Sitz im Leben*), is presented as quite different from that of the ancient martyrs: contrary to the persecution of Christians in ancient Rome, the Soviet anti-religious persecutions are described as all-pervasive. As Archbishop Yuvenaliy has pointed out, even renouncing their faith did not spare the victims their lives. They were charged with anti-Soviet propaganda and not with being Christians, which was formally permitted by law. Therefore, whether the new martyrs renounced God or not is not a decisive criterion for canonization. They were never forced to do so, so they did not. But those victims whose canonization was rejected did other things: witnessed falsely against strangers and people close to them, lied, agreed to become informers, etc. So instead, refraining from these actions has become a decisive criterion for the canonization of the new martyrs. By informing on others, those found unworthy of canonization denounced the ideals of their religion and thereby, in a way, they equally renounced their God.

As explained by Papkova, the saintly ideal of the new martyrs is not as widespread in Russian society – even among practising Orthodox Christians – as the Church might have wished. I see two main reasons for this. The first is connected to the general lack of interest in the Soviet repression. The second is more specifically that contemporary Russians may find it hard to identify with the new martyrs after all, even if they lived closer in time to our days than the ancient martyrs or the Old Russian saints. The question is whether it is at all possible to grasp the reality of the omnipresent terror in Stalin's Soviet Union. Either way, in order to understand the deeds of the new martyrs, it is equally necessary to understand the nature of Soviet repression. The story of the new martyrs is inseparable from Soviet repression; had it not been for the repression, there wouldn't have been any new martyrs. Therefore, as the analysis in this chapter has shown, the Church has become involved in constructing the memory of the Soviet repression and propagating its version of the story.

I find it important to distinguish clearly between the commemorative actors presented in this chapter: the Memorial Society, the Russian Orthodox Church, and the Russian state. The state and the Church do not speak with one voice. The "persecution discourse" of the Church, to use Bogumil's terminology, is tolerated by the Russian state, but it is not encouraged. The story of the new martyrs might be *triumphant* in its religious sense, since the new martyrs have overcome the suffering and entered the eternal kingdom and now shine before men as holy persons to be imitated. However, from the secular point of view of the Russian state, it is hard to find anything edifying in the story of a state killing millions of its own citizens in what Etkind has called a collective suicide; all the more so since the Russian state has legally succeeded the Soviet state and thereby "inherited" the responsibility for the Soviet repression. The patriotic and optimistic state ideology of sixteenth-century Russia seems hardly applicable to the propagation of today's new martyrs, even seen through the glasses of the "religious logic". The repentant interpretation of the repression is too dominant for this to be possible. From the viewpoint of the Russian state, the less is said about the Soviet repression, the better. The absence of state-erected monuments to the repression speaks for itself and underlines the indifference of the state. Still, the persecution discourse of the Church is much "safer" for the state than the persecution discourse of the Memorial Society. This is precisely because the main focus of the Church is the ideal of the new martyrs and their veneration, whereas the main focus of the human rights organizations, as shown by Bogumil, is justice, the assigning of responsibility, and a continuing vigilance over human rights in Russia.

The state does little to support the commemoration of the new martyrs, just as it does little to support the work of the Memorial Society. For the state, a much more advantageous twentieth-century story is that of the victory in the Great Patriotic War. The parades celebrating "Victory Day" (*Den' Pobedy*) on 9 May have become increasingly spectacular since 2000 (Ryazanova-Clarke 2008: 223ff.). As in Soviet times, thousands of soldiers now participate in an impressively choreographed parade culminating when the military "hardware", in the form of missiles and tanks, rolls over Red Square, as in the old days. And the people willingly participate in the event. The popularity of the state-supported celebration of Victory Day stands in contrast to the unpopularity of remembering the Soviet repression. The city centre around Red Square is closed to traffic, there are concerts, mass-produced artefacts such as flags and pilots' caps (with the red star) are sold, and the remaining veterans are praised as thousands upon thousands of people enjoy the holiday. It seems that this is a story that serves to unite rather than separate the Russian people today. The darker chapters of the recent history are forgotten. Let us recall Igor Garkavy's words: "Memory is hard work. Memory is a struggle. Memory is effort. If we don't make an effort in our organizations, it will actually be forgotten…"

Notes

1 For a comprehensive analysis of the chuch–state relation in contemporary Russia, see Papkova, *The Orthodox Church and Russian Politics* (2011).

2 Today, around 75% of the population consider themselves to be Orthodox Christians, according to a poll carried out in 2010 (VTsIOM: Russian Public Research Center 2010). At the same time, only 4% claim to attend church at least once a month.

3 "Repression" is used in Russia as an overall term for the various types of persecutions that went on in the Soviet Union, and the terminology is therefore preserved here.

4 A local church council means a church council for the entire Russian Orthodox Church, as opposed to the seven ecumenical church councils held from the fourth to the eighth centuries.

5 Patriarch Nikon wished to reform church services according to a Greek model, but the Old Believers were against it. They perceived the Greek Orthodox Church as heretical, due to the role of the Byzantine Church during the Church Council of Florence-Ferrera a couple of centuries earlier, in 1439. At the Council, the Byzantine Church had agreed to recognize the pope as the leader of Orthodox Christianity in return for a promise of military help to keep the Ottomans out of Constantinople. Although this decision was retracted after the fall of Constantinople in 1453, the Byzantine Church had lost its authority in the eyes of many Russians, and the memory of the Greek Orthodox Church as "heretical" was preserved among them.

6 When taking their monastic vows, monks and nuns in the Orthodox Church receive a new name. They are no longer presented by their surname, but it is often written in parentheses so as to distinguish which monk or nun is referred to.

7 "Boyars" were the aristocrats of Kievan and Muscovite Russia.

8 For a saint's life I use the term *hagiography*, rooted in the Greek Orthodox tradition, rather than the synonym *vita*, rooted in the Latin tradition. In Russia, either the Church Slavonic *zhitie* or the Russianized Greek *agiografia* are used.

9 The archives mentioned by the Foundation are: The Synod's Fund, the Local Council, the Office of the Patriarch, private foundations of the clergy, the Standing Central Committee on Cults of the Presidium TsIK USSR (1921–1938), the Council for Religious Affairs in the SM USSR (1943–1974), the People's Commissariat for Justice of the Russian RSFSR, FSB and its regional offices.

10 The *martyrs* were directly killed by the state, whereas the *confessors* were persecuted, possibly imprisoned and sent to Gulag camps, but died a natural death.

11 An *akathist* is a short service addressed to a particular saint.

12 A Russian prince from the fourteenth century, famous for winning the Battle of Kulikovo over the Mongolian Army in 1380.

13 The positive attitude of Father Dmitriy Smirnov towards the canonization of Evgeniy Rodionov was thus treated in an article on the Russian website "e-islamic" (e-islam. News of Islam every day 2011).

14 The Russian Orthodox Church Abroad (*Russkaya Pravoslavnaya Tserkov' za Rubezhem*) was an alternative Church structure of exiled archbishops, priests and lay people. They broke with the patriarchate in 1927, after the *locum tenens* of the patriarch, Metropolitan Sergiy, published his declaration of loyalty to the Soviet government, which caused tensions both in Russia and in the Russian diaspora.

15 A "polygon" is a shooting range used for the training of police officers. This particular polygon in Butovo, south of Moscow, was used as an execution site in the 1930s and is today a commemoration site, as is described in the chapter's third section. In the following, I will refer to it as the Butovo Polygon.

16 Evidently, there are other religious communities involved in remembering the Soviet religious persecutions, but this chapter will be restricted to analysing the activities of the Russian Orthodox Church.

17 In 1990, this monument – a stone brought from the former Gulag camp on the Solovki Islands – was placed on the square in front of yet another Gulag symbol in the centre of Moscow: Lyubyanka, the headquarters of the NKVD (later the KGB), where many victims of Soviet repression were interrogated and tortured.

18 One sign of this is that there are members of both the Memorial Society and the Memorial Centre "Butovo" among the contributing editors of the eight-volume project *The Butovo Polygon: A Memory Book for the Victims of Political Repression* (Golovkova 2003).

19 *Radonitsa* is a popular Orthodox feast-day held in the cemetery nine days after Easter, where the Orthodox symbolically celebrate the joy of Easter together with those who have passed away.

20 See the organization's website, memo.ru/hr/hotpoints/caucas1/index.htm.

21 The concept "Moscow – the Third Rome" derives from an often quoted letter by the monk Philotheos written to Tsar Vasiliy III in 1511, in which he praises the tsar and his tsardom: "And now there is the Holy synodal Apostolic church of the reigning third Rome, of your tsardom, which shines like the sun in its Orthodox Christian faith throughout the whole universe." Philotheos concludes: "Two Romes have fallen, a third stands, a fourth there shall not be" (Cherniavsky 1961: 619).

References

Anon (2011): Intercessors of our Salvation (Molitvenniki o nashem spasenii), *Pokrov*, 481): 15–17.

Assmann, Aleida (2008): Canon and Archive, in Astrid Erll & Ansgar Nünning (eds): *Cultural Memory Studies. An International and Interdisciplinary Handbook*, Berlin: Gruyter.

Bagger, Hans (2007): The Study of History during the Post-Soviet Identity Crisis, *Scando-Slavica* 2007 (53): 109–125.

Bagger, Hans (2008): History Consumption in post-Soviet Russia (Historiekonsum i det postsovjetiske Rusland), *Den Jyske Historiker*, 117–118: 185–202.

Bodin, Per-Arne (2007): *Eternity and Time. Studies in Russian Literature and the Orthodox Tradition*, Södertälje: Almqvist & Wiksell.

Bodin, Per-Arne (2008): How to Remember a Dead Soldier, *Memory Studies*, 3(2): 95–111.

Bodin, Per-Arne (2009): *Language, Canonization and Holy Foolishness. Studies in Post-soviet Russian culture and the Orthodox Tradition*, Stockholm: Stockholm University.

Bogumil, Zuzanna (2010): Crosses and Stones. Solovki-symbols in the Construction of the Memory of Gulag (Kresty i kamni. Solovetskiye simvoly v konstruirovanii pamyati o GULAGe), 71. Available at: http://magazines.russ.ru/nz/2010/3/zu3.html (Accessed 23 August, 2011).

Cherniavsky, Michael (1961): *Tsar and People. Studies in Russian Myths*, New Haven: Yale University Press.

Church of the New Martyrs and Confessors of Russia (Khram svyatykh novomuchenikov i ispovednikov Rossiyskikh): *The Butovo Polygon. The Russian Golgatha (Butovskiy Polygon. Russkaya Golgofa).*

Damaskin (Orlovskiy) (2009b): Methodological and practical Particularities in the Investigation of the Deeds of the New Martyrs and Confessors of Russia (Metodologiya i prakticheskie osobennosti issledovaniya podviga novomuchenikov i ispovednikov rossiyskikh), in 17th International Educational Christmas Readings. Canonization and Veneration of Saints (*XVII Mezhdunarodnye Rozhdestvenskie Chteniya. Proslavlenie i pochitanie svyatykh*).

Damaskin (Orlovskiy), (2010): A Comparison of the Martyrdom of the Saints of the ancient Church and the New Martyrs of Russia (Sopostavlenie podviga muchenichestva svyatykh drevney Tserkvi i novomuchenikov Rossiyskikh), in 18th International Educational Christmas Readings. Canonization and veneration of saints (*XVIII Mezhdunarodnye Rozhdestvenskie Chteniya. Proslavlenie i pochitanie svyatykh*).

Demina, Anastasiya (2011): To Draw the Names of the Perished out of Non-existence (Izvlech' iz nebytiya imena bogibshikh), *Pokrov*, 481: 26–29.

Dorman, Veronika (2010): From Solovki to Butovo. The Russian Orthodox Church and the Memory of the Soviet Repression in post-Soviet Russia (Ot Solovkov do Butovo. Russkaya Pravoslavnaya Tserkov' i pamyat' o sovetskiykh repressiyakh v postsovetskoy Rossii), *Laboratorium*, 2010 (2): 327–348.

Etkind, Alexander 2009: Post-Soviet Hauntology. Cultural Memory of the Soviet Terror, *Constellations*, 16 (1): 182–200.

Golovkova, Lidiya (2003): The Butovo Polygon. A Commemoration Book for the Victims of Political Repression, vol. 7 *(Butovskiy Polygon. Kniga Pamyati zhertv politicheskikh repressiy, tom 7)*, Moscow: Izdatel'stvo Also.

Golovkova, Lidiya (2005): The Moscow Saint John the Forerunner Convent. Pages of history *(Moskovskiy Ioanna-Predtechenskiy Zhenskiy Monastyr'. Stranitsy istorii)*, Moscow: Izdatel'stvo Leto.

Golovkova, Lidiya (2007): The Butovo Polygon. A Commemoration Book for the Victims of Political Repression, volume 8 *(Butovskiy Polygon. Kniga Pamyati zhertv politicheskikh repressiy, tom 8)*, Moscow: Izdatel'stvo Also.

Golubinskiy, Evgeniy (1903): A History of the Canonization of Saints in the Russian Church *(Istoriya kanonizatsii svyatykh v russkoy tserkvi)*, Moscow.

Greene, Robert (2010): *Bodies Like Bright Stars. Saints and Relics in Orthodox Russia*, Illinois: Northern Illinois University Press.

Iannuariy (Ivliev) (2011): The Biblical View on the Sanctity of God and the Sanctity of People (Bibleyskiy vzglyad na svyatost' Boga i svyatost' lyudey), in 19th International Christmas Readings. Canonization and Veneration of Saints (*XIX Mezhdunarodnye Rozhdestvenskie Obrazovatel'nye Chteniya. Proslavlenie i pochitanie svyatykh*).

Kaleda, Kirill (2007): Memories of Grandfather Volodya (Pamyati dedushki Volodi), in The Priest-Martyr Vladimir Ambartsumov, presbyter of Moscow *(Svyashchen-nomuchenik Vladimir Ambartsumov, presviter moskovskiy)*, Moscow: Izdatel'stvo Zachat'evskogo Monastyrya.

Kaleda, Kirill (2011): The Celebration of the Assembly of the New Martyrs and Confessors of Russia (Prazdnik Sobora novomuchenikov i ispovednikov Rossiyskikh), *Pokrov*, 481: 18–21.

Knox, Zoe (2005): *Russian Society and the Orthodox Church. Religion in Russia after Communism,* London: Routledge Curzon.

Lenhoff, Gail (1989): *The Martyred Princes Boris and Gleb. A Socio-cultural Study of the Cult and the Texts,* Columbus, Ohio: Slavica Publishers.

Lobanov, V. (2008): *Patriarch Tikhon and the Soviet Power 1917–1925 (Patriarkh Tikhon i sovetskaya vlast' 1917–1925 gg.),* Moscow: Russkaya Panorama.

Malakhova, N. (2010): Orthodox Calendar 2011 *(Pravoslavny kalendar 2011),* Moscow: Izdatel'stvo Moskovskogo Podvor'ya Svyato-Troitskoy Sergievoy Lavry.

Mordasheva, Evgeniya (2011): The Holy Martyr Apollinariya Tupitsyna (Svyataya muchenitsa Apollinariya Tupitsyna), *Pokrov,* 481: 34–35.

Moscow Patriarchate, (1950s): *The Russian Orthodox Church. Organization, Situation, Activity,* Moscow: Moscow Patriarchate.

Moscow Patriarchate (2001): *The Archbishops' Jubilee Council of the Russian Orthodox Church (Yubileyniy Arkhiereyskiy Sobor Russkoy Pravoslavnoy Tserkvi),* Moscow: Izdatel'skiy sovet Moskovskogo Patriarkhata.

Optina Monastery (Vvedenskiy Stavropigial'ny Muzhskoy Monastyr' Optina Pustyn') & Damaskin (2008): *Hagiographies of the New Martyrs and Confessors of the Optina Pustyn' Monastery (Zhitiya novomuchenikov i ispovednikov Optinoy pustyni),* Optina Pustyn'.

Orekhanov, G. (2002): *On the Way to the Council. Church Reforms and the First Russian Revolution (Na puti k soboru. Tserkovnye reformy i pervaya russkaya revolyutsiya),* Moscow: Pravoslavny Svyato-Tikhonovskiy Bogoslovskiy Institut.

Papkova, Irina (2011): *The Orthodox Church and Russian Politics,* Oxford: Oxford University Press.

Papkova, Irina (2008): *The Freezing of Historical Memory? The Post-Soviet Russian Orthodox Church and the Council of 1917,* Washington D.C: Indiana University Press.

Pospelovskiy, Dmitriy (1995): *The Russian Orthodox Church in the Twentieth Century (Russkaya Pravoslavnaya Tserkov' v XX veke),* Moskva: Respublika.

Pospielovsky, Dmitri (1998): *The Orthodox Church in the History of Russia,* New York: St. Vladimir's Seminary Press.

Rogova, R.M. (1986): *Atheist Education of School Pupils (Ateisticheskoe vospitanie shkolnikov),* Moscow: Prosvyashchenie.

Rousselet, Kathy (2007): Butovo. La création d'un lieu de pèlerinages sur une terre de massacres, *Politix,* 77 : 55–78.

Rousselet, Kathy (2011): L'Église orthodoxe Russe et la mémorialisation de la Terreur, in David Kenz & François-Xavier Nérard (eds): *Commémorer les victimes en Europe. XVIe–XXIe Siecles.* Seyssel: Champ Vallon.

Russian Orthodox Church's Commission on the Canonization of Saints (Kommissiya Svyashchennogo Sinoda Russkoy Pravoslavnoy Tserkvi po kanonizatsii svyatykh) (1999): *Canonization of Saints in the twentieth Century (Kanonizatsiya Svyatykh v XX veke),* Moscow: Izdatel'stvo Sretenskogo Monastyrya.

Ryazanova-Clarke, Larissa (2008): Re-creation of the Nation: Orthodox and Heterodox Discourses in Post-Soviet Russia, *Scando-Slavica,* 2008 (54), pp. 223–239.

Semenko-Basin, Ilya (2010): *Sainthood in the Russian Orthodox Culture of the twentieth Century: A History of Personification (Svyatost v russkoy pravoslavnoy kulture XX veka: istoriya personifikatsii),* Moscow: Rossiyskiy Gosudarstvenny Gumanitarny Universitet.

Zubov, Andrey (2009): *The History of Russia, the Twentieth Century (Istoriya Rossii, XX vek),* Moscow: Astrel.

Internet sources

Arendarenko, Antonina (2004): Father Dmitriy Smirnov about the possibility of canonizing Evgeniy Rodionov (Prot. Dmitriy Smirnov o vozmozhnosti kanonizatsii Evgeniya Rodiova), *Radonezh*. Available at: http://www.radonezh.ru/text/8501.html (Accessed 9 February 2012).

Church of the Nativity of the Theotokos in Krylatskoe (Khram Rozhdestva Presvyatoy Bogoroditsy v Krylatskom) (2012): Available at: http//hramnaholmah.ru/ (Accessed 6 February 2012).

Communication service of the Department of Inter-Christian relations (Sluzhba kommunikatsii OVTsS) (2011): The head of the Russian Orthodox Church met with the ambassador of Japan in Russia Masakharu Kono (Predstoyatel' Russkoy Pravoslavnoy Tserkvi vstretilsya s poslom Yaponii v Rossii Masakharu Kono). Available at: http://mospat.ru/ru/2011/04/06/news39348 [Accessed 28 April 2011] Damaskin (Orlovskiy) (2009a): Who does the Church canonize as its saints? Particularities of the research of the new martyrs' deeds. Orthodoxy and the world (Kogo Tserkov proslavlyaet vo svyatykh svoikh? Osobennosti issledovaniya podviga novomuchenikov. Pravoslavie i mir). Available at: http://www.pravmir.ru/kogo-cerkov-proslavlyaet-vo-svyatyx-svoix-osobennosti-issledovaniya-podviga-novomuchenikov/ (Accessed 29 April 2011).

Demidov, Pavel (2010): Becoming saints on earth (Svyatymi stanovyatsya na zemle). Available at: http://www.fond.ru/index.php?menu_id=375&menu_parent_id=358&show_date=1&category_id=15&article_page_content=0&show_preview_img=0&show_file_list=0&flag=ajax&page=1&regime=site&content_id=158 (Accessed 29 April 2011).

e-islam. News of Islam every day (e-islam. Novosti islama den' za dnem) (2011): Priest Dmitriy Smirnov believes that the Soldier Evgeniy Rodionov is a Saint (Protoierey Dmitriy Smirnov schitaet svyatym soldata Evgeniya Rodionova). Available at: http://www.e-islam.ru/mainnews/?ID=2833 (Accessed 8 February 2012).

Foundation (2010): About the Foundation (O Fonde). Available at: http://www.fond.ru/index.php?menu_id=367&menu_parent_id=357 (Accessed 30 December 2010).

Information Service of the Archbishops' Council (Informatsionnaya sluzhba Arkhiereyskogo Sobora), 2011. The Patriarch of Moscow and all Russia's report on the Archbishop's Council (2 February 2011): The Department of Inter-Christian Relations (Doklad Patriarkha Moskovskogo i vseya Rusi Kirilla na Arkhiereyskom Sobore Russkoy Pravoslavnoy Tserkvi (2. fevralya 2011): Russkaya Pravoslavnaya Tserkov'. Otdel vneshnykh tserkovnykh svyazey). Available at: http://www.mospat.ru/ru/2011/02/03/news35626/ (Accessed 28 April 2011).

Kishkovsky, Sophia (2007): An Orthodox shrine rises on a Russian killing field, *The New York Times*. Available at: http://www.nytimes.com/2007/06/07/news/07i-ht-journal.4.6042382.html [Accessed 6 February 2012].

Krayniy, Aleksey (2011): Warrior Martyr (Voin-Muchenik). Available at: http://pravoslavie58region.ru/index.php?loc=evgeniy-rodionov-block9-300111.htm (Accessed 9 February 2012).

Maksimov, Maksim (2003): About the activities of the Synodal Commission on the Canonization of Saints (O deyatel'nosti sinodal'noy komissii po kanonizatsii svjatykh). Available at: http://www.fond.ru/index.php?menu_id=394&menu_parent_id=358# (Accessed 29 April 2011).

Memorial (2011): Who and What Is Memorial? Available at: http://www.memo.ru/eng/about/whowe.htm (Accessed 28 April 2011).

Nérard, François-Xavier (2009): The Butovo Shooting Range, Online Encyclopedia of Mass Violence. Available at: http://www.massviolence.org/The-Butovo-Shooting-Range?decoupe_recherche=nerard%20shooting%20range%20butovo (Accessed 7 February 2012).

Ovchinnikov, A. (2011): What are saints canonized for in Russia? (Za chto na Rusi svyatymi stanovyatsya?). Available at: http://kp.ru/daily/25620/787714/ (Accessed 29 April 2011).

True Orthodox Church (2012): Official website of the Department of External Church Affairs. The Official website of the Russian Orthodox Church (Ofitsial'nyy sayt Otdela Vneshnikh Tserkovnykh Del. Ofitsial'ny sayt Rossiyskoy Pravoslavnoy Tserkvi). Available at: http://www.sinodipc.ru/ (Accessed 9 February 2012).

VTsIOM: Russian Public Research Center (VTsiom: Vserossiyskiy Tsentr Izucheniya obshchestvennogo Mneniya) (2010): Do we believe in God? (Verim li my v Boga?). Available at: http://wciom.ru/index.php?id=268&uid=13365 (Accessed 1 June 2011).

On site recordings of speeches

Dunaeva, Valeriya (2011): Butovo Polygon, 3 May 2011
Garkavy, Igor' (2011): Butovo Polygon, 3 May 2011

CHAPTER 9

The Role of Orthodox Christianity in Greece

Victor Roudometof

The field of memory studies has been a booming academic industry since the second part of the twentieth century (for a useful introduction to the social scientific literature, see Olick, Vinitzky-Seroussi & Levy 2011). More specifically, the use of history in Church and lay discourse is a significant aspect of the culture of European societies. Debates about heritage and memory provide an important means for shaping the self-image of European nations and their evolving relationship towards "Europe" and the European Union (EU). Concern with heritage is an aspect of the broader theme of collective memory, but this link is rarely acknowledged explicitly in the literature (Roudometof 2007).

In traditional society, memory was directly experienced in several realms, but in modern societies modernization erodes the realms of memory, and therefore memory becomes disembodied (Nora 1996–1998). While in pre-modern societies heritage was confined to the upper classes, modern societies have caused the democratization of heritage – by redefining it specifically as *national heritage*: the shared repository of national culture that is important because it preserves the people's sense of identity and continuity across history (Lowenthal 1998: 60–68). This nationalization of heritage is partly responsible for the proliferation and dispersion of the concern with the topic of (national) heritage across most societies around the globe (Graham et al. 2000: 13). It is important to note that this is a relatively newfound concern that is specific to modern societies organized into nation-states that hold out historically specific images of the national past, which in turn operate as key elements for creating, reproducing and amplifying the people's sense of their past and their belonging to their nation's "imagined community" (Anderson 1991).

Religious actors often play a key role in the national debates about heritage and memory. From France's *l'affaire de Mandil*, to the publication of cartoons of the Prophet Mohammed in Denmark, to the decision to ban the construction of a mosque in Switzerland, religion has made a return to the European public scene, raising a spectrum of important cultural and political considerations. These intense "culture wars" (Hunter 1992) feature new battle lines that often – but not invariably – cut across the conventional political spectrum. The new battle grounds include the orientation of European societies vis-à-vis the European project, the role of national heritage, national memory, religion and culture in national identity, and the way national identity is impacted by Europeanization, by immigration and, more generally, by all the multitude of real or imagined processes that are typically subsumed under the rubric of globalization. In the USA, such debates have been framed in terms of Taylor's (1994) original formulation about the "politics of recognition". However, the situation is different in Continental societies, where different states exhibit considerable variation in their efforts to come to terms with multiculturalism (Cornwell & Stoddard 2001).

Greece's debates on these issues mirror the broader European engagement with these issues. Both in Greece's own debates and in debates throughout Europe, the necessity to walk a fine line between the demands of multiculturalism and those of protecting national identity from real or perceived threats is a critical imperative. In this chapter, I examine some of these debates and place them within the broader cultural and political context of the dilemmas facing the Greek nation-state and Greek society in the early twenty-first century. In the chapter's first section, I outline some key contemporary topics in which the role of Orthodox Christianity and of the Church of Greece has occupied centre stage. Next, I briefly outline the polemical standpoints that pertain to the debate about contemporary Greek culture, and situate the role of the Orthodox Church of Greece in the context of this broader debate. Last, I address the issue of nationalism, which is of particular significance for Greece – especially because of its connection to ongoing geopolitical rivalries vis-à-vis neighbouring states.

The Orthodox Church of Greece in Contemporary Debates

Over 90% of the population of Greece are Orthodox Christians, and therefore speaking about the role of religion in modern Greece is in many respects identical to addressing the role of Orthodox Christianity in the country's public life and national culture. Just as with other forms of Christianity throughout Europe, in the course of the last few centuries, Eastern Orthodox Christianity has been absorbed into the fabric of Modern Greek national identity (Roudometof 2001). Although Greece has a long history of engagement with Western Europe, its social, economic and cultural trajectory follows not that of the developed Western European societies but, rather, the semi-peripheral societies of South-eastern Europe. It is only since the Second World War that most of these societies – including Greece – have become *urban societies* (that is, the majority of their inhabitants live in urban as opposed to rural areas) for the very first time in their modern history (Stoianovich 1994:212–15, 223–25). Their steadfast urbanization altered the traditional moral bases of their cohesion. In the Greek case, this trend is manifested in the post-Second World War statistics on religious attendance that show a clear decline in the rates of regular church attendance (for data and analysis, see Georgiadou & Nikolakopoulos 2001; Makrides 1995). But this decline does not by any means suggest a decline in the public role of the Orthodox ecclesiastical leadership in Greece.

On the contrary, during the 1967–1974 military dictatorship, the regime's official policy was the pursuit of the creation of a "Greece of Christian Greeks" (as was the official state slogan during the *junta*). This association between modern Greece and Christianity dates back to the nineteenth century, when the fusion between Orthodoxy and Greekness assumed its contemporary format (Roudometof 2010). The military dictatorship aptly applied this ideology of "Hellenic Christian civilization" to the realm of public culture and state policy (Gazi 2004: 34–50). The 1974 restoration of democracy caused the overnight collapse of this ideology, which was almost instantly delegitimized. It took more than a decade for religion to resurface forcefully back into the public realm.

In 1998, the election of Archbishop Christodoulos to the leadership post of the Orthodox Church signalled a new era for the Orthodox Church of Greece. During his ten-year reign, the late archbishop promoted a multifaceted programme of Church modernization, and his charisma and TV-friendly persona turned him for a period into one of the most popular public figures in the country (Makrides & Roudometof 2010; for an analysis, see Oulis, Makris & Roussos 2010). Certainly, during Christodoulos' rule, official pronouncements and other forms of action by the Orthodox Church of Greece enhanced its status as a key agent participating in a series of clashes (or "cultural wars") involving both state agencies and non-state constituencies. For Christodoulos (1999) as well as other defenders of the modern synthesis of Church and nation, Orthodoxy is a chain of national memory (Hervieu-Léger 2000). The late archbishop routinely reminded his audience of the critical role of religion for the preservation of Greek national identity in past centuries:

> Hellenism cannot live without visions and hope. Only if the castle of our memory remains unconquered and maintained by our legends and those who incarnate our National Idea, only then can our *Genos* [Race or Progeny] become glorious. And our *Genos* can survive only if embraces again the life-giving Greek-Orthodoxy. (Christodoulos 1999: 52)

This perspective earned the late archbishop both ardent supporters and vehement critics. Public reception was marked by a strong and unusual polarization of views. To the Right, the public reception of such statements has certainly been mostly positive. Historically, and just as in many other Southern European states, most Greek conservative political and social actors have been on amicable terms with the Church's leadership. But this should not be misconstrued as a unanimous agreement. For example, the former minister and free-market promoter Andreas Andrianopoulos (2001) expressed reservations about the strong advocacy of the Church–Nation link asserted in Christodoulos' discourse and the siege mentality often evoked in his speeches and other forms of public communication. To the Left, public reaction consisted mostly in interpreting Christodoulos as an epigone of the mentality of the nationalists, the ultra-right-wing faction of the Right and other anti-communist forces. Predictably, the Left's reaction was overwhelmingly negative and dismissive. In their view, Christodoulos' open assertion of the Church–Nation link was tantamount to right-wing propaganda.

Still, the assertion of the Church–Nation link is actually far less unusual than the Left's perspective assumed (for example, see Aliv-izatos 1999). The late archbishop's position was neither idiosyncratic nor isolated from the broader tenets of conventional ecclesiastical discourse. In an analysis of the encyclicals of the Holy Synod of the Orthodox Church of Greece for the period between 1833 and 2000, Papageorgiou (2000) finds that this assertion has always informed the self-image of the Church hierarchy. In the eyes of the hierarchy, reli-gion, family and homeland are thus the cornerstones of Greek society as such. Papageorgiou (2000: 284) concludes that the Church's image is that of traditionalism, and the past, "a closed system that is connected to the values of the past without attempting openings towards ... the present and the future." In fact, the encyclicals reveal the synod's iden-tification of itself with the Church as an institution, thereby excluding the laity from being active members in the workings of the institu-tion. In conjunction with the legal ethics that prevail in the texts, the Church's self-image is that of a bureaucracy that exists in collaboration with the state and often acts as an extension of public authority in a hierarchical manner vis-à-vis its members. So, Christodoulos was far less exceptional in the substance of his approach and thinking than critics often assume. Defending the modern synthesis of Church and nation is an approach consistently voiced by the Church hierarchy in Greece for most of its modern history.

By far the most visible and the most well-publicized controversy of the Christodoulos era (1998–2008) was the 2000 ID crisis, when the Church of Greece publicly disagreed with the Greek government over whether the new ID cards should include an entry for religious affilia-tion. The state openly supported the introduction of new ID cards for Greek citizens that would no longer include religious affiliation on them. Although the Greek government insisted that EU regulations prohibited such a disclosure, the Church opted for voluntary disclosure, leading to a protracted public crisis (for analyses, see Danopoulos 2004; Prodromou 2004; Roudometof 2005; Stavrakakis 2003). The images of Greek bishops and believers protesting against the Greek govern-ment's effort to institute new ID cards that would exclude an entry for religious affiliation were widely circulated among the European public (see Makrides 2004; Molokotos-Liederman 2003, 2007a, 2007b). This episode marked not only a new era of Church–state relations but also a turning point in the relationship between the Orthodox Church and the Greek public. Outside Greece, the ID crisis also contributed greatly to the proliferation of a negative image of the Orthodox Church. The Church's image was that of an anti-modern institution set against the forces of modernization and Europeanization.

It is important to note that the ID crisis was part of a broader range of topics that have marked the forceful reappearance of the Church into public life. The list of "hot issues" includes the prohibition of the catechism, the public operation of mosques and denominational churches, the issue of cremation, and the issue of burial rites and baptism for individuals who have chosen to have a civil wedding ceremony (which the Church does not officially recognize as valid) instead of the religious ceremony (Dimitropoulos 2001; Mavrocordatos 2003). Underneath the emergence of these topics as areas of public contestation lies Greece's post-1981 participation in the European Economic Community (EEC) and post-1992 in the European Union (EU). Since 1990, these topics have surfaced as a result of the state facing the necessity to implement policies consistent with the EU's vision of cultural (including religious) pluralism, while the Church's own stance has been to attempt to prevent the loss of its privileged position in society and in its dealings with the state.

In addition to the aforementioned list of issues, since 2000 there have been some additional controversies that have evolved around the Orthodox Church of Greece, either as part of the public debate or directly, through the actions of its hierarchs. The following is a brief overview of these cases.

The Mosque Debate over the Construction of an Islamic Temple in central Athens

This debate has its origins in government-sponsored legislation introduced in anticipation of the 2004 Athens Olympic Games. Needless to say, more than a decade has passed since the introduction of legislation, yet no temple has been built. Part of the rationale was the necessity to accommodate the religious needs of a growing immigrant Muslim constituency in Athens, who, up to this day, lack a mosque and Islamic cultural centre. The mosque issue was entangled with the broader and bitterly politicized public debate about immigration in contemporary Greece. This entanglement did not contribute to the resolution of the mosque issue. Instead, the construction of an Islamic temple became the subject of protracted political and ideological controversy (for an analysis, see Anagnostou & Gropas 2010). Public debate, inclusive of parliamentary discussions, often assumed that the Church's official position was against the construction of the Islamic temple. Alas, this perception was far from accurate. In June 2002, Archbishop Christodoulos met with European Commissioner Mr. Alvaro Gil-Robles, to whom he said the following:

> We, being Greeks, were subjected to the [rule of the] Turks for 400 years. And this occupation (*katohi*) by the Turks was paid for with sacrifices in blood. We had hundreds of victims who were sacrificed for the freedom of this land. Our religion played the primary role in protecting our language, history, religion and identity, for at that time it had no political power. In the mind of the Greeks, everything Islamic is Turkish ... Thus there is this hatred which, I would say, we do not cultivate. We are trying to silence it and this is also known to the government. For this reason, [the government] has chosen a place outside the city of Athens [Peania], so that [the Muslims] are not right in the middle ... we are afraid that such a mosque right in the centre of Athens with a minaret ... and a muezzin who will be heard five times a day performing the prayer, will provoke a reaction from the Greek people, the extent of which we cannot know. (Quoted in Antoniou 2010: 157)

As the above statement makes abundantly clear, for the late archbishop the mosque issue is deeply intertwined with Greece's historical legacy of Ottoman rule. Moreover, the archbishop was quick to highlight the religious dimension of the Turkish–Greek relationship ("In the mind of the Greeks, everything Islamic is Turkish"), thereby establishing a niche for the Church. The Church–Nation link previously mentioned is prominently displayed here ("Our religion played the primary role in protecting our language, history, religion and identity"). The archbishop also highlights the extent to which reaction to the mosque rests at the popular level – and that it is *not* the Orthodox ecclesiastical establishment that is its source. In fact, an ethnographic study of the anti-mosque mobilization (Antoniou 2010) has revealed that the archbishop's representation was actually rather accurate. The Church hierarchy attempted to navigate between state agencies and a popular grassroots right-wing constituency of fundamentalist-like Christians that was adamantly opposed to the mosque project. The hierarchy attempted to do so by adopting a flexible perspective that would thus enable the preservation of amicable relations with all parties.

The Parthenon Video Affair

Following the opening of the Athens Acropolis Museum in 2009, a major controversy erupted over the video presentation that was prominently featured in the museum. The video was the work of French-Greek director Costa Gavras. It contained a reference to damage done to the Parthenon in the first Christian centuries and, for a brief period, it showed images of people dressed in seemingly religious attire (which was common clothing during those centuries) destroying the Parthenon's sculptures. Upon the opening of the museum, members of the Church's hierarchy protested over what they deemed to be an inappropriate reference to the Church. In effect, they argued that the video insinuated that the Church was responsible for damage done to the Parthenon. The government's initial reaction was to censor the video by deleting its controversial images. But this action in turn led to Costa Gavras' public and vocal protests in which he called for his work to be removed altogether. Finally, after a year and an online protest campaign, the government reversed its initial decision and let the entire video be shown in its original version (Ng 2009).

The Textbook Affair of 2007

During the 2006–2007 academic year a major debate erupted in the Greek media on the occasion of the introduction of new history text-books in Greece's elementary and middle-level schools. The scandalous issue pertained to the issue of a new history textbook for sixth-graders (a copy of the textbook is available from Antivaro 2007). Critics claimed that the new textbook was full of mistakes and that it was also insulting to Greece's national memory. At issue was the attempt to provide a less nationalistic account of past historical events by presenting Greek history in schools differently than it had been. The Orthodox Church was implicated in the affair inasmuch as the textbook did not contain references to such cherished topics as the legend of the "secret school". According to this national legend, Greek educational institutions including schools were closed down during the period of Ottoman rule. Orthodox clergy schooled Greek students at night in secret. Suffice it to say, this national myth originated in nineteenth-century public commemorations of the Greek War of Independence. In the context of such occasions, poetic licence gradually gave rise to a powerful national myth (see Angelou 1999). When the new history textbooks were sent to elementary schools in 2006–2007, parents, intellectuals and journalists complained that these failed to make any reference to this sacred national myth. When history professors proceeded to publicly explain that the secret school is but a myth, journalists, politicians and many intellectuals reacted with dismay and disbelief, creating a media frenzy that swept the Greek television talk shows for the better part of March 2007. Mrs M. Giannakou, Minister of Education at the time, defended the process and tried to appease the opposition (see her 2 August 2007 interview posted on her website, *Marietta Giannakou* 2007). Her successor to the Ministry of Education moved swiftly to postpone the circulation of the new textbooks, thereby bowing to public sentiment. In fact, press reports attributed her failure to get re-elected to parliament in the subsequent national elections to the impact of this affair.

Battle Lines in Contemporary Greek Culture

As the above examples illustrate, in Greece the debate over national heritage and cultural identity includes not only the role of the Orthodox Church of Greece in broader society, but also the attitudes and policy vis-à-vis the millions of Greece's legal and illegal immigrants, the teaching and interpretation of history in the Greek schools, and so on. In these intense ideological and cultural conflicts, public intellectuals play prominent roles. As a result, culture wars between self-styled conservative and progressive intellectuals often centre on issues of national heritage – such as those described above.

Although strongly coloured by political partisanship, these cultural-political contests feature relatively well-defined groups of intellectuals with competing public agendas. On the one hand, there are the "defenders of the nation", who routinely suggest that Greece is under siege by forces aiming to undermine its national identity, territorial integrity, state sovereignty and the central role of Orthodox Christianity for defining Greekness. On the other hand, there are the "modernizing intellectuals", who suggest that their opponents are reactionaries bent on keeping Greece away from the European project and social, political and cultural modernization. Their vision is one of engagement with the EU and supranational institutions, with the clear goal of adjusting Greek institutions to international norms. For them, such norms include a multicultural society, acceptance of immigrants as full participants in modern Greek society, the expulsion of nationalistic rhetoric both from foreign policy and from public life (including schools), the endorsement of minority rights, and the conviction that the Orthodox Church of Greece needs to be disentangled from the state (what is usually presented as "Church–state separation").

Perhaps a partial list of names would help the reader gain a better understanding of these debates and their various protagonists. Those belonging to the camp of the "defenders of the nation" include the philosopher Christos Yannaras, the law professor I. Konidaris, and the former university professor Costas Zouraris, as well as the clergyman Ft. Georgios Metallinos. The late Archbishop Christodoulos was perhaps the most charismatic public-opinion maker from within the ranks of this group. Those belonging to the second, "modernizing" camp are themselves split between liberals and Leftists. Liberals include the historians Thanos Veremis and Ioannis Koliopoulos, and the professor of education Maria Repousi. Leftists include the historians Th. Liakos and Effie Gazi, the sociologist Constantine Tsoucalas, the education professor Thalia Dragona, and the political philosopher Giannis Stavrakakis. This list of names is only a partial one, offered here simply for illustrative purposes. It is meant to clearly establish the intellectuals' split along these lines, but also to clearly show that these cultural debates cannot be reduced to the conventional liberal versus Leftist division – and even less so in terms of political allegiances to the Left or Right.

These two public agendas have been competing for the hearts and minds of Greece's public for nearly two decades. The narratives of history woven by each side are meant to provide the template for rendering their respective positions acceptable to the public. This ongoing struggle over issues of national heritage carries with it important implications about Greece's immigration policy, its foreign policy and role in a future EU, and the nature of its public sphere in the twenty-first century.

With regard to Orthodox Christianity in particular, there are two clearly demarcated and radically different paradigms of thinking. The first of these is conventionally referred to as the conservative or "neo-Orthodox" camp. The label is certainly somewhat misleading, because there are neo-Orthodox thinkers of diverse views. But since the late

1990s, the two most prominent public intellectuals affiliated with this camp have been Christos Yiannaras and Costas Zouraris. Using the media in a particularly skilful fashion, they have advanced a populist interpretation that blends Greek nationalism, anti-Western attitudes, anti-modernism, and Orthodoxy. Accordingly, the foundation of the modern Greek state and construction of modern Greek identity in the nineteenth century was an attempt to Westernize the Greek Orthodox people. This political and cultural project is thus seen as a threat to the broader historical and cultural unity of Greeks with the Eastern Orthodox religious heritage. The modernization of Greece undermines the foundations of authentic Greek culture and alienates Greek people from their traditional values.

Against this interpretation stands the conventional academic one of Eastern Orthodoxy as a historical barrier to Greek modernization (Lipowatz 1993; Mappa 1997; Pollis 1999). According to this perspective, Greek Orthodoxy has been a significant obstacle to the success of modernization because of the lack of institutional separation between Church and laity as well as the failure to differentiate the holy and secular domains as such. Following the 1833 establishment of the autocephalous Orthodox Church of Greece, both hierarchs and the modern Greek state sought to cultivate a highly symbiotic relationship in which the state used the clout of the Church to foster its nation-building efforts, while the Church hierarchy used the state to maintain its hegemonic position in society as well as its financial security (through salaries received from the state). Invariably, the end result was a tendency of the Church hierarchy to side with the state and a failure to register an autonomous voice in civil, political and cultural affairs. This trend has been severely criticized by those who attribute this tendency to the lack of institutional differentiation between the Church and broader society (see Fokas 2000).

Unlike its Catholic and Protestant counterparts, the Orthodox Church of Greece (like its sister Eastern Orthodox Churches throughout Eastern Europe) does not differentiate between the institutional structure of the organization and the religious community of believers, but instead maintains the organic unity of original *Ecclesia* inherited from early Christianity. For example, the Church considers the entire body of those publicly affiliated with Orthodoxy as Church members – no meaningful distinction is made between religious adherents (that is, those who regularly attend services and participate in the Eucharist) and those who do not (and hence are only nominally associated with the faith). Maintaining such a holistic approach, critics argue (Mappa 1997: 38–39), does not allow Orthodox Christianity, or more broadly, the Orthodox culture of East European nations, to recognize and accept the Other as an autonomous agent. The Other is not accepted as equal, and social life is not organized on the basis of rational procedures derived from the necessity to coexist with the Other. For example, religious sects and denominations can be accepted if deemed part of Greece's historical legacy, but the free, unrestricted and open operation and competition of rival religious entities within the context of a competitive religious economy is considered sacrilegious. Unlike the historical experience of several West European states (with France as the most famous historical example), the modernization of the Greek state did not entail the separation of Church from state (Karagiannis 2009). Consequently, the argument goes, no room is left for the impersonal principles of Law, Rationality, and Order to assume a status independent of the persons associated with them. Hence, the Greeks' attitude and cultural value system constitute an obstacle to the successful modernization of Greek state and society.

It is important to view this internal cultural debate as reflecting policy positions and orientations, and not necessarily as an accurate reflection of historical events (Roudometof 2005). Orthodox Christianity at large (i.e. the various national Churches, the patriarchates, and the monastic orders) has had an ambiguous and multifaceted relationship with these ongoing struggles over national identity and the European project. It is often both an agent of resistance and an agent of engagement with topics of public discourse (for examples, see Makrides 2009). There is considerable ambivalence in the relationship between the Orthodox Church of Greece, or even more broadly, Orthodox Christianity, and modernity; and the attitudes of the ecclesiastical leadership, as well as individual hierarchs, priests or theologians, cannot be easily grouped into a single camp. Rather, this debate effectively narrows down the entire range of interactions between Orthodox ecclesiastical institutions and the broader Greek society into two different and polarizing options: the Orthodox Church is *either* an agency of protecting traditional values (both religious and secular) from unwarranted intrusions of modernity; *or* it is a reactionary institution that holds back progress and modernization.

In order to gain a better and far more sound understanding of the Church of Greece's reactions, one needs to go beyond the rhetoric of the above-mentioned polarizing interpretations. To do so, one has to take into account the shifting fortunes of Greece after the 1989 collapse of Communism. The 1990s featured a new phase in EU developments – including the Maastricht Treaty (1992), the introduction of the euro, and the EU's Eastern European enlargement in 2004. As a result, the Orthodox Church of Greece found itself in a new and evolving social and cultural landscape. Following the collapse of communist regimes in Eastern Europe, the influx of close to a million legal and illegal immigrants into Greece severely affected Greek society by producing serious challenges on issues of religious pluralism and multicultural coexistence. Simultaneously, the European Union and various Europeanization projects spearheaded by the state and other supranational institutions sought to provide a legal and institutional framework for registering this new situation in state legislature and administrative practice.

The Orthodox Church reacted to these new multiple challenges by re-entering the public domain forcefully in order to reassert its traditional privileged legal, social and cultural status. Its efforts have been variously referred to as "politicization" of the Church or "de-privatization" of Orthodoxy (Alivizatos 1999; Roudometof 2005; Stavrakakis 2003). This politicization of Orthodoxy has been expressed in a variety of issues raised in the context of church–state relations: cremation, catechism in Greek public schools, the status of civil versus church weddings, the Church's role in providing welfare for ethnic Greeks alone (vs. Muslim Greek citizens), the construction of a mosque in Athens, the status of the oath in public ceremonies, and the rights of religious minorities are all topics of great concern that involve the state and its relationship to the Orthodox Church.

But the de-privatization of religion has also been expressed in a tapestry of topics pertaining to the relationship between Orthodox Christianity and the broader Greek society and culture; for example, the Church's new-found role in welfare, the use of popular music to convey religious messages, and the efforts to come to terms with the role of women in the Church are all examples of a refashioning of the relationship between Orthodoxy and modern Greek society and culture (for examples, see Molokotos-Liederman 2010; Fokas 2010; Sotiriu 2010). In other words, the ecclesiastical institutions' engagement with social issues has been multifaceted and far from uniformly negative (or entirely positive).

The Church agents' rhetoric operates against the background of this active engagement. To the extent that compliance with the EU's norms and its famous "culture of compromise" is understood as compromising Greece's national heritage or the nation's "traditional values", intellectuals and Church leaders are likely to voice their opposition – typically expressed in terms of harsh criticism of "globalization" and Europeanization. To the above, it is necessary to add the cultural influx of new mass media that have further added to the impression of a siege upon traditional "local" institutions like the Church – a siege allegedly waged by broader "global" forces. The need to defend the nation against the "globalization threat" was voiced by the late Archbishop Christodoulos (1999: 127), who suggested that globality means "a common hindsight and prospect based on the choices of the powerful. [It means] the decline and perhaps even disappearance of locality." Against this vision of locality, Christodoulos posited Greek-Orthodox particularity.

In this respect, Church discourse at times has echoed concerns typically associated with left-wing criticism of global neo-liberalism. This is certainly ironic – especially since in reality the Church's rhetoric has been routinely opposed by the Greek Left. There is of course a considerable difference between the Left's response and that of the Church. While the Left attempts to rally the people to resist global capitalism and cultural commodification, in the late Christodoulos' view, the Orthodox Church is the only institution of Greek culture that is capable of resisting the centralizing impulses of state-sponsored Europeanization and other global forces that would otherwise undermine Greek national identity (see Oulis, Makris & Roussos 2010: 198–201). It is the issue of nationalism that provides the major battleground between the Church and the Left; for in the latter's view, the intertwining of religion and nationalism so typical not only of Christodoulos' own discourse but also of other hierarchs is reminiscent of a troublesome past. This recourse to the nation has been used in the course of twentieth-century Greek history to justify the persecution of the Left by right-wing governments – most famously during Greece's post-Second World War period (1944–1974). Hence, in spite of their surface similarities in rhetoric opposing new "global" threats to the nation, in reality a great gulf separates the Church from the Left. It is precisely because Greece's Left has been persecuted in the recent past in the name of the national interest that its response has been to look upon Christodoulos as a right-wing nationalist cleric more interested in partisan politics than in ecclesiastical affairs (see Alivizatos 1999; Stavrakakis 2003).

With regard to the Church's overall stance to this range of topics that have consistently emerged in the public debate over the last decades, it is important to comprehend the complex strategy of the Orthodox Church of Greece. Generally speaking, by grounding its self-image in Greek national identity, the Church adopts a flexible strategy with respect to state policy; *viz.*, insofar as the state legislature confirms the Church's privileged position, the Church does not complain about the state's oversight of its own affairs. In fact, the Church is willing to invoke such legislation in order to protect its own interests (Roudometof 2008). But whenever the state enacts legislation that would undermine the Church's privileged position, the Church is capable of publicly criticizing state authorities or campaigning against the politicians who sponsor such legislation. The Church's stance vis-à-vis various legislative efforts has been to declare such secularizing initiatives as inherently "anti-Christian" – a hard-line position that has often led to a complete surrender of the Church's position (see Nikolopoulos 2005 for a review of various cases).

Geopolitics, Nationalism and the Orthodox Church

The 1990s agenda of turning the EU into the United States of Europe has caused various and contradictory responses from the European public. For example, the Habermas-Derrida "Core Europe" proposal (see Levy et al. 2005) called for delaying or postponing the expansion of full membership benefits to the new post-2004 East European EU member states. This proposal was greeted with hostile remarks that such strategies of exclusion are to a degree anti-European, or that they pave the way towards a segmentation of European unity. It is not accidental that East European reaction centred precisely on this issue of Eastern Europeans being made to feel like second-class citizens.

Geopolitical, cultural and religious considerations have played and continue to play a major role in determining each country's response to and understanding of the European project. Csergo and Goldgeier (2004) point out that the European states' strategies vis-à-vis the EU are shaped to a considerable degree by whether the EU is viewed as an alliance of states or as a union of nations. Even more so, the public of states like Greece often expresses a positive evaluation of Europe or the EU, not due to supranational sentiment, but rather because it views

Europe and the EU as shields against geopolitical instability or real and perceived threats emanating from Turkey or other states. Issues of "national interest" and national identity provide important arenas in which to register discontent with the accelerated pace of Europeanization and also to assert the necessity for protection of national difference.

It is not accidental that since the early 1990s the Orthodox Church of Greece has publicly sided with the Serbs in the wars of the Yugoslav succession (Michas 2002). Public support for the Serb Orthodox brethren has been consistent with popular post-Cold War geopolitical thinking in Greece, whereby the goal of forming a Balkan-wide Orthodox alliance against Muslim, or more accurately Turkish, "threats", was widely circulated and discussed. The late Archbishop Christodoulos also favoured this line of thinking (see Oulis, Makris & Roussos 2010: 202). His writings over time reveal a consistent image of Turkey as the "organic successor" to a barbarian Ottoman Empire that enslaved the Greek nation for nearly 400 years. Predictably, EU membership is not considered to be a realistic option for Turkey.

These geopolitical issues connected directly geopolitical matters with religious rhetoric, and were extremely influential during the 1990s – especially in light of the wars of the Yugoslav succession. Of greater importance for Greece itself, however, was the 1991 declaration of independence of the former Yugoslav Republic of Macedonia. The claim to use the term "Macedonia" (which is also the name of the adjacent Greek province) and the historical national mythology of the new nation clashed directly with Greek national narrative (Roudometof 2002). Greece objected to the recognition of the new state on the grounds that the use of the name Macedonia is an infringement upon Greece's cultural heritage. This engendered a diplomatic and geopolitical confrontation that remains unresolved to this day.

Within Greece, ecclesiastic leaders lent their support to the Greek "cultural warriors" (journalists, amateur historians, activists, etc.) who set out to defend the nation's honour against those with softer viewpoints (who were accused of being less patriotic). Metropolitan Anthimos of Thessaloniki (which is the second largest city in Greece and is located in the Greek part of geographical Macedonia) is a well-known outspoken (and would-be) opinion-maker, who routinely uses his Sunday oratory (broadcast regularly by Greece's state television channel ERT-3) to rally nationalist sentiment in favour of hard-line views on the Macedonian issue.

Moreover, in 2000, a new ultra-right-wing political party entered Greek politics: Popular Orthodox Rally (*Laikos Orthodoxos Synagermos*, or LAOS), which was created by former Conservative MP G. Karatzaferis. Unlike its predecessors in the Greek political scene – the National Democratic Union (NDU) and the National Party (NP) – LAOS succeeded in capturing sufficient votes to establish itself in Greece's political landscape. While its predecessors were partly motivated by a romantic gaze towards Greece's pre-1974 authoritarianism, LAOS has a clear-cut agenda that has not been predicated upon a nostalgic view of the recent past. Its agenda is similar to that of other European right-wing parties – including featuring nationalism and anti-immigrant sentiments as key elements. The political use of Orthodoxy is quite explicit in the party's official title, and Karatzaferis himself has repeatedly highlighted his amicable relationship with the late Archbishop Christodoulos. The party naturally adopted hard-line positions on the Macedonian issue as well.

It seems reasonable to suggest the existence of a certain ideological alliance between Orthodox Christianity and political conservativism. Such an overlap is also displayed in the public opinion data (Georgiadou & Nikolakopoulos 2001) but of course this is a global phenomenon. Religious adherents tend to be conservative and, therefore, they are far more likely to support politically conservative parties (see, for example, Jelen 1993). It is however quite mistaken to consider that the viewpoints on the Macedonian issue or similar geopolitical issues (such as the Athens–Ankara disagreements over the Aegean) can be reduced to the conventional political division between the Left and the Right.

More specifically with regard to the post-1991 Macedonian controversy, it might be quite convenient to use Metropolitan Anthimos' numerous and colourful statements as indicators of the nationalist posture of the Church of Greece. What such an exercise leaves out, however, is an inconvenient truth that is quite important: unlike the culture wars over Greece's identity politics, when it comes to issues of "national interest", policy positions are not easily reducible to Left versus Right dichotomies. In fact, as far as public debate on these issues is concerned, one has to concede that the existence of pluralistic perspectives that vary across party lines offers evidence of a vibrant public sphere, where discourse and debate do not degenerate into predictable partisanship. Just like many other European democracies, the division between "hawks" and "doves" in foreign policy is one that, while it sometimes overlaps with political partisanship, nevertheless cannot be reduced to a mere appendage of party politics.

Consider the following comments made in an interview by Mikis Theodorakis, the world-renowned Greek composer and an icon of the Greek Left (Gilson 2010):

> *Q: Many view the word patriotism as an insult today. How do you define it and how does it differ from nationalism?*
>
> *A:* An insult from whom, and for whom? I declare myself a patriot and I adore the Greek nation. Simultaneously, I am an internationalist and a utopian communist. Let anyone come and challenge me. I remind you that all these concepts – homeland, nation, internationalism and communism – were my guides in my every step, work, decision and act from the very beginning, in 1940, when we entered the war, until today. That gives me the right, for my part, to consider whoever battles these concepts as mudslingers.

The above is not an isolated comment. Theodorakis has consistently adopted what is often considered a "hard-line" Greek nationalist attitude with regard to the Macedonian issue. As far back as 2004, he stunned many among Greece's more progressive intelligentsia by issuing a public statement in which he clearly and openly took the so-called "nationalist" position with regard to the infamous Athens–Skopje "name dispute" (i.e. whether the former Yugoslav Republic of Macedonia should be recognized as the "Republic of Macedonia" by Greece and the international community). In that statement, Theodorakis (2004) declared that:

> With regard to Skopje, it will be necessary to underline, I think, that the element which makes us rise and be like one man against the name *"Republic of Macedonia"*, is naturally not with the words but with what some factions visibly signal behind these words, namely *the irredentist claims against our country's territorial integrity* [emphasis in the original]. This is something that unfortunately was not made sufficiently known, with the well-known results. Today, it is therefore time to resoundingly shout in every direction, and chiefly to Skopje itself, so that there will be no delusion regarding our future stance – which in every instance will be what it always has been whenever our national integrity has faced dangers.

Conclusions

In this chapter, I have offered an overview of the Orthodox Church of Greece's engagement with the politics of heritage and memory. Discussion was not restricted only to the specifically ecclesiastical issues, however, but also touched on the polarization of views within Greece's broader public debate on these matters. It is important to view Greece as part of the broader European engagement with this problematic, and not as an exception to presumed European tendencies. The collapse of communism in Eastern Europe, which had a dramatic impact on European social, economic, and political affairs, provided the general context for the reassertion of religion in Greece's cultural politics. This should not be viewed in isolation from broader trends. During the post-1989 period, the most popular response among Orthodox national Churches throughout Eastern Europe has been to cling to their version of the modern synthesis of Church and nation in the face of contemporary globalization (for discussions of individual cases, see Roudometof et al. 2005). Orthodox intellectuals and religious leadership within Greece are not an exception.

In this chapter, I have offered only a sketchy – and not an exhaustive – account of the specific hot issues of ecclesiastical involvement in public culture, the politics of memory, and issues of national heritage. These various hot topics provide arenas where two competing groups of intellectuals offer radically opposite interpretations of them. In this chapter's second section, I offered an overview of the stances and the attitudes of these two opposing groups. Specifically, in the course of this chapter's discussion, I have argued that, in order to gain a balanced perspective on their confrontation, one needs to view their cultural battles as a form of ongoing public negotiation of the relationship between Greece and the broader European project. In other words, the specific cultural battles (over an elementary-school textbook or the mosque or the ID crisis) all provide important sites that offer the occasion to debate the extent and nature of European integration as it should be applied in Greece's case. In these and many other instances, the rhetoric of European values versus the rhetoric concerning the necessity for the protection of national heritage provides the basic cleavage between the opposing sides. In this respect, Greece's debates on these hot topics are expressions of similar disputes that take place throughout Europe – as this volume's other chapters aptly illustrate.

Just as in other European states, political partisanship colours these debates. The proponents of the Church tend to be mostly on the Right, whereas progressive intellectuals tend to be mostly on the Left. However, this is an imperfect generalization with many exceptions. Certainly, political parties take advantage of the Right for political purposes – as is the case with the Greek ultra-right party LAOS.

In Greece's case, I believe, it is useful and relevant to suggest the existence of three different levels of generality with respect to the range of issues where the Church and religion in general are implicated. First, there are the specific ecclesiastical issues (such as cremation or burial rites and baptism for those who have had a civil wedding). These are topics about which the Church enjoys an authoritative position. Some of these issues have more to do with the interpretation of Canon Law and less with national history *per se*.

Second, there is a broad range of more diffuse topics – such as the listing of religious affiliation on ID cards, the operation of mosques, or the Costa Gavras video. These are topics that do not concern the Church exclusively, but about which other constituencies – including the state – have at least equal say in their outcome. In these topics, the Church has to compete for the legitimacy of its viewpoints vis-à-vis other parties. It is in this category that the "use of the past" becomes a highly contested and publicly deliberated issue.

Third, there are broad political issues, such as geopolitics or nationalism and foreign policy. Although the perspectives expressed on such topics – like the Macedonian issue – are certainly coloured by considerations of national memory and heritage, this is not the only consideration. Foreign policy issues are often decided with realism and geopolitical considerations in mind, and the state plays an important role. In this domain, the Church has only limited ability to influence outcomes, as it is only one of several agents in the public scene. Certainly, it can voice its own perspectives, but with far less appeal than on ecclesiastical issues.

Needless to say, the ecclesiastical leadership will undoubtedly persist in voicing their opinions on this entire range of topics. In 2008, after the passing of Christodoulos, the election of Ieronimos to the Archbishopric of Athens and all of Greece signalled a new course in the Church's public involvement. Ieronimos has been soft-spoken, far more liberal and less openly nationalistic than was his predecessor, and unwilling to turn himself into a television personality. His election signalled a victory for those hierarchs who considered that the Church had suffered from media "overexposure" during the former archbishop's tenure and that it was time to adopt a more subdued public persona. Still, as the Pantheon affair demonstrates, the Church's hierarchs remain quite vocal whenever they feel the need to protect the Church's reputation from criticism that they perceive as unjust or biased.

References

Alivizatos, Nicos C. (1999): A New Role for the Greek Church?, *Journal of Modern Greek Studies* 17 (1): 23–39.

Anagnostou, Dia and Ruby Gropas (2010): Domesticating Islam and Muslim Immigrants. Political and Church Responses to Constructing a Central Mosque in Athens, in Victor Roudometof and Vasilios N. Makrides (eds): *The Orthodox Church of Greece in the 21st Century. The Role of Religion in Culture, Ethnicity and Politics.* Aldershot: Ashgate.

Anderson, Benedict (1991): *Imagined Communities. Reflections on the Origin and Spread of Nationalism* (2nd edition). London: Verso.

Andrianopoulos, Andreas (2001): *Hellenism and Orthodoxy,* Athens: Kaktos. (in Greek)

Angelou, Alkis (1999): *The Underground School. Chronicle of a Myth.* Athens: Hestia. (in Greek)

Antivaro (2007): *Special on the New School Textbook for the 6th Grade of Elementary Schools,* http://palio.antibaro.gr/istoria.php#biblio (Accessed 27 August 2010).

Antoniou, Dimitris (2010): The Mosque That Wasn't There. Ethnographic Elaborations on Orthodox Conceptions of Sacrifice, in Victor Roudometof and Vasilios N. Makrides (eds): *Orthodox Christianity in 21st Century Greece. The Role of Religion in Culture, Ethnicity and Politics,* Aldershot: Ashgate.

Christodoulos (Paraskeuaidis), Archbishop of Athens and All Greece (1999): *Of Soil and Heaven,* Athens: Kastaniotis. (in Greek)

Cornwell, Grant H. and Eve Walsh Stoddard (eds) (2001): *Global Multiculturalism. Comparative Perspectives on Ethnicity, Race and Nation,* Lanham: Rowman and Littlefield.

Csergo, Zsuzsa and James M. Goldgeier (2004): Nationalist Strategies and European Integration, *Perspectives on Politics,* (2) 1: 21–37.

Danopoulos, Constantine P. (2004): Religion, Civil Society and Democracy in Orthodox Greece, *Journal of Southern Europe and the Balkans* (6) 1: 41–56.

Dimitropoulos, Panagiotis (2001): *State and Church. A Difficult Relationship,* Athens: Kritiki. (in Greek)

Fokas, Efterpie (2000): Greek Orthodoxy and European Identity, in Achilleas Mitsos and Elias Mossialos (eds): *Contemporary Greece and Europe*, Aldershot: Ashgate.

Fokas, Efterpie (2010): Religion and Welfare in Greece. A New, or Renewed Role for the Church?, in Victor Roudometof and Vasilios N. Makrides (eds): *The Orthodox Church of Greece in the 21st Century. The Role of Religion in Culture, Ethnicity and Politics.* Aldershot: Ashgate.

Gazi, Efi (2004): *The Second Life of the Three Hierarchs. A Genealogy of the "Graeco-Christian Civilization",* Athens: Nefeli. (in Greek)

Georgiadou, Vasiliki and Ilias Nikolakopoulos (2001): The People of the Church, in C. Vervardakis (ed.): *Public Opinion in Greece,* Athens: VPRC-Livanis. (in Greek)

Giannakou, Marietta (2007): 2 August 2007 Interview, *Marietta Giannakou*, http://www.giannakou.gr/index.php?page=view_article&news_id=4 (Accessed 27 August 2010).

Gilson, George (2010): Interview with Mikis Theodorakis, *Athens News*, June 21: 10–11, http://www.athensnews.gr/articles/13367/07/12/2009/24111 (Accessed 28 August 2010).

Graham, Brian, Gregory John Ashworth and J. E. Turnbridge (2000): *A Geography of Heritage. Power, Culture and Economy*, London: Arnold.

Hervieu-Léger, Danièle (2000): *Religion as a Chain of Memory*, New Brunswick: Rutgers University Press.

Hunter, James (1992): *Culture Wars. The Struggle To Control The Family, Art, Education, Law, and Politics in America*, New York: Basic.

Jelen, Ted G. (1993): The Political Consequences of Religious Group Attitudes, *The Journal of Politics* 55: 178–190

Karagiannis, Evangelos (2009): Secularism in Context. The Relations Between the Greek State and the Church of Greece in Crisis, *European Journal of Sociology* 50 (1): 133–167

Levy, Daniel, Max Pensky and John Torpey (eds) (2005): *Old Europe, New Europe, Core Europe. Transatlantic Relations after the Iraqi War*, London: Verso.

Lipowatz, Thanos (1993): Orthodox Christianity and Nationalism. Two Aspects of the Modern Greek Political Culture, *Greek Political Science Review*, 2: 31–47. (in Greek)

Lowenthal, David (1998): *The Heritage Crusade and the Spoils of History*, Cambridge: Cambridge University Press.

Makrides, Vasilios N. (1995): The Orthodox Church and the Post-War Religious Situation in Greece, in Wade Clark Roof, Jackson W. Carroll and David A. Roozen (eds), *The Post-War Generation and Establishment Religion. Cross-Cultural Perspectives*, Boulder: Westview.

Makrides, Vasilios N. (2004): L'"Autre" Orthodoxie. Courants du Rigorisme Orthodox Grec, *Social Compass*, 51 (4): 511–521.

Makrides, Vasilios N. (2009): *Hellenic Temples and Christian Churches. A Concise History of the Religious Cultures of Greece from Antiquity to the Present*, New York: New York University Press.

Makrides, Vasilios N. and Victor Roudometof (2010): Tradition, Transition and Change in Greek Orthodoxy at the Dawn of the Twenty-First Century. Introductory Considerations, in Victor Roudometof and Vasilios N. Makrides (eds), *Orthodox Christianity in 21st Century Greece. The Role of Religion in Culture, Ethnicity and Politics*. Aldershot: Ashgate.

Mappa, Sofia (1997): *Orthodoxy and Authority in Greek Society*, Athens: Exantas. (in Greek)

Mavrocordatos, George T. (2003): Orthodoxy and Nationalism in the Greek Case, in John T. S. Madeley and Zsolt Enyedi (eds), *Church and State in Contemporary Europe. The Chimera of Neutrality*, London: Frank Cass.

Michas, Takis (2002): *Unholy Alliance. Greece and Milosevic's Serbia*, College Station: Texas A & M University Press.

Molokotos-Liederman, Lina (2003): Identity Crisis. Greece, Orthodoxy, and the European Union, *Journal of Contemporary Religion*, 18 (3): 291–315.

Molokotos-Liederman, Lina (2007a): Looking at Religion and Greek Identity from the Outside. The Identity Cards Conflict through the Eyes of Greek Minorities, *Religion, State and Society*, 35: 139–161.

Molokotos-Liederman, Lina (2007b): The Greek ID Card Controversy. A Case Study of Religion and National Identity in a Changing European Union, *Journal of Contemporary Religion*, 22: 187–203.

Molokotos-Liederman, Lina (2010): Sacred Words in a Secular Beat. The Free Monks Phenomenon at the Intersection of Religion, Youth and Popular Culture, in Victor Roudometof and Vasilios N. Makrides (eds), *The Orthodox Church of Greece in the 21st Century. The Role of Religion in Culture, Ethnicity and Politics.* Aldershot: Ashgate.

Ng, David (2009): Acropolis Museum Backs Down in Costa Gavras Film Row, *Reuters News Agency*, http://uk.reuters.com/article/idUKTRE5733W020090804 (Accessed 4 August 2010).

Nikolopoulos, Panagiotis D. (2005): *Privatization of Religion and Secularization of the Church,* Athens: Kastaniotis. (in Greek)

Nora, Pierre (1996–1998): *Realms of Memory. The Construction of the French Past,* New York: Columbia University Press.

Olick, Jeffrey K. Vered Vinitzky-Seroussi and Daniel Levy (eds) (2011): *The Collective Memory Reader.* Oxford: Oxford University Press.

Oulis, Dimitris, Gelasimos Makris and Sotiris Roussos (2010): The Orthodox Church of Greece. Policies and Challenges Under Archbishop Christodoulos of Athens (1998–2008), *International Journal for the Study of the Christian Church* 10 (2–3): 192–210.

Papageorgiou, Niki (2000): *The Church in Modern Greek Society,* Thessaloniki: Pournaras. (in Greek)

Pollis, Adamantia (1999): Greece. A Troublesome Secular State, in Dimitris Christopoulos (ed.): *Legal Issues of Religious Difference in Greece,* Athens: Kritiki. (in Greek)

Prodromou, Elizabeth H. (2004): Negotiating Pluralism and Specifying Modernity in Greece. Reading Church-State Relations in the Christodoulos Period, *Social Compass* (51) 4: 471–485.

Roudometof, Victor (2001). *Nationalism, Globalization, and Orthodoxy. The Social Origins of Ethnic Conflict in the Balkans,* Westport: Greenwood.

Roudometof, Victor (2002). *Collective Memory, National Identity and Ethnic Conflict. Greece, Bulgaria and the Macedonian Question,* Westport: Praeger.

Roudometof, Victor (2005): Orthodoxy as Public Religion in Post-1989 Greece, in Victor Roudometof, Alexander Agadjanian and Jerry Pankhurst (eds): *Eastern Orthodoxy in a Global Age. Tradition Meets the 21st Century,* Walnut Creek: Alta Mira Press.

Roudometof, Victor (2007): Collective Memory and Cultural Politics. An Introduction, *Journal of Political and Military Sociology,* 35 (1): 1–16.

Roudometof, Victor (2008): Greek-Orthodoxy, Territoriality and Globality. Religious Responses and Institutional Disputes, *Sociology of Religion,* 68 (1): 67–91.

Roudometof, Victor (2010): The Evolution of Greek-Orthodox Christianity in the Context of World-Historical Globalization, in Victor Roudometof and Vasilios N. Makrides (eds): *Orthodox Christianity in 21st Century Greece. The Role of Religion in Culture, Ethnicity and Politics,* Aldershot: Ashgate.

Roudometof, Victor and Vasilios N. Makrides (eds) (2010): *Orthodox Christianity in 21st Century Greece. The Role of Religion in Culture, Ethnicity and Politics,* Aldershot: Ashgate.

Roudometof, Victor, Alexander Agadjanian and Jerry Pankhurst (eds) (2005): *Eastern Orthodoxy in a Global Age. Tradition Meets the 21st Century,* Walnut Creek: Alta Mira Press.

Sotiriu, Eleni (2010): "The Traditional Modern". Rethinking the Position of Contemporary Greek Women in Orthodoxy, in Victor Roudometof and Vasilios N.
Makrides (eds): *The Orthodox Church of Greece in the 21st Century. The Role of Religion in Culture, Ethnicity and Politics*. Aldershot: Ashgate.

Stavrakakis, Yannis (2003): Politics and Religion. On the "Politicization" of Greek
Church Discourse, *Journal of Modern Greek Studies*, 21 (2): 153–182.

Stoianovich, Traian (1994): *The Balkan Worlds. The First and Last Europe*. New York:
M. E. Sharpe.

Taylor, Charles (1994): The Politics of Recognition, in Charles Taylor, K. Anthony
Appiah, Jurgen Habermas, Steven C. Rockefeller, Michael Walzer, and Susan Wolf
(eds): *Multiculturalism. Examining the Politics of Recognition*, Princeton: Princeton
University Press.

Theodorakis, Mikis (2004): Public Statement, 10 November, *Theodorakis*, http://
en.mikis-theodorakis.net/index.php/article/articleview/398/1/10/ (Accessed 28
August 2010).

CHAPTER 10

Exploring the Particular in the Global World

Three Contemporary Bosnian Theological Writers on Islam, Sufism, Authenticity and National Belonging

Catharina Raudvere

In 1966 the novelist Meša Selimović (d. 1982) used the Sufi environment around the Hadži Sinanova Sufi lodge (*tekija*) in Sarajevo to provide an eighteenth-century frame for criticism of the contemporaneously rigid socialist society in which the author lived. The depiction of the Ottoman administrative hierarchies in the novel *Dervish and the Death* (English transl. 1996) was far from a flattering historical mirror image for the Yugoslav federation. This particular setting provided Selimović with space to discuss moral integrity and the lack of it, group loyalty versus individual needs, and strategies for navigating hierarchies in an authoritarian society. Parallels were quickly drawn by readers, and later by critics too, to the time immediately after the Second World War when Partisan committees had gained power over individuals' lives in the absence of a functional state administration; a situation which had consequences for Selimović's own family (Cooper 1996). The spiritual life of the dervishes plays an insignificant role in the plot of the novel, and Selimović is definitely not a religious writer. Nevertheless, to many readers then, and later, the book was not only criticism in disguise, it was also the first encounter with a venture to include the world of the dervishes in a shared cultural background for people living in Yugoslav Bosnia – although from a literary perspective, not a historian's.

In the long run, the widely read novel sparked awareness among general readers of Sufi traditions as part of a regional cultural heritage, but it was not primarily among the Sufi circles that religion became part of the political agenda when opposition to the authoritarian rule became noticeable towards the last decades of the Tito era. As will be discussed below, the influences of the 1980s and 1990s were more of a global Sunni mobilization for Islamic authenticity in which Sufi-orientated actors did not play any prominent role.

The decline of the socialist federation after Tito's death in 1980, and the cruel war after the independent states were proclaimed in the early 1990s, constitute the necessary background against which contemporary debates on religion, identity and belonging must be viewed. The authors discussed in this chapter had received their academic schooling during the last decade of the Yugoslav era; a period ending in a war (1992–95) that saw ethno-religious political mobilization in general growing steadily stronger and the space for alternative understandings of Muslim identities diminishing. This did not result in any general radicalization after the war in any profound sense as the media image sometimes implies, but the political development and foreign religious influences definitely pushed public discourse on identity and belonging in a more conservative religious direction (Öktem 2010; Raudvere 2012a).

The specific aim of this chapter is to discuss some examples where references to Sufism appear in the writings of three Bosnian Muslim theological writers in the period after the war in the 1990s. The authors, Enes Karić, Rešid Hafizović and Adnan Silajdžić, have taken positions that cannot be inscribed on a theological conservative–liberal scale, and a common feature is their search for religious answers to the disruption caused by politics. The five selected collections of essays by the three authors are in many ways examples of how a shared world of multicultural and inter-faith dialogues is explored by means of references to selected parts of Bosnian Muslim heritage.

Religion and National Belonging in Contemporary Bosnia

The Muslims of Bosnia constitute a fairly small community, even if its large diaspora is added. Nevertheless, certain of the trends observed in the books discussed here are relevant for global discussions in the Muslim world, or for that matter certainly also among other denominations.

Trine Stauning Willert's chapter on Greek Orthodox theologians in the present volume indicates a similar striving towards universalism as a stand against chauvinistic nationalism. The Bosnian writers discussed here indicate a complex relation between conceptions of heritage, identity and authentic religion.

From the 1980s a pronounced new interest in religion was noticeable among urban Muslims in the Yugoslav federation. Religious belonging and background became a key instrument when the issues of the time were formulated in ethno-national categories. This trend was perhaps first more apparent in Catholic and Orthodox circles in the 1960s and '70s, when many Muslim activities were still, if not underground, then at least inconspicuous in terms of more large-scale mobilization (Karić 2011a; Lučić 2012). As a reaction to the Yugoslav anti-religious politics, Muslim Bosnians did not cultivate nostalgic perceptions of an Ottoman past to the extent one might suppose. Instead, since the 1980s young active Muslims were under the increasing influence of globalized Islam and its more conservative views of "folkreligion" and local customs, in which Sufi rituals were included by some young imams who came back from studies in Egypt, Saudi Arabia or Malaysia.[1] This condition highlights an apparent paradox that follows the increased visibility of Islam in Bosnia for more than three decades: on the one hand there is an emphasis on cultural heritage and regional identity, and on the other a general quest for Islamic authenticity that does not provide space for the Balkans' Sufi traditions. Or in other words, there is a stress on underlining Muslim life in the Balkans as part of European history as well as an emphasis on Islam's Arabic origin. Both positions have been used to define Bosnian Muslim identities, and conceptions of Sufism play a role for them both.

The early pre-war political use of religion was an issue for a limited group of Muslims. Alija Izetbegović, whose "Islamic Declaration" (1970) was formulated already in the late 1960s and thereafter circulated to a great extent underground, became the most prolific voice for opposition based on Islamic arguments.[2] In 1983 the trial in Sarajevo of thirteen Muslim intellectuals attracted international attention, and already then the image of Bosnian Muslim life as being under strong Arab influence began to conquer foreign media, although there was not a large movement around Izetbegović at the time. As the conflicts grew more severe, it was hardly the time for complexity – neither in rhetoric nor in analyses. Religious discourses were inevitably drawn into politics. As an engineer, rather than an Islamic scholar, the late Alija Izetbegović is an example of shifts in authority and leadership in the contemporary Muslim world. With his at the same time both ideological and more pragmatic political influence, Izetbegović embodied a split attitude to Sufism and the particularities of Bosnian Islam that often returns, hailing this more mystic aspect of Islam as historical legacy and wanting to purify it at the same time. Izetbegović was one of the founders of the Democratic Action Party (SDA) that formulated Muslim identity issues politically and was in power between 1990 and 2000. This period was formative for the issues brought up in the essays studied here.

Sufism – Theology, Ritual Practice and Textual Motif

Sufism (*tesavvuf*) often appears at the core of what is generally held up as the significant regional characteristics of Balkan Muslim life (Popovic 1994, 2009; Raudvere 2012b). The references to Sufism function as a recurring motif that offers a literary figure with which to approach history as well as visions and ideas for the future.

Sufism and the ritual life connected with its meeting places and local pilgrim sites have been criticized, if not attacked, as "folk Islam" from two very different ideological angles. For more than a century, both secular liberals and representatives of purist Muslim interpretations have raised objections against what they find over-emotional and irrational. Some regard Sufism as lingering superstitious folk religion, impossible to integrate with what is perceived as modern Islam, and therefore turn to more purist alternatives, quite often among proselytizing Arab, Arabized or Turkish groups. To complicate the picture even more, the Sufi legacy, despite its connection to folk religion, is nevertheless highlighted as significant for a particularly European feature of Islam prevalent in the Balkans. An ambiguity in relation to what many experience as "Bosnian tradition" is therefore apparent, as it is thought, on the one hand, to remain authentic and stand independent of any Arabization of the original message. On the other hand, is it also considered to represent qualities that could easily be integrated with modernity: liberal, open to other denominations, and focused on personal piety. In short: As much as a mode of religious expression, Sufism is also a tool when the cultural memory of the Muslim Balkans is defined.

The importance of the Sufi orders (*tarikat*) in the Muslim history of the Balkans is undeniable. The orders constituted, beside their obvious religious role, important social, cultural and economic networks across urban and rural divisions. With their transnational contacts and strong cohesion within the groups, the Sufi orders provided adaptation to changes within a framework of traditionalism. They have therefore become emblematic among detractors as well as sympathizers for their ability to change and at the same time survive. The resurgence of the historical orders of the region, and the appearance of new groups and networks, is telling of the role of Islam and religious belonging in contemporary Bosnia and Herzegovina. This chapter will, however, discuss the role of Sufism as a signifier of intellectual alliances in the work of some contemporary theological writers. Taking up the theme of Sufism appears to be a way of both being able to connect to regional Muslim history as well as linking to an international non-Muslim audience and its image of Sufism as a more spiritual mode of Islam, and to certain intellectual trends of universalism. The recent war and its aftermath is the inescapable background to the books discussed, both at a political level and a more personal one for the individual authors. Their focus on Sufism can be seen as a way of reacting to politicized national identities based on formal religious belonging, and a mode of connecting with non-political spirituality throughout history, and both inside and outside the Muslim world.

As intellectuals, in this particular case academics and public voices, the authors base their authority in their field of expertise – but comment on topics of general interest, and communicate to a broader audience than academia. However, they are only partly critical, as they speak from an ambiguous position of being both part of and seeing this from a distance. Muslim intellectuals have by tradition been men of learning who have based their authority on their formal education and their theological and juridical positions. In these capacities, they have for centuries been part of local and regional power structures in terms of accepted religious expressions, legal interpretations and theological alliances. The twentieth century saw new types of leadership all over the Muslim world competing for influence (Cooper et al. 1998; Esposito & Voll 2001). In the Yugoslav case there were dissidents, such as Alija Izetbegović, in pronounced opposition to the regime, and men holding official offices in the Islamic Community who were defenders of traditional values, but still part of an administrative body with close links to the state (Bougarel 2001, 2007; Popovic 2006; Lučić 2012). In the introduction to his edited volume *Producing Islamic Knowledge*

(2011),[3] Martin van Bruinessen discusses the shifting conditions for contemporary Muslim authorities and points out both social changes in many Muslim communities and new modes of communication and access to information for groups not necessarily linked to the men of learning.

Based on Talal Asad's reasoning about Islam (and other denominations) as a discursive tradition, van Bruinessen discusses the strategies for these new conditions for authority to formulate tradition are met and the means to gain legitimacy are accepted in local communities. Zygmunt Bauman's distinction between legislators (who build authority on tradition and accepted truths) and interpreters (who in postmodernity challenge established truths) is to some extent relevant for the cases here, as they indicate active uses of history and the search for authenticity (1987). At the same time they are too categorical to be applied unconditionally to the present cases, as just a quick glance at their CVs and publication lists of the authors shows. For intellectuals in post-war times and in globalized modernity, Bauman's terms appear to be positions to navigate between rather than characteristics of specific forms of exercised authority. Stephen Leonard makes an important point on Bauman's categorization: "the authority of the modern legislator intellectual may be derived in part from his epistemic claim ... that rounds out the justification for his intervention in social and political activities" (1986: 16f.). The Bosnian cases do not necessarily indicate a shift in Bauman's chronological sense from high to late modernity, but point at the discursive advantage of addressing different crowds in a global world with different modes of communication.

Three Muslim Theological Writers on the Concept of Authentic Religion and Bosnian Heritage

The objective of this chapter is to discuss how Sufism is used by three individual voices in the debate about which cultural heritage can be useful in the construction of the foundation for Bosnian Islam. These three theological writers, Enes Karić (b. 1958), Rešid Hafizović (b. 1956) and Adnan Silajdžić (b. 1958), have several features in common. They hold positions at the Faculty of Islamic Sciences in Sarajevo (FIN);[4] they have published academic essays and books in English with a clear ambition to reach out to an international audience and debates beyond the national borders. They are close in age and have adult experience of the late Yugoslav era and the war in the 1990s, which forms an important background to several of the essays and books discussed below.[5] The authors are all well known to the more educated readers in Bosnia for their public opinions on contemporary issues and theological stances. However, they address different themes from slightly different theological positions, and they publish with different publishing houses; a detail that bears some significance. The writers and their individual networks connect at several points, not only because of their academic positions at FIN, and they appear crosswise as each other's peer reviewers in the colophons of the books.

The selected books are essayistic, and not academic studies in the strict sense of the term. They can to a great extent be characterized as post-war projects for the public debate, as the wars in the 1990s and their consequences in one way or the other constitute a point of departure for the arguments put forward: lingering traumas after the atrocities, failed reconciliation, and the constitutional predicament of Bosnia and Herzegovina following the Dayton Accords that has set many borders between ethno-religious groups. It must be noted from the beginning that none of these authors represents any chauvinistic nationalism or expresses any excluding definition of who is a Bosnian Muslim. They are not Muslim nationalists, but defenders of Muslim religious heritage as formative for the region's past and future, and all three of them distinctly emphasize Islamic authenticity as the root of Sufism when the topic is approached. In the following, I do not argue that the three writers are representative of any general trends in Bosnia or that they have had a substantial influence by means of these five books, but that they are in many respects symptomatic of the post-war period. Their work indicates an identification of the need to seek new alliances that are adapted to a global discourse on spirituality, and with this new context come different conditions for the exercise of religious authority.

Enes Karić is perhaps the most prolific public figure of the three selected authors, as he served as Minister of Education and Culture from 1994 to 1996 (in a government led by Haris Silajdžić, a relative of Adnan Silajdžić); he has been the dean of the Faculty of Islamic Sciences at the University of Sarajevo, and he ran for the position as head of the Islamic Community in 2005 (Bougarel 2007: 105ff.). Furthermore, he has translated and introduced the Iranian-born Sufi scholar Seyyed Hossein Nasr, and in 1995 he published his translation of the Quran into Bosnian. Karić is also the one who has most international publications, and he has also published one novel and a travelogue from a pilgrimage to Mecca (the latter has been translated into English, *The Black Tulip*).[6]

The chapters of *Essays (on Behalf) of Bosnia* (1999) were all published first in Bosnian during the war and the immediate post-war period (1992–1999). Before they were collected in one volume, the English pieces were published and presented not only in Europe and the USA, but also in Turkey, Pakistan and Malaysia. This indicates that the texts, already as oral presentations, were aimed at varied audiences, which is also apparent from the way the arguments are put forward. The war provides the resonance, and in the acknowledgements Enes Karić tells of losses and the siege of Sarajevo as a motive for publishing the book. The volume was published by El-Kalem, the publishing house of the Islamic Community in Bosnia, and in cooperation with FIN. The peer reviewers of the book, as indicated in the colophon, were the historian Zdravko Grebo and the author and essayist Dževad Karahasan, who are also addressed in the acknowledgements.

Enes Karić positions himself with a passage from Meša Selimović's *Death and the Dervish*, which precedes the chapters as a vignette. A sentence in the middle of the quotation reads, in Karić's translation: "We live at the crossroads of the worlds, on the border of nations; we bear the brunt for everybody, and we have always been guilty in the eyes of someone."[7] The quotation does not indicate who "we" are, but judging from the following essays it is the Bosnian Muslims and their position in a regional border zone, where identities never completely fit the expectations of others, neither east nor west. In the essay "Islam in Contemporary Bosnia: A Personal Statement", that starts with the Selimović quotation again, Karić returns to the border zone as the homeland of the Bosnian Muslims and its importance for Europe at large (1990:90ff.).

In the third section of the collection ("The Universe of the Quran") a long essay is dedicated to Sufism: "The Significance of Sufism in the History of Islamic Civilization: Its Place and Value in the Universal and Perennial Process of Spiritual Inquiry". The title alone tells us that the perspective is not ethnographic, but rather that Sufism is promoted here as the Islamic contribution to perennial philosophy, and the choice of terminology leads the reader's associations to traditionalist writers like Réne Guénon and Frithjof Schoun. A note at the end of the chapter indicates that the text was presented at a UNESCO conference in Paris in 1999 on "Different Aspects of Islamic Culture" and confirms that Karić has served as a voice of intellectual Bosnian Muslims at several points.[8]

The point of departure for Karić's essay on Sufism is an emphasis on the unity between two classical theological concepts, *sharia* (law) and *haqiqa* (truth), as a hallmark of Sufi stances or positions, and that the fundamental base is in the Quran. The focus on canonical scripture and divine law is in line with the arguments of the previous chapters. Enes Karić expresses an ambiguous attitude towards Sufism, as does Rešid Hafizović. The initial confirmation of the Quranic foundation of Sufism and its place at the core of Islamic tradition is essential to his reasoning. The ambiguity mirrors not only the historical debates as to whether Sufism is an innovation (*bida*) or originally Islamic, but also contemporary conflicts about what constitutes authentic Islam.

The Sufi classic Ibn Arabi (d. 1240) and the contemporary liberal theologian Nasr Hamid Abu Zayd (d. 2010) are present in the text from the beginning, as is a reference to Seyyed Hossein Nasr (b. 1933), one of the leading philosophers of the *sophia perennis* school (Stenberg 1996: 97ff.). This signals Karić's basic understanding of Sufism. Perennialism, sometimes referred to as the traditionalist school, is a particular course in the intellectual and religious history of Europe, and with connections to all the world religions as well as to more spiritualistic currents (Wasserstrom 1999; Sedgwick 2004, 2011). The basic theological doctrine is the conviction in one universal religion which has manifested itself in various ways in different religions. Leading figures like Réne Guénon, Frithjof Schoun, Martin Lings and Seyyed Hossein Nasr have all emphasized Sufism as the particular exponent of *philosophia perennis* in Islam (Rawlinson 1997: 25ff., 543ff.). The universalism of the traditionalists is often combined with a more or less pronounced anti-modernism and anti-materialism which makes it a useful tool for cultural criticism.

The printed version of the essay as it stands is rather closed, as it does not introduce Sufism or the Sufi works referred to and leaves the completion of the full picture to the reader. Karić does not aim to introduce Sufism, but to hold it up as a reflection of universal insights not bound to any specific historical context. In Karić's chapter, it is rather the Quran interpretations of Ibn Arabi and Abu Zayd that structure the reasoning in the text and thus relate to the other chapters in the section. The Sufi methodology connects to the broader hermeneutical theme of the book, as Karić underlines the eternal and symbolic meanings of the Quran and thus opens for a connection to universal and perennial philosophy and quotes Ibn Arabi: "Pass from the forms seen by your eyes to the essence offered to you by those forms" (1999: 247). Nasr Hamid Abu Zayd's symbolic understanding of the Quran is also quoted at length: "Ordinary human language points to the Divine language, and the Divine language to the Reality, to the Absolute"; and he continues: "The Divine language, the Quran for example, contains symbols which can be understood only by God's chosen admirers" (1999: 249). Enes Karić's comment underlines that Sufis see the internal meaning of every possible perception, and thus perceive meaning in the smallest expression.

If the first of the four sections of the chapter are focused on the legitimacy of Sufism and its implications for Quran hermeneutics, the last one is more specifically directed towards a non-Muslim audience and in many respects connects to the following chapter with its critical reflections on modern science. The role of Sufism in Islamic civilization is defined as: "the courses of eternal wisdom, perennial thought and spirit" (1999: 256); it is constituted by God-inspired wisdom of perennial quality. Sufism is "washing Islamic theological systems from outside and strengthening them by its new live sap from inside" (1999: 258). But nothing from the discussions of wartime Bosnia in the first sections of the volume recurs in the discussions of Sufism. Instead, an eternal perspective is introduced, and with a reference to the Quran 21:30, but with no quotation or comment: "Man is predisposed to the perennial wisdom which has been stored in him as a seed, a spark" (1999: 256). Karić writes of and ascribes to Sufism a universal trait, in that this inextinguishable spark is to be found in other religions, though with a proviso: "provided they are truly traditional".

Like all three writers, Enes Karić bases his understanding on Sufism as an exponent of perennial philosophy, and at the end of the essay he opens up for an understanding of Sufi traditions as something that provides sapient qualities to conventional theology. The criticism is mild, and the focus is rather on promoting a priori categories of unambiguous cultural units such as "traditions", "religions", "civilizations" from more of a value-conservative perspective than an esoteric traditionalist one.

In the introductory note to his second collection, *Essays on Our European Never-Never Land* (2004),[9] Enes Karić reflects on the title, which he assumes the reader might find pessimistic. Nevertheless, he finds it appropriate for Bosnia's ambiguous relation to Europe: something foreign in the back yard, but still within the compound; and it connects well to the Selimović epigraph in the first volume. The choice of metaphors underlines once again the fringe position of the Muslims of the Balkans as their particular situation. Karić raises the issue of whether Europe really wants the Muslims from the region as parts of a shared cultural legacy: "The Balkans has committed genocide against us, and Europe will not want us like this, indigent, state-less and wretched" (2004: 6). Here, Enes Karić identifies three significant areas of problems: poverty, the lack of political structure in Bosnia and Herzegovina after the Dayton Accord, and the destructive role of victimhood after the atrocities in the 1990s. But rather than defining the situation in political and social terms, Enes Karić chooses wording as if he were characterizing a person, not the conditions of a nation, and deems it "an unhappy theme".

At several points in the volume, Karić refers to leading traditionalists, and the main chapter of Sufi relevance is the introduction to the philosopher Seyyed Hossein Nasr, whom Karić has translated and introduced to Bosnian audiences since the 1980s. In Nasr's extensive writings there are especially two fundamentals that are underlined by Karić: the base in *philosophia perennis* and the criticism of "Western science", and "the Moderna" that has effectively hindered contemporary individuals from reaching their traditional roots within their religious tradition.

Rešid Hafizović is the only one of the three writers who addresses Sufism in the very title of his book, *The Human Image in the Mirror of Sufism* (2005), and develops it as the main motif throughout the volume. In this case, the reviewers of the book were Enes Karić and Adnan Silajdžić. The writer is well known in Bosnia as the translator of Ibn Arabi and Persian classics of Sufi relevance. Hafizović is also well known to the general public for his outspoken criticism of the Islamic Community for not taking a clear enough stance against radical Islamist groups. These immediate debates are, however, not present in the volume.

The book about Sufism was published by the Ibn Sina Institute in Sarajevo, an institution funded by the Iranian Ministry of Education and led by staff from Iran. This fact is not so much an indication of the theological inclination of the author as an example of the century-long importance of Persian literature for Bosnian Sufis, as well as an indication of how comparatively well-funded foreign institutions were in contrast to Bosnian ones in the immediate post-war period, and that this also had an impact.[10]

The essays appear in a bilingual volume, in a design similar to one of Adnan Silajdžić's (2006), and can be read in English from one cover and in Bosnian from the other; this mode of approach signals an openness to many kinds of readers.

In a personal foreword, Rešid Hafizović, with his family roots in Srebrenica, calls Sufism "my real sanctuary" in wartime (2005: 9), and dedicates the book to his killed brothers and their mother. The war has brought the worst and the lowest of humans, and Hafizović's quest for a spiritual alternative that can meet the human condition leads him, like Enes Karić, to the roots. The book presents a coherent motif throughout the text: Adam, who represents what the author labels the diffracted face of the human soul on its way up the spiritual ladder towards God and unity (*tevhid*).

In a short chapter, a particular character is introduced: "Homo bosnia-cus: The Image of the Dismembered Purushe" (2005: 65ff.). Here the Bosnian Muslims are compared to the "heavenly Purushe – Metaphysical Man", although the Vedic background of the slaughtered primordial being (Purusha) is never clearly stated. It is highly unexpected imagery, and Bosnia's position is defined as: "Caught between the stake and the cross, between the curved Turkish blade and the incense-burner, like the spirit of the wandering Jew, *Homo bosniacus* was forced to keep seeking a new spiritual abode on the map", and Hafizović continues: "and at the same time to discover and don a new spiritual garment in which he would recognize the metaphysical and moral plenitude of his primordial spiritual genius" (2005: 66). This being is placed in parallel with "the primal genius of the pregnant Abrahamic tradition" and "the authentic Semitic gnosis with which the spiritual taste and aroma of Moses, Jesus and Muhammad's unchanged law is imbued" (2005: 67). As in the argument of Enes Karić, the three religions share the spark; the human quest is to regain it. Even so, it is highly unusual with references like these to non-monotheistic religions.

The Vedic Purusha myth of the slaughtered primeval being, "the Man", is obviously a metaphor for war-torn Bosnia, and Hafizović ends the chapter with the only hint to a Hindu reality when arguing why this myth is a relevant comparison to *Homo bosniacus*: "the dismembered Purushe, the cosmic Man, who has long since lost his head, shoulders and trunk, so that his existence has been reduced to the lowest horizons of his Vaisya-Sudra [low cast] limbs" (2005: 72). In this reference to the two lowest groups in the Hindu caste system – which requires the reader to have some knowledge of Vedic/Hindu mythology – Bosnia's victimhood is given a brutal image. At the same time it is an image of the human condition when separated from "authentic gnosis".

With the chapter "Sufi Hermeneutics of the Heart as the Recipient of Initiatory Wisdom", Hafizović connects to a theme at the core of Karić's and Silajdžić's writings too: the genealogy of Abrahamic religions and the shared spiritual tradition that is possible to reach despite the contamination of modernity. This is, according to Hafizović, the "sacrohistorical and hierohistorical self-epiphany" (2005: 120) that provides "the ripe, bursting fruits of the olive trees of Sinai, the vines of Carmel and the date palms of the Hijaz" (2005: 121). Sufi literature is in this respect a major tool for reaching the core of the three world religions and, viewed from the point of departure of the book, a way to distance oneself from the rifts and conflicts of contemporary times. There is still an obvious connection between identity and belonging, and to the Sufi legacy of Bosnian traditions.

Both Adnan Silajdžić's collections of essays, like Karić's, were published in cooperation between the Faculty of Islamic Sciences and the publishing house of the Islamic Community, el-Kalem. His are the only two books of the five that have figurative covers which comment on the issues dealt with. *Muslim Perceptions of Other Religions* (2006) uses Tarik Jesenković's picture "Muslim Identity: Homage à Magritte", based on the often reproduced painting "La reproduction interdite", where the man reflected in the mirror has a fez on his head, but the man looking in the mirror does not. In this case, both the title and the cover clearly illustrate the identity issues brought up in the book: resemblance, but not sameness. As mentioned above, this volume too can also be read in English from one cover and in Bosnian from the other. On the cover of the other volume, *Muslims in Search of an Identity* (2007), there is a stylized courtyard of a mosque in the shape of a labyrinth with a minaret in the corner, hinting at arabesque tradition and its playful blend of figurative and non-figurative art, and designed by the same artist as above.

Adnan Silajdžić's books are of a somewhat different character from those discussed above, as they are more academic and more frequently relate to works from the humanities and anthropology. The presence of Sufism is also more indirect, but the references to Guénon, Nasr, Schoun and Renan are there as guides to the traditionalist sources, though also Ahmed Akbar, William Chittick and other names from perennialist Sufi circles. Both books were reviewed by Enes Karić and Haris Silajdžić.

Muslim Perceptions of Other Religions deals in four chapters (one of which is in French) with the necessity of inter-faith dialogue, and is based on presentations in international groups.[11] Silajdžić's point of departure is the necessity to find answers to what he calls "the signs of our times": globalization, materialism, uprootedness and rejection of tradition. Together with Christian theologians such as Rowan Williams and Hans Küng, and with references to social scientists like José Casanova and Peter Beyer, Adnan Silajdžić defines the platform for possible communication as the loyalty to tradition and the search for mystic common roots. The Magritte illustrations in the volume underline the human condition in modernity: people in little communication with one another and eternity at a distant horizon.

Muslims in Search of an Identity has a foreword by Enes Karić, in which he connects to themes in his own work; among them the critical reflections over the deficiencies in modernity despite its technological advancements. The answer is tradition and Muslim modernity, represented by S. H. Nasr among others. In a global world, Karić praises Silajdžić for connecting to other believers, also non-Muslim, and states that it is the interpretive achievements that "will determine whether Muslims will find the strength to define their own trajectories of modernity" (2007: 12). In his own foreword, Adnan Silajdžić emphasizes the balance between the absolute and constant, on the one hand, and historical and cultural change, on the other. He provides, like the two other authors, a personal background, when referring to his own crisis over the nature of contemporary cultural identity.

To meet the challenges when faith and knowledge must interact, Silajdžić's twofold theological strategy is the same as that of the previous authors. The base is the legitimate interpretation of the sacred scriptures, represented by Islamic reformers, and faithful loyalty to tradition; the reverse is not only opposition to God, but disconnecting from one's culture. Tradition is also by this author defined as the roots connected to a specific people, and in a perennalist mode regards this as stable cultural categories (2007:54). Silajdžić even uses the Sufi term for the remembrance of God, *dhikr*, as a means to guard tradition (2007:58). When he recognizes diversity it is not in the postmodern appraisal of hybridity, but "difference, including religious difference, is a God-given state of humanity, and we must respect it" (2007:106). In order "to realize our essence" (2007:106), contemporary interpretation can never diverge from tradition.

Religious Heritage in Times of Ethno-Religious Divides

Taken together, it is hard to define what audience(s) the books discussed above are aimed at. Connected to certain educational institutions and legal offices, the authors represent official interpretation, which is noticeable in their mode of claiming authority and in their way of referring to theological authenticity; the authors also address readers further out in the public sphere and beyond their homeland Bosnia. They nevertheless focus on Bosnian issues and are defenders of Bosnian heritage. Influence and reception are therefore hard to measure, and the economic limitations for book production in the years after the war, and still, make it hard to read too much into the choice of publishers. There are many references to Sufism as a philosophical tradition with links beyond the Muslim world and universal philosophers, but with no mention of its Balkan representations and cultural variations. The reader of the five books is left with little insight into the writers' understanding of regional cultural legacy as lived practice. Rather, the references to Sufism are means to emphasize a strong belief in authentic and pure traditions, which are made to stand out as alternatives to the politicized religion that has so willingly served as a tool in aggressive identity projects.

The essays were written during the war or in the immediate post-war period, and the versions in English were published during a distinct period (1999–2007); and although the authors have continued to publish, recently it has not been writings of this outreaching character and, with one exception, not aimed at this kind of a broader international readership. The texts could therefore be read as comments on the collapse of a multi-religious society and the aftermath of horrific violence between neighbours. The writers aim to discuss the Bosnian predicament based on local experiences, but with a double European link: communicating the connection of the Bosnian legacy with the rest of Europe and emphasizing that Islam has a place there too, as well as introducing European perspectives to the Bosnian readers – the shared moral values of the world religions and especially the Abrahamic ones. All three writers touch on the area of inter-faith dialogue, in which they have been more or less involved as public figures, at home and abroad. However, their presentations of Sufism as an introduction to Islam that connects with other monotheistic traditions to a great extent remain closed to readers without previous knowledge of this particular form of mysticism. They mostly give the theological terminology in Arabic, rather than its Bosnian equivalents, and rarely present the particularities of the Bosnian way of being Muslim, to speak with Tone Bringa (1995), rather than emphasizing the multi-religious background of the region. There are no ethnographic descriptions (or accounts of local historical character) and there are no theological arguments in favour of Sufi forms of piety.

There are very few references to contemporary academic literature on related topics (with the exception of Silajdžić 2007), which gives the texts an even more closed character. There is an apparent absence of more political or sociological analyses or any wish to argue against or in favour of specific theories. True, their point of departure is theological, not an ambition to place religion in society. Although identity issues and reconciliation call for political analyses, the writers instead provide theological interpretations.

The emphasis on traditionalism and *philosophia perennis*, in which Sufism is underlined as the specific Islamic contribution, both opens and closes their texts. All three authors argue from the perspective that religion is the prime criterion for identity, collective as well as individual. Moral universes without religion do not find a place in their works. It is an important principle in Islamic theology that Islam is not a new religion, but the original and true one. This is a standpoint that through history has left space for a special relation to the Abrahamic religions in comparison to other religions, and it fits well with the quest for authenticity in perennialist and traditionalist thinking. To some extent it does imply a contradiction between the unique and the universal, but it nevertheless leads to a vaguer and more general Muslim position that opens up for more universalistic encounters (especially Karić and Hafizović). References to Sufism function as an argument in the works discussed above, as they identify the common roots of the Abrahamic religions as well as the primordial spark in the sense of traditionalism.

The field of Islamic studies has seen a lot of interesting work trying to define "the new Muslim intellectuals" (Esposito & Voll (eds) 2001; Cooper et al. (eds) 1998). Not that there is anything new about Muslim intellectuals as such; and certainly not in Bosnia, with its rich Ottoman legacy. Rather, the issue is the conditions in which the new intellectuals communicate: globalization and access to spaces with less dependence on the traditional authoritative institutions have seen agents of other backgrounds play a more important role.

But the aim of the English texts presented here is perhaps not primarily to formulate arguments inside a Muslim discourse, nor are they focused on critical analysis. The need for religion as an argument in contemporary debate appears in these texts as a way of emphasizing the necessity of religious identities without siding with chauvinistic nationalist positions. The link they establish with their non-Muslim readers is the one among believers where the genealogical link between the Abrahamic religions is the prime argument, along with an understanding of "traditional civilizations" as monotheistic.

The writers discussed here are traditional intellectuals in the Gramscian (but also conventional) sense, speaking from clearly defined academic positions and in their argumentation drawing from a long Islamic tradition of learning and mode of establishing authority. They combine two platforms of authority: the academic rank and that of international representatives of Bosnian Islam. The latter position brings them into new modes of communication.

The impact of the changes in (late) modernity when it comes to shifts in authority and new arenas of communication is substantial, as observed by Zygmunt Bauman, when identifying/characterizing different types of intellectuals. The way in which the three writers construct arguments falls between Bauman's categories of legislators and interpreters (1987), as they balance their use of epistemic authority and positions at an influential institution of learning with addressing issues of a more universal character. The three authors cannot easily be put into Bauman's original interpreter category, as the writers' conceptions of Sufism do not relate to postmodern relativism and multiple discourses. The absolute claim is there in the definitions of traditional and civilizational, but the references to Sufism are still made in a way that opens for alliances outside the structures of institutional borders. To a great extent they are arguing as legislators when the category of Islam is to be confirmed as the legal point of departure (the relation between Sufism on the one hand and the Quran and Sharia on the other), but they act as interpreters when Sufism is discussed. This strategy apparently provides them with the space needed to uphold legitimacy within the local discourse, and at the same time reach out for inter-religious/cultural dialogue. Rather than references to Sufism as practised in Bosnia and the Balkan region, it is

Sufism as a prism of universal mysticism that constitutes the intellectual outreach to non-Muslim international readers.

Sufism appears here as a tool to open discussions across religious borders, in search of an apolitical alternative that is not time-bound, but possible to anchor with eternal truth claims; the writers regard Sufism as part of regional traditions that could be an alternative to the disruption of fundamental values in modern times. Their definition of themselves as contemporary theologians emphasizes the role of the custodian and the defender of an authenticity that is possible to reach, despite materialism and moral decline.

Talal Asad's notion of religion as a discursive practice (1993, 2003) can serve as a tool to make Bauman's categories less polarized. This can open up for a discussion of how authority is constructed by the three writers in the midst of harsh debates about national identity and belonging soon after a war. They have maintained their positions as legitimate speakers for Islam, and at the same time acquired spaces for new alliances (with the traditionalists and the non-Muslim readers).

The conventional image of the dissident intellectual has been discussed for a long time. Irrespective of their self-definitions, the institutional affiliation as professors at FIN, the writers represent in one way or another the Islamic Community and public interpretations of Islam. The Bosnian case highlights an often neglected aspect in the taxonomy of the intellectuals: the receivers of the perennial message. The way the texts seek to establish authority is also a clear indication of the audience, i.e. the mode in which Islamic knowledge is produced and consumed. In these books Islam is regarded as theology, as a system of ideas, not as practice. The question of whether these essays are to be regarded as teaching or reasoning is consequently hard to answer. In any case, both modes of communication fit with the image of the public intellectual and the production of Islamic knowledge.

Intellectuals are conventionally associated with progressive attitudes and criticism of authorities, although terms like more moderate or liberal interpretations of Islam are seldom (or never) used by the authors themselves. Instead, they are advocating positions defined by national particularities in opposition to foreign and radical elements. But their public stance against the radicals makes international readers regard them as "Muslim liberals". In the ongoing conflicts in Bosnia today, historical continuity and claims of authenticity are major tools, and the positions of the selected writers can be hard to pinpoint in ideological terms, especially when some of them are pointed at by international bodies as representatives of (liberal) Euro-Muslims. The selected authors, liberal in comparison to more radical elements, can still be part of conservative structures, and their perspective on regional culture is quite homogenizing and does not emphasize diversity within the Muslim community; rather, it presupposes stable cultural categories, with a terminology like "peoples", "cultures", "traditions" and "civilizations". The absent themes in the texts discussed above could be summarized as a tendency to avoid difference. Social and economic differences within the nation/community are not discussed; nor are gender and generation: perspectives that would contradict the universalist stand.

Religious Heritage in Times of Ethno-Religious Divides

Another of the Yugoslav period's great novelists also used the Ottoman era to stage his plots and issues: Ivo Andrić (d. 1975). Being a modernist in the ideological, but not the literary, sense of the term, religion, and especially practised religion, was something that belonged to time past and the uneducated countryside (Hawkesworth 1984; Buturović 2002: 8ff., 34ff.). In his epic novels like *The Bridge on the Drina* and *Bosnian Chronicle*, religion does not stand out as a tool to think with or build a complex plot around. Andrić, from a Catholic family, saw the future in South Slav unification already in his youth. Religion could do nothing but divide people. In an early academic work, Andrić describes his period in Bosnia as an exile, and the old-fashioned manners he encounters are bound to disappear in favour of reason and modernity. His controversial doctoral thesis, *The Development of Spiritual Life in Bosnia under the Influence of Turkish Rule*, from 1924, was translated and published in a commented edition shortly before the break-up of Yugoslavia (ed. Juričić & Loud 1990). Critics have argued that this text openly displays Andrić's condescending attitudes towards Muslims and should be read as a correlate to the later novels. It could also be read as a more general representation of how the urban elite regarded life in rural areas and their hopes for what modernity would sweep away. Andrić's realistic novels leave little space for the marvels of religion, and when he uses the same Sarajevan Sufi lodge as Selimović in his short story "Death in Sinan's Tekke" (1924), it is to tell of the Sufi environment as hierarchical and hypocritical in its views on norms and reality; the opposite of the naturalistic enlightenment of a modern citizen (Hawkesworth 1984: 79ff.).

Selimović and Andrić wrote for an audience in a comparatively closed society where the Yugoslav unity was a coat that fitted no one perfectly, except the opportunists. Read today, the two novelists do not necessarily give ethnographic accounts of old Bosnia, and, even if they have the atrocities during the Second World War as an implicit backdrop to their major works, conflicts are defined in terms of ideology, hierarchies and authority, or human moral matters. Religion as everyday practice seems to belong to a faraway land in history. Their representations of Sufism and Sufi lives are images of what modernity leaves behind, not "tools to think with" or modes to communicate with.

The three contemporary Muslim authors discussed in this chapter belong to a very different public sphere than the novelists, where religious difference is apparently easier to discuss with foreigners than with countrymen, as none of them touches upon differences within the Bosnian Muslim community. Rather than pointing out regional particularities, it is eternal spiritual values that are held up as unambiguous cultural and civilizational units which stand out as a theological alternative to political and social analyses of the situation in Bosnia in the decade after the war. Sufism appears in their work as a tool for communicating both with fellow Bosnian Muslims and with international non-Muslim readers, whereby Sufism connects Bosnian heritage with a universalistic discourse.

Notes

1 The so-called imam movement of the 1980s is sometimes written of as solely part of radical trends, but to most of the young men who received Islamic education and training abroad, this was an encounter with the broad variety of contemporary Muslim theology. Periods of closed Islamic schools (*medrese*) had to a great extent left Bosnian Muslims isolated from the Islamic world of learning, and the possibilities to go abroad meant a reconnecting to Islamic debates; for many of them this was the beginning of productive international networking. For a few it was also a definitive step towards radicalization, with puristic interpretations of religion, although not for the majority (Babuna 2004; Bougarel 2001, 2007; Bougarel et al. 2007; Clayer & Bougarel 2001; Öktem 2010, 2011).

2 Alija Izetbegović (1925–2003) was a well-known Muslim dissident in Yugoslavia and was Bosnia's first president after the disintegration of the federation (1996–2000). Izetbegović left behind an extensive collection of texts, besides *The Islamic Declaration*. Several of these works are in dialogue with texts by dissidents such as Havel, Kolakowski and Milosz, and with authors such as Beckett, Emerson and Sartre. The degree of radicalism in his thinking and publications is still a very much-debated issue. Irrespective of this, he was a unifying symbol for the Muslims of Bosnia during

the war in the 1990s and is still to many a representative of Bosnian resistance under the siege, even if his political-religious ideas are not embraced.

3 As the subtitle indicates, *Transmission and Dissemination in Western Europe*, the focus of the volume is on Muslim diaspora communities. Nevertheless, several of the arguments and observations proposed are relevant to the Bosnian case as well as the Muslim world at large.

4 The Faculty of Islamic Sciences (Fakultet islamskih nauka, FIN), originally founded in 1882, was (re-)established in its present form in 1977, and is associated with Sarajevo University, but funded by the Islamic Community of Bosnia and Herzegovina. For the Faculty of Islamic Sciences, see: www.fin.ba; for the Islamic Community of Bosnia and Herzegovina, see: www.rijaset.ba; and for Sarajevo University and its associates, see: www.unsa.ba.

5 Another internationally well-known writer could have been included: Rusmir Mahmutćehajić (b. 1948), a trained engineer by profession. In several books and articles he has discussed the relationship between Sufism and the Bosnian heritage, but has not done so from an Islamic scholar position at FIN. Mahmutćehajić's platform has been the foundation for Forum Bosnia. See: www.ifbosna.org.ba.

6 Enes Karić's novel *Pjesme divljih ptica* ("Songs of Wild Birds") (2009) clearly alludes to Selimović's *Death and the Dervish* and is set in a similar environment.

7 The same passage and the preceding lines read in Bogdan Rakić's and Stephen M. Dickey's translation referred to above: "We have been severed from our roots, but haven't become part of anything else; foreign to everyone, both to those who are our kin and those who won't take us in and adopt us as their own. We live at a crossroads of worlds, at a border between peoples, in everyone's way. And someone always thinks we're to blame for something" (1996: 330). The vignette starts with a quotation from a later chapter in the novel: "Not to anyone else has history played the kind of joke it's playing on us. ... We've been torn away from our roots, but haven't become part of anything else. Like a tributary whose course has been diverted from its river by a flood, and no longer has a mouth or a current; it's too small to be a lake, too large to be absorbed by the earth" (1996:408).

8 This theme was a priority area of UNESCO's culture sector and its organized dialogues in general and regional history, 1999–2007.

9 The volume was published by OKO (in a series called "Foreigner-Étranger-Ausländer-Straniero-Extranjero", edited by Zdravko Grebo and Rešid Hafizović, that was, according to one of them, never continued).

10 The Ibn Sina Institute has published several titles related to Sufism and translations of Sufi classics by Hafizović and other scholars of Oriental languages at Sarajevo University. See www.ibn-sina.net. Rešid Hafizović has been a member of the Iranian Academy of Philosophy in Tehran since 2005.

11 The book was originally published in Bosnian a year before by Council of the Congress of Bosnian Intellectuals.

References

Andrić, Ivo (1924/1977): Smrt u Sinanovoj tekiji, in *Žed* (Sabrana djela Ive Andrića), Sarajevo: Svjetlost.

– (1990): *The Development of Spiritual Life in Bosnia under the Influence of Turkish Rule* [*Entwicklung des geistigen Lebens in Bosnien unter der Einwirkung der türkischen*

Herrschaft, 1924], ed. and transl. Zelimir Juričić and John F Loud, Durham: Durham University Press.
– (1992): Death in Sinan's Tekke, in *The Damned Yard and Other Stories*, transl. by Celia Hawesworth, London: Forest Books.
Asad, Talal (1999): *Genealogies of Religion. Discipline and Reasons of Power in Christianity and Islam*, Baltimore: Johns Hopkins University.
– (2003): *Formations of the Secular. Christianity, Islam and Modernity*, Stanford: Stanford University Press.
Babuna, Aydin (2004): The Bosnian Muslims and Albanians. Islam and Nationalism, *Nationalities Papers*, 32: 287–321.
Bauman, Zygmunt (1987): *Legislators and Interpreters. On Modernity, Post-modernity, and Intellectuals*, Cambridge: Polity Press.
Bougarel, Xavier (2001): "Trois définitions de l'islam en Bosnie-Herzégovine", *Archives de sciences sociales des religions*, 115: 183–201.
– (2007): Bosnian Islam as European Islam. Limits and Shifts of a Concept, in Aziz Al-Azmeh and Effie Fokas (eds): *Islam in Europe. Diversity, Identity and Influence*, Cambridge: Cambridge University Press.
Bougarel, Xavier et al. (eds) (2007): *The New Bosnian Mosaic. Identities, Memories, and Moral Claims in a Post-war Society*, Aldershot: Ashgate.
Bringa, Tone (1993): *Being Muslim the Bosnian Way*, Princeton: Princeton University Press.
Bruinessen, Martin van (2011): Producing Islamic Knowledge in Western Europe. Discipline, Authority and Personal Quest, in Martin van Bruinessen and Stefan Allievi (eds): *Producing Islamic Knowledge. Transmission and Dissemination in Western Europe*, London: Routledge.
Buturović, Amila (2002): *Stone Speaker. Medieval Tombs, Landscape, and Bosnian Identity in the Poetry of Mak Dizdar*, Gordonsville: Palgrave Macmillan.
Clayer, Natalie and Xavier Bougarel (eds) (2001): *Le nouvel Islam balkanique. Les musulmans, acteur du post-communisme 1990–2000*, Paris: Maisonneuve et Larose.
Cooper, Henry R. (1996): Introduction [to Meša Selimović' *Death and the Dervish*]" (Writings from an Unbound Europe), Evanston, Ill.: Northwestern University Press.
Cooper, John Nettker et al. (1998): *Islam and Modernity. Muslim Intellectuals Respond*, London: I.B. Tauris
Esposito, John and John Voll (eds) (2001): *The Makers of Contemporary Islam*, Oxford: Oxford University Press.
Hafizović, Rešid (2005): *The Human Image in the Mirror of Sufism*, Sarajevo: Ibn Sina Institute.
Hawkesworth, Celia (1984): *Ivo Andrić. Bridge between East and West*, London: Athlone.
Izetbegović, Alija (1970): *Islamska deklaracija. Jedan program islamizacije Muslimana i muslimanskih narodna* [*The Islamic Declaration. A Programme for the Islamization of the Muslims and the Muslim Nation*], s.l.: s.n.
Karić, Enes (1999): *Essays (on Behalf) of Bosnia*, Sarajevo: El-Kalem.
– (2004): *Essays on Our European Never-Never Land*, Sarajevo: El-Kalem.
– (2009): *Pjesme divljih ptica* ["Songs of Wild Birds"]: Sarajevo: Tugra.
– (2011a): *Contributions to Twentieth Century Islamic Thought in Bosnia and Herzegovina*, Sarajevo: El-Kalem.
– (2011b): *The Black Tulip*, Sarajevo: Connectum.
Kersten, Carool (2011): *Cosmopolitans and Heretic. New Muslim Intellectuals and the Study of Islam*, London: Hurst.

Leonard, Stephen (1986): Introduction. A Genealogy of the Politicized Intellectual, in Leon Fink, Stephen T. Leonard and Donald M. Reid (eds): *Intellectuals and Public Life. Between Radicalism and Reform*, Ithaca: Cornell University Press.

Lučić, Iva (2012): In the Service of the Nation. Intellectuals' Articulation of the Muslim National Identity, *Nationalities Papers*, 40: 23–44.

Öktem, Kerem (2010): *New Islamic Actors after the Wahhabi Intermezzo. Turkey's Return to the Muslim Balkans*. Oxford: European Studies Centre, University of Oxford.

– (2011): Between Emigration, de-Islamization and the Nation-State. Muslim Communities in the Balkans Today, *Southeast European and Black Sea Studies*, 11: 155–171.

Popovic, Alexandre (1994): *Les derviches balkaniques hier et aujourd'hui*. Istanbul: Isis.

– (2006): Muslim Intellectuals in Bosnia-Herzegovina in the Twentieth Century. Continuities and Changes", in Stéphane A. Dudoignon, Komatsu Hisao and Kosugi Yasushi (eds): *Intellectuals in the Modern Islamic World. Transmission, Transformation, Communication*, London: Routledge.

– (2009): *L'Islam balkanique. Les musulmans du sud-est européen dans la période post-ottoman*. Istanbul: Isis.

Raudvere, Catharina (2012a): Textual and Ritual Command. Muslim Women as Keepers and Transmitters of Religious Knowledge Contemporary Bosnia, in Hilary Kalmbach and Masooda Banu (eds): *Women, Leadership and Mosques: Changes in Contemporary Islamic Authority*, Leiden; Brill.

– (2012b; forthcoming): Claiming Heritage, Renewing Authority. Sufi-Orientated Activities in post-Yugoslav Bosnia-Herzegovina, *European Journal of Turkish Studies*.

Rawlinson, Andrew (1997): *The Book of Enlightened Masters. Western Teachers in Eastern Traditions*, Chicago: Open Court.

Said, Edward (1994): *Representations of the Intellectual. The 1993 Reith Lectures*, New York: Pantheon Books.

Sedgwick, Mark (2004) *Against the Modern World*, Oxford: Oxford University Press.

– (2011): Guénonian Traditionalism and European Islam, in: Martin van Bruinessen and Stefan Allievi (eds): *Producing Islamic Knowledge. Transmission and Dissemination in Western Europe*, London: Routledge.

Selimović, Meša (1966): *Derviš i smrt*. Sarajevo: Svjetlost.

– (1996): *Death and the Dervish*. Transl. by Bogdan Rakić and Stephen M. Dickey. (Writings from an Unbound Europe), Evanston, Ill.: Northwestern University Press.

Silajdžić, Adnan (2006): *Muslim Perceptions of Other Religions*, Sarajevo: El-Kalem.

– (2007): *Muslims in Search of an Identity*, Sarajevo: El-Kalem.

Stenberg, Leif (1996): *The Islamization of Science. Four Muslim Positions Developing an Islamic Modernity*, Lund: Lund University.

Wasserstrom, Steven M. (1999): *Religion after Religion. Gershom Scholem, Mircea Eliade, and Henry Corbin at Eranos*, Princeton: Princeton University Press.

Websites

Faculty of Islamic Sciences at Sarajevo University: www.fin.ba
Forum Bosna: www.ifbosna.org.ba
Ibn Sina Institute in Sarajevo: www.ibn-sina.net.
Islamic Community of Bosnia and Herzegovina: www.rijaset.ba
Sarajevo University and its associates: www.unsa.ba

MYTHS AND MUSEUMS —
OLD STORIES, NEW USES

CHAPTER 11

Framing Uses of the Past

Nations, Academia and
Museums Conjuring History

Peter Aronsson

The process of nation-making and nationalism framed the creation of a long-standing division of labour between an array of humanistic and social science university disciplines. The role of cultural inquiry and representation was determined by their productive relation to the corresponding spheres and logics of politics, market and religion. The compound result of that interaction produced a strong set-up for naturalized narratives about the world from the eighteenth century until late in the twentieth century, replacing a world view that measured values in the face of eternity with one measuring progress in terms of utility in this world.

The frame was not only a complex set of eventually naturalized institutions representing the spheres of a world order, but also necessarily a set of tools to negotiate intrinsic contradictions producing legitimacy, meaning and historical change while securing the continuity of the wider cultural and political frame. In this process history became a central mode of explaining change, creating meaning; i.e. setting up spaces of experiences and hence creating horizons of expectations, as theorized by the conceptual historian Reinhart Koselleck. With him we can emphasize not only the power of past actions to form the setting for contemporary action, but the power of our fears and hopes to structure the way the past is recollected as a relevant history (Koselleck 1985). These insights bring an old philosophy of time into the professional realm of historians again. Augustine stated in AD 397:

> But what now is manifest and clear is, that neither are there future nor past things. Nor is it fitly said, "There are three times, past,

present and future;" but perchance it might be fitly said, "There are three times: a present of things past, a present of things present, and a present of things future." For these three do somehow exist in the soul, and otherwise I see them not: present of things past, memory; present of things present, sight; present of things future, expectation.[1]

This frame of shared understanding and using of the past as history is located beyond individually relevant pasts, often grasped in contrast to concepts like memory and experience.

When specialist multi-disciplinary fields of research and education, such as museology, heritage and memory studies, tourism, branding and storytelling increasingly establish themselves as professionally relevant spaces of knowledge, I like to argue the importance of understanding the transportation and translation of concepts and values *between* these more specific fields of knowledge, on the one hand, and their societal counterparts, on the other. Hence there is a need for a more overarching conceptualization of uses of the past which encompasses new and old, existential as well as institutionalized, modalities of utilizing the past for understanding the power of these as outcomes of interactions and translations between different spheres of using the past.

I will argue that the act of bringing meaning to and communicating the destiny of the individual sets it in an immediate relation to collective forms of understanding, both in more informal and more institutionalized formats. The role of the latter as provider of negotiating between opposites and bridging time gives institutions a central role in this argument.[2] Communal framing of individual emotions and collectively organized performance of meaning such as religion and scientific methods are different modes of legitimizing understanding of the world to rescue us from the frightening contingency of the world.

The movement of history provides direction and providence, if nothing else by its narrative form. Heritage simultaneously provides material proofs and invaluable relics of the existence and importance of the past and the community it is inscribed as evidence for. The national context in turn provides a comprehensive and mighty institution to carry and defend ideas of this community – and is reciprocally legitimized and produced by its very defence.

Historians and other academics of culture became an increasingly professionalized priesthood of this trade, and hence secured their legitimacy as custodians of objective truth as the basis for their usefulness in the process of nation-making. Every nation developed a system for protecting national heritage and art and making it part of national education in schools and museums. National traumas of war and crises gave new energy to these collective frames.

With its scientific logic, the practise of academic disciplines tended to become more technical and less accommodating to new desires. This set of institutionalized relations and meanings is here labelled the old division of labour in uses of the past, formatting distinct but structurally quite similar national historical cultures. The quest for reformation and search for meaning beyond science was born with the success of academic professionalization. This took on various forms, such as public history, community archaeology, but also a wide political and popular history interest more or less out of reach of the academy, in history wars, popular books, journals, TV and films.

Challenged in the twentieth century first by competing epistemes of synchronic and instrumental social science and later by constructivism and deconstructivism, professionalized disciplinary history reacted by diversifying and expanding its thematic focus, historicizing ever wider realms of the world. Cultural processes paralleled by market penetration and neo-liberal victories, epitomized by events in 1989–2001, shifted the balance of power, unleashed various uses of the past in popular and institutional historical cultures and a new division of powers. The response came in academic disciplines as an interest in memory studies, heritage, identity politics and uses of the past by people other than academics, on the one hand, and as an exploration of alternative framings of narratives, on the other (Aronsson 2004; Jenkins et al. 2007). These changes open for a new division of labour still under negotiation between the old institutions, market forces, tourism as an expanding global industry; and individualized desires, presenting new contexts for culture research and policymakers.

Examples of these ongoing negotiations could be taken from any heritage site. In the early nineteenth century the Swedish city of Visby, and especially its medieval ring-wall, became a heritage site of both medieval trade and Sweden's eventual victory over Denmark in the battle over Gotland. Romantic painters and visitors have interacted with heritage boards and tourist markets, local and national framing over the centuries. Visby was declared a UNESCO World Heritage site in 1995 as the main Hanseatic city of the Baltic region and "the best-preserved fortified commercial city in northern Europe".

The city, entrepreneurs and NGOs have also looked for ways to turn the tide of migrants, prolong the short summer season, and mobilize the inhabitants to be proud of their past. More medieval facades than ever have since then been restored, medieval festivals initiated and nourished to provide a setting for tourists, learning, historical re-enactment and fantasies of a radically different world; and these attract more visitors and money since the medieval golden age. This epoch stands today less for the beginning of Swedish national unity to be explored by scientific means, as the medievalism of the nineteenth and early twentieth centuries did, but more as a playground for experiencing the radical otherness of the Middle Ages: religious, naive, collective, pre-national, ecological, and a time when a man was a knight and a woman a virgin (Ronström 2007; Johansson 2009; Sandström 2005; Gustafsson 2002; Aronsson 2002). The transportation and translation of cognitive, existential, emotive, political and economic values are enacted by loosely set up networks of traditional cultural heritage institutions, educational organizations, entrepreneurs and political bodies. This complexity illustrates well the need to make use of the trans-disciplinary perspective suggested here to grasp the overall working of these negotiations and division of labour. After doing that, it might of course be valid and indeed necessary to use more specific tools to understand and explain performances of museums or identity-making.

In this chapter, these dynamic relationships explaining the role of historical inquiry will be framed by the new interest in *uses of the past* developing in several disciplines of culture studies. Through the text runs an argument for the viability of research also participating in a reflexive way in the production of meaning. Critical research cannot only be deconstructive, but reflexive, and hence enhance the productive capacity of culture research. I will present a theoretical perspective on uses of the past and show how research into one field of great relevance to policy, national museums, might add to a deliberative dialogue with existential, ethical and political implications.

National museums were once created, and interact with the wider historical culture to negotiate contradictory values and change. Since they should encompass the totality, they have always needed to negotiate more values than, on the one hand, academic practice or, on the other, outright ideologies or market logics of using the past.

The actual change of state-making, while framed by national ideology, needs to utilize transnational narrative tropes such as Europe, the Nordic or Hellenic to produce visions of competing and possible national futures, and still build distinctly divergent pasts with similar material. Politics and ideology were to be built on objective truth and material evidence of cultural belonging and unicity. The interplay between an older regime of identity politics and contemporary challenges means that new approaches are added to negotiate meaning in cultural policy and visitor experience. A set of national institutions responding to market demands, individualization, and the desire for community demonstrates the value of the prestigious setting of heritage, where meaning has been and is negotiated between science, politics, and the existential desires of citizens.

The transformation of Athens, and especially the Acropolis, is a good example: a complex but living part of the Ottoman Empire was by the Greek War of Independence in 1830 physically cleared from its complex heritage and made into a symbol of the Greek golden age, fourth century BC. Since then it has been a symbol of Greek nationalism, shared European values, and one of the tourist sites par excellence. Historians criticize the monomanic re-creation of one epoch, Greek politicians demand the Elgin Marbles be flown back from the British Museum to their natural context and has built a new aestheticized Acropolis museum with copies of the missing pieces as a silent accusation to stress their standing demand for repatriation. The museum in turn declares the acquisition to have been legal, and say they will keep it by the right of law, to safeguard preservation, and to give universal access to the knowledge as part of their duty as a universal museum (Aronsson 2011b).

The Old Division of Labour – and New Uses of the Past

There is no doubt that academia played a decisive role in the earlier integrative dynamic of nation-making. To put it bluntly, the traditional division of labour between the disciplines has enhanced the integrative function of the nation: history forgets internal differences of regions and class and naturalizes the borders and orders of contemporary nation-states. Archaeology roots community in the ground, with silent proofs of Stone Age axes and traces of Neolithic soil toiled by early peasants, our forefathers, speaking loudly of the genesis of the land and people and their gradual evolution. Ethnology culturalizes the same regional and class differences ignored by history, making them into a beautiful composition of a national concert or a bouquet of different colours assembled in coffee-table books and heritage institutions to enjoy on a

Sunday afternoon. Simultaneously, the past is honoured as the definite and unchangeable roots of contemporary society and made different to communicate the pastness of its history, releasing the present from the past. Past and present connect either through contrast or a line of evolution of the group and society thus defined and presented.

The peasant society represented by regional differences at museums like the open-air Skansen in Stockholm or its counterparts in Riga or Bucharest, instituted by the upcoming industrial and urban bourgeoisie to limit tensions created by a rapid industrialization and urbanization, is a perfect case for this argument. In fact the present-day conflict between a coherent ethnic narrative of the nation and a more multicultural preference reproduces these two options in modernized versions. Eventually, in the mid-twentieth century, the social sciences produced (allegedly) instrumental knowledge with which to deal with problems of difference, in need of very little historical reflection – it is the future ahead of us for sociology or behavioural sciences. This corresponds to the idea of the national community as a rational contract based on civic values and effective solutions of practical problems – a third option to balance the more historical ones. The net sum of this division of labour is a massive naturalization of the present order, using all three modes of rationalizing the present, but in varying degrees emphasizing the rational choice, the ethnic homogeneity, or multicultural dynamics as the most vital basis for security and progress.

Against the self-understanding of critical inquiry that dominates the self-image of many academic researchers, I would argue that this dynamic of stabilization still dominates the role they play in the wider society. Furthermore, the dominance of a constructivist approach is in phase with flexible capitalism – teaching citizens reflexivity and the ability to change and adjust, which today is more valuable than the capacity to sacrifice the lives of soldiers in war (Sennett 1998; Aronsson 2000). The question and real challenge is not one of simply safeguarding autonomy and objectivity, but the more awkward one of transforming the role of academic knowledge and adding to its former dominating role of producing national coherence, to a broader set of values ranging from existential to economic and political in a globalized world.

Developments in science, with ever-widening constructivisms and culturalisms, and contemporary history have led to an increased interest in new pasts. More areas are brought in from nature to culture and hence historicized – gender and other previously naturalized relationships, for

The monk football had an informal place in the Medieval Week of Visby. It was perceived as too much of a joke to be part of the programme. After having been appreciated in research as an authentic example of the medieval spirit of the carnival, it was transported into the official programme. Photo: Peter Aronsson.

instance. A generational distance to the Second World War and the end of the Cold War, a heightened sense of uncertainty and epochal shifts in economy and politics, produce new challenges to be dealt with. With the increasing power of the media as a window of perception and an area of experience, the interest in and need to know how history is (re)-created in other arenas than academic has become obvious. The relative power and legitimacy of not only traditional institutions such as museums, but also new media such as film, TV, popular journals, the Internet and social media, add to the historical culture. Relating to identity issues beyond the quest for national delineation and responding to demands for individual experiences has reshaped the field for history to work in, making it possible to talk of an adjusted set of "values of the second order"; values not discussed but taken for granted: local, regional, European in addition to national framing; gendered, generational, life-styled, universal or multicultural human rights. Identity negotiations are diverse and contested, building new versions of the past to match new ideas of the present and the future (Taylor 1989).

This has led not only to the addition of a new thematic field to cultural history, but has also brought out a new perspective in many cultural sciences and society at large. When studying what uses of the past are reshaping community, it is not possible to stay confined within disciplinary historiographies. The life-world of any visitor using the past combines too many dimensions to be truthfully assessed by a perspective from just one academic discipline. The relationship between disciplinary historiography and cultural uses of the past in society has rapidly changed from predominantly having been formulated as abuses (lies, vulgarization) (Lowenthal 1998) to active ethical and political cultures of regret and sorrow – *Vergangenheitsbewältigung* in the German context – and exploring more openly the historical impact of uses of the past as a historical force in its own right (Rüsen 2002).

In more theoretical terms I would argue that this entails a possibility of repositioning professional historical reflection in the productive gap left by existential historicity, *Geschichtlichkeit* in the phenomenological sense, on the one hand, and more objective epistemologies and metaphysics of history and historical explanation, on the other. If it does not close the gap, it does at least expand the area of historical reflection and open it to multidisciplinary collaboration in ways that change the meaning of cultural sciences by placing them on a par with other actors in the historical culture, whether as suppliers of data or reusers of shared discourses and practices.[3] For too long, too simple strategies have been suggested for dealing with the tension presented by existential motivation and intersubjective communication, either denying the viability of the first in objectivist discourse or collapsing the two in vulgar post-modernism.

This space between the subjective and the objective is the place where several interactions between the logic of intersubjective, scientific enquiry of "wie es *eigentlich* gewesen", and the ethical use, "*wie* es eigentlich gewesen", give both existential and collectively meaningful interpretations of the past. The normative force of culture research has rightly been criticized for naively playing into the hands of nationalism. The ethical turn in research responds to the challenge by not only criticizing this but acknowledging the ethical potential in culture research, and also in historical research, and opening the way to study and engagement in the production of more, not less, meaning. Adding multidimensional reflexivity is the academic duty, not the vain ambition to abstain from participating.

Using the Past

I have suggested that concepts such as the culture of history and the uses of history are just as potentially important concepts in historiography as are social aspects, culture, mentality and gender in terms of their potential for changing the perspective and relevance of research.[4]

The culture of history can be defined as being constituted of the artefacts, rituals, customs and assertions with references to the past which allow us to link the relationship between the past, present and future. Occasionally, they are direct and explicit interpretations of this link. *Uses of history* connotes the processes whereby parts of the culture of history are activated to form definite opinions and action-oriented totalities. Through the uses of the past, more precise formations take form, such as collective memories and heritage. These define a link between the past, present and future which directs the setting up of a useful past out of the possibilities provided in the culture of history. Institutionalized practices of schools, universities and heritage institutions are important for the stability of these framings, but ongoing negotiations of the meaning and viability are part of the performance where they interact with political, economical and existential logics and desires. The presentations of Visby and Athens testify to the persistence of certain elements in the culture of history of these places, but also to the plasticity of the motives that are mobilized to make them meaningful in new eras. The utopias and tensions of the nineteenth century are not exactly the same as the ones in the twenty-first century.

A certain selection of the culture of history is activated as communities of memory are formed; a regime or frame of how history is thought to be meaningful. Here, I diverge for specific reasons from other uses of the term cultures of history to label these more specific sets of uses. While not denying that these are possible to delineate and discuss in order to understand the process of reproduction, I think this way of framing historical cultures gives them too reified and homogeneous a character for my purpose, whereas I would like to emphasize the role of ongoing negotiation, the need for activity to procure meaning, the process of making specific formations, such as heritage, re-enactments or politics of identity and development around Visby or the Acropolis out of the potentialities and possibilities at hand in the wider historical culture.

The concept of the categories *space of experiences* and *horizon of expectations*, taken from Reinhart Koselleck, fits well into this framework. Knowledge and descriptions of the past create opportunities for certain assumptions about the future. The hopes and fears created by images of the future in the present influence the relationship between what is memorialized and what is forgotten, framed into a space of experience. The uses of history take place in the dynamic process that links the spaces of experience and horizon of expectations in a specific situation (Koselleck 1985). Making history is a specific performative art of using the past. I do not, however, share Koselleck's theory of a radical break with the Enlightenment shaping History as an independent entity, but work with a theory of transhistorical productive tensions that are negotiated in the uses of the past as history (Aronsson 2011a).

The field of cultures of history might be separated into communicating spheres, some of them more explicit and some more implicit in their use of history, but with the references to the past made according to different logics:

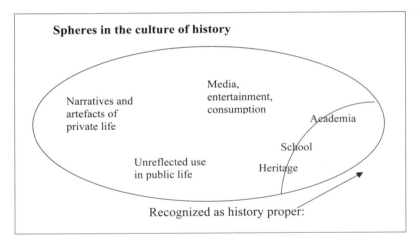

The past in private life is recollected to bring meaning and coherence into the biography of the individual and is usually thought of as memories rather than history. In the public sphere and politics, references to the past are more often made as statements and judgements of facts in order to justify the present order of things or plans for the future. The formal institutions in the right corner of the diagram are assigned the power of legitimate care, protection and communication of the past to citizens, students and children. Consuming and communicating the past is of course in some sense done in all these spheres, but when the logic becomes predominantly market-oriented, the need to build on facts, adhere to political orders, and still attract the desire of the individual becomes intensively negotiated to bring about the necessary profit.

Two hypotheses related to this diagram are:

- The impact of a specific use of the past is dependent on the intertwined combination of uses in several spheres. When an epoch like the medieval era reaches a pivotal interest above others, or when a regional level is articulated more than national or local levels, this is possible because it speaks through all these channels. The net production of meaning is often enhanced, rather than undermined, by contradictory combinations.
- The power of legitimacy heavily invested in the right side of the diagram has spread more evenly during the last few decades. Legitimate uses of the past are publicly recognized as private experiences, political community-building, and commercial goals; the striving for knowledge being only one special interest. The interaction between them seems to be a matter of legitimacy by cross-reference rather than contradiction, which used to be the foundation of the traditional evaluation of critical science.

A good example of this are the many sites, like the World Heritage medieval Visby of Gotland introduced earlier, developing strategies for combining university research, heritage management, tourism, local and regional development, live re-enactment to meet a desire to be entertained, negotiate gender issues and religious interest by staging the medieval city as a different continent: men and women were different, life close to death and nature, religion an absolute reality.

Heritage as Communication

The interplay between actors and logic does change over time, even if they are bound to each other more than is usually recognized. Traditional fears that the cultural industries and heritage industry have nourished about the power of market logic have given way in recent decades among many actors to hopes for the development of visiting industries, but also to the boosting of values such as trust, inclusion, health and creativity (Florida 2002; Putnam et al. 1992; Dicks 2000; De Groot 2009).

This hope for the utility of the past looks new compared to the ideal of scientific history, but continues traditions of history as *magistra vitae* in the classical and early modern period, the utility of knowledge of cultural history for civic development in the eighteenth century, and the burgeoning genre of historical novels in the nineteenth century. It is one of the positions in the long-term negotiations between the justified need for a disinterested position and the fact that historical enquiry is from the start directed by fears and longings rooted in ethics and aesthetics (Aronsson 2010; Grafton 2007; Aronsson 2011a).

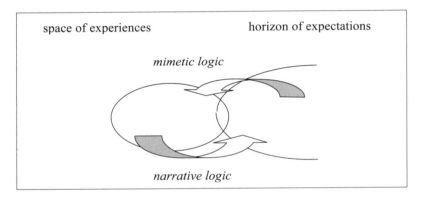

The communicative framework for meaningful history is multi-dimensional. Firstly, history needs only to be told where there is a public – hence the high-tide for the creation of histories in fifth-century BC Athens, in Renaissance Italy and Enlightenment Europe. This opens for reflection on the dynamic between uses of the past in the making and changing of community. The division of labour between experts and audiences, participants and spectators, is part of this sphere. Following from that, the second dimension concerns how uses of the past connect ideas of how utopias and dystopias work on the contemporary mind to set up memory and history prepared to deal with the threats and longings of people and society. The circulation between mimetic and narrative logic is best read from right to left, although the opposite is used in the persuasive logic of historians: we explore the past to be better equipped in the present to deal with the future. However, the present action of forming the space of experience out of the multitude of possibilities available is already informed by the horizon of expectation, what we need most badly: comfort and nostalgia in a world of rapid change; tools for inventing a new nation or excuses for our inability to care for our fellow human beings?

Thirdly, and as a result of the first two dimensions, the multitude of possible narratives are moulded into a set of genres of communication, such as books, films, storytelling, museums, and into the possible narrative tropes available for recognizing meaningful stories (White 1987). The formation of narratives connecting the past with contemporary desires and ideas of the future belongs to the structural features of uses of the past. The storyline, the inner meaning, can change over time, but the forms are restricted to four logically possible narratives. At the same time they resemble some of the mythical genres of grand narratives about the past. These four can be logically constructed by their way of relating past–contemporaneousness–future:

1. The past as the *Good Old Days*, where the good, beautiful and true were readily present. The classical period and the heritage of Greek and Roman culture created from the Renaissance are paradigmatic of this trope.

2. The story about continuing *Progress*, where the bad old days develop into our own time, little by little or by revolutionary acts, with ourselves as the crown of historical development: from poverty to welfare capitalism (the main story of the Western world).

3. History as a *Never-Never Land*, indisputably and qualitatively separated from our own presentness (tourist landscapes).

4. And the opposite idea: *There is nothing new under the sun.* Humans are basically the same, and we live in one time-space of experiences to learn from, be seduced and horrified by (providing the subjective opportunity of empathy) (Aronsson 2004: 77–85).

Many good stories contain a combination of these four narrative genres, thereby allowing the tale to respond to different needs. For example, many national narratives begin with people in a paradisiacal Stone Age or communal past, threatened by various external enemies, struggling hard to expel the enemies and restore the natural borders of the nation. Eventually, through heroic actions by individuals and collective action, this is successful, and contemporary society is at the top of the curve towards progress and eternal bliss, which means more or less keeping things as they are (Berger & Lorenz 2008).

These four types designate the formal connection between the past and the present in the narratives. However, their meaning is not restricted to the storyline but is also attached to their capacity to work as symbols and metaphors. As such, they can be used as inspirational monuments or as locations for critical perspectives.

The need to use these tropes to make an intelligible past into history applies on both individual and community level. The impact of a specific formation of uses of the past is dependent on the capacity to integrate meaning across logics of circulation, between actors, to create relevance for understanding, legitimacy and power relating to contemporary change.

A good example of long-standing institutional investment in building meaningful narratives on facts, for political and educational purposes, and communicated to large audiences, are national museums. The narrative performed by and in museums has a corresponding mimetic logic, where strategies for collection and preservation define the heritage and artefacts to be preserved. These change over time as a consequence of the need to integrate difference and represent unity in the midst of change. They are rich enough to allow for various narratives to be built, all duly proved and illustrated by material evidence. Built as secular cathedrals honouring their national patrons, scientific progress and the public sphere, they interact with traditional academic disciplines but go beyond them to make a difference in the production of communal meaning also in the experience economy of late-modernity. History needs a public and collective dimension to be reaffirmed as real and fulfil its meaning-building capacity – too much is invested in these old institutions not to make them viable in contemporary society as well. They are worth a chapter because of their character as crossroads for several logics and powers at play in using the past to pursue visions of the future.

National Museums Negotiating Heritage

National museums refer to those collections and displays claiming, negotiating, articulating and representing dominant national values, myths and realities. They need therefore to be explored not as created once and for all, but as historical and contemporary processes of institutionalized negotiations of what values will constitute the basis for national communities, individual meaning and dynamic state formation. This is a crossroads for many of the processes mapped above.[5]

The scene for the use of history in dealing with the simultaneous needs for integration and power enhancement was set in early-nineteenth-century Europe. The parallelism between the way religions and cultural heritage create values is intensive and entangled in many ways, as nationalism has been acknowledged as secular religion, capable of providing a whole context of meaning. Artefacts from the Catholic age were put on display as early as the nineteenth century, not as relics or heretical items, but as objects of a triumphantly overcome era in cultural history and as art treasures of olden days. Ideological dimensions of religion, such as ideas of the chosen people, are transferred into modernity by heritage bodies, in museums of both Protestant and Catholic countries. The sacred order of power and societies was translated into a historically motivated order of things, interplaying with general narratives of heritage but also with the precise interpretation of material culture. In Sweden the State Church was abolished in the year 2000, making it necessary to draw a line between substantial costs to be covered by the state for churches as "heritage" to be preserved, and costs to be covered for spiritual needs by the Church on its own.

Artefacts appear as pre-modern art in museums in Protestant countries, religions of "other" peoples placed in ethnographic exhibitions, and so on. In many situations, churches themselves become ambiguous sites of both religious and heritage worship, visited by tourists/congregations. In some settings the presence of religion becomes more nationally explicit than in others. This has been the case of Orthodox Christianity as a Greek heritage confronting Ottoman occupation from the nineteenth century. The Byzantine epoch centres around church heritage and is at the heart of Greek national self-understanding. During the Balkan wars of the 1990s, the destruction of religious heritage was at the centre of them – and restoration projects are at the heart of reconciliation efforts. In contemporary Iran, the national museum was transformed into a more Islamic representation to fit new political powers. These diverse examples demonstrate the affinity, competition and complementarity that participate in negotiating the value systems of the religion and the museum with political powers.

The overarching urge for the rapid creation of national museums, however, was to secure and naturalize the idea of a national existence.

The Finnish National Historical Museum is in its architecture recollecting both the worldly and spiritual powers: A Renaissance castle and a church frame the national romantic themes of the museum. Photo: Peter Aronsson

In states formerly occupied by Napoleon, but also in old sovereign states like Denmark and Sweden, it was an essential task in the face of rapid changes and the secession of major parts of the old realms. For Norway and Finland, set half-free by the same turmoil, possibilities to articulate national community gradually widened.

Similarly, Europe was part of the framing, from the high esteem of the classical heritage as part of a Golden Age to presentations of the nation as part of international trade patterns with roots in the Bronze Age, and shared intellectual history from Christianity to the Enlightenment. Even dominant narratives are never completely closed, but keep some doors open for ambiguous reading, to accommodate possible changes, while others need to be more securely locked to avoid catastrophe (Aronsson 2010). The idea of a Nordic communal past and heritage has been more readily demonstrated in Denmark and Sweden, the old competing empires, and ignored by the more vulnerable new nation-states of Norway and Finland (Aronsson & Gradén 2012, forthcoming).

Within these challenges there were other tasks to deal with concerning integration and positive stimuli: making regional, class, gender and ethnic differences into a positive part of heritage, and not into sources of conflict, fragmentation and contention. One good example is the representation of regional diversity as a matter of aesthetic values and skills as they appear in regional costumes (female emphasis) and building culture (male sphere).[6]

Much of this agenda was also valid throughout the twentieth century. The change of emphasis concerns the kind of differences that ought to be the primary focus of integrationist efforts. Region and later class, which were the main concerns of nineteenth-century cultural policy, gender and ethnicity, are moving to the centre as we move further into the twenty-first century.

Referring to the theoretical model presented above, national museums are highly organized bodies in the historical culture of a society, representing the level of knowledge as well as the essence of its nature and art, its political and cultural unity, to be collected, systematized, guarded and narrated. The format for the national story is very similar, although always told as a unique experience in each nation-state. It starts as far as possible in the distant past as a primitive but Golden Age, through troubles and tribulations caused by enemies, after which the nation is eventually liberated and can begin its road to progress in the contemporary era (Berger & Lorenz 2010).

However firmly institutionalized in its own right, the museum does communicate with the other spheres of circulation (politics, market, and personal experience). The successful exchange and transportation of values (knowledge, economy, meaning) is part of the resulting power of its representations to convey a legitimate and meaningful world view. The exchange is not without tensions. Most antagonistic is the museums' explicit relation to the market. Bringing objects from the market into the heritage sector means permanently declaring them beyond the system of value attached to demand and supply. Musealization makes objects priceless evidence of the past. Laws in all countries are enacted to protect historic objects from crossing that border, and many attempts are made to repatriate objects that wrongly crossed the line. In practice there is, of course, a huge economy trading in antiques, natural history specimens and works of art. Farthest away from the market are material proofs of the ancient history of the nation, declared universally to be the property of the nation. Closest to the market, and in reality competing with it, is the art trade. The parallels between the museum and the nation and the Church and religion are striking. Two central systems of transcendent reference and inner-worldly existence meet similar dilemmas to negotiate. A structural similarity to some uses of the concept of religion is the mythical character of history as a source of meaning-guiding world views, values and action. It also produces sacred objects and places not possible to reduce to commercial values, and hence protected by law and belief from market circulation or individual misuse. These similarities can be traced back to their location as mythical, in the sense that they are fundamental in the establishment of meaning, not only of facts. They make empirical statements about the nature of the world in the path of history. These similarities made history a possible secular structure of meaning, partly shifting position with religion in the nineteenth century.

The closeness and competitive standing of the market forces co-varies with the fluid relation to donors and patrons. This is partly a practical issue of acquiring good objects without breaking the budget, but it also establishes a relationship between the museum and the nation, understood as being composed of its good citizens. The act of donating to as well as visiting the museum can be compared with other gifts and performances creating a communitas (Mauss 1954), such as in the congregation and the parish. Simultaneously, a difference between the generous and mighty donor and the still honourable but smaller contributor is communicated, and a relation to the more or less grateful citizen and ever more important tourist is established. Social inclusion and market penetration add to traditional heritage values.

Naturally, a more intensive relationship does develop with the political sphere for a national museum. This may be a clear-cut relationship where national museums are part of the government structure, as in Greece and Turkey; but at the other end of the spectrum, making the museum might be a way to construct the nation as a public sphere before the actual political structure exists. The first purpose-built national museum was set up for Hungary in Budapest, while the country was still part of the Austrian Empire. A Polish national museum was set up in Rapperswil in 1869 while Poland was still under Russian rule.

Since modern museums are not only scientific archives but also, and successively more so, public exhibitions, they need to address the desires of the audience, be it their engagement in the national cause of the country, pressing existential issues for the individual, the excitement about advanced multimedia presentations, or the structuring of a museum visit as a desirable outing for the family on holiday, with a café and special arrangements for children's entertainment.

Even if the exhibitionary grammar of heritage was once influenced by the heritage of religious culture, the idea of relics and representation, the flow of influence has for a long time gone mostly in the other direction: sacred spaces and objects turned into museums. Through imperialism and cultural transfer, Western culture has set a standard for national museums and cultural heritage, even codified in UNESCO, as part of a normality standard for the nations of the world. With globalization, the growing business of travel and tourism as an industry and new identity projects, they are subject to change (Harrison 2010; Smith 2006).

Negotiating with the Museum

Many of the negotiations and conflicts behind the scenes in the museums have long-standing trajectories; they are indeed not mishaps but part of the value of the institutions in creating them as relevant cultural forces at play over the last two and a half centuries. Having now looked into the empirical dynamic, we might formulate these negotiations in more theoretical terms.

The first negotiation made by any museum is pointing to an object and arguing that it represents a unique or typical value. From this follows the authoritative and sometimes contested decision about what type of reality or value the object represents: the natural world, outstanding art, a craft tradition, a historic event, or a *foreign* culture. The struggles of indigenous people to move the representation of their cultures from the natural history collection to other departments are part of that negotiation. The movement of aboriginal artefacts from ethnographic collections to art exhibitions marks a change in the apprehension of their culture. Being represented in and by themselves is a goal for many nations: The Ájtte museum of Sami culture and mountain region in Sweden moving objects from Stockholm to Jokkmokk, and the Museum of the American Indian recently opened on the Mall in Washington, demonstrates this drive for national museums connected to minority rights.

This is one of the dimensions where knowledge and politics interact explicitly, the second long-standing negotiation of national museums. A political community in the making needs scientific support for its ancientness, its coherence and qualities over time. The quality and unity of the culture is composed through the museums into an orchestration as the third negotiation dealing with differences within the nation. "United in diversity" is not only the motto of the European Union but also a strategy for all societies, since they are compounded of various groups, however strong the political centralization they live under. In highly centralized states like Stalin's Soviet Union, as well as the democratic Turkey under Atatürk, cultural diversity was represented; which meant toning down political controversies and reducing differences to aesthetic pleasures of high art or the admiration and presentation of class and regional difference as part of the stability and beautiful variation harboured in the culture of an allegedly stable and even naturalized national community. In more self-confident and old imperial cities, the multicultural representation takes on a universalist coat. "Do you want to see the world? Visit the British Museum!" Built on Enlightenment traditions, museums in London and Paris, and also in Vienna, claim to represent the world and a universal aspiration for pure and free knowledge about everything. This just happens to be done best where the assemblage of great artefacts has ended up through contingencies of world history. Universalism can be a successful national strategy legitimizing power and centrality.

Dealing with external enemies is a delicate issue, if it is not secured by a great distance in time. The museum answers explicitly or quietly by interplaying voices and silences in dealing with old conflicts. The dissolution of the Swedish Empire in 1809 and 1905 was commemorated in 2005 and 2009, but the victories of imperial Sweden in 1658, which were great occasions for jubilees before the 1920s, are nowadays quietly forgotten in the capital. In Germany, the nineteenth-century victories of the Empire cannot be celebrated any more – the Holocaust has become the central commemoration of a shared and dark past to be counteracted. In Greece and Turkey, the conflict over Cyprus is explicit. Civil wars and fascism in Italy and Greece are not highlighted, to put it mildly, while the role of these countries as the cradle of Western civilization is. The role of the nation towards its neighbours – as part of Europe, a Western tradition, and in the world community – is communicated differently. In Eastern Europe, an array of Occupation museums are dedicated to dealing with the recent past due to changing political circumstances (Sarkisova & Apor 2008).

Museums deal with change as a fourth negotiating dimension. By creating periods pointing to evolution, they eventually place the recent past in the historic museum. What part of the economy, after agriculture, is ready to be the next in line to end up in a historical museum, and which parts point towards the future? The question is not always answered *post facto*, but established as an argument about where to place hopes and investments for the future. National museums as investments in the experience economy, and competition between nations and metropolises in that field, is a contemporary factor adding to older objectives of securing heritage.

The level of investments in national museums is high in contemporary society. The motives and hopes are often a mixture of a will to secure a scientific and relevant understanding of the national heritage, achieving community integration, stimulating creativity and cultural dialogue, and creating attractions for a burgeoning experience economy. The Netherlands is planning for a new national museum communicating a stronger ethnic canon; a path also chosen in Denmark. Many other museums, from Canada and New Zealand to Sweden, hail a more multicultural approach, playing down the traditional national aspect of narrative, inviting new citizens to a more diverse idea of society. Ethnographic museums open with a post-colonial invitation to dialogue all over the world, in tension with strong demands for the restitution of objects, from the human remains of Sami, to the Elgin Marbles of the Acropolis. It is a contested billion-dollar cultural industry, creating, negotiating and reinforcing ideas of values, belonging and ownership.

The narrative about these issues treats questions of historical change in many ways. It is not by chance that the EU, troubled by disputes about European integration, in/with the Lisbon Treaty, calls for knowledge about how the authoritative institutions of national museums create long-standing values and identities in need of attention. A free market, along with ideas of universal human rights, is in fact localized, embedded and negotiated in institutions like these.

Transnational Framings

When does heritage become the foundation for aggression, and when is it used to go beyond borders to reconciliation with former enemies? When do societies suffer from "too much history" or histories enhancing hostilities, and when is heritage part of the solution, creating more secure, tolerant and inclusive political cultures? This problem could be discussed by using material from the contemporary Balkans or South Africa, but I will draw on a longer time frame to elucidate the problem.[7]

In Scandinavia, as in most of Europe, history is a sad story of internal and external warfare, providing plenty of fuel for bitter struggles. Historiography was aggressive and hostile in early modern times, but changed dramatically in the nineteenth century. This change was instrumental in producing a cultural transnationalism able to temper hostility in the history of secession in the Nordic countries in the nineteenth and twentieth centuries. The establishment of Nordic museums competed with national ones in the early and more vulnerable phase of nation-making.

Internally, the heritage of potential injustice for most of the provinces was not used for aggressive nationalist purposes in the age of nationalism, or later in the age of regionalism. There have been plenty of traumatic experiences between neighbours in Scandinavia's past, but after the generations that experienced the actual trauma, there seems to have been effective negotiation and integration to prohibit civil war. The capacity of the state to skilfully combine the use of force with the power of political negotiation is no doubt of vital social and political importance, but it is not enough to suppress possible discontent. It is my argument that a triple integrative strategy has been at work on the cultural level.

The establishment of a Nordic cultural nation and historical culture is the first important factor in the process of building Nordic nation-states. In eras of open aggression, this dimension becomes more articulated, and in times of less stress it becomes more of a silent strategy. The presence of Nordic culture is on one hand represented by "banal Scandinavianism" in names, interpretations and maps. On the other, it is stated by mostly leaving the other countries' territory in silence, leaving room for as few territorial claims as possible between the neighbours. The Scandinavian dimension is mainly there in a respect for the present-day borders, creating silence or marginalizing issues of restitution. An earlier strong discourse on Nordic or Germanic tribes has perhaps also been put in disrespect by Nazi abuses. It survives in some remarks on culture and Viking endeavours.

Hidden behind these is the second integrative strategy, which is less appreciated. The ability to deal with regional differences as a national cultural orchestration was a very important aspect during the nation-formation period. Later, it was transformed into a purely administrative aspect of allocating equal opportunities, and the question of diversity moved from a potential political arena of identity and power to that of cultural heritage and personal sentiment. Instead, the European dimension is strong in the interpretation of communication and trade. These have a long tradition in classic learning, but are now of course resonating well with European integration. In the EU, regional issues have in recent decades become a more urgent matter in negotiating power between the EU and nation-states, but this is not openly addressed in national museums, other than through the more frequent regional mapping of past phenomena on the European scale.

The third and corresponding aspect is the successful investment in a national (historical) culture in many spheres of life: sports, language, politics, literature, and welfare politics are parts of everyday historical culture. They enforce a greater impact on mentality, while national museums are important explicit markers of ideology, negotiating also with visitors and other nations as part of cultural diplomacy.

There is no doubt that academia has played a decisive role in this integrative dynamic. History forgets regions and naturalizes nation-states, archaeology roots community in the ground, ethnology culturalizes differences, and social science produces instrumental knowledge to solve problems.

The fact that Denmark has a comprehensive national museum needs explaining, since as a state it belongs historically to the group of imperial conglomerate states like Sweden and the United Kingdom, which are usually prone to universalize their diversities strongly in the Enlightenment tradition, and to undercommunicate the making of the nation-state. There are four dimensions to explaining the Danish case: its autocratic rule until 1848; the Napoleonic Wars, with the bombardment of Copenhagen; the strong German threat and expansion in the nineteenth century, and the Nazi occupation in the Second World War. This made the transformation, nationalization and centralization of royal collections determine the imperial tradition, still part of the existing Danish state in relation to the Faroe Islands and Greenland.

The national museum is also a mix of a universal museum of the British Museum kind, typical for old multi-cultural empires, and a more focused national museum like that in Finland, typical of a recently created state.

Denmark and Sweden exemplify two different strategies in relation to the late modern challenges in cultural policy. In Denmark, a strong reinforcement of the national narrative, both in the recent establishment of an official cultural canon and in more rigid immigration policies, is part and parcel of the overall cultural heritage policy (Jensen 2008; Kulturministerium 2006; Jönsson et al. 2008). These differences are also reflected in the profile and ambition of the research activities in the two national museums. The National museum of Denmark has a substantial research department concerned with the periods and material covered by the museum. The Historical Museum in Sweden has instead a much smaller volume of research and focus within the museum on a critical perspective on the creation and working of the institution itself.[8]

The absence of an official reflexive relation to the nation-state, evolution, and highlights of the collections is in fact a hallmark of the Danish National Museum and its most recent exhibitions on prehistory. It reflects an urge to meet individuals, religious issues, aesthetic preferences, and everyday life, which opens for other readings by late-modern Danes and foreign visitors alike. In Sweden, the national narrative is obvious in the selection of material, but denounced in rhetoric and by the division of labour between several museums. The net result is that in Sweden the national dimension is met with avoidance and hypocrisy, but in Denmark embraced with naivety and pride. This is well in tune with contemporary variations in the political culture of the two countries, and testifies to the space for strategic choices in meeting similar challenges. In mitigating globalization and migration, the quest for integration can be met with either stronger demands for national explication, as has been stated in many Eastern European countries but also in the Netherlands and Denmark, or with more cosmopolitan, enlightened or multicultural approaches. The multicultural approach is stronger in the USA, Canada, New Zealand and most of Western Europe, with a mixture of universalism and politics of recognition. Scandinavianism was part of the negotiation between former hostile neighbours, and still has a small role to play in the negotiation of the place of Nordic countries in their European context (Aronsson 2012, 2008).

The net result is a massive naturalization of the present order, as regards both the nation-states and the established museum institutions. The challenges of globalization, migration, and climate change present a new context for the negotiation of identity. My suggestion is that the challenges are partly new, but the answer – integration into a national political system – is still the main vision and programme for cultural and political institutions. This is not surprising, but contrasts with the self-understanding of many museum professionals and reform-oriented politicians, who agree on a discourse about the need for a radically new function for the institutions.

Conclusions

In collecting, reshaping and creating meaning for the past, the use of strong narratives of continuity and change, threats and survival, challenges and heroic endeavours, is commonplace. National museums as prestigious institutions at the centre of capitals, close to the traditional castles, parliaments and cathedrals, work as part of complex division of labour between disciplines and between knowledge and politics in the creation of meaning and legitimacy, dealing with fundamental ideas of order, difference and unity. They need to address the desires of individuals, the politics of identities, public representations of values, the state of knowledge in several disciplines, and market conditions for reaching out to audiences. This has been true for many centuries, but over time shifts do occur in where the power of initiative lies: from civic elites to government bodies, from heritage institutions to popular media and the travel industry.

An expanding culturalization and secularization of the world opens for historicization and public representation of the world as heritage: natural history museums, evolution, cultural history and art history. Medialization enhances the value of places and artefacts, and cheap travel makes them accessible for a transnational audience.

National museums, tourist destinations, and more mundane heritage sites are places for negotiating contradictions of values hidden and materialized as descriptive representations of the true, the beautiful and the good (knowledge, aesthetics and ethics). They are expressions of simple narrative tropes where good and evil, eternal values and progress create meaning; and at the same time repositories of possible reinterpretations, hybrid interpretations, precisely because they harbour contradictions and negotiate them into a situated legitimate understanding of the world and the destiny framing both the individual and the nation.

The path taken for state-making, and the force of the actual traumas that need to be tackled, determine to a certain degree the making and working of national museums. Old empires tend to represent national grandeur and community through universal values of Enlightenment origin, to encompass a multicultural citizenry and make the most legitimate use of the amassed riches from colonies. The power and resources of the centralized state set limits to representation in the capital.

Recent conflicts, threats, and active state-making processes make nations more active in forming national historical cultures and representing them in national museums in a coherent and all-encompassing mode. Both migration and other aspects of globalization challenge traditional national narratives; but responses differ according to the desired horizon of expectation, and hence the space of experience in museums is restructured accordingly. As long as individuals fear and long for something, and need to corroborate these visions in a shared narrative of the past as a tool to orient themselves in the present, histories will be made out of the past, and values negotiated with facts and artefacts as evidence not only of what the world was like, but of what it ought to be.

Notes

1 Augustin 1886, Chapter XX. "In What Manner Time May Properly Be Designated", Book XI.

2 This means that strong statements about the disparity of memory and history, individual and collective memories, are apprehended here as polarities that stand in a dialectic and in fact necessary organic relation to each other. Historicity as a part of existential predicaments ought to be closely related to the justification for historical epistemologies.

3 Carr 2005. In a way, this is moving reflection to a position similar to the organic relationship it once had in the national framing, but more in tune with contemporary desires. No doubt the gain in relevance might have its downsides needed to be balanced by critical reflection. This is precisely why it should be pursued in the academia, and not exclusively developed by market response as otherwise might be the case.

4 This introduction to a theory of uses of the past is an abbreviated version of Aronsson 2004. It can be found in English in a context of regional uses of the past in Aronsson 2007.

5 Several dimensions of these negotiations and their consequences are explored in the research project "European National Museums: Identity politics, the uses of the

past and the European citizen" (EuNaMus), running 2010–2013, www.eunamus.
eu. Knell, Aronsson & Amundsen 2011.
6 For more elaborate work behind this conclusion, see Aronsson 2012.
7 The theme of this discussion is part of a more detailed comparison between Denmark and Sweden in ibid.
8 See ongoing research presented at www.shmm.se and reports on www.natmus.dk,
although the most recent research report (Forskningsberetning) is from 2004. Of
course, critical discourse is present in the public and academic domains in Denmark
as well. See e.g. Jensen & Varberg 2008.

References

Aronsson, Peter (2000): Regionbegreppets funktion för skilda akademiska discipliner
och samhällsutvecklingen, in Lars-Erik Edlund and Anna Karolina Greggas (eds):
Kontinuitet och förändring i regionala rum, Umeå: Umeå Universitet.
Aronsson, Peter (2002): Att uppleva historia, in Irene Johansson, Kenneth Andersson,
and Marie Lindstedt Cronberg (eds): *Tid och tillit. En vänbok till Eva Österberg*,
Stockholm: Carlsson.
Aronsson, Peter (2004): *Historiebruk. Att använda det förflutna*, Lund: Studentlitteratur.
Aronsson, Peter (2007): The Old Cultural Regionalism – and the New, in Bill Lancaster,
Diana Newton and Natasha Vall (eds): *An Agenda for Regional History*, Newcastle:
Northumbria University Press.
Aronsson, Peter (2008): Representing Community. National Museums. Negotiating
Differences and Community, in Nordic Countries, in Kathrine J. Goodnow and
Haci Akman (eds): *Scandinavian Museums and Cultural Diversity*, New York: Berg-
hahn Books.
Aronsson, Peter (2010): Uses of the Past; Nordic Historical Cultures in a Comparative
Perspective, *Culture Unbound, Journal of Current Cultural Research*, 2: 553–563.
Aronsson, Peter (2011a): *Historia*, Malmö: Liber.
Aronsson, Peter (2011b): Explaining National Museums. Exploring Comparative
Approaches to the Study of National Museums, in Simon J. Knell, Peter Aronsson
and Arne Amundsen (eds): *National Museums. New Studies from Around the World*,
London: Routledge.
Aronsson, Peter (2012): Exhibiting Scandinavian Culture. The National Museums
of Denmark and Sweden, in Stefan Berger, Chris Lorenz and Billie Melman (eds):
Popularizing National Pasts. 1800 to the Present, London: Routledge.
Aronsson, Peter and Lizette Gradén (eds) (2012, forthcoming): *Performing Nordic
Heritage*, London: Ashgate.
Augustin, Aurelius (1886): *The Confessions of St. Augustine. Translated and annotated
by J G Pilkington*, New York: Christian Literature Publishing Co.
Berger, Stefan and Chris Lorenz (eds) (2008): *The Contested Nation. Ethnicity, Class,
Religion and Gender in National Histories*, New York: Palgrave Macmillan.
Berger, Stefan and Chris Lorenz (eds) (2010): *Nationalizing the Past. Historians as
Nation Builders in Modern Europe*, Basingstoke: Palgrave Macmillan.
Carr, David (2005): Phenomenology of Historical Time, in Maria Sa Cavalcante
Schuback and, Hans Ruin (eds): *The Past's Presence. Essays on the Historicity of
Philosophical Thinking*, Huddinge: Södertörns högskola.

De Groot, Jerome, (ed.) (2009): *Consuming History. Historians and Heritage in Contemporary Popular Culture,* London: Routledge.

Dicks, Bella (2000): *Heritage, Place and Community,* Cardiff: University of Wales Press.

Florida, Richard (2002): *The Rise of the Creative Class. and How It's Transforming Work, Leisure, Community and Everyday Life,* New York: Basic Books.

Grafton, Anthony (2007): *What was History? The Art of History in Early Modern Europe,* Cambridge: Cambridge University Press.

Gustafsson, Lotten (2002): *Den förtrollade zonen. Lekar med tid, rum och identitet under Medeltidsveckan på Gotland,* Nora: Nya Doxa.

Harrison, Rodney (2010): *Understanding the Politics of Heritage,* Manchester: Manchester University Press.

Jenkins, Keith, Sue Morgan and Alun Munslow, (eds) (2007): *Manifestos for History,* London: Routledge

Jensen, Benard Eric (2008): *Kulturarv. Et identitetspolitisk konfliktfelt,* København: Gad.

Johansson, Carina (2009): *Visby visuelt. Föreställningar om en plats med utgångspunkt i bilder och kulturarv,* Klintehamn: Gotlandica förlag.

Jönsson, Lars-Eric, Anna Wallette and Jes Wienberg, (ed.) (2008): *Kanon och kulturarv. Historia och samtid i Danmark och Sverige,* Göteborg och Stockholm: Makadam.

Knell, Simon J., Peter Aronsson and Arne Bugge Amundsen (2011): *National Museums. New Studies from Around the World,* London: Routledge.

Koselleck, Reinhart (1985): *Future's Past. On the Semantics of Historical Time,* Cambridge: MIT Press.

Kulturministerium, Dansk (2006): *Kulturkanon,* København.

Lowenthal, David (1998): *The Heritage Crusade and the Spoils of History,* Cambridge: Cambridge University Press.

Mauss, Marcel (1954): *The Gift. Forms and Functions of Exchange in Archaic Societies,* Glencoe, Ill.: Free Press.

Putnam, Robert D., Robert Leonardi and Raffaella Y. Nanetti (1992): *Making Democracy Work. Civic Traditions in Modern Italy,* Princeton: Princeton University Press.

Ronström, Owe (2007): *Kulturarvspolitik. Visby. Från sliten småstad till medeltidsikon,* Stockholm: Carlsson.

Rüsen, Jörn (2002): *Geschichte im Kulturprozess,* Köln, Weimar and Wien: Böhlau.

Sandström, Erika (2005): *På den tiden, i dessa dagar. Föreställningar om och bruk av historia vid Medeltidsveckan på Gotland och Jamtli historieland,* Östersund: Jamtli.

Sarkisova, Oksana and Peter Apor (eds) (2008): *Past for the Eye. East European Representations of Communism in Cinema and Museums after 1989,* Budapest and New York: Central European University Press.

Sennett, Richard (1998): *The Corrosion of Character. The Personal Consequences of Work in the New Capitalism,* New York: W.W. Norton.

Smith, Laurajane (2006): *Uses of Heritage,* New York: Routledge.

Taylor, Charles (1989): *Sources of the Self. The Making of the Modern Identity,* Cambridge: Harvard University Press.

Varberg, Jeanette (2008): Nationalmuseets nye udstilling. Danmarks Oltid, *KUML:* X: 291–296.

White, Hayden (1987): *The Content of the Form. Narrative Discourse and Historical Representation,* Baltimore: Johns Hopkins University Press.

CHAPTER 12

Recycling Ancient Narrations on a Post-modern Market

Some Questions about Myth Today

Stefan Arvidsson

The conditions for creating, communicating, and receiving myths are currently very different from the situation before the advent of modern societies. The idiom and content of myths also look different today, besides which the dominant interpretative ideology is not the same as it was in the medieval or early modern period. In a previous work I have studied how the medieval stories of Sigurd (Siegfried) Fafnisbani, Brynhild and Gudrun (Krimhild) were adapted by Richard Wagner and J. R. R. Tolkien and transformed to suit a modern audience (Arvidsson 2007). This chapter aims to discuss some conclusions drawn from that study, along with bringing to the fore some questions that emerged in the course of the work: Are there at all myths today? Where? If so, what is meant by "myth"? What are the conditions for creating, disseminating, and receiving them? Is there a market for myths today?

Since the question of which of the various existing definitions of myth is appropriate when studying contemporary myths is partly dependent on the description of characteristics of our society, I will not start from that end. But we still need some provisional guidelines to "myth": A basic model of communication consists of sender, message, and receiver, and a definition of myth can proceed from any of these components.[1] If we proceed from the sender component, we can enlist the aid of the American historian of religions Bruce Lincoln, who has vitalized the study of myth in numerous ways. First in *Discourse and the Construction of Society: Comparative Studies of Myth, Ritual, and Classification* (1989) and then in *Authority: Construction and Corrosion*

(1994), Lincoln argues that we ought to assess myths as narratives to which religious, political, or cultural leaders try to lend authority, and which they try to get other people to perceive as true, as sensible, or at least as guidance for their understanding of themselves and the world (Lincoln 1989:15–26, 1994:1–13). It is not necessary for the people to perceive the story as being literally true, only that in one way or another it contains some kind of wisdom. A myth may therefore be defined as a narrative that is recognized as having an exemplary truth. Here is how Lincoln puts it: "a narrative possessed of authority is one for which successful claims are made not only to the status of truth, but what is more, to the status of *paradigmatic* truth" (Lincoln 1989:24). Myth is thus, seen from the sender component, something made up by people with power or authority with the conscious aim to influence the consciousness of a larger number of people.

If we instead define myth in terms of the message component, we end up in the classic folkloristic position on myth as narratives that take place before the creation of the world and of mankind; as stories with gods, demons, and chaotic beings as their main actors.[2] We shall return later to whether it might be meaningful to talk of myths even if the actors are not gods and demons but rather other kinds of ahistorical entities. Finally, if we look at the receiver component of the communication model, we can define myth as a narrative that *de facto* shapes the consciousness and conceptions of individuals,[3] no matter whether the senders intended this or not, and no matter whether the narrative includes supernatural actors or not. Let us bear these three alternatives in mind as we now turn to the actual inquiry.

The Symbolistic Interpretation

The possibilities to lend authority to a narrative, to elevate it into some kind of supposedly eternal truth, have changed in modern times. The most important reason for this is what can be called, in a broad sense, the Enlightenment; that is, the intellectual ambition to check all narratives against reason. This reason is supposed to examine the claims of the narrative with the aid of the senses, logic, source criticism, and other critical rules of thumb. The natural sciences and the closely allied modern technology, along with scientific medicine, have been the main pioneers and the strongest arguments for the Enlightenment project. In the heyday of the Enlightenment in the eighteenth century, people attacked not only rituals, magical ideas, and the power of the Church, but also questioned religious narratives. Like Plato a couple of thousand years earlier, the champions of the Enlightenment chose the side of *logos* against *mythos*. Ancient cosmologies were refuted with the aid of science. Myths became lies, and were not infrequently condemned as deliberate deceptions by priests.

Romanticism was the cultural reaction to the Enlightenment. The Romantic writers argued against the Enlightenment philosophers, declaring that traditions and customs can have an intrinsic value and that they cannot be simply assessed in terms of reason. As regards myths, Johann Gottfried Herder and others stated that they could not be apprehended literally – and thereby refuted by scholarship – but that their content was more ethical and aesthetic.[4] Myths *symbolized* something. Behind the story that the Enlightenment and science had exposed as a lie, a deeper truth was concealed. To benefit from a fantastic tale, then, the receiver had to practise the use of a symbolic gaze; the ability to see that the one thing can and should take the place of the other. The receiver of myths must disregard historical contexts as well as the literal meaning of the stories. Myths are not about what they might seem at first sight to be about. There is a symbolic significance hidden deep in them.

In 1835, David Friedrich Strauss tried in *Das Leben Jesu* to save the New Testament from the criticism of the fantastic tales of Jesus' miracles by Enlightenment philosophers and scientists.[5] Strauss did so by referring to the New Testament narratives as "myths". But people believed, with the Enlightenment view of myth current in their minds, that Strauss with this choice of word was dismissing the scriptural stories as lies. Yet Strauss' actual purpose was to show that the literal meaning of the narratives was irrelevant and that they actually symbolized moral attitudes. Later, this became the stance of the influential liberal theology school of thought (although one must say that liberal theology in general has been much more inclined to express its religiosity in philosophical and not in mythical form).

In modern times, the pre-understanding of a symbolistic interpretation of myths has become so firmly established that there is no need to argue for it. The prominent twentieth-century theologian Rudolf Bultmann, for example, claimed that "whenever a myth has been taken literally its sense has been perverted" (Bultmann 1959:27). But myths are not symbolic or allegorical narratives. Myths *might be* interpreted symbolically, but there is nothing in the mythical narratives themselves which automatically sanctions that perspective. This is actually trivial, but it must be stated because the general perception of mythical narratives has become so impregnated by the symbolic perspective. Historically speaking, however, the symbolistic interpretation of myths is an exception, since most people who have passed on the myths of their people have actually believed in their literal meaning. Even today there are billions of people who believe in the literal message of myths. Many Hindus actually believe that the god Rama was born a number of centuries ago in the South Asian city of Ayodhya, and that he performed great deeds on Sri Lanka together with the monkey god Hanuman. Many Christians, probably the majority of them, believe that Jesus could make the lame walk. Indeed, that belief is one of the main reasons for remaining a Christian.

Myths of Nationalism

The tradition of liberal theology launched the idea of Christian stories as allegories about moral issues, but in reality avoided all language that was too symbolically overloaded. There was, however, in the late nineteenth century another arena for mythopoetic imagination: nationalism. Already Herder had declared that myths and traditions should be perceived as expressions of a *Volksgeist*; they were the cultural forms of a people. Nationalism, which started as a liberal and social liberation programme and ended as an anti-liberal chauvinistic movement, picked up old narratives and not infrequently concocted new ones.[6] Richard Wagner's recasting of Old Norse and medieval legends is probably the most successful example of the vitalization of mythical expressions in modern time.[7]

If we go back to my introductory discussion of the definition of myth, we may note that, in the case of nationalism, we are dealing with myth no matter where we begin. The stories of nationalism were created and told by politicians and authors with the intention of getting people to perceive them as instructive and true. They were created with the sole purpose of shaping people's consciousness, not least in light of the rapidly increasing organization of the working class, which risked shaking the very foundations of the bourgeois society. At the end of the nineteenth century, the newly established institution for the education of every citizen, schools, succeeded the Church as the chief institution for transmitting myths in this sense. We know from history that this nationalistic, mythical propaganda was actually successful – even a great many of the Social Democratic Party cadre in Germany and France quickly forgot about international solidarity when the Fatherland called in 1914.

But can stories about the history of a nation really be called myths in the folkloristic sense? They are surely not about gods creating the cosmos. No, but they are about supposedly ahistorical entities. When Gustav Vasa liberated Sweden from Danish lordship, according to nationalistic histories he was not laying the foundation for the nation-state of Sweden but rather redeeming the Sweden that already existed as a Platonic idea.[8] The myths of nationalism are about eternal nations and their fates. It is telling that the National Socialist scholar Walter Wüst disliked the talk of how Germany had "come into being", finding that phrase a gross insult:

> Even today, they speak with soft, calculating stubbornness, for example, about the becoming [Werden] of the German people, and take their pleasure by enumerating mongrelized material to superstitious students and comrades, as if the German Being had been formed from them as a homunculus: late classical antiquity, and the declining Roman world with its landholding feudalism – poor Odal! –, the Church and France, Arabic and Jewish philosophy as well as the Renaissance, and finally the Counter-Reformation and parliamentarism. … Whoever attacks the basic building material of German and Germanic exist-ence, to them let it be said: we want – also cultural-historically – to be the master and not the lover in our own house![9]

Post-war Demythologization

It is worth pointing out that it was not just the nationalistic Right that used mythological propaganda language. Let me take two examples of dragon slayers. No one did more at the end of the nineteenth century to show the usefulness of mythical language than Richard Wagner. After the election successes in 1912, when their party gained 35% of the votes, the German Social Democrats published a postcard where we can see "Rote Siegfried" after killing the dragon of the bourgeois parties.[10] This Wagnerian symbolism was comprehensible to most Social Democratic sympathizers at the time, we may assume.

Before socialist realism became the official language of art and

German Social Democratic post-card printed after the successful election in 1912.

propaganda in "the world's first workers' state", the Bolsheviks, to take the second example, expropriated older Christian myths. In this picture, presumably from some time between 1918 and 1920, Leon Trotsky, the organizer of the Red Army, is acting like Saint George by killing the dragon of counter-revolution.[11] Perhaps we might label the years from 1918 to 1945 as the period of "mythical politics"? The post-war era became, on the contrary, a time of radical demythologization: mythical politics was identified with "totalitarian" politics, which included Nazism as well as Communism.[12] The demythologization of the post-war era can, if you will, be associated with two radically different philosophers.

The year 1945 saw the appearance of Karl Popper's *The Open Society and Its Enemies*. In this work on the history of philosophy, Popper criticizes Plato, Hegel, and Marx because, when they think they have discovered a teleological meaning in the evolution of history ("historical prophecies"), they use it to justify coercive totalitarian politics (Popper 2005:xix). Although Popper does not expressly call the three philosophers' outlook "mythical", it would have made perfect sense.[13] The antidote to totalitarian politics is, according to Popper, "piecemeal social

Leon Trotsky, the founder of the Red Army, replacing Saint George.

engineering" (Popper 2005:xviii). With *La condition postmoderne* from 1979, Jean-François Lyotard became world-famous. Lyotard claims in the book that the era of *le grand narratif*, overarching meta-narratives about History, Truth, and Liberty, is over – and that there is nothing to mourn (Lyotard 1984). For both Popper and Lyotard, it was Marxism, very influential during this post-war era, both in the labour movement and at the universities, that was the quintessential symbol of a mythical and essentially totalitarian view of history. Perhaps it would not be unfair to see the crucial final step in this demythologization in Francis Fukuyama's *The End of History* (1989), where he puts forward his famous thesis that not only the ideological perspectives and conflicts of the period are over, but that the whole of history in the strict sense is over:

> … what we may be witnessing is not just the end of the Cold War, or the passing of a particular period of postwar history, but the end of history as such: that is, the end point of mankind's ideological

evolution and the universalization of Western liberal democracy as the final form of human government.[14]

The warnings against the use of mythical and utopian ideas, as issued by today's political hegemony, against the background of Popper, Lyotard, and others, are due to the belief that such ideas inevitably lead straight to "totalitarianism". According to the Slovenian philosopher Slavoj Žižek, it is not only the case that we no longer have "mythical politics", but that we are even living with a "post-political" political discourse.[15] By this, Žižek is referring to the fact that the politicians no longer declare any ideals, or any real goals for their political actions; instead, everything is about practical, administrative solutions expressed in a bureaucratic-instrumental language. The normal political discourse today is therefore stripped of the mythological words that used to be a part of every politician's terminology. Even words which are used as a kind of invocation (such as "liberty") and which had a certain mythical lustre not so long ago (in the case of liberty, this was coloured by things like Eugène Delacroix's famous painting) are today only bleak words.[16] The political discourse consists of dry statements, of thin, bureaucratic phraseology, with the imprecise philosophic concepts of representative democracy, "liberty", "the individual", "rights" and "security" as talismans against all "mythical" and utopian ideas.

New Age Myths

If myths are no longer alive in the political discourse (but let us consider at the end whether this is really true), then where are they? In the decades after 1900, in soil not so far removed from where nationalism grew, the seeds were sown of what would be called New Age. This spirituality was made up of a mixture of the search for a non-Christian religious world-view, anti-bourgeois lifestyle, and romantic sentiments. It was in this counterculture movement that yet another way was found (alongside the ethical interpretations of liberal theology and the nationalistic usages of myth) to reveal the true symbolic content of myths. In this New Age spirituality – one source of which was the legendary Monte Verità in Ascona, where all kinds of turn-of-the-century hippies mixed with revolutionaries and occultists, and where from the 1930s onwards the famous Eranos conferences under the aegis of Carl-Gustav Jung took place – the old myths were interpreted in therapeutic terms.[17]

Under the influence chiefly of Jung, but also of historians of religions such as Mircea Eliade, and authors such as Joseph Campbell, myths came to be perceived as a kind of map to the soul. Secularization meant enlightenment – that is, the triumph of *logos* over *mythos* – but also differentiation, and the parts of culture that remained for religion during the secularization of the West were mainly concerned with pastoral care (whereas things like politics, ethics, medicine, and law became secular spheres). It is therefore no wonder that a movement arose in which old religious expressions were interpreted in psychological terms. Stranger, perhaps, is that so many people have found it reasonable to project this therapeutic interpretation of the myths – myths exist to make a person healthy and grow mentally – back in history. When reading books about popular scholarship on myth and New Age spirituality (two genres that seem to merge), one can be led to believe that the old Vikings did nothing but try to "find themselves".

The myths that are read and studied by people interested in the New Age movement and by a more general interested public might, for example, be taken from traditional Celtic or African mythologies, and are in that way myths in the folkloristic sense of the word ("narratives about gods"). Since the nineteenth century there have been a few works with a major impact reproducing ancient religious stories (for example, the Brothers Grimm, Thomas Bulfinch's *Mythology*, and Robert Graves' versions of Greek and Celtic myths), and a huge number of popular works that have taken their interpretations and retellings further. When these stories are taken up by New Age seekers and neo-pagans in their theologies and rituals, they become myths also in the sense of narratives whose content actually influences the receivers. As regards the question of whether these stories are also myths in the sense of narratives that the senders intended to function as "paradigmatic truths", the matter is a little more complicated.

The translators, editors, and authors of the mythologies that circulate in the New Age and neo-pagan movements probably have different aims. Some wish to educate, others to entertain; some want to make money, and others want to save people. The fact that the storytellers are agents on the market also affects their chances of functioning as redeeming prophets (the optimal position of authority). It is still the case that the world is full of prophets, that is to say, people who claim to channel divine words, but the royalties go to ordinary mortals. Helen Schucman, for example, has become a multimillionaire from conveying

Jesus' message in the New Age bestseller *A Course in Miracles*. Copyright takes priority over the divine mission.

In traditional societies, myth appeared as a form of narrative that was linked in various ways to the interests and viewpoints of the elite. It expressed the outlook of those in power, and the storytellers, troubadours, and poets were in debt to them. When mythical imagination lives on different terms, it is spread in other ways and therefore is presumably better able to express the author's own personal world. A myth-maker like Richard Wagner – the first who vigorously succeeded in bringing the old myths into the modern world – certainly still belongs in high culture, although he himself wanted to be a leader of the people, and even though his music today is said to be the most frequently used in video and computer games, he had much greater opportunity to "put himself into" his art than, say, the anonymous author of the *Nibelungenlied*. But what does that really tell us? Nietzsche diagnoses Wagner in this sardonic way:

> He instinctively avoided a psychological plot – but how? – by always putting idiosyncrasy in its place... Very modern – eh? Very Parisian! very decadent! ... "But the substance of Wagner's texts! their mythical substance, their eternal substance!" – Question: how is this substance, this eternal substance tested? The chemical analyst replies: Translate Wagner into the real, into the modern, – let us be even more cruel, and say into the bourgeois![18]

Regardless of whether the sender wants to be a redeeming prophet or not, his or her books today are at the mercy of the market. It is no longer, as in traditional societies, the ethical, aesthetic, or intellectual qualities of the narratives that determine their success among the audience; instead, as with all other cultural products, the mythical narratives are adapted, packaged, and advertised for the market. What this means for the consumers is something we can only speculate about: does the situation allow the best religious narratives, whatever that might mean, to emerge? Do the market mechanisms allow a wide range of literature about the philosophy of life, or do they lead instead to identical and predictable messages and aesthetic forms? We can be fairly sure that the culture producers will be less inclined (or, if you wish, as little inclined as before) to endeavour to express and respond to genuine human needs, and that they will instead have their eyes firmly fixed on the sales success of rival culture producers. In a situation where, for example, the published legends about human encounters with aliens are as similar to each other as one pair of jeans is like another pair, the first task of research on myth is to show how the idea of consumers making "free choices" from a smorgasbord of philosophies of life is largely a chimera.

The Myths of the Culture Industry

Myth-making has been heavily influenced by the mass production of the culture industry, which to some extent presupposes a uniform audience, while simultaneously homogenizing culture consumers by toning down or eliminating regional peculiarities. Today we see a virtual monopoly on the production of fantastic stories. The Dream Factory, Hollywood, and the Walt Disney Company account for an overwhelming majority of all the fantastic narratives that are spread. Even if these films and other products are rarely about gods and demons, they almost certainly influence the receivers. The films and the associated merchandise – the children's books, t-shirts, toys, tea towels, etc. – shape dreams, ideas, desires, and emotions. If we use another of Bruce Lincoln's definitions of myth – as "ideology in narrative form" – these products of the culture industry are no doubt myths (Lincoln 1999:149). One scholar who has studied them in this way is the folklorist Jack Zipes.[19] As the title of one of his books suggests, *Fairytale as Myth & Myth as Fairytale* (1994), not only have old folktales, via Charles Perrault and the Brothers Grimm, been transformed into American myths ("ideology in narrative form") by Walt Disney and others; the myths have simultaneously been "fairytalized". By this I mean, in the spirit of Zipes, I hope, that the ideological messages are no longer being sent by serious religious and political leaders, packaged as "authoritative paradigmatic truths", but now come in the form of entertainment. Just for fun.

The fact (if it *is* a fact) that ideology today is distributed in the form of entertainment must entail a methodological switch: as long as a culture is provided with authoritative narratives, these are essential to study, regardless of whether or not ordinary people may know them by heart, or even if they deliberately refrain from interpreting and leading their lives according to the values expressed in the narratives. But if no narratives are authoritative and all are "equal" in the realm of entertainment, we cannot pick some films or television programmes or detective novels at random and analyse them. We must instead – in an almost Lévi-Straussian way – view the products as variants of one and the same product and collect a large number of variants (for example, all vampire films) so that we can then identify the bearing mythemes and decode their messages and values. Only then can we get a clear view of the ideology conveyed by "the myths".

The Reception Situation

The culture industry has encouraged the emergence of a series of new media: books with colour illustrations and cartoons, live-action and animated films, video and computer games, the Internet, live theatre, and so on. These all have genre-specific features in the way they communicate myths and fantastic stories, and presumably they differ as regards the degree to which they fairytalize them: the film *Jesus Christ Superstar* (1970), from the musical by Tim Rice and Andrew Lloyd Webber, seems to be able to arouse religious feelings, which I find it hard to believe that the comic book *The Book of Genesis according to R. Crumb* (2009) by Robert Crumb can do. Another thing that ought to be investigated when it comes to the mythicality of the products of the culture industry is the reception situation. When you see a "mythical" film in the cinema – think of *Black Hawk Down* (2001) by Ridley Scott or *300* (2007) by Zack Snider and Frank Miller – you are in a situation that presumably is not so unlike the traditional reception of myth: sitting passively in an audience. How different it is to sit at home in your armchair and read the stories of the gods in a book like Diana L. Paxon's *Essential Ásatrú: Walking the Path of Norse Paganism* (2006) while the children pester you to think of something for them to do. Or to get help from the supernatural strength of Anubis when playing the computer game *Age of Mythology* (2003) with a friend. Does the reception situation of myths affect us to such an extent that it should also affect the way in which we classify something as myth?

Advertising Myths

A sphere that is closely associated with the culture industry is the pictorial world of advertising. We cannot find anything mythical in the sense of stories of the gods here, but if we regard myth as "ideology in narrative form" which shapes individuals' will and ideals, one can turn to the world of advertising and commerce. There is quite a lot of interesting research in this field. One example: in the article "Supermarkets as Libraries of Postmodern Mythology", the economists Maria Kniazeva and Russell W. Belk analyse the small stories printed on packages – stories that can begin like this, for example:

> Uncle Ben's® – original manfacturer [sic] of "The rice that never sticks" – has for more than 60 years used its expertise too [sic] produce rice that tastes good and maintains a superior high quality.[20]

> The product that has given the world its best-known taste was born in Atlanta, Georgia, on May 8, 1886. Dr. John Stith Pemberton, a local pharmacist, produced the syrup for Coca-Cola®, and carried a jug of the new product down the street to Jacobs' Pharmacy, where it was sampled, pronounced "excellent" and placed on sale for five cents a glass as a soda fountain drink.[21]

Kniazeva and Belk succeed in classifying the receivers of these mythical microtexts about the essence of the products into four types: "caregiver", "cosmopolitan", "tradition-bound", and the sensible "frugal student" (Kniazeva & Belk 2010:752). In times when the profit calculations and market surveys of the big corporations profoundly affect citizens' self-images, these and similar studies seem highly fruitful ground for the search for today's myths.

Myth in Politics or Culture

I want to end by trying to tie together the basic questions that have arisen. First: is today's political discourse totally demythologized? If we compare today's "post-political" discourse with the excesses of fascism and Stalinism in aestheticizing propaganda and symbolically charged rhetoric, the answer seems obvious. Mythical politics is dead – and with it also utopian dreaming, it may be added.

But can a society really do without myths altogether? Have we not known, at least since Durkheim, that no society survives without a cement of values, of shared ideological convictions, to hold it together? And don't we need narratives through which to communicate these values? Couldn't political key words and commonly used expressions like "freedom", "what the market demands", or Adam Smith's "invisible hand" be called elements in mythical narratives? Perhaps we demand too much of myths if we require them to be a kind of elaborated symbolistic universe? Or is it the case that there actually is a political ideology, liberalism, that manages without mythical narratives? Can myths still perhaps be found among communist and right-wing movements? Among neocons and Islamists? But not among liberals? That would be very strange.

The solution to the dilemma of "a-mythicality of liberalism" could either be that we are not looking for the right things when we look for liberal myths, or that the liberal society is held together by other means than ideological narratives. Marxists sometimes claim that the significance of ideology decreases in today's "new world order".[22] Ancient slave-owning societies, like the feudal societies with their serfdom, needed their narratives about the will of the gods and about the divine genealogies of the privileged families. But societies ruled by a market economy need them much less. The reason for this is said to be that the organization of the economy itself has the effect of cementing people together, since workers are free in the sense of owning their own bodies but are simultaneously caught in a trap since they have to sell themselves to survive. The economy *itself* therefore occupies the position that ideology had in pre-capitalist societies.

Another alternative is to claim that the emotions and values previously implanted with the aid of religion and mythology are no longer implanted via the political sphere in our times. Ideology has ceased to function as authoritative statements about right and wrong, and now occurs as entertainment instead. If myth has vanished from the political discourse that concerns how market forces govern the citizen-as-labour-and-consumer, then there has been a discursive distribution of labour through which the production of myths has been outsourced to the culture industry. Mythical imagination is thus expressed less by people "in leading positions" in official public contexts. It is instead conveyed through lifestyle magazines, films, advertisements, television programmes, and music. Art and culture have become the most important arenas for ideological-mythical communication.

The culture industry still creates old-fashioned mythical-heroic films acclaiming violence, power, and neo-colonialism, but the most striking thing in our times is nevertheless the production, distribution and consumption of the mythical world that can be captured in the terms fantasy literature, New Age, and new media. In these cases we come closer to an almost utopian, or at least dreamy or fairytale-like, aspect of the mythical imagination. If the fantastic has left politics and moved to culture, it means that not only ideologically cementing narratives have moved, but also that the utopian energies have ended up in the sphere of culture. Everywhere in the "pop mythology" landscape, images of Arcadia are flourishing; think, for example, of Peter Jackson's staging of the world of the Hobbits in *The Lord of the Rings* (2001–3) or the image of the Na'vi culture in James Cameron's film *Avatar* (2009).

The path of mythology from the mainstream of culture – where it had tentacles reaching not only into private, existential life but also into art, politics, and science – to culture consumption in the private sphere, is a part of secularization. For those who, like Karl Popper, fear mythical structures, and perhaps think about the line of ideas running from Georges Sorel's propaganda using myths to incite rebellion, to fascism, which excelled in mythical symbolism, this is a sign of a mature and rational cultural climate.[23] The division between, on the one hand, political considerations and, on the other, mythical perceptions of history, fantastic legends, and utopian infatuation, is something they think enables wise social engineering and keeps extremism in check. Or should we lament the separation between politics on the one hand and myth and utopia on the other? Have the New Age myths and the fantasy culture become an insidious escapism seeking to get away from a harsh social reality, or have they become the opium providing illusory therapy to the individual monadist? Does pop mythology offer a haven where dreams can still be formulated and expressed? Or is it the other way around: that it prevents individuals from trying to understand and change their politically controlled reality? Do the fantasy novels, the epic films, and the historical video and computer games correspond to a genuine desire for something else; perhaps for community, authenticity, meaning, and justice?

For some people, the distinction between politics and mythology is a sign of poverty; a reflection of a society where discussions of purpose and meaning disappear in a maelstrom of choices between different consumption habits, company shares, and charter trips. J. R. R. Tolkien, who in many ways successfully continued Wagner's work of lending new life to old myths and legends, belonged to this minority:

> Why should a man be scorned if, finding himself in prison, he tries to get out and go home? Or if, when he cannot do so, he thinks and talks about other topics than jailers and prison-walls? ... Not only do they confound the escape of the prisoner with the flight

of the deserter; but they would seem to prefer the acquiescence of the "quisling" to the resistance of the patriot. To such thinking you have only to say "the land you loved is doomed" to excuse any treachery, indeed to glorify it (Tolkien 1983:148).

For Tolkien, fantasy, myth, and fairytales were correlates to reality. It is only in this light that we can determine whether our civilization is something to take pride in or not. As R. J. Reilly puts it with reference to Tolkien, perhaps we should not understand the immersion in mythical and fantastic narratives as escapism, but as "a time to regroup one's forces for the next day's battle" (Reilly 1969:147).

These concluding questions and discussions have brought us to the end of our sketch of myth today. We are approaching the field outside the scholarly questions. Whether we contentedly sit down at home and enjoy life as it is today or, like the wounded Frodo, feel forced to search for alternative fantasy worlds and utopian landscapes – this is a choice that lies outside the enclosure of the academia.

Notes

1 An excellent introduction to the study of myth can be found in Segal 2003.
2 For a orderly account of the folkloristic view of myth, see Bascom 1984.
3 One of few who, in connection with attempts to define myth, discusses how a narrative is received (whether as credible or not) is Lincoln 1989 (esp. 24f.).
4 On Herder's view of myth, see the comments, contextualization, and excerpts in Feldman & Richardson 1972: 224–240.
5 On Strauss' view of myth, see the comments, contextualization, and excerpts in Feldman & Richardson 1972: 450–462.
6 A good survey of nationalistic myths can be found in the richly illustrated *Mythen der Nationen: Ein Europäisches Panorama* (1998), edited by Minoka Flacke.
7 See Arvidsson 2007:99–141.
8 In passing on the Swedish myth of Gustav Vasa, Lincoln touches on the theme (1989:22f.).
9 "Mit sanft berechnender Hartnäckigkeit sprechen sie, auch noch in diesen Jahren, zum Beispiel vom Werden des deutschen Volkes und haben ihre Freude daran, gläubigen Studenten und Volksgenossen die Mischstoffe aufzuzählen, aus denen sich deutsches Wesen homunculusartig geformt werden: die Spätantike und das ausgehende Römertum mit Grundherrschaft und Lehenswesen – armes Odal! –, die Kirche und Frankreich, die arabische und jüdische Philosophie sowie die Renaissance, schließlich Gegenreformtion und Parlamentarismus. ... Wer sich so an dem ewigen Grund- und Baustoff deutschen, germanischen Daseins vergreift, dem sei gesagt: wir wolle, auch kulturgeschichtlich, Herr, nicht Liebhaber im eigenen Hause sein!" (Wüst 1942:11f.)

10 Information about "Rote Siegfried" from http://search.iisg.nl/search/search? action=transform&col=marc_images&xsl=marc_images-detail.xsl&lang=en&docid=11039014_MARC (Accessed 1 February 2011).

11 The picture alludes to the arms of the Russian Empire, which had St George and the dragon in the escutcheon. The picture comes from http://commons.wikimedia. org/wiki/File:TrotskySlayingtheDragon1918.jpg (Accessed 1 February 2011).

12 On important pieces making up the historical puzzle of the term "totalitarian", and the term "authoritarian" that pre-dated it, see Lincoln 1994, chapter 8.

13 In an introductory chapter, however, Popper talks about "the myth of destiny"; that is, the belief that one can find historical laws and thus deduce future events (2005:3ff.).

14 Fukuyama 2006:107. The article constitutes the framework for Fukuyama's book *The End of History and the Last Man*, from 1992.

15 Žižek often considers this topic, perhaps expressed most simply in the phrase "cynicism as a form of ideology"; e.g. Žižek 1994:28ff.

16 I was surprised when Carl Bildt, Sweden's most internationally renowned politician, on the last day of December 2010, in an article in *Dagens Nyheter*, which was otherwise written in standard bureaucratic-administrative political jargon, called "Europe" the "torchbearer of liberty". Such mythical symbolism is rare these days.

17 On Ascona and Monte Verità, see Green 1986; on the Eranos conferences, see McGuire 1989.

18 "Er wich instinktiv der psychologischen Motivirung aus – womit? damit, dass er immer die Idiosynkrasie an deren Stelle rückte... Sehr modern, nicht wahr? sehr Pariserisch! sehr décadent! ... 'Aber der Gehalt der Wagnerischen Texte! ihr mythischer Gehalt, ihr ewiger Gehalt!' – Frage: wie prüft man diesen Gehalt, diesen ewigen Gehalt? – Der Chemiker antwortet: man übersetzt Wagnern in's Reale, in's Moderne, – seien wir noch grausamer! in's Bürgerliche!" (Nietzsche 1969:27f.)

19 See Zipes 1994:72–161; 1997:89–128; 2002:1–22, 104–145.

20 From Uncle Ben's® long-grain rice, bought in 2010. See Kniazeva & Belk 2010.

21 Quoted from http://www.thecoca-colacompany.com/heritage/chronicle_birth_refreshing_idea.html (Accessed 12 August 2012).

22 Eagleton (1991:33–43) lists several variants of the thesis "late capitalism manages without ideology".

23 On Sorel's view of myth, see e.g. Tager 1986. The scholar of myth Ken Dowden (1992:89) expresses a wholly Sorelian idea when he writes: "Myth, like propaganda, is worthwhile because people believe in it. Enemies must be prepared to counter it within the rules of the game it establishes."

References

Arvidsson, Stefan (2007): *Draksjukan. Mytiska fantasier hos Tolkien, Wagner och de Vries*, Lund: Nordic Academic Press.

Arvidsson, Stefan (2010): Greed and the Nature of Evil. Tolkien versus Wagner", *Journal of Religion and Popular Culture*, 22 (2).

Bascom, William (1984): The Forms of Folklore. Prose Narratives, in Alan Dundes (ed.): *Sacred Narrative. Readings in the Theory of Myth*, Berkeley: University of California Press.

Bultmann, Rudolf (1959): New Testament and Mythology, in Hans Werner Bartsch (ed.): *Kerygma and Myth. A Theological Debate*, London: SPCK.

Dowden, Ken (1992): *The Uses of Greek Mythology.* London and New York: Routledge.

Eagleton, Terry (1991): *Ideology. An Introduction.* London: Verso.

Feldman, Burton and Robert D. Richardson (1972): *The Rise of Modern Mythology. 1680–1860.* Bloomington: Indiana University Press.

Flacke, Monika (1998): *Mythen der Nationen. Ein europäisches Panorama.* München and Berlin: Koehler & Amelang.

Fukuyama, Francis (2006 [1989]): The End of History? in Gearóid Ó Tuathail, Simon Dalby and Paul Routledge (eds): *The Geopolitics Reader*, 2nd ed. London: Routledge.

Green, Martin (1986): *Mountain of Truth. The Counterculture Begins, Ascona, 1900–1920.* Hanover: University Press of New England.

Halliday, W.R. (1933): *Indo-European Folk-Tales and Greek Legend.* Cambridge: Cambridge University Press.

Kniazeva, Maria and Russell W. Belk (2010): Supermarkets as Libraries of Postmodern Mythology, *Journal of Business Research*, 63: 748–753.

Lincoln, Bruce (1989): *Discourse and the Construction of Society. Comparative Studies of Myth, Ritual, and Classification.* Chicago: University of Chicago Press.

Lincoln, Bruce (1994): *Authority. Construction and Corrosion.* Chicago: University of Chicago Press.

Lincoln, Bruce (1999): *Theorizing Myth. Narrative, Ideology, and Scholarship.* Chicago: University of Chicago Press.

Lyotard, Jean-François (1984 [1979]): *The Postmodern Condition. A Report on Knowledge.* Manchester: Manchester University Press.

McGuire, William (1989): *Bollingen. An Adventure in Collecting the Past.* Rev. ed. Princeton: Princeton University Press.

Nietzsche, Friedrich (1969 [1888]): *Der Fall Wagner*, in *Nietzsche Werke. Kritische Gesamtausgabe*, part 6, vol. 3. Berlin: Walter de Gruyter.

Popper, Karl (2005 [1945]): *The Open Society and its Enemies, vol. 1 The Spell of Plato*, London & New York: Routledge.

Reilly, R.J. (1969): *Tolkien and the Fairy-Story*, in Neil D. Isaacs and Rose A. Zimbardo (eds): *Tolkien and the Critics. Essays on J. R. R. Tolkien's The Lord of the Rings*, London: University of Notre Dame Press.

Segal, Robert A. (2003): *Myth. A Very Short Introduction*, Oxford: Oxford University Press.

Tager, Michael (1986): Myth and Politics in the Works of Sorel and Barthes, *Journal of the History of Ideas*, vol. 47 (4): 625–639.

Tolkien, J. R. R. (1983): On Fairy-Stories, in *The Monsters and the Critics and Other Essays.* London: George Allen & Unwin.

Zipes, Jack (1994): *Fairy Tale as Myth. Myth as Fairy Tale.* Lexington: University Press of Kentucky.

Zipes, Jack (1997): *Happily Ever After. Fairy Tales, Children, and the Culture Industry.* London and New York: Routledge.

Zipes, Jack (2002): *Breaking the Magic Spell Radical Theories of Folk and Fairy Tales.* Lexington: University Press of Kentucky.

Žižek, Slavoj (1994 [1989]): *The Sublime Object of Ideology.* London and New York: Verso.

About the Authors

Peter Aronsson is professor of Cultural Heritage and the Uses of History at Department of Culture Studies, Linköping University. His research interests focus on the uses of the past in National Museums, the role of historical narratives in mobilizing people and creating a durable democratic culture. He is a main contributor to a major European crossdisciplinary project on historical consciousness, exploring the general concept of history.

Stefan Arvidsson is professor of History of Religions at Stockholm University. His main research field is comparative religion with a special focus on myth and mythology. He has also done research on Old Norse religion, New Age, religious strategies in modern times and applied the perspectives of the History of Religions on secular ideologies, especially National Socialism and Communism.

Karin Vibeke Hyldal Christensen is a PhD-student in Russian Studies at the Department of Cross-cultural and Regional studies, University of Copenhagen. Her main research areas are Russian culture and national identity with a particular focus on the role of the Russian Orthodox Church in contemporary Russian society.

Jörg Hackman is DAAD Alfred Döblin Professor of East European History at the Department of History and International Relations, University of Szczecin. His research interests cover the fields of social change, civil society and nation building in multicultural regions of North Eastern Europe.

Peter Lambert is lecturer in history at the Department of History and Welsh history, Aberystwyth University. His research interests include the Weimar Republic and the uses of the past in constructions of German identities, especially during the Third Reich era.

Marko Lehti is senior researcher in Peace, Mediation and Conflict Research at the School of Social Science and Humanities, University of Tampere, and senior lecturer in history at the University of Turku. His research focus is the history of the Baltic countries, the legacy of the West in the region, and memorial sites there.

Jitka Malečková is head of the Turkish Studies Program and associate professor at the Department of Middle Eastern and African Studies at Charles University, Prague. Her main research fields are modernization processes in the Muslim world, and the role of women in Czech intellectual history and historiography.

Catharina Raudvere is professor of History of Religions at the Department of Cross-cultural and Regional Studies, University of Copenhagen. Her research focuses on contemporary Muslim life, especially in Turkey and the Balkans, religion and politics. She is currently leading the research centre The Many Roads in Modernity.

Victor Roudometof is associate professor in Sociology at the Department of Social and Political Sciences, University of Cyprus. His research interests include globalization, transnationalism, migration and diaspora, especially nationalism and ethnicity in the Balkans.

Krzysztof Stala is associate professor in Polish Studies at the Department of Cross-cultural and Regional Studies, University of Copenhagen. His research fields include modern Polish literature and culture, nationalism and national identity, and representations of Holocaust in modern European literature.

Adrian Velicu is associate professor in the History of Ideas at the Department of the Humanities and Gender Studies, Karlstad University. His research interests include the history of the French Revolution, the development of the civil society and civic ideas in Europe, and Romania's cultural legacy.

Trine Stauning Willert is assistant professor in Modern Greek Studies at the Department of Cross-cultural and Regional Studies, University of Copenhagen. Her research is focused on national identity, religion and education in contemporary Greece, and the cultural relationship between Greece and Europe in a historical and contemporary perspective.